NEGOTIATING NATIONALISM

For Chantale

Negotiating Nationalism

Nation-building, Federalism, and Secession in the Multinational State

WAYNE NORMAN

This book has been printed digitally and produced in a standard specification in order to ensure its continuing availability

OXFORD
UNIVERSITY PRESS

Great Clarendon Street, Oxford OX2 6DP

Oxford University Press is a department of the University of Oxford.
It furthers the University's objective of excellence in research, scholarship,
and education by publishing worldwide in

Oxford New York

Auckland Cape Town Dar es Salaam Hong Kong Karachi
Kuala Lumpur Madrid Melbourne Mexico City Nairobi
New Delhi Shanghai Taipei Toronto
With offices in
Argentina Austria Brazil Chile Czech Republic France Greece
Guatemala Hungary Italy Japan South Korea Poland Portugal
Singapore Switzerland Thailand Turkey Ukraine Vietnam

Oxford is a registered trade mark of Oxford University Press
in the UK and in certain other countries

Published in the United States
by Oxford University Press Inc., New York

© Wayne Norman 2006

The moral rights of the author have been asserted

Database right Oxford University Press (maker)

Reprinted 2008

All rights reserved. No part of this publication may be reproduced,
stored in a retrieval system, or transmitted, in any form or by any means,
without the prior permission in writing of Oxford University Press,
or as expressly permitted by law, or under terms agreed with the appropriate
reprographics rights organization. Enquiries concerning reproduction
outside the scope of the above should be sent to the Rights Department,
Oxford University Press, at the address above

You must not circulate this book in any other binding or cover
And you must impose this same condition on any acquirer

ISBN 978-0-19-829335-4

Contents

Preface		vii
Acknowledgements		xix
1	**Thinking through Nationalism**	1
	1.1 Defining our concepts	3
	1.2 What is nationalism? Or, who is a nationalist?	5
	1.3 Nationalism and liberal theory	9
	1.4 Looking ahead	16
	Appendix: Nationalism without Nations?	18
2	**Forging Identities: The Politics and Ethics of Nation-building**	23
	2.1 Self-determination versus determining the self	23
	2.2 The benefits of *having* a national identity versus the dangers of *trying* to forge a national identity	29
	2.3 What is a national identity?	33
	2.4 Constructing, deconstructing, and reconstructing national identities	37
	2.5 Cataloguing the *methods* of nation-building	43
	2.6 *Evaluating* the methods of nation-building	49
	2.7 The moral and political relevance of the *content* of national identities	57
	2.8 Conclusion	66
	2.9 Looking forward: from nationalism to federalism	69
3	**Should Nation-building be Federalized? Reconsidering the Role of Federalism in Normative Political Theory**	73
	3.1 Introduction: self-determination and federalism	73
	3.2 Federalism and federalist theory: for whom?	77
	3.3 Federalism as a parallel universe in the history of political thought and practice	80
	3.4 Reconsidering the rejection	85
	3.5 Conclusion: reconciling the disciplinary solitudes	92
4	**Federal Constitutionalism I: Options for Federal Design**	95
	4.1 Federal versus non-federal institutions	97
	4.2 Basic components and options for federal design	100
	4.3 Symbolic terms of federation	120

	4.4 Conclusion	130
	Appendix: Canada's Constitutional Odyssey: Bold Adventures and Cautionary Tales	131
5	**Federal Constitutionalism II: Evaluating and Justifying Options for Federal Design**	**139**
	5.1 Introduction: hybrid theories for hybrid states	139
	5.2 Principles drawn from 'classic' liberal-democratic traditions: their utility and limits for multinational federalism	141
	5.3 Constitutional recognition	156
	5.4 Conclusion	168
6	**A Federalist Theory of Secession**	**170**
	6.1 Background context in international law	170
	6.2 Domesticating secession	173
	6.3 Theorizing secession, theorizing nationalism, and theorizing federalism	180
	6.4 Conclusion	214
Afterword		**216**
Bibliography		223
Index		241

Preface

This book grew up in the murky shadows of two '9/11s', either of which could mark the political birth of the new century. On 9 November 1989, the Berlin Wall, and the empire it symbolized, began to crumble. By the time the millennium began in earnest the Wall would exist primarily in the form of kitschy, fist-sized souvenir fragments snapped up by tourists in the early 1990s. These things are now available, complete with a certificate of authenticity, for less than a dollar on eBay. Rather pricier on eBay these days are trinkets associated with the attack against the World Trade Center and the Pentagon that took place on the other plausible date for the beginning of our new era, 11 September 2001.

There is no question that in the years immediately following each of these '9/11s' the world—and just as significantly, our perceptions of, and theories about, the world—changed dramatically. The book is primarily concerned with a political phenomenon exposed, in different ways, by both of these events: namely, nationalism. In the 1990s, across Eastern and Central Europe, the Balkans, and the former Soviet Union, nationalist conflicts were tearing apart states and even an empire; whereas in the USA, after its '9/11', nationalism was a large part of the explanation for how a country seemed to pull itself together, and how it justified fighting two wars on foreign soil. The full story of these two post-9/11s is of course a good deal more complicated, in part because of the complexity and elusiveness of the idea of nationalism itself.

The study of nationalism, and of cultural pluralism more generally, exploded in political theory circles in the 1990s. I hope this book benefits from a certain degree of hindsight on the pioneering attempts by political philosophers and political theorists to come to grips with this subject matter. We are now in a position to recognize the achievements of these efforts by laying numerous questions and debates quietly to rest. We can also now see that certain enquiries led us down blind alleys, while other potentially useful paths of enquiry have still gone largely unexplored. By and large, any intellectual post-mortem will be confined to the Preface and Chapter 1. The lion's share of the book will be devoted to the still neglected questions of how rival minority and majority nationalist projects can be accommodated within the democratic constitutional structures of a single (federal) state.

Back in the day, as we first gazed at the world on the other side of the fallen Wall, we were struck not by the manifest shortcomings of state communism—something that virtually every Western political theorist had long since taken for granted—but by the cascading waves of nationalism that rushed in to fill the power vacuum. And what a dreadful disappointment that was. 'When the Berlin Wall came down, when Václev Havel stood on the balcony in Prague's Wenceslas Square and crowds cheered the collapse of the Communist regimes across Europe, I thought, like many people, that we were about to witness a new era of liberal democracy.... We soon found out how wrong we were. For what has succeeded the last age of empire is a new age of violence' (Ignatieff 1993: 5). The violence would get worse before it got better; but we do now have some reason to think that, at least in Eastern and Central Europe, there was a *period* of interethnic violence, with intermittent episodes here and there, but not an *age* or *epidemic* of it. As it turns out, this was but one of the many 'myths' or 'misconceptions' about nationalism that blossomed when we intellectual tourists moved into what was for almost all political theorists a new field. (According to Brubaker 1998, it is myth number two of six.)

And mere tourists in the field of nationalism we surely were. No matter what your discipline, if you were educated in the English-speaking world in the post-war period, you were very unlikely to have learnt much of anything about this seemingly most passé of 'isms'. Philosophers of my generation (I was born in the same month as the Berlin Wall), for example, were raised on a steady diet of John Rawls, Ronald Dworkin, and Robert Nozick. But not one of the three major books by these authors from the 1970s has an index entry for 'nationalism' or a use of the word 'nation' that is not synonymous with 'state'. The communitarian wave did little to redress this neglect, despite the fact that nationalism can be considered to be one the most successful forms of communitarian politics in the modern world.[1] Again, the communitarian textbooks of the 1980s by Alasdair MacIntyre, Michael Sandel, and Michael Walzer contain not a single index entry for 'nationalism'.[2] The same is true even of the leading political philosophy textbook of the 1990s, published in 1990 (though surely written before the Wall came down) by Will Kymlicka—the philosopher most responsible for putting issues of ethnocultural identity back on the agenda of liberal political theory.[3] Throughout this period political philosophers almost always took the frontiers of the culturally homogeneous nation-state as the frontiers of their discipline. It was barely noticed, and hardly a point of contention, that Rawls had taken for granted that society is a 'cooperative scheme in perpetuity', in which 'membership is a

---

[1] See Posner (2002), discussed below. For communitarian scepticism about nationalism, see O'Neill (1994).

[2] MacIntyre did address some of the relevant issues in his essay, 'Is Patriotism a Virtue?' (1984).

[3] It is noteworthy that the second edition of Kymlicka's text, published in 2001, contains chapters on citizenship theory and multiculturalism, with a substantial section on nationalism.

given' and 'fixed', and in which the citizens 'will [all] lead their [entire] lives' (Rawls 1971). We worried about how citizens could get along if they had different concepts of the good, and even, heaven forbid, of justice; but that they might speak different languages or have different cultural identities—the norm in 90 per cent of states, and the very building blocks of nationalism— was never entertained in mainstream debates.[4]

The situation was not a lot better in the social sciences, although here at least many large departments of, say, sociology or political science may have had *someone* who specialized in nationalist or ethnic-conflict studies. There was in fact something of a resurgence in the study of nationalism throughout the 1980s, though it remained a relatively ghettoized area of inquiry.[5] And perhaps these theorists could be excused for a certain amount of gloating about the return of ethnicity to a central place in their disciplines, given the years or decades of sneering they must have endured from colleagues convinced that particularistic, tribal, cultural identities were no match for the modernizing and integrating powers of the modern state.[6]

By the early 1990s these pre-trendy scholars of nationalism must have felt like well-settled ex-pats greeting a flood of tourists from their native land. The affirmation of having been onto something special is welcome at first, but soon the tourists are littering the landscape and putting up garish hotels. Brubaker is surely being polite, for example, when he describes the new centrality of nationalism to so many disciplines as a 'mixed blessing'. 'On the one hand,' he grants, 'the robust demand for knowledge about—and "fixes" for—nationalism brings new opportunities, resources, and attention to the field. On the other hand, the rapid expansion of the field has strengthened analytically primitive currents in the study of nationalism, threatening to erode...the analytical gains previously made in sophisticated works by Benedict Anderson, John Armstrong, John Breuilly, Ernest Gellner, Anthony Smith, and a number of other scholars.'[7] Perhaps he doth protest too much. Some of the central

---

[4] This is not to say that there were no discussions of nationalism by philosophers in the English-speaking world during the cold war era. We can obviously point to the numerous important works in the history of ideas and sociology, respectively, of two men trained in (and alienated by) analytic philosophy, Isaiah Berlin and Ernest Gellner. Among the noteworthy normative discussions of nationalism written while the Wall was still intact are Barry (1983), McCormick (1982), and Taylor (1979). To say that these debates were not part of the mainstream is, nevertheless, an understatement.

[5] See Gellner (1983), Smith (1983, 1986), Anderson (1983), Breuilly (1982), Armstrong (1982), and the numerous articles by Connor (1994).

[6] For a critique of the 'nation-building' and 'national integration' bias of the social sciences in the 1960s and 1970s, see the classic 1972 essay by Connor, 'Nation-building or Nation-destroying?', reprinted in Connor (1994); and Brubaker (1996: 79–83).

[7] Brubaker (1998: 233). Donald Horowitz, the dean of ethnic-conflict studies, betrays similar grumpiness with philosopher-tourists buzzing through his domain. Reflecting on some of the

disputes between the five authors of the 1980s that he mentions were bound up with conceptual, epistemological, and occasionally ontological theories about the nature of nations and nationalism, and explanations of how they arose historically. While the philosophical tourists have certainly been guilty of naive understandings of the history and sociology of nationalism, it must also be said that they were often less than impressed by the awkward handling of many of these essentially philosophical and methodological debates among the social scientists.

It is not part of my project in this book to either rework or replace existing sociological theories of nationalism. Although I will sometimes be required to take sides where these theories diverge, I shall generally be seeking empirically uncontroversial starting points. My aims here are normative. I am concerned with *how we ought to act, and what sorts of institutions we ought to give ourselves, when we live in societies where nationalism is current.* And in particular I shall focus on these questions in states in which more than one group considers itself to be a nation or national community; where there is more than one nationalist discourse, more than one nation-building project. Most states, as it turns out, are like this; and this is the sort of place where nationalism and the consequences of nationalist politics tend really to matter. Following Kymlicka, I will refer to such states as 'multination' or 'multinational' states to distinguish them from 'nation-states' or (awkwardly, for the sake of clarity) 'uninational states'. There is, of course, tremendous variety in the configurations of multinational states: we can find anywhere from two or three different communities with competing national self-conceptions sharing the state (as in Belgium or the UK) to dozens or even hundreds (as in Russia or India); both majority and minority national groups can have more or less developed senses of nationhood (and I am including under the rubric of 'multinational states' those in which the constituent ethnocultural groups may not yet have a fully developed *national* consciousness); different national communities within the state may or may not compete for the hearts and minds of some of the same citizens (in other words, there may or may not be citizens who feel the pull of more than one national identity, such as Catalan and Spanish); some multinational states have one dominant majority nation that sees the state as its own, where others have a majority group that sees the state as belonging to all of the citizens and constituent groups, and still others

---

early writings by philosophers on secession he tries not 'to exhibit hostility to the efforts of philosophers on such issues in general—for moral reasoning is needed'. But his years of studying the dynamics of actual conflicts between ethnic groups leave him with no patience for 'a priori methods that seem appropriate for other problems [of political philosophy but are] utterly unsuitable to this problem' (Horowitz 1998). We shall discuss Brubaker's critique in the Appendix to Chapter 1, and Horowitz's in Chapter 6.

(in fact, around one-third of states) have no ethnocultural group that constitutes a majority; and so on.

At the heart of this book is a plea for the continued existence of flourishing, peaceful, democratic multinational states. Indeed, there should be more of these: not by independent nations banding together to create more multinational states, but by greatly expanding the number of existing multinational states that are flourishing, peaceful, and democratic. I shall argue that it is something like a necessary condition for true democracy and flourishing—and justice—in multinational states that they provide a substantial realm of self-determination for the minority national communities within their borders. At a basic level, such a plea for multinational states is part and parcel of the desire for the spread of democracy around the world. You cannot have one without the other. Simple arithmetic tells much of the story. There are, by conservative estimate, something like 5,000 ethnocultural groups in the world, and around 200 states; or on average 25 per state.[8] These are the kinds of groups, distinguished by language, dialect, religion, culture, race, etc., that either *have* (in the case of perhaps one-fifth of these groups) or *could develop* a national self-identification. As a matter of fact, most states in the developing world have many more than two dozen ethnocultural groups. One of the first things to happen when democracy arrives in such states is that long-suppressed groups can begin to mobilize and make demands (for either autonomy, inclusion or both) upon the state.[9] Since most ethnocultural groups in the world are intermixed in the way that those in the former Yugoslavia and in Rwanda are, the 'globalization of secession' is quite clearly not even a candidate solution for the challenges posed by legitimate demands for minority rights and self-determination. To carve up existing multination states on ethnic lines in this way would either (*a*) create new minority groups in the new states or (*b*) avoid this problem only through massive and, in most cases involuntary if not terrorized, transfers of populations.[10] The first result exacerbates the 'problem' of national minorities rather than solving it; and the second 'solves' the problem in a way that is in practice horrific and in result morally tragic. The plea for multinational states is also in part a revulsion with the idea that it is impractical or otherwise undesirable for peoples who do not share the same culture, religion, language, or skin colour to cooperate within the same political community.[11] The international community is right to

---

[8] For estimates of the ethno-demographics of modern states see, e.g. Connor (1994: 29–30).

[9] For the classic discussions of these phenomena, see Horowitz (1985) and Lijphart (1977). For analysis of more recent data, see Reilly (2001).

[10] On the ethics of so-called 'ethnic cleansing', see Nickel (1995).

[11] This is, if you will, a negative desire, against the triumph of intolerance and the potential for violence it encourages. Like Jacob Levy, I can announce that '[T]his book does not celebrate

resist indulging the most small-minded nationalists in fantasies of national (if not ethnic) purity; and its moral authority to do so is strengthened considerably by the existence of thriving, polyglot, multinational democracies in the developed world.

That said, this book does not pretend to be offering direct prescriptions for dealing with nationalism in the newly democratizing, radically multinational states of the developing world. It is a work of relatively abstract political philosophy ensconced firmly within the broad tradition of liberal-democratic theory as it has evolved since the publication of Rawls's *A Theory of Justice* (1971). Since we are dealing here with nationalism as a kind of political discourse and political culture, and since I will be spending much of the book looking at institutional 'solutions' for housing competing nationalist projects within multinational states, this book will also incorporate rather more political sociology than is typical for a work in this tradition. There is always a tension (a 'dialectic'?) within this approach between the attempt to make some *general, abstract claims* about the forms and limits of a liberal nationalism, on the one hand, and the need to evaluate forms of nationalist politics and constitutional arrangements in terms of their consequences and dynamic implications *in particular historical settings*, on the other. There are nationalist strategies and institutional responses to nationalism that would work impressively within one liberal-democratic political culture, and yet be either disastrous or ideologically unthinkable in another. To speak only at the very general, abstract level is to gloss over this fact; and yet to focus too closely on the way a particular state might deal with competing nationalisms is to risk saying little of relevance for other political cultures. There is little one can say in the abstract about how to resolve this tension or dilemma. The selection of issues and the range of institutional possibilities I consider will look most familiar to citizens in relatively affluent multinational states with strong traditions of constitutional democracy and a history of democratic minority-nationalist movements: in short, in countries like Belgium, Canada, Spain, Switzerland, or the UK. By implication, it will also be indirectly relevant to multinational states that may be seen as evolving in at least some aspects of their political cultures in this direction; for example, India (which may simply belong on the preceding list) or some of the multinational states in Eastern and Central Europe and the Balkans.

It is also hoped that some aspects of the conceptual and normative scheme presented here will be seen as relevant in states and political cultures, such as the

---

ethnic and cultural identities, the beauty of diversity they add to the world, or the meaning they add to the lives of many.... But neither does this book advocate or even look toward the transcendence of ethnic or cultural identities in favor or a cosmopolitan ethic' (Levy 2000: 7).

USA and France, that resist interpreting themselves as 'multinational' despite the continued existence of rooted ethnocultural or ethnolinguistic minorities. Of course, in many ways a dominant national culture has triumphed in the USA, France, and Germany, although this was by no means a foregone conclusion, say, two centuries ago. If we can count these countries among the few 'unination' states in the world today, it is thanks to the success of deliberate nation-building projects designed specifically to eliminate or dominate sources of cultural diversity that might have threatened (and in some cases did threaten) the unity, authority, and effectiveness of these states. Given the success of these three powerful republics, citizens of many newly democratic multinational states—particularly in Eastern and Central Europe—can be forgiven for asking why this kind of nation-building should not be considered the best long-term strategy for dealing with the 'inconvenience' of having more than one people 'warring in the bosom of a single state'.[12] We will explore this issue in Chapter 2, on the ethics of nation-building, and in the subsequent chapters on federal constitutionalism. The short answer is that much has changed since the heyday of nation-building a century ago. On the one hand, to put it bluntly, ethnocultural minorities do not go quietly any more; assimilationist nation-building projects tend not merely to be ineffective—they also usually backfire by reinforcing and 'nationalizing' minority cultural identities.[13] And, on the other hand, many of the heavy-handed 'methods' that 'worked' a century or two ago (from military conquests and annexations to the banning of minority languages and the colonizing of minority territories) are now universally condemned in democratic societies.

The legacy of nationalism in the great nation-states is also instructive, in part because of its very invisibility from the inside, so to speak. Like fish unaware of the water they swim in, citizens and even intellectuals in both France and the USA tend not to see their political cultures as nationalist.[14]

---

[12] This image comes from an official report by Lord Durham in 1839 on the future of two of Britain's Canadian colonies. He recommended the deliberate assimilation of French Canadians as the best way to avoid this figurative, and potentially literal, warring. See the abridgement of the report in Craig (1982).

[13] In his classic and oft-cited discussion of this process, Connor argues: 'No examples of significant assimilation [of ethnocultural minorities into a larger national community]...have taken place since the advent of the age of nationalism and the propagation of the principle of self-determination of nations' (Connor 1994: 54).

[14] Conservative intellectuals may be less prone to this particular form of blindness or aversion to a nationalist self-conception. In an article that questions Iraq's readiness for American-style democracy, George Will writes: 'The American revolution was, at bottom, about the right of a distinctive people, conscious of itself as a single people, to govern itself in its distinctive manner, in nationhood.... Most Americans [today] are not merely patriots; *they are nationalists, too*. They do not merely love their country; they believe that its political arrangements, and the values and understandings of the human condition that those arrangements reflect, are superior to most other nations' arrangements' (Will 2004: 20, my italics).

Indeed, they may even contrast their forms of democracy, republicanism, or patriotism, with the more disturbing manifestations of nationalism found elsewhere. That is, until some extraordinary event disturbs or muddies the otherwise transparent water—most dramatically of all via the spilling of their own blood. In a book on nationalism published in 2000, the sociologist Michael Hechter could write that 'everyone recognizes that nationalism is much more prevalent in...Canada...[than in] the United States' (Hechter 2000: 3–4). But before the following year would be over—i.e. after 11 September 2001—few would take that claim about the comparative weakness of nationalism in the USA to be obvious. Observations at that year's end by the judge and legal philosopher, Richard Posner, are telling:

American race relations, which a few months ago seemed the nation's most serious problem, now seem almost benign, and concerns about 'lifestyle' trivial. We see that black Americans have the same basic values as white Americans, and homosexual Americans the same basic values as heterosexual Americans. The category 'American' suddenly seems spacious and lofty, transcending the petty divisions that so preoccupied the politically active and the ideologically obsessed. We now can see the virtue in concepts such as 'Americanism' and 'nationalism'. (There's nothing like a common enemy for making friends.) We discover that left-leaning communitarians, who decried the loss of community, overlooked the *American* community. We are learning that social diversity and social homogeneity, extreme individualism and national community, are compatible. (Posner 2002: 22–3)

Posner is not claiming, I take it, that terrorists from abroad *provoked* a rise in nationalism or generated a new national identity. His point is that their acts revealed the surprising strength and importance of the bonds that already existed.[15] Without even trying, in some sense, America had managed to thoroughly incorporate successive generations—including those who came of age in the 1960s questioning everything America stood for, those who came of age in the 1990s with a 'totally, like, whatever' attitude to politics, and those who immigrated to the USA after coming of age somewhere else—into the vast imagined community that is the American nation. This nation continues to build or rebuild itself without apparently resorting to the crude techniques from the golden age of nationalism. But the resulting nationalism

---

[15] Posner's words provide a strikingly genuine example of a phenomenon described and predicted by David Miller in his 1995 book, in which he writes that 'genuinely momentous events', including armed conflicts, and even some natural disasters or international sporting triumphs, provide 'the occasions on which we are suddenly confronted with the ties that bind us to our fellow nationals, ties which in everyday life remain hidden from view.... [E]ven those who profess their indifference to nationality under ordinary circumstances are very likely to find that, at those exceptional moments when the fate of the whole nation is determined collectively, their sense of identity is such that they see their own well-being as closely bound up with that of the community' (Miller 1995: 14–15).

is no less capable of mobilizing a population behind a political or military project. We will explore this phenomenon in detail in Chapter 2.

The title of Chapter 1, 'Thinking Through Nationalism', is also a central theme for the entire book. The phrase is deliberately and multiply ambiguous. As a philosophical work this book begins with an attempt to reflect on the concept of nationalism and the special challenges this most slippery of 'isms' poses for liberal-democratic theory. As a work in applied normative theory, it is also an attempt to resolve some of the challenges nationalism as a political phenomenon poses for liberal-democratic societies. The phrase may even hide an unrealistic hope that we can think our way *through* and even, to some degree, *past* nationalism, to some form of 'post-nationalist' political culture. At the same time, it reveals a confession: that the author, and most readers, cannot escape the fact that they have come of age within political cultures that can be described as more or less nationalist. It is difficult to reflect upon political society without using some kind of nationalist lens or mirror. Or to put it less generously, 'thinking through nationalism' is difficult in the sense that, like any good ideology, nationalism invariably clouds and obscures one's thoughts. As Miller (1995: 6) notes: '[I]deas of nationality are the conscious creations of bodies of people, who have elaborated and revised them in order to make sense of their social and political surroundings, and we too are involved in this process. We cannot properly distance ourselves from it and treat nationalism as a force of nature that afflicts others but not ourselves.'

Well, we can and should *try* to distance ourselves from our own nationalist conditioning, and hence the other meanings available in this phrase 'thinking through nationalism'. But few writers on nationalism fail to betray their own national origins and aspirations; and this may be especially true of the 'tourists' who rushed into the field through the gaps in the Berlin Wall. While some of us may have been around long enough now to have picked up the idiom of nationalist scholarship, we invariably betray our old accents and have to rely all too often on our mother-tongue vocabulary. My accent, if it is not already apparent, is Canadian—'English Canadian' (to use a phrase that, like many group names in multinational states, is highly contested) to be exact; although I have also spent a significant amount of time throughout my academic career in francophone and bilingual milieux in Canada, and in the (English part of the) UK, (the Catalan-speaking part of) Spain, (the French-speaking part of) Belgium, and the (liberal-speaking parts of) the USA. In addition to the standard textbook cases, such as the founding of the American federation, the Third Republic in France, and the familiar 'front page' or CNN cases from the recent past, I will draw many examples of nationalist politics from the political cultures with which I am most familiar. My aim is to argue for some relatively generalizable normative, conceptual, and institutional claims about politics of nationalism in democratic multinational states. I shall for the most part leave it to readers in other lands to decide whether these philosophical claims clarify the political stakes with which they are more familiar.

My modest aim, in short, is to be more a tour guide than a tourist—even if, like almost all of the tour guides to nationalism who speak the language of liberal political theory, I was a mere tourist myself when the Wall came down. As I will explain in Chapter 1, this book arrives in what we might call the 'second wave' of recent philosophical and normative discussions of nationalism. The first wave, which ran through the 1990s, focused on legitimizing the very subject matter of nationalism as a domain of normative enquiry, on exploring the basic concepts of nation and nationalism, on explaining the compatibility or incompatibility of nationalism with other basic principles of liberal democracy, as well as on justifying a primary or remedial right to secession. All of these issues remain alive (at least in the somewhat embarrassing sense in which most philosophical questions never truly die). But many have also been sufficiently settled to enable us to proceed beyond them. There was, in other words, significant progress during the 'first wave', and with it the emergence of substantial pockets of consensus. For the purposes of normative theorizing, I believe that most of what *has to be said* about the meaning of concepts like 'nation', 'nationalism', and their cognates *has been* said. I will not rehearse all of these issues laboriously, although of course every writer must be clear about how, and to some extent *why*, he or she is using such protean concepts (as I shall try to be in Chapter 1).

So much then for the general intellectual, political, and even autobiographical background to this book and to the debates it is attempting to advance. Allow me to finish these prefatorial remarks with a brief and necessarily polemical and truncated sketch of the narrative structure of the argument to come (with relevant chapter numbers appended in [square brackets]):

- The idea of nationalism defies any brief summary or reduction. [1]
- And in particular, we will miss much of what is interesting about nationalism if we think of it primarily as the ideology of national communities seeking self-determination. [1]
- Among other things, nationalism is a kind of a political culture: it colours how we identify ourselves, how we justify policies and political programmes, and how we mobilize support for such programmes. It is a way of doing politics. [1]
- Nationalist political cultures and nationalist politics are compatible with liberalism when they involve identities, policies, discourses, and activities that do not violate standard liberal-democratic norms. It is, in principle,

permissible to pursue liberal ends using some nationalist political means. [1, 2]

- A central issue for a liberal nationalist is the question of what the state, and political actors more generally, are permitted to do to deliberately shape and strengthen the national identities of citizens. In short, what forms of *nation-building* are permissible, or perhaps even obligatory? This has been a surprisingly neglected issue in the recent literature. [2]
- Routine functions and activities of the state have significant effects on the content and strength of citizens' national identities, so we cannot pretend that the state can be neutral about identity the way it can be about, say, religion. [2]
- We need to develop a series of criteria and tests that allow us to evaluate nation-building activities and discourses. I will argue that plausible criteria do indeed endorse certain nation-building projects by the state and by political actors more generally. [2]
- And since most states contain more than one community with a national identity, it follows that we can expect a plurality of legitimate nation-building projects in such states. Typically, these will also be *rival* nation-building projects, because they are competing for the hearts, minds, and identities of some of the same citizens (e.g. both Scottish and British nationalist leaders will compete for the loyalty of ordinary Scots). [2]
- Such a rivalry gives rise to conflicts and tensions in the state, as well as to charges of injustice when some national communities feel themselves to be unfairly disadvantaged in their ability to shape and nurture their own identities and projects. [2]
- Federalism can serve as an institutional response to this rivalry and conflict. By dividing sovereignty, a federal system makes it possible for majority and minority communities to have exclusive control over specific political jurisdictions, such as the education system or the military, that are useful for nation building. In other words, federalism facilitates the distribution and sharing of nation-building tools between national minorities and majorities. [3]
- But how do we decide what federal arrangements are appropriate and just in any given multinational state? Again, contemporary political philosophers have offered surprisingly few answers to this question. [3–5]
- We can gain a few limited insights from the history of federalist thought from the early Renaissance through the twentieth century; but it must be said that almost none of these theorists was thinking of federalism as a way

to manage a plurality of national communities and nationalist projects within a common political space. [3]

- We can also gain a certain amount of insight into just federal design from traditions of democratic and constitutional theory used to justify other kinds of political institutions. But these theories were not designed to deal with competing nationalisms either. [5]

- In order to develop a fully adequate normative theory of multinational federalism, we must supplement these traditional democratic and federalist theories with principles of recognition. [5]

- I catalogue an array of constitutional options for federal design [4], and sketch a normative federal theory incorporating principles of mutual recognition that could be endorsed by national majorities and minorities alike. [5]

- I apply this theory to one specific aspect of a multinational federal constitution, namely, the design and justification of a clause for regulating secession and secessionist politics. [6]

- Virtually all national minorities in advanced democratic states prefer continued membership in their multinational state to secession. But most also seek greater autonomy and recognition. [3, 6]

- A well-designed and well-negotiated secession clause—one that makes a democratic secession difficult but not impossible—can paradoxically reduce incentives for secessionist politics while enhancing recognition and autonomy for national minorities, and political stability for the national majority. [6]

Most of these claims are controversial. With added nuance, caveats, and explanation, I obviously hope they will seem less so over the course of the book. At the heart of this project are the inevitability, and also the legitimacy, of rival nation-building projects within the multinational state. The challenge for both political leaders and political philosophers is to design and justify a federal system in which the rivals can be partners. There are no a priori, top-down solutions to this challenge. In a democratic society we must envisage an institutional framework in which these rival nationalisms can negotiate the terms and limits of their partnership.[16] Or to put it the other way, the partners must negotiate the terms and limits of their own nationalisms. This book aims to sketch out the options, stakes, and principles appropriate for such 'negotiations'.

---

[16] See Blattberg (2003: especially chs. 1 and 2), for a rich discussion of different metaphors of conversation and negotiation in multinational constitutional politics.

Acknowledgements

Recognition plays a pivotal role in the argument of this book: it facilitates the 'negotiation' of rival nation-building projects within a federal state. I must, however, begin by recognizing the role of a very large cast who have contributed to both my understanding of the subject matter and my will to persevere with the project. One of the dilemmas of recognition in multinational states is that if only a small number of groups are recognized, the others will feel slighted; but if many groups are recognized, the significance of the recognition will seem diminished for the groups who feel themselves to be more 'fundamental'. I hope the same dilemma does not apply for colleagues, since there are almost as many who have helped me as there are ethnocultural groups in India. I can very honestly say that every single person about to be name-checked has, through conversation or written comments, influenced my thoughts on at least some point, assumption, or argument in this book.

Special thanks go out to several colleagues who read and commented on the entire first draft of the manuscript: Josep Costa, Martin Blanchard, an anonymous reader from the Press, Avigail Eisenberg, Andrew Potter, Hilliard Aronovitch, Will Kymlicka, and Chantale LaCasse. I must also thank under this heading several graduate students who put me through the paces during a semester-long seminar using the manuscript at the Université de Montréal in 2005: Dominic Martin, Alexandre Doire, Paul Journet, Xavier Landes, Tony Patoine, Nick Sagos, Andrea Connors, and Carolyne Chagnon. The final draft evolved considerably because of this rigorous but generous feedback.

My views on nationalism and federalism have been shaped profoundly by my interactions with colleagues from around the world, especially from the countries I discuss frequently in the book: Ross Poole, Ferran Requejo, Philippe Van Parijs, Guy Laforest, Phil Resnick, Margaret Moore, Allen Buchanan, David Miller, Manuel Toscana, Pablo da Silveira, Axel Gosseries, Ronald Beiner, Dimitri Karmis, Kai Nielsen, Attracta Ingram, Adrian Favell, Filimon Peonidis, Samir Khordoc, Agust Ingthorsson, Dominique Leydet, Michael Freeman, Michael Milde, Jacob Levy, Rainer Baubock, Matthias Kaufmann, Eamonn Callan, Rob Reich, Eve D'Onofrio, Caroline Ford, Sima Godfrey, Daniele Conversi, David Schmidtz, Alan Patten, Michel Seymour, Daniel Turp, Alain Dieckhoff, Charles Taylor, Alain Gagnon, Stéphane Dion, Yael Tamir, Adrian Favell, Anthony Smith, Hervé Pourtois, Robert Howse, Melissa Williams, Francisco Colom, Ramon Maiz, Ronald Watts, Jon Erik Fossum, Andreas Føllesdal, Ibrahim Ouattara, Brian Anderson, Chris

MacDonald, Bryn Williams-Jones, and Don Lenihan. I owe a special shout-out to two colleagues and friends with whom I have discussed these topics off and on for almost fifteen years, and who coincidentally were the founders of the two research centres that have served as my academic havens over the last decade, Michael McDonald (Centre for Applied Ethics) and Daniel Weinstock (Centre de recherche en éthique).

I have held regular faculty positions at three different universities during the course of this research project: University of Ottawa, University of British Columbia, and Université de Montréal. Along with the Social Sciences and Humanities Research Council of Canada, and the patrons of the Chairs I have held at my last two institutions, Mary and Maury Young, and the McConnell Foundation, these three universities have contributed essential resources, including human resources in the form of very able research assistants: Paolo Prosperi, Sangeeta Mishra, Jason Blahuta, Fiona Stewart, Mickey Fabry, Pierre-Yves Néron, and especially Nick Sagos, whose help was indispensable over the final months of writing, revising, formatting, and indexing. I have also benefited immensely from visiting positions lasting from a few weeks to several months at the Department of Philosophy at the LSE, the Chaire Hoover at the Université Catholique de Louvain, the Institut des études européenes at the Université de Paris VIII, the Department of Political Science at the Universitat Pompeu Fabra, the Center for Social Innovation at Stanford University, and the Department of Philosophy at the Universidad Católica de Uruguay.

Many authors have thanked particular libraries, and in one of his books Brian Barry thanked radio stations he listened to while writing. Like anyone nowadays who prefers to work at home (close to his or her CD collection) I would be remiss if I did not acknowledge two commercial websites that have greatly facilitated this research: one, named after a very long river, that lets you search inside books, then delivers them the next day; and one named after a very large number, that lets you search for almost anything anywhere, including your own long-forgotten thoughts stored on your own hard-drive. I am also indebted to two other sites of special significance to this project: constitution.org and the host site of the International Constitutional Law Project (http://www.oefre.unibe.ch/law/icl/info.html) both of which provide English translations of constitutions from around the world and back in time.

Some of these chapters began life as articles, even if they now bear only a family resemblance to the original publications. Chapter 1 uses material from 'Theorizing Nationalism (Normatively)', in R. Beiner (ed.), *Theorizing Nationalism*, New York: SUNY Press, 1999, 51–66; Chapter 2, evolved out of 'From Nation-building to National Engineering: The Ethics of Shaping

Identities', published in both A. Dieckhoff (ed.), *The Politics of Belonging: Nationalism, Liberalism, and Pluralism*. Lanham, MD: Lexington Books, 2004, 87–105; and in Ramon Maiz and Ferran Requejo (eds.), *Democracy, Nationalism and Multiculturalism*, London/New York: Routledge, 2005, 79–95. This paper had been earlier published in Spanish and French as: 'La Ética y la construcción naciónal', in R. M. Suárez and J. M. Rivera Otero (eds.), *Construcción de Europa: Democracia y globalización*, Vol. 1, Santiago de Compostela: Prensa de la Universidad de Santiago de Compostela, 2002, 905–23; and 'La nation en construction', in A. Dieckhoff (ed.), *La constellation des appartenances: Nationalisme, libéralisme et pluralisme*, Paris: Presses de Science-Pô, 2004, 125–52. Chapter 6 uses material from 'Domesticating Secession', in S. Macedo and A. Buchanan (eds.), *Secession and Self-Determination*, NOMOS XLV, New York: New York University Press, 2003, 193–237; and it draws on ideas first published in 'The Ethics of Secession as the Regulation of Secessionist Politics', in M. Moore (ed.), *Self-Determination and Secession*, Oxford: Oxford University Press, 1998, 34–61; and 'Secession and (Constitutional) Democracy', in F. Requejo (ed.), *Democracy and National Pluralism*, London: Routledge Press, 2001, 84–102. I am grateful to these publishers for permission to incorporate any previously published passages into this book.

I would like to thank the Cohen-Rese Gallery in San Francisco for introducing me to the work of the extraordinary figurative painter, Tatiana Zaits; and I am forever indebted to the artist herself for allowing us to use her painting 'Lambarena' on the cover. I could not have commissioned a more evocative representation of the contents of this book.

An author, especially a chronically tardy one, has no right to expect the level of patience and encouragement that I am most grateful to have received from my editors at OUP, Dominic Byatt, Claire Croft, and Lyndsey Rice. Finally, I must thank again two individuals mentioned at the outset: the person most responsible for starting me down this road, and keeping me from veering off it, Will Kymlicka; and the person who ensured that the book would indeed be completed before the road ran out (or vice versa), and so much more, Chantale LaCasse.

W. N.
Université de Montréal

1

Thinking through Nationalism

> Nationalism is the starkest political shame of the twentieth century, the deepest, most intractable and yet most unanticipated blot on the political history of the world since the year 1900. But it is also the very tissue of modern political sentiment, the most widespread, the most unthinking, and the most immediate political disposition of all at least among the literate populations of the modern world.
>
> —John Dunn (1979: 55)
>
> It is incontestable that the resurgence of nationalist sentiment in many areas of the world is one of the most important and least anticipated phenomena of contemporary international politics.
>
> —Robert McKim and Jeff McMahan (1997: 3)
>
> Nationalism is not a 'force' to be measured as resurgent or receding. It is a heterogeneous set of 'nation'-oriented idioms, practices, and possibilities that are continuously available or 'endemic' in modern cultural and political life.
>
> —Rogers Brubaker (1996: 10)

Very soon after political philosophers redirected their attention towards nationalism in the early 1990s, the very idea of 'liberal nationalism' went from being an oxymoron to a pleonasm. Philosophers in this 'first wave' were faced with the burden of proving that it was *not impossible* to be a liberal and a nationalist at the same time.[1] As a result of their efforts the burden of proof

---

[1] As far as I am aware, the first book (at least, the first one published on a major academic press) on the evaluation of nationalism by a political philosopher in the 'post-Rawlsian' era was Tamir's *Liberal Nationalism* (1993). After a series of important articles and chapters in the late 1980s and early 1990s, Miller followed with *On Nationality* (1995). I take these to be the exemplary works of what I am calling the 'first wave' of recent philosophical analyses and evaluations of nationalism, as are the two major books by Kymlicka (1989, 1995a) during this period, which covered a larger range of issues of concern for cultural minorities in liberal states. There was also around this time and shortly after a flurry of articles—an important one by Margalit and Raz (1990), and many collected in edited volumes such as McKim and McMahan (1997), Couture, Nielsen, and Seymour (1998), Moore (1998), and Beiner (1999)—that staked out a wide variety of competing positions on a broad range of issues, and that obviously belie any notion that there was a unified research project or consensus in the literature on nationalism.

soon shifted to fall upon those who wished to deny that the liberal tradition had always, in practice, incorporated basic elements of nationalism. This was quite a feat, given that television was showing us 'nationalist' mortar shells exploding in crowded marketplaces during this period. Not to mention the fact that the last time political philosophers had taken any interest in nationalism it was with Hitler, Mussolini, Franco, and Tojo in mind.[2] What accounts for this rather spectacular revision of philosophical attitudes to an ideology that was once—and again in the popular opinion of many Western states—so widely condemned?

The answer to this question is manifold, and has little to do with the political landscape of post-Communist Eastern Europe or inter-war Germany. For one thing, coincidentally, the early 1990s saw the overly abstract liberal–communitarian debates refocus on two more concrete issues: minority rights and citizenship. The first issue began with a concern for the salience of the most rooted forms of communal identity: those provided by ethnicity and culture, particularly for minority groups. Following Kymlicka's lead, many liberal theorists were receptive to the idea that a liberal concern for individual autonomy required an equal and prior concern for a healthy cultural context in which valued choices could take place.[3] This in turn sanctioned liberal discussions of minority rights up to and including the rights of minority nations to self-determination. The second arena for transformed debates among liberals, communitarians, republicans, and others was over the issue of citizenship, including the all-important though long-neglected question of the source of social cohesion in diverse modern states. The urgency and difficulty of this question bred a renewed interest in the

---

Also noteworthy in the 'first wave' were Ignatieff (1993) and a book on patriotism covering some of the same issues, Nathanson (1993). Several journals devoted special issues to nationalism, including *Critical Review* (1996: 10/2), and *Philosophical Forum* (1996–7: 28/1–2). Constitutional dramas and the rise of Québécois and Aboriginal nationalism in Canada in the early 1990s gave rise to numerous works and edited volumes of interest, including Taylor (1993), Baker (1994), Weinstock (1994), Blais, Laforest, and Lamoureux (1995), Carens (1995*a*), Tully (1995), Seymour (1995), and Kymlicka (1998*c*). The Yugoslav tragedy inspired a small library of works, many of which contain reflections on nationalism tagged to detailed explanations of how things went so terribly wrong (see, e.g. Denitch 1994; Akhavan and Howse 1995, Pavkovic 2000). We must also not forget Hardin's *One for All: The Logic of Group Conflict* (1995), which surfed brilliantly on a wave of its own. There is no clear starting point for what we might call the 'second wave', but by 2000 many political theorists were engaging in debates as much with the 'first wave' as with the theories of social scientists from the 1980s. Early 'second wavers' include Poole (1999), Levy (2000*a*), Aronovitch (2000*a*), Moore (2001), and a number of the essays in Miller (2000), Kymlicka and Norman (2000), Kymlicka and Opalski (2002), Gagnon and Tully (2001), Dieckhoff (2004), Eisenberg and Spinner-Halev (2005), Seymour (2004), and Macedo and Buchanan (2003).

[2] See, e.g. Barker (1942), Popper (1944).
[3] Kymlicka's earliest version of the argument is in his 1989 book (ch. 8).

utility of national identities as a form of 'social cement'. A further factor in this rehabilitation of nationalism was a bit of scholarship (in a discipline that had become very ahistorical during the post-war period) revealing that, at least until the advent of National Socialism, liberal thinkers had always paid a fair bit of attention to what we might call the fabric of majority national cultures. In retrospect, it is odd that we had missed this fact: that we had read, for example, J. S. Mill's *Considerations on Representative Government* for what it said about utilitarianism and participatory democracy while ignoring entirely its gem of a chapter, 'Of Nationality'; or that we read *The Federalist* as a treatise on liberty and faction politics and not also as a blueprint for nation-building, and so on.

A final explanation for the positive gloss that so many of the 'first-wave' treatments applied to nationalism is conceptual. Enquiries into the possibility of 'liberal nationalism' have two very protean 'isms' to play around with. Suffice it to say that the vision of nationalism or national identity embraced by the cautious 'first-wave' supporters of liberal nationalism had little in common with the visions of nationalism that bear the face of Hitler, Milosovic, or Le Pen. For this reason, many of the early debates between liberal nationalists and critics of liberal nationalism were hardly debates at all: the critics were condemning things the supporters were not supporting.

1.1 DEFINING OUR CONCEPTS

When normative debates are miscast in this way it is often tempting to focus on the key terms involved: to believe that only if we can find the best definition of the central concepts in the debate—or at least agree upon how we are all going to use the terms for the purpose of our debates—can we ever expect to make progress on the substantive normative issues.[4] This background assumption seems to inform the work not only of most of the political philosophers and theorists of the 'first wave', but also of the social scientists whose work in the 1980s and 1990s served as these theorists' primary textbooks. In their influential Oxford Reader on nationalism, Hutchinson and Smith (1994: 3–4) declare on their opening page: 'Perhaps the central difficulty in the study of nations and nationalism has been the problem of finding adequate and agreed definitions of the key concepts, nation and nationalism.' Most recent books on nationalism have sections on 'what is a nation?' and

---

[4] For one of the later defences of this essentially positivist methodology, see Oppenheim (1981). For a critique see Miller (1983) and Norman (1991).

'what is nationalism?' in the first chapter. But it is rarely appreciated what different sorts of questions these are. The first one does call for a definition of a concept that can be articulated in the space of a few lines; this partly explains why there is now substantial agreement among political theorists about what we mean by 'nation'. However, as I shall argue presently we run into problems when we seek a similarly concise definition of 'nationalism'.

First 'nation'. Most definitions of the concept of nation in the writings of both the social theorists of the 1980s and the political philosophers and theorists since 1990 converge on the following points:

- Nations are a kind of human community.
- They are not by definition coextensive with states, although there are a few nation-states; they are also not the same as mere ethnic groups, although there are some ethnic nations and many national identities with ethnic 'elements'.
- They cannot be identified by any particular set of properties, although they tend to be named communities, with a homeland, common myths, shared memories, and a shared language.

Following J. S. Mill and Renan in the nineteenth and Weber in the early twentieth century, most contemporary writers on nationalism also emphasize the importance of subjective properties of nationhood.

- They are 'communities of sentiment' or 'imagined communities'.
- Communities qualify as nations when most of their members believe and feel them to be nations, i.e. when there is a critical mass within the community of individuals with a particular national identity[5] and a desire among their members to be self-governing.

As Gellner (1983: 7) puts it: 'Nations are the artefacts of men's convictions and loyalties and solidarities.'

Now this basic level of conceptual agreement leaves open many legitimate disputes concerning, for example, whether some given community properly qualifies as a nation, when various nations first appeared as such, what causal forces bring about particular nations, whether it makes sense to distinguish different kinds of nations (such as so-called ethnic or civic nations), and so on. We will discuss some of these issues at various points in this book when they are relevant to specific normative or institutional issues.

Before moving on, however, it is worth reflecting briefly on the last two conditions in the above list. In effect, virtually all theorists of nationalism now

[5] In Chapter 2 I will discuss at length the components of national identity and how these are promoted or reinforced by political discourse and state institutions.

agree that a necessary condition for a community's qualifying as a nation is a goodly percentage of its members believing it to be a nation deserving of self-government and self-determination. This 'self-reflexiveness' built into the concept should give us pause. Jacob Levy sketches one particularly striking implication for normative theories making use of the concept of nation:

'Nation' does not denote a kind of community describable apart from nationalist projects and the claim of national self-determination. Once we have a sociologically persuasive account of where a 'nation' is, we find that one way or another the political mobilization that nationalist theory is supposed to *justify* is already part of how we've picked the community out. In other words the political program of nationalism is built into the category of nation to begin with; the normative argument is always circular. (Levy 2004: 160)

The implications of the subjective or self-reflexive content of the concept of nation are more radical than many political philosophers—and certainly most in the 'first wave'—have supposed. In fact, all the remaining chapters of this book are devoted to exploring these implications for nationalist projects and the constitutional order of states housing more than one such project. For the time being we can note simply that we should not assume that 'nation' is a more primitive concept than 'nationalism', since the former cannot be properly understood until we are clearer about the latter. To this task we now turn. (In the appendix I explore a much more radical suggestion about the implications of the alleged 'circularity' Levy describes: i.e. Brubaker's argument that we should drop the language of idea of 'nation'—or even deny the existence of nations—when explaining and evaluating nationalism, in order not to be co-opted by the nationalists.)

1.2 WHAT IS NATIONALISM? OR, WHO IS A NATIONALIST?

'Nationalism' is conceptually messier than 'nation'. In the language of ontology, nations are social substances, a kind of thing. As we noted, all theorists willing to grant existence to nations agree what kind of thing they are: a kind of human community. The term 'nationalism', however, can refer to several distinct sorts of things, properties, mental states, abstract entities, and processes. Consider the following oft-cited list of ways Smith (1991: 72) has noticed the term being used:

1. the whole process of forming and maintaining nations or nation-states;
2. a consciousness of belonging to the nation, together with sentiments and aspirations for its security and prosperity;

3. a language and symbolism of the 'nation' and its role;
4. an ideology, including a cultural doctrine of nations and national will and prescriptions for the realization of national aspirations and national will;
5. a social and political movement to achieve the goals of the nation and realize its national will.

In short, 'nationalism' has been used to refer to a *process*, a kind of *sentiment* or *identity*, a *form of political rhetoric*, an *ideology*, a *principle* or set of principles, and a kind of *social-political movement*. And we could add to this list. Moore, for example, writes of 'nationalism...as a normative *argument*' and nationalism as 'a normative *theory*' (2001: 5, my italics). Obviously, these sorts of things are related, and we can see how—even if we decided that only one of these things should properly be called 'nationalism'—we would still want to use the adjective 'nationalist' to describe phenomena of the other sorts. Now if this multiplicity of things that can be called nationalist does not make the concept of nationalism confusing enough, we must remember that for each kind of thing (e.g. an ideology, political movement, or identity) there is considerable debate about what precisely are the necessary or sufficient conditions for its being nationalist.

This book is addressed to the predicament of the political philosopher trying to get enough of a handle on the nature of nationalism to begin to pick out and pursue the normative and institutional issues to which it *(it?)* gives rise. Our primary concern here is not conceptual. It is not 'What does "nationalism" mean?', but rather 'What should a normative theory of nationalism be about?' The short answer to this question is: All of the things mentioned in Smith's list. Or to put it another way, *whatever we may, on grounds of conceptual propriety, decide to call 'nationalism'*, a normative theory of nationalism should be concerned with the nature of national identities, the political attempts to forge and shape them, the rhetoric and ideologies that are used in such attempts, and the principles nationalists use to justify these kinds of politics, among other things.

That said, what conceptual resources do we have for privileging one or more of these uses of 'nationalism'? It would be helpful if we could reserve the term 'nationalism' for only one or two of Smith's categories (he himself uses it for ideological movements). At the same time, we want to take care because it is clear that the hasty identification of nationalism with just one of these categories has often resulted in an unfortunate narrowing of the agenda of normative issues for a political theory of nationalism.

For example, consider Gellner's famous dictum: 'Nationalism is primarily a *political principle*, which holds that the political and national unit should be congruent' (1983: 1, my italics). If we were to take this claim seriously (more seriously than Gellner himself does), then a normative theory of nationalism could quickly be reduced to a justification of the principle of national self-determination. I believe this would be a *serious* mistake. It would lead us to ignore much that is interesting in nationalist politics, for example, the fact that nationalist movements may be in existence generations before the ('unawakened') nations they will claim to represent, and that much of their political activity may be focused on goals that have little direct connection with making the national and political units congruent.[6] Given the familiarity of political philosophers with the project of justifying principles, it should come as no surprise that many of their initial attempts to come to grips with nationalism in the 1990s were reductionist in just this way.

What is the significance of the 'ism' in 'nationalism'? It is commonplace to concede that nationalism is 'by far the most potent ideology in the world' (Barry 1987: 353; see also Hechter 2000: 3), but also that it is alone among major political ideas or systems in lacking a great theorist. As Anderson (1991: 5) observes, theorists of nationalism are often perplexed by the '"political" power of nationalisms vs their philosophical poverty and even incoherence. In other words, unlike most other isms, nationalism has never produced its own grand thinkers: no Hobbeses, Tocquevilles, Marxes, or Webers.' Not to mention Rousseauxs, Kants, or Rawlses, to give more philosophers their due. Of course, some great philosophers have written on nationalism, even in its favour. But none of these can be read as a grand theory of the sort that, say, Kant, J. S. Mill, or Rawls provide for liberalism, or Marx for socialism. The nationalist writings of Fichte or Heidegger read more like *exercises* in nationalism (and rather delusional exercises at that) than generalizable theories of nationalism. Herder, who is often cited as an intellectual founder of a certain brand of tolerant, universalistic cultural nationalism (perhaps even the inventor of the German word for 'nationalism'), in fact produced but a few pages on the subject. J. S. Mill's best-known thoughts on it boil down to a chapter in which he views common nationality and language as necessary conditions for social unity and democracy; and Rousseau's ideas can be read mainly out of his advice to the government of Poland.[7] According

---

[6] Nationalist leaders of a minority nation can attempt to foster discontent with the status quo by criticizing almost any policy of the central government. The terms of these criticisms may be internal to the policy domain (education, health care, or what have you), but part of the intended effect is to shift the loyalties and trust of the members of the minority nation away from the larger state and the central government. To 'hear' nationalist discourse only when nationalists are calling explicitly for political autonomy may make one deaf to 95 per cent of the content of a nationalist political culture.

[7] As Bernard Yack put it so pithily, 'there are no great theoretical texts outlining and defending nationalism.... Only minor texts by major thinkers, like Fichte, or major texts by second-rate thinkers, like Mazzini' (quoted in Beiner 1999: 2).

to Anderson, we should not regard the poverty of nationalist theory as a sign that the idea has been unduly neglected by political theorists, or that it is too feeble to support a sustained theoretical enquiry. Rather, we are being misled simply by thinking about this 'ism' as primarily an idea or ideology. It would, he says, 'make things easier if one treated it as if it belonged with "kinship" and "religion", rather than with "liberalism" or "fascism"' (Anderson 1991: 5).

Anderson provides an important insight here, even if it is overstated. It is overstated because nationalism surely does qualify as an ideology (or a family of ideologies) on common interpretations of that term. Nobody—Anderson included—would deny that nationalisms are (to cite a typical definition of 'ideology') 'patterns of symbolically charged beliefs and expressions that present, interpret and evaluate the world in a way designed to shape, mobilize, direct, organize and justify certain modes or courses of action and to anathematize others' (Kettler 1987: 235). As we have already seen, important aspects of nationalism can also be cast as a political doctrine of assigning rights and duties to nations and their members. Nevertheless, Anderson is surely correct to point out the difference between the kinds of 'isms' involved in, for example, nationalism and liberalism. Nationalism is not merely a different set of principles and background empirical assumptions vis-à-vis liberalism the way, say, conservatism or socialism is. It is a different kind of 'ism', more akin in many ways to categories like capitalism, feudalism, or tribalism. (For example, like capitalism it arose in certain places at certain times, and then spread around the world with technological progress; it is modern but has obvious primordial roots; it arose without any theorist thinking up a grand idea; it mingles with and modifies other political doctrines; it reorients people's world views in profound ways; it demands an institutional and political framework, which in turn requires justification.) Thus, 'nationalism' clearly refers as much to social, cultural, political, and anthropological *phenomena* as it does to a system of beliefs or principles. (Some 'isms' refer merely to phenomena or activities, and not to any real doctrine at all, e.g., 'hooliganism' or 'sado-masochism'—Sade's own theorizing [1795] notwithstanding.) In effect, Anderson's point underscores the importance of the first item on Smith's list of the things to which the term 'nationalism' can refer: 'the whole *process* of forming and maintaining nations or nation-states'.

So again I ask: Where does this leave the philosopher trying to clarify the idea of nationalism enough to generate an agenda of normative issues? First, we can reaffirm that we should not define nationalism in a narrow way (e.g. merely as a set of political principles) that excludes from view much of what is interesting about the *phenomena* of nationalism. Second, it seems clear that it is acceptable and normal to use the term to refer both to kinds of cultural–political phenomena and to kinds of principles or ideologies. Third, we should realize that the question 'To what does the term "nationalism" properly refer?' is neither necessary nor sufficient for an answer to our more basic question, 'What should a normative theory of nationalism be about?' Of course, we *do* need a thorough understanding of nationalism to answer this primary question. But we need the knowledge contained in a book, or bookshelf, on nationalism, not merely that given in a sentence- or paragraph-length definition of the term. This is because we need a sense of the range of elements within a political culture that can be coloured by nationalism. We need to know the difference between nationalist and non-nationalist versions of political discourse, institutions, political projects, political movements, identities, and sentiments. It is the evaluation of these sorts of things that will ultimately be the business of a normative theory of nationalism. What we want is a way of evaluating when it is legitimate (if ever) to be a national*ist*; to feel like one, to talk like one, to justify political arguments like one, and to act like one.

1.3 NATIONALISM AND LIBERAL THEORY

More specifically, this book enquires about when, or in what ways, it is legitimate for a *liberal* to be a nationalist. The remaining chapters concern the justification of various institutional and constitutional responses to nationalism within a liberal–democratic framework. Although generally more concerned about background principles than institutions, most of the 'first wave' of recent normative discussions of nationalism were also anchored in the liberal tradition in this way. I am inclined to begin with a caveat offered by Tamir (1993: 4) in her ground-breaking study: 'The treatment of nationalism and liberalism in this book is not symmetrical. Liberalism is taken as a starting point, and there is no attempt to justify the set of liberal values in light of which this work aims to reflect on, evaluate, and structure a theory of nationalism.' Like Tamir, I will not be spelling out and justifying liberal first principles. But to be honest, this caveat requires a caveat. Enquiry into the nature of nationalism and the challenges it poses for the liberal state quickly reveals fundamental issues on which liberal theory has had surprisingly little to say. This should be obvious in the ensuing chapters on the morality of nation-building, federalism, and secession, where almost nothing had been written by political philosophers until very recently. To work on these issues is therefore necessarily to attempt to augment the understanding of liberal theory in the same way that theorizing about institutions from punishment (in the eighteenth and nineteenth centuries) to the welfare state (in the post-war years) did in previous generations. These enquiries tend to pose challenges at a deeper level for the 'foundations' or basic assumptions of liberal and democratic theory, some of which, potentially, require some basic theoretical rethinking and recasting. We saw this process at work in the 1990s, when enquiries about identity and minority rights pushed debates about liberal–democratic citizenship to new levels of sophistication.[8] Issues concerning the recognition of national minorities, secession, and federalism have a similar potential to breathe new life into stale or neglected assumptions about liberal–democratic constitutionalism. Among other things, all three of these issues, in one way or another, challenge the presumption that there is one people, or polity, within the state, and with it the cherished liberal ideal of equal citizenship. Like Tamir, my treatment of liberalism and nationalism here will be asymmetrical in the sense that I will not have the space to pursue systematically the issues that nationalism raises for liberal theory as such. But in an important sense this book (like Tamir's in fact) aims to reflect on liberalism (and the liberal state) as much as it does on nationalism (and nationalist political culture). This is especially true of the chapters on federal constitutionalism (Chapters 3–6). Throughout these chapters I will refer to some powerful general liberal, democratic, and federalist principles as these are used without much controversy in 'uninational' states. They will be modified as necessary—and in particular, with principles of mutual recognition—for the multinational state.

The remainder of this chapter is devoted to spelling out a range of issues for a liberal theory of nationalism; to put it more accurately, to recall the chapter title for a liberal trying to *think through* nationalism. It should soon become obvious that once we begin to think of nationalism as a kind of political culture rooted in a certain kind of discourse, public justification, and sentiment, there is almost no aspect of a functioning liberal democracy that cannot be affected by nationalism.

1.3.1 Nationalism as Political Culture

Let us begin with an issue that will arise in the context of every chapter to follow, but which I will not be exploring systematically in the abstract. It surfaces in the understanding of nationalism as a *phenomenon*, and for this reason it has been largely neglected by the 'first wave', which concentrated on the implications of nationalist principles and identities. One way of

---

[8] See Kymlicka and Norman (2000) for a survey of these debates, and Barry (2001) for an old-school liberal reaction.

understanding the phenomenon of nationalism is to see it as a characteristic of a *political culture*. The concept of political culture is of course a complex and rich one, and it has been relatively neglected in the Rawlsian tradition (among others) in recent political philosophy, which has focused largely on the justice of institutions. The following broad characterization of the notion of political culture is a helpful starting point:

> Involving both the ideals and the operating norms of a political system, political culture includes subjective attitudes and sentiments as well as objective symbols and creeds that together govern political behaviour and give structure and order to the political process. (Pye 1993)

Both liberal democracy and nationalism are types of political culture in this sense. To put it another way, a given political culture can be shaped by either or both of liberalism and nationalism. These two 'isms' are associated with a somewhat different range of 'subjective attitudes and sentiments' as well as 'objective symbols and creeds'. Among the ways to understand the question of whether 'liberal nationalism' is a coherent notion is to explore in what ways it is possible for a healthy political culture to share elements of both 'creeds'. In multination states this question is complicated by the fact that states 'generally have both elite and mass political cultures, along with further subcultures that are rooted in regional, occupational, class, ethnic, and other differences' (Pye 1993).

For our purposes here it is sufficient to note that democratic political cultures are constituted in part by the kinds of discourses, public arguments, and justifications that are current and that carry weight in politics and that they carry weight in large part because of the presence of certain sentiments and attitudes. A political culture is nationalist, then, to the degree that nationalist rhetoric and justifications are current and effective in political discourse. What qualifies rhetoric, justifications, and other kinds of political discourse as nationalist? Again, this is a surprisingly neglected question in recent forays into the evaluation of nationalism. In some basic sense, it is a necessary and sufficient condition for being a nationalist that one uses (and is moved by) nationalist discourse. To *be* a nationalist is to *speak* like one. So to decide whether or when it is morally acceptable (say, qua liberal) to be a nationalist, it will be necessary (*a*) to identify the basic features of nationalist discourse, and (*b*) to explain how liberalism determines which forms of discourse are acceptable or ideal in a liberal polity.

1.3.1.1 *What is nationalist discourse?*

I have already suggested that it is a big mistake to look for nationalist discourse by focusing entirely on the policies, institutions, or demands being argued for (e.g. on the Gellnerian demand that the national and political units become congruent). Again, in a nationalist political culture, virtually *any* political issue (even issues such as health care or the eradication of rabies) can become imbued with nationalist meaning and value. Almost any issue can be used to shape or reinforce a national identity, evoke national sentiments, or mobilize nationalist opinion. *What makes a demand or justification* nationalist *are not so much the things demanded but the* grounds *or the* sentiments *that are appealed to either explicitly or implicitly.*[9]

Consider the following partly hypothetical illustration. Roughly speaking, all provinces in the Canadian federation have the same legislative and administrative competencies. The federal government is sovereign in some competencies (e.g. foreign affairs, the issuing of currency, and the military) and provincial governments are sovereign in others (e.g. education and health care); other competencies are shared between the two orders of governments. Now consider the positions of two provincial governments that decide to demand a measure of control over a power that is constitutionally allotted to the federal government, e.g. immigration. The government of British Columbia, an anglophone province on the Pacific coast, could demand some administrative control over immigration on the grounds that it has to cope with special issues—a very large influx of Chinese-speaking immigrants who are, among other things, accounting for over half of the students in some school districts—and that it is in a better position than the authorities in Ottawa, 5,000 km away, to deal effectively and fairly with this challenge. Note that this demand can be made on entirely liberal-democratic grounds: that justice would be better served if those most affected by and knowledgeable about a problem were the ones entrusted to deal with it. Now the government of Quebec, the one predominantly francophone province, could make exactly the same demand for more control over immigration, and it could even use some of the same arguments. Its concern, however, is primarily one of identity: it wants to control immigration in order to increase the likelihood that immigrants to Quebec will integrate into the French-speaking majority culture in Quebec, since a steady stream of immigrants integrating into the English-speaking community in Quebec would, in time, give Montreal, Quebec's principal city, an anglophone majority. Although the basic demand is the same as the one used by British Columbia, the grounds, or rationale, not to mention the sentiments appealed to when it tries to sell this demand to its own people, are very different. I submit that this would be a *nationalist*

---

[9] The fact that such grounds are so often implicit rather than explicit, and concern issues that often have no obvious connection to 'the national question', is one reason why it is so difficult for outsiders to easily interpret political cultures in which they are not immersed.

justification, since it is grounded in the desire by the Québécois to preserve a national culture and national identity.[10]

There are two upshots to this partly hypothetical example. First, the point I have been arguing for: nationalist discourse is not determined only or necessarily by the issue or the demand as such, but by the grounds or sentiments appealed to. Second, it also illustrates a very useful, if (again) underused, way of posing the issue of whether liberalism is compatible with nationalism by focusing on the ways in which liberalism and nationalism can imbue the same political culture. For Quebec's nationalist demand here is not in any sense anti-liberal (see Carens 1995*b*). Indeed, the demand itself is the same as one that can be made in a thoroughly liberal way by any province. There does not seem to be anything fundamentally illegitimate about the demand. I have never read a liberal theorist who argued that the central government, rather than the provincial governments, in a federation must always have full control over immigration policy; more to the point, there is no necessary reason why a Quebec government would have to use any power it gained over immigration in an illiberal way. Quebec in this example is asking for the power to do something that the most progressive 'national' government do, namely handle immigration in a way that encourages the full integration of immigrants into the mainstream culture. By looking at the relations between liberalism and nationalism *as forms of political discourse and political culture*, we find a lively and open question about how much and when they are or are not compatible.

1.3.1.2 *Are there liberal duties and virtues of discourse?*

Liberal theorists have also been relatively silent on the issue of what we might call the *virtues of political discourse*.[11] How ought liberal political actors ideally debate and justify matters of public policy in the public domain (and how should liberal-democratic institutions attempt to structure such debates)? What duties do they have not only to argue for just policies and institutions—most of liberal theory has been developed to help us decide

---

[10] And even more subtly, if we take this actual case in Quebec, the demand for more control over immigration is part of a general discourse meant to reveal to Québécois citizens that Quebec does not have the powers it requires for the Québécois to be 'masters of their own house'. Within a nationalist political culture like Quebec's, the demand for any federal power—even one as apparently insignificant, from a traditional nationalist perspective, as manpower training—can become imbued with nationalist significance in this way. Incidentally, as a result of a special administrative arrangement, Quebec gained control over most of the process of immigration in the early 1990s.

[11] I am not talking here of 'discourse ethics', that abstract Kantian foundation of ethics developed by Habermas, Apel, and others in the 1980s.

these sorts of questions about justice—but also to argue for them in good, liberal ways?

Rawls gives us some idea of what would happen in the ideal, 'well-ordered' liberal society. Such a society is 'designed to advance the good of its members and [is] effectively regulated by a *public* conception of justice' (Rawls 1971: 453). Members acquire a 'skill in judging things to be just and unjust, and in supporting these judgments with reasons' (46), as well as a *sense of justice*, which is 'a normally effective desire to apply and to act upon the principle of justice, at least to a certain degree' (505). 'Moreover, we ordinarily have some desire to act in accord with these *pronouncements* and expect a similar desire on the part of others.... One may regard a theory of justice as describing our sense of justice' (46; all italics in these quotes are mine). The picture of virtuous liberal discourse here is pretty clear. Ideally, liberals would like a society in which people *understood* the requirements of justice, were *motivated* to act upon and accept the demands of justice, and *participated* in public debates by making arguments that appeal to their fellow members' *sense of justice*.[12] This is a picture, if you will, of the ideal liberal political culture.

The problem is *all* large political cultures diverge considerably from this ideal. There are usually competing conceptions of justice, some of which might even claim not to be liberal. People sometimes argue for policies or institutions that are in their self- or group-interest, even when they know that this is not necessarily what justice requires (with NIMBY arguments being one of the clearest examples). And skilled political actors appeal routinely to sentiments other than the 'sense of justice', even when they do have the goal of justice in mind. These sentiments include greed, fear, self-interest, religiosity, partisan political affiliation, class, gender, ethnicity, nationality, race, and so on. There has been some discussion among liberal theorists, especially in America, about limits on the use of religious discourse by various kinds of actors in the liberal state.[13] There has also been an explosion of literature on civic virtues and deliberative democracy. But in all three of these areas, it is often difficult to make a tight connection between the *virtues* of political discourse for model citizens on the one hand and *institutional* and *constitutional* recommendations on the other. For one thing, it is obvious that the free

---

[12] This picture is clarified (or perhaps complicated) by the 'political liberalism' of the later Rawls (1993) in order to give further guidance for the public discourse in pluralistic societies with diverse conceptions of the good. Here we are advised to be sure to appeal to common principles of justice, rather than to deep and contested conceptions of the good, in order to secure widespread agreement and support.

[13] See, e.g. Audi (1989). See Nootens (1998) for a pioneering discussion of how these reflections on liberalism and religious discourse might be adapted to deal with the issue of liberal-nationalist discourse.

use of arguments appealing to religion (and to national identities or ethnicity) is the sort of thing that any liberal state will want to protect constitutionally.

So while it may be an ideal in a liberal society to have people appealing to grounds and sentiments of justice in their political arguments, it is also far from an aberration when liberal political actors appeal to more particular sentiments and identities. In principle, liberal nationalists fall into this latter category. They support policies and institutions that lie within a range that is generally acceptable within a liberal-democratic society, but they are willing (or eager) to justify these publicly with arguments that appeal to national sentiments of citizens identifying with either majority or minority national cultures. They will also engage in activities, and support policies or institutions that aim to shape or reinforce these identities. I shall focus on the question of how to evaluate this kind of political objective in Chapter 2, on nation-building. But I signal here, once again, how unfamiliar this kind of question is for liberal theory: there has never been much discussion about what limits there are on the liberal state's (or the liberal politician's) attempt to favour, promote, or create certain identities, especially when compared to the volumes and volumes that have been written on the issue of the limits on the state's favouring or promoting certain conceptions of the good. Political philosophers today are most indebted to the 'first wave' in the 1990s for the rich and sophisticated understanding some of these theorists gave to the nature of national identities and to the altogether healthy way these can mingle with other identities and values in the hearts of modern democratic citizens.[14] So when we worry about what political actors and the state are permitted to do to shape identities, we need not be questioning the legitimacy of national identities. (Obviously, as I discuss in Chapter 2, there can be national identities with odious contents; but these are relatively rare in the political cultures of contemporary democracies.) The concern is in part about whether the state can or should try to be relatively neutral in certain realms of identity politics and in part about the potential dangers of a political culture in which nationalist forms of justification and rhetoric carry more weight sometimes than liberal forms, even in the cause of advancing liberal institutions. This way of evaluating nationalism, then, is consequentialist: it asks us to try to weigh the potential costs (risks) and benefits of liberal actors 'playing the nationalist card'. On the one hand, nationalism may help mobilize people to sacrifice for a good cause (e.g. redistributing their wealth, standing up for minority rights, or repelling a foreign invasion), but on the other, it may legitimize a form of rhetoric or political currency that can be more effectively

---

[14] See, e.g. Taylor (1993: ch. 3), Kymlicka (1989: ch. 8), Tamir (1993: chs. 4 and 5), Miller (1995: chs. 1 and 2) and, Callan (1997: ch. 5).

spent by non-liberals in the future. For example, many American liberals were horrified when the groundswell of national(ist) sentiment that followed the terrorist attacks of September 11, 2001 was used by the Bush administration to mobilize support for a military adventure in Iraq that seemed unrelated to the 'war on terrorism'.

In the spirit of the quote from Tamir with which I began this section, I shall not be developing anything approaching a full-fledged liberal theory of political discourse here. And without this I cannot pretend to answer the question of how liberal theorists, liberal actors, and the liberal state should evaluate and deal with nationalist discourse in a liberal-democratic political culture. I shall, however, attempt to explore some of the issues at stake here, and also some of the ways that institutional choices can either foster or discourage the development of nationalist or liberal discourses and sentiments.

1.4 LOOKING AHEAD

The rest of the book is concerned with the way major institutional arrangements can be used to regulate and influence various kinds of nationalist politics in the liberal multinational state. Chapter 2 looks at one of the most direct manifestations of liberal nationalism: the attempt to use the institutions of state (including the schools, the state-controlled media, and the military service) to forge or 'engineer' national identities at either the state or the substate level. (This is typically done at the substate level when a minority national community has control over the government of a federal subunit, like a province or canton.) What limits should liberalism impose on state attempts to shape identities, and what constitutional mechanisms (if any) can be put in place to encourage respect for these limits? These questions are especially difficult in the context of states housing competing nation-building projects by a national majority and one or more minorities.

Chapters 3–5 explore the way the tool kit of constitutional engineering can be used to reconcile competing national communities and their nation-building projects within a common political space. For shorthand I will group most of these arrangements (especially for states with national minorities that are territorially concentrated) under the rubric of *federalism*. Some form of federalism or territorial autonomy is in fact the preferred arrangement of self-determination for virtually all national minorities in modern democratic states, i.e. it is generally preferred to either escape through secession or submersion within a centralized state. These chapters explore principles that are useful for identifying and justifying concrete federal arrangements in the multinational state; and also the challenges that these kinds of arguments and arrangements pose for more traditional models of liberal-democratic constitutionalism. The traditional 'rulebook' for justifying democratic and federal arrangements in uninational states need not be tossed away in the multinational state. On the contrary, as I will argue in Chapter 5, a number of familiar and relatively uncontroversial liberal-democratic patterns of argument can be used to justify realms of autonomy for rival nation-building projects in a federal state. But given that these traditional patterns of argument were not originally developed to regulate nationalist conflicts, it is hardly surprising that they are not sufficient for the task. It often goes unnoticed that the constitutional order in unitary nation-states is buttressed with forms of symbolic recognition that go beyond what is strictly justified by liberal and democratic theory. More than anything it is these patterns and principles of recognition that must be modified if we are to conceive of rival nationalists agreeing to negotiate limits on their own nation-building in the multinational state.

Chapter 6 continues this discussion, since I will argue for the advisability (at least in some favourable cases) of entrenching some kind of secession procedure in the constitution of the multinational federation. This recommendation comes not from any enthusiasm for secession as a solution to the problems of multinational states. More often than not secession would simply lead to the creation of new multinational states with even more vulnerable minorities. I will argue that there are several pragmatic and principled advantages to a carefully designed legal secession procedure—not least of which is that it may make secession *less* realistic as a goal for minority-nationalist entrepreneurs, and thereby reduce the incentives for disruptive ongoing secessionist politics. In addition, I try to illustrate why a secession clause would 'fit' with a number of the principles of recognition for multinational federal constitutions that are developed in Chapter 5. In other words, a properly formulated and negotiated secession clause could facilitate the forms of autonomy and recognition that minorities would demand as their conditions for free and fair and 'loyal' participation in a multinational state.

Chapter 2 on the ethics of nation-building is the lynchpin for all of these arguments for federal constitutionalism. The freedom to 'nation-build', i.e. to use political means to reinforce and to shape a national identity, is a large part of what it is for a community to be self-determining. It is time, therefore, to explore what exactly is involved in nation-building, and how we should evaluate its legitimacy in a liberal-democratic state.

But first, we have a brief appendix dealing with some unfinished business concerning the nationalist 'corruption' of the concept of nation. (The natural flow of the argument will not be interrupted for the reader who wishes to skip past this appendix.)

APPENDIX

NATIONALISM WITHOUT NATIONS?

Rogers Brubaker, 'the most brilliant of the younger generation of the scholars of nationalism',[15] implores us not to ask or attempt to answer the question 'What is a nation?' The problem with the question is that 'the very terms in which it is framed presuppose the existence of the entity that is to be defined. The question itself reflects the realist, substantialist belief that ' "a nation" is a real entity of some kind...' (Brubaker 1996: 14). He calls this a 'realist ontology of nations', a 'reification', and a 'political fiction'. In so doing, Brubaker would seem to be in direct conflict with David Miller, to name but one theorist. Miller not only posits this ontology, he *argues* for it: '[N]ations really exist, i.e. they are not purely fictitious entities, so that someone who believes that they belong to one is not simply the victim of error.... A person who in answer to the question "Who are you?" says, "I am Swedish"... is not saying something that is irrelevant or bizarre in the same way as, say, someone who claims without good evidence that she is the illegitimate grandchild of Tsar Nicholas II' (Miller 1995: 10–11). There would appear to be a substantial point of disagreement here. Is there?

Brubaker gives several indications that he has *ontological* concerns about 'nation' (i.e. concerns about whether or not nations *exist* or are 'real, enduring entities'). But nowhere does he come right out and claim that there is no such thing as nations, or that nations do not exist. Although he quickly rehearses 'four developments in social theory [that] have combined to undermine the treatment of groups as real, substantial entities' (Brubaker 1996: 13), he does not even begin to engage in the kind of abstract, metaphysical argumentation that would be required to make a credible claim about what kinds of things are or are not woven into the 'fabric of the universe'.[16] Instead, I think it is

---

[15] According to Professor John A. Hall of McGill University on the back cover of Brubaker (1996).

[16] I believe that the phrase 'the fabric of the universe' comes from John Mackie. For an extremely rigorous and thorough guide to the 'metaphysics of the social world' see the book bearing that title by Ruben (1985). Ruben gives good reasons for thinking that 'social substances like France, Ealing and the Red Cross' really exist in ways that are not reducible to non-social, individual entities or properties (see his ch. 1). Incidentally, if we are being careful in our

pretty clear that his real concerns are *methodological* and not ontological. Indeed, methodological in quite a normative, almost moral, sense. He is concerned with how we as scholars *ought to think* about nationalism in order to better understand such a complex social phenomenon and ideology—one that constantly threatens to subvert and corrupt the researcher. He is not denying 'the reality of nationhood' or 'nationness'. Brubaker's aim (1996: 16) is

> to focus on nationness as a conceptual variable..., not on nations as real collectivities. It is to treat nation not as a substance but as institutionalized form; not as collectivity but as practical category; not as entity but as contingent event. Only in this way can we capture the reality of nationhood and the real power of nationalism without invoking in our theories the very 'political fiction' of 'the nation' whose potency in practice we wish to explain.

The basic idea here, I take it, is that researchers need not automatically adopt the vocabulary and conceptual scheme used by those they are researching. That nationalists, and even ordinary citizens, believe they are members of real nations is, of course, indisputable. But we do not need to begin by endorsing the existence of these nations in order to explain or understand their nationalist beliefs, identities, or emotional attachment. As Brubaker puts it:

> Nationalism is not engendered by nations. It is produced—or better, it is induced—by *political* [and cultural and economic] *fields* of particular kinds. Its dynamics are governed by the properties of political fields, not by the properties of collectivities.[17]

It is not immediately clear what the methodological benefits will be for sociologists who heed Brubaker's advice. Presumably, he has in mind numerous fallacies the empirical investigator is likely to commit while trying to explain such phenomena as, in Brubaker's words, the slow development or sudden crystallization of national identities and nationalisms among groups of people.

In the abstract, there are two reasons to reserve judgement about the significance of Brubaker's methodological counsel. First, one might question whether Brubaker's approach is really such a radical departure given that it does not seem to be incompatible with the now-standard 'imagined communities' response to the question 'What is a nation?' Indeed, it would actually

---

ontology, we may note that Miller's argument for the existence of nations (as entities) relies entirely on the existence of nationalities that are merely properties of individuals. It is at least possible that social properties like 'being Swedish' could exist even if social entities, like the country or nation Sweden, do not.

[17] Brubaker (1996: 17, the italics are his) and the interpolation comes from his footnote attached to this sentence. For an exposition of the concept of a political field, Brubaker recommends Bourdieu and Wacquant (1992: 94ff).

seem *to follow* from this approach to the nature of nationhood that one would adopt a methodological or investigative response like Brubaker's. According to Anderson (1991: 6): 'All communities larger than primordial villages of face-to-face contact (and perhaps even these) are imagined.' In other words, they exist only in the minds of their members (and others), and different kinds of communities are distinguished 'not by their falsity/genuineness, but by the style in which they are imagined'. Anderson, no less than Brubaker, should be led from this way of answering the question 'What is a nation?' to investigate how it is that people in large, anonymous societies come to hold the images, beliefs, and sentiments of nationhood or 'nationness'.

Second, it would seem that one can more or less directly translate claims about the *properties of nations-as-social-entities* into claims about the *property of nationness*, which Brubaker prefers. In both cases we are talking about abstract social properties. Brubaker actually shows us how this is done, e.g. when he takes Anthony Smith to task for referring to our world as a 'world of nations'. Instead, Brubaker suggests, we should consider our world to be 'a world in which nationhood is pervasively institutionalized in the practice of states and the workings of the state system. It is a world in which nation is widely, if unevenly, available and resonant as a category of social vision and division. It is a world in which nationness may suddenly, and powerfully, "happen"' (Brubaker 1996: 21). I see no reason why Smith would not agree with this. In other words, it is a world of nations! If we can always translate our references to nations in terms of the beliefs and sentiments of individuals (or the properties of institutions), then there should be nothing methodologically suspect about referring to nations. All forms of scientific enquiry do this kind of thing as a matter of course. Physicists and chemists do not really believe that electrons are little negatively charged planet-like substances orbiting around a star-like nucleus (as we were all once taught in school). But they still talk about electrons in this way as a kind of shorthand that is useful for many of their purposes.

Despite these two 'abstract' criticisms, we should not dismiss Brubaker's methodological counsel out of hand. While it may be overstated as either a metaphysical position or a theory in the philosophy of social science, there are good grounds for thinking it to be a useful guideline for fair and effective writing about nationalism. Just about every historian and sociologist of nationalism has highlighted the role that 'intellectuals' play in the invention, development, and promulgation of national identities and individual political theorists writing on nationalism have to choose what kind of intellectual they want to be.[18] Their

---

[18] For a very concise description of the role of intellectuals in nation-building see Hroch (1993).

writings have the potential to influence nationalist debates and projects in their own states or in those of their foreign readers. For example, to refer to some particular group as a nation may not be a neutral observation. As Levy (2000*a*: 70) points out: 'Nationalist projects are dedicated to convincing some people that they belong to this nation rather than that one—that they are French rather than German, Turkish rather than Kurdish, Québécois rather than Canadian (or, in each case, vice versa).' In cases where there is still a lively contest about the national status of a particular group, or of who counts as a member of that putative nation, a reference to them as a nation may unwittingly take sides or treat as a 'fact' a social understanding that is still very much contested. This may be the real brunt of Brubaker's complaint with Smith's assumption about seeing our world as 'a world of nations'. It gives the impression that most of the contests for defining the national status of groups (especially minority groups) have already been decided. Or at any rate, it is a view of the world that may encourage us to overlook all of the vigorous political effort devoted everywhere to affirming or denying the existence of different minority and majority national communities, and of contesting the 'true' national membership of various groups of people. Of course, it is true that we simply cannot avoid referring to particular groups as either nations or things that are very closely related, such as national minorities, national communities, minority nations, and peoples. The same goes for using proper names, like 'the Flemish', 'the French', or 'the Kosovars', which carry with them in many contexts a kind of national or quasi-national status. But the least we can do when attempting to explain or describe the political world of nationalism is to try to remain aware of the stakes involved.

When we move from the social–scientific project of *explaining* and *describing* to the normative–philosophical task of *evaluating* and *prescribing*, these stakes are raised. Consider three basic normative issues for which the concern about being 'co-opted' by the nationalist's vocabulary is germane. First (as we shall see particularly in Chapter 5), the demand for recognition as a nation or a people within the constitutional framework of the state (as well as within international institutions) is itself one of the central missions of minority nationalist movements; so political philosophers need to be able to take a stand on when such recognition is appropriate (if ever) and what forms it should take. Second, a normative political theory of nationalism should have something to say about what we might call the 'virtues of political discourse', and in particular about when it is appropriate for different kinds of political actors to speak like nationalists and to justify policies, actions and institutions with nationalist arguments. (As I argued in this chapter, *speaking like* a nationalist is a large part of what it is *to be* a nationalist in a democratic culture.) Third, a political theory of nationalism must address the issue of what kinds of normative arguments are appropriate to justify or criticize certain major institutional questions of concern to nationalists in both majority and minority groups within multinational states e.g. the question of when secession is justified and what constitutional procedure should be available to a secessionist region, or when federalization is appropriate and what form it should take. Of particular importance here is the question of the relevance of demonstrating that the group demanding secession or federal autonomy is a bona fide nation or people.[19] Simply to refuse to acknowledge the very existence of things called 'nations' is barely to engage in these three central issues for a normative theory of nationalism. Brubaker is obviously correct when he warns against 'unintentionally reproducing and reinforcing' concepts and categories found in the practice of nationalism with concepts and categories in a theory of nationalism (Brubaker 1996: 22). But sometimes we might actually have to do this intentionally.

---

[19] In an argument that tries explicitly to heed Brubaker's call not to reify nations, Levy (2004) tries to show that the best case for granting autonomy to national minorities does not require agreeing that they qualify as nations or that nations per se have any rights to self-determination.

2

Forging Identities: The Politics and Ethics of Nation-building

2.1 SELF-DETERMINATION VERSUS DETERMINING THE SELF

There are two closely related (and interrelated) ways of articulating the basic desires and projects of nationalists: in terms of *self-determination* of the nation in question, and in terms of *nation-building* or literally the attempt to determine the 'self' of the nation. Put another way, these are two basic nationalist ambitions that are sometimes, but not always, pursued together. A normative theory of nationalism concerns what political actors and institutions can legitimately do in pursuing self-determination or nation-building. Nationalists themselves (especially minority or colonial nationalists) are much more likely to talk explicitly and passionately about self-determination than about nation-building. And indeed, when engaged directly in nation-building projects they are likely not to speak about it at all. It would presumably not surprise Brubaker that political philosophers too have been much more likely to discuss and evaluate nationalism in terms of self-determination than in terms of nation-building. It is not implausible that we have borrowed part of our agenda and vocabulary from nationalists even if we profess scepticism about nationalism ourselves.

For example, I could describe the chapters following this one as concentrating on the evaluation of the two broad avenues of self-determination for national minorities: territorial autonomy within a larger federal state (Chapters 3–5) and secession from the larger multination state in order to form a new 'unination' state (Chapter 6). A Brubakerian danger with this way of evaluating nationalist projects is that we will be co-opted into acquiescing in the nationalists' contention that particular minority communities are in fact nations, and that nations (and perhaps only nations) qualify for particular kinds of rights to self-determination. With this Brubakerian danger in mind, this chapter will begin to stake out an alternative language for articulating and justifying minority demands for autonomy and self-government—one that mines the darker and less well discussed side of nationalism, namely nation-building. The modern state possesses enormous powers to shape the national identities of its citizens. Sometimes these powers are used *deliberately* to create or reinforce a unified nation; but often identity-shaping consequences are *unintended* effects of policies and institutions that seem otherwise in accord with justice. This opens up a 'non-self-determination' argument for minority rights and federal autonomy (and perhaps even secession): minority communities may have a right to resist intended and unintended nation-building by the majority and considerations of fairness may require that such communities be given the means, through self-government in a federal subunit, to conduct their own nation-building projects. Such an argument would not presuppose that any given minority community was a nation, that nations as such have special rights or even that it is a good thing to build a nation. Most of these arguments, however, will be developed in later chapters. This chapter is devoted to unpacking the neglected notion of nation-building and to proposing some elementary ways we might evaluate nation-building practices using standard liberal-democratic principles and arguments.

The topic of self-determination for minorities clearly does not exhaust the problem-space of nationalism. For one thing, there are questions about how *majority* national communities seek (and ought or ought not to seek) self-determination. This is the other half of Gellner's principle of nationalism as aiming to make national and political units 'congruent'. Minority nationalists can seek a political unit within or outside of the state, and majority nationalists can seek to expand the boundaries of their national community until it kisses the boundaries of the state in which they already form a majority. They can do this in obviously evil ways, such as genocide, mass expulsions of minority communities, forced conversions, and other forms of coercive assimilation, including the banning of languages, religions, minority ethnic names, and so on. Or they can do it in more progressive ways that invite individuals from minority communities to integrate into the cultural mainstream, perhaps by modifying or thinning out the majority identity in ways that make it possible for all citizens of the state to feel a part of the national community.[1]

This project of getting a nation to expand to the borders of its state (or substate political unit) is one way of understanding the idea of nation-building.[2] It can be related to national self-determination—especially if the majority perceives the minorities to be frustrating its attempts to be master of

---

[1] For discussions of the ways of 'managing diversity' in the ethnic conflict literature, see Kymlicka and Norman (2000: 12–18) and McGarry and O'Leary (1993: 4–38).

[2] The preceding sentences refer to nation-building practices by national majorities; but similar forms of nation-building are also conducted by national minorities who form the majority of a territorial unit like a federal province.

its own house. But in many ways nation-building by both majority and minority communities should be seen as distinct from overt quests for self-determination. As we shall see, it both *precedes* and *follows* successful attempts by national communities to become self-determining.

This last claim would seem to be at odds with the conception of nationalism at the heart of an important recent book by Michael Hechter. Hechter (2000: 7) adopts a very Gellnerian definition of nationalism as 'collective action designed to render the boundaries of the nation congruent with those of its governance unit', where the 'governance unit' is defined as 'that territorial unit which is responsible for providing the bulk of social order and other collective goods...to its members' (9). This understanding turns out to equate nationalism with the quest for self-determination, and self-determination with the quest to make the national and governance unit congruent. As a consequence, nationalism should literally disappear when this congruence is achieved. 'There is no motive for nationalism when the boundaries of the nation and the governance unit are congruent, for then the nation *already* has self-determination.... The motive for nationalism only exists when the boundaries between the governance unit and the nation are not congruent' (Hechter 2000: 26).

This way of looking at, or looking for, nationalism is as misleading as it is widespread (especially within the cultures of successful nation-states). Both reductions are problematic: the reduction of nationalism to self-determination-seeking, and the reduction of self-determination to seeking the congruence of the national and political unit. Surely there is nothing oxymoronic about the idea of a nationalist nation-state, a 'unination' state with a nationalistic political culture. Indeed, this is surely how we would want to describe three of the clearest examples of nation-states: Argentina, Japan, and Iceland. Each is nationalist in different ways, but in all three we find, for example, a state school system that places a high priority on reinforcing a national identity through selective and mythologized understandings of history. All three societies take pride in a glorious past. Argentina and Japan have both used military adventures to stir up nationalist emotions, and even Iceland puffed up a bit after its plucky 'Cod War' with the UK in the 1970s. All three continue to use international sporting events (including, in the Icelandic case, chess and beauty pageants) to bolster the national self-image; and so on. Similar things could be said for somewhat more contested examples of nation-states, like France, the USA, and Greece.

Nationalism sometimes *precedes* national-self-determination-seeking because (as all theorists now agree) the national 'self' has to be created, nurtured, shaped, and motivated. People who previously thought of themselves as having various sorts of identities—including religious, linguistic, and regional identities—have to be convinced, perhaps over generations that their primary identity is as a member of *this particular* nation. And that the project of building and shaping an identity is an aspect of nationalism independent of the fact that this form of identity 'engineering' is useful for pursuing the self-determination project. Having a national identity pervasive within a community enables another manifestation of nationalist politics, namely the attempt to rally support for political causes and policies by appealing to this identity and the sentiments that go along with it. Certainly, such causes can include explicit demands for self-determination; but they can also include the cause of simply getting one's party elected (by wrapping it in the flag, so to speak), or even of selling one's product (perhaps by literally wrapping it in a flag or flag-like motif) or promoting one's TV show or newspaper. Again, when it comes to the nationalist activity of mobilizing support for a cause, project, policy, party, product, or what have you, it could be that you will miss 95 per cent of the nationalist discourse if you are paying attention only to nationalist mobilization for self-determination per se. In other words, nation-building (creating, spreading, or shaping a national identity) and nation-mobilizing (generating support for a project or policy by appealing to national identities and national sentiments) are distinct realms of nationalist politics whether or not they are being used explicitly to make the nation congruent with the 'governance unit'.

Another common confusion is explicit in Hechter's definition of self-determination as the congruence of national and governance units; but it is implicit in much of the literature on nationalism that has focused on the demands of national minorities for autonomy, on the one hand, and on the brutal behaviour of national majorities (such as the authorities acting on behalf of Serbs, Croats, or Hutus in the early 1990s) attempting to rid their political space of non-nationals on the other. The quest for self-determination—and all of the nationalist mobilization that brings it about—surely does not end once the goal of 'congruence' is met. The core idea of self-determination, whether for individuals or communities, involves being able to do what you want; or in the words of J. S. Mill, it is 'pursuing our own good in our own way'. And nations (or nationalists) cannot simply want to have their own political space (such as a state) for its own sake; they presumably want that in order to accomplish other things of value. What else might national communities value? Everything from collectively increasing or securing their power internationally to satisfying basic desires of their individual members, including desires for a better standard of living and a just society. At least part of the explanation for why many nation-states retain nationalist political cultures is that strong national identities and sentiments in the population make it easier for political leaders to mobilize support for policies etc. that they consider to be in the national interest.

'September 11' and its immediate aftermath in the USA provided a dramatic illustration of the extent of nationalist 'preconditioning' among both ordinary Americans and their political and media elites. First, the terrorist attacks revealed to ordinary Americans something that they had taken for granted to such an extent that many had come to believe the contrary: that they had a significant sense of kinship with their fellow Americans, even those who lived thousands of miles away and voted for a different presidential candidate in the previous election.[3] (This is nicely illustrated in the quote from Posner in the Preface.) Second, this sense of kinship, combined with a patriotic tradition of defending America and 'American values' or 'American interests', allowed political leaders immediately (within a day) to be able to convince 'the nation' that the events qualified as an act of war (even though it was not yet known who carried out the attacks, and even though it transpired that they were not carried out by another state), and that the only possible answer was to respond militarily. It was also significant that all of the private news networks crafted graphic backdrops with headings such as 'America under Attack', and 'America's New War', complete with Star-Spangled Banner motifs, within minutes or hours of the attacks. In other words, it could never have been considered an attack on two office towers filled with private-sector firms; it was necessarily an attack against the nation.[4] All of the spontaneous gestures of grief and mourning by ordinary citizens were also accompanied by the national flag, rather than, say, some randomly coloured single-twisted ribbon or symbol of Christianity. It is not my concern to decide which parts of these responses were justified. Although the attack itself was unprecedented for this generation of Americans, nobody should have found their response surprising. If your nation and state wants to be a superpower with a global reach and with significant 'national interests' around the globe—if this is what the nation has 'determined itself' to want—then it is crucial that the citizenry be mobilized on an ongoing basis to support policies necessary to realize this desire. That includes, in this case, a continuous willingness, even in times of peace, to devote a significant amount of the gross *national* product

---

[3] As part of an explanation for why George W. Bush was really a popular president (even though his rival in the election of 2000 had garnered more votes), an educated gentleman from the American Midwest once told me half-jokingly: 'New York and California [two states that had voted heavily against Bush in the 2000 election] were not really part of America, and Bush had a solid majority of support in the "real" country.' This conversation took place on an airplane in the first week of September 2001. A week later, such a thought would have been unthinkable for this fellow, or certainly unmentionable.

[4] Of course, there was also an attack against the Pentagon on 11 September 2001. This added to the death toll on the day, but there is no reason to think that Americans would have had a significantly different reaction if this essentially military target had not been hit. The collapse of the Twin Towers and the devastation in lower Manhattan were the enduring images of the day. The loss of thousands of fellow citizens' lives was the source of pain and anger.

(GNP) to a standing military with global reach. But just as importantly, it supports ongoing state and non-state activities to nurture the kinds of national sentiments and 'patriotic' responses to foreign provocation that will enable political leaders to act decisively on the nation's behalf.

Again, September 11 is a dramatic example. Consider the very different kind of nation-state nationalism found in Iceland (see, e.g. Karlsson 2000). Iceland used to have a typical 'self-determination-seeking' nationalist project that enabled it to secede peacefully from Denmark in 1944. But the fact that it was then perhaps the most 'congruent' and ethnically homogeneous nation-state in the world was no reason to think that there would be, as Hechter's theory would imply, no more motivation for nationalism. Icelanders lived, and continue to live, in a precarious environment at the edge of the Arctic Circle. Within the memory of the eldest citizens today, most Icelanders were desperately poor and large populations were prone to famine. The country is now very prosperous, thanks ultimately to its successful harvesting of one primary resource: fish. But fish stocks, and the world price for fish, can fluctuate dramatically from one year to the next. And there is always the possibility that from one decade to the next the fish stocks could virtually disappear. The strong sense of state-sponsored national identity and national solidarity is functionally important for Icelanders in many obvious ways: it keeps educated and highly mobile Icelanders from emigrating even if there are sharp drops in their incomes some years, and even if they could find a more agreeable climate to the south;[5] it generates broad support for an egalitarian form of redistribution that allows almost all members of the nation to enjoy the wealth that is generated by a fishing industry that employs less than 10 per cent of the population. I do not mean to imply that there is an elitist plot to keep Icelanders nationalistic for utilitarian purposes. Iceland's famously paternalistic political class may even be primarily concerned with ensuring that new generations of Icelanders are simply able to enjoy the rich heritage of their cultural identity. As Ross Poole (1999: 69) puts it, a national identity

[5] Of course, we should never underestimate the role of hardship in general, and harsh climate in particular, in formation of national identity. This is certainly a feature of Norse mythology, and is confirmed anecdotally by Icelanders I have met. It also figures prominently in the early American and Canadian settlers, as well as in the stories of how these people 'settled' their western territories. A folk song that became a nationalist hymn during the so-called Quiet Revolution in Quebec, 'Mon pays' (word and music by Vigneault 1966) proclaims:

> Mon pays ce n'est pas un pays, c'est l'hiver
> Mon jardin ce n'est pas un jardin, c'est la plaine
> Mon chemin ce n'est pas un chemin, c'est la neige...
> Mon refrain ce n'est pas un refrain, c'est rafale
> Ma maison ce n'est pas ma maison, c'est froidure
> Mon pays ce n'est pas un pays, c'est l'hiver.

[p]rovides us with a land in which we are at home, a history which is ours, and a privileged access to a vast heritage of culture and creativity. It not only provides us with the means to understand this heritage; it also assures us that it is *ours*. If on occasion the nation may require that we endure losses and hardships on its behalf, it also makes available a fund of meanings, pleasures and rewards beyond anything that we are likely to find in our individual lives.

This idea of national identities providing a context of meaningfulness for individuals suggests a paternalistic motive for nationalism that is not directly related to self-determination for the group. But the fact that Icelanders do have a strong sense of national identity and national pride also enables both Icelandic political leaders and Iceland as a congruent nation-state to do things it might not be able to do otherwise.

I have focused very briefly on these anecdotes involving nation-states in order to give a functional illustration of the motivations for ongoing nationalist politics even in national communities enjoying full self-determination in the formal sense. Michael Billig calls this 'banal nationalism', stressing that 'banal does not imply benign'. It consists of 'ideological habits which enable the established nations of the West to be reproduced.... [T]hese habits are not removed from everyday life, as some observers have supposed. Daily, the nation is indicated, or "flagged", in the lives of its citizenry. Nationalism, far from being an intermittent mood in established nations, is the endemic condition' (Billig 1995: 6).

The rest of this chapter focuses on understanding and evaluating nation-building and nation-mobilizing as it is carried out in both nation-states and multination states. The latter type of case can be significantly more complicated, since multinational states involve rival nation-building projects (i.e. from the centre and within the minority regions), often competing for the hearts, minds, and identities of the same citizens. But for both multinational and uninational states, we will ask the following question: *what should political actors and state institutions be permitted, encouraged, required, or forbidden to do in the attempt to shape people's national identities?*

2.2 THE BENEFITS OF *HAVING* A NATIONAL IDENTITY VERSUS THE DANGERS OF *TRYING TO FORGE* A NATIONAL IDENTITY

The most significant project in the 'first wave' of normative theorizing about nationalism in the 1990s was the attempt to expose just how much of traditional liberal-democratic theory and practice presupposes the bonds of national identity. Political philosophers throughout most of the post-war period had taken for granted that 'citizens' or 'individuals' would be motivated to cooperate democratically with their anonymous fellow citizens and be willing to have their personal wealth 'redistributed' in order to fulfil the demands of liberal egalitarianism. Rawls devoted much of the third part of his *Theory of Justice* to speculations about the social-psychological mechanisms supporting this kind of cooperation, but this was one aspect of his theory that generated very little subsequent discussion. Most philosophers were content to debate what rights, including welfare rights, there should be in the liberal state, while paying very little attention to the question of why or how citizens would be motivated to support such institutions. Central to Rawls's motivational account is that 'the citizen body as a whole is not generally bound together by ties of fellow-feeling between individuals, but by the acceptance of public principles of justice' (Rawls 1971: 474; quoted in Miller 1995: 94). This sort of claim would be roundly rejected in the central texts of the 'first wave'—especially Tamir (1993), Miller (1995), and Kymlicka (1995*a*). Their 'liberal nationalism' would be based on claims about the necessity of 'ties of fellow-feeling', and on the belief that national or cultural identity provided the best way in modern societies to secure those ties.[6] A shared national identity, it is argued, engenders 'mutual trust' among citizens, which 'makes it more likely that they will be able to solve collective-action problems, to support redistributive principles of justice, and to practice deliberative forms of democracy' (Miller 1995: 98).[7]

It is not at all clear how one would set out systematically to defend this last claim as a matter of sound sociological explanation or fact. Certainly, none of the principal texts in the 'first wave' ever laid out independent criteria to measure, on the one hand, the extent to which a national identity is shared within a given society, and, on the other, the extent to which such a society exhibits 'mutual trust', solves collective-action problems, supports redistributive principles of justice, practices deliberative democracy, and so on. One suspects that among the developed democratic states in the world one would not find a significant correlation between strength of national identity and any of these other characteristics (in part because the sample size of this group of states is relatively small). Belgium, with its relatively weak or fractured national identity, may well do a better job on all these fronts than, say, France, which surely has a stronger sense of national identity. Something similar

---

[6] As Weinstock (1996) has rightly pointed out, two of the members of this liberal-nationalist troika shy from the label: at least in the texts cited above, Kymlicka does not call himself a nationalist and Miller does not call himself a liberal.

[7] For a concise discussion of a wide variety of the benefits, as well as some of the dangers, of a national identity, see Smith (1991: 15–18).

might be said of Canada and the USA.[8] I shall not be pursuing this line of objection here, however. I suspect that relatively little of interest can be said at that level of generality about the alleged causal relations between national identity and other political or sociological facts. Political identities are very complex and the explanations for why a particular political culture supports certain practices, conventions, and institutions are vastly more complex still, not to mention contested. National identities and social cohesion are not kinds of things that bang into each other like billiard balls. In a moment I will propose an analysis that distinguishes a wide variety of beliefs, values, and sentiments that make up one's national identity. And when we look at these various components, it is not hard to see why many will be conducive to the sorts of liberal-democratic goods mentioned in the quote from Miller, above. (Of course, some of these elements are also conducive to some famous liberal-democratic 'bads', like intolerance and chauvinism.) The point is not whether there is some general causal link between national identity and, say, support for distributive justice, but whether the best explanation for why some particular state was able to institutionalize a laudable scheme of distributive justice will take bonds of national identity into account. The very informal anecdotes I discussed above, concerning the USA after September 11 and present-day Iceland, give some indication of why such explanations might seem appropriate. It does not seem crazy to explain the relative lack of emigration from Iceland (despite splendid foreign-language skills, state sponsorship for students wishing to pursue higher education abroad, and a truly miserable climate) by making reference to the depth and bonds of Icelandic identity.[9] And this despite the fact that it probably *would* be crazy to suggest that national identity per se lessens emigration (since, of course, it would be easy to point to many nationalistic societies with high rates of emigration, along with many states with a relatively weak national identity, like Belgium, that have very little emigration).

We would also have a hard time explaining the persistent role of national identity in the politics of democratic nation-states if it were not the case that these identities facilitated the successful mobilization of citizens. In the first round of the 2002 presidential elections in France, there was no doubt that the existence of a certain ethnoreligious conception of French national identity among a sizeable minority in France propelled the far-right 'nationalist', Jean-Marie Le Pen, into second place. But it is even more significant that the

---

[8] Miller (1995: 94–6) addresses just this objection, though not by giving any empirical evidence for a correlation between national identity and these other liberal-democratic goods.
[9] Iceland permits very little immigration, and in most recent years has averaged a net emigration of fewer than 2.5 persons out of 1,000. (*Source*: http://www.indexmundi.com/iceland/net_migration_rate.html).

centre-right candidate, Jacques Chirac, was able to win the run-off by mobilizing the support of left-wing voters who despised him and his party less than they cherished the more open-minded conception of French identity that he represented in the head-to-head contest against Le Pen. (To put it differently, they were literally embarrassed and ashamed *as Frenchmen* that Le Pen had done so well and might yet manage a 'respectable' showing in the second round.) It is not so much that national identities necessarily dispose citizens to mutual trust and solidarity; but if a particular 'liberal' conception of national identity has evolved in a democratic political culture, i.e. if members feel pride in thinking of their nation as exemplifying liberal-democratic values and traditions, it will serve as a valuable resource for political actors who want to mobilize support for policies and institutions that can be shown to be consistent with that identity and its aspirations.[10]

The vague claims about the potential benefits of a healthy national identity by the theorists of the 'first wave' were necessary primarily because of the near-complete silence on these issues by political philosophers in the post-war/cold war period. It is now time to move on. In particular, I shall be rather less concerned about the general benefits for a society that happens to find itself with a healthy sense of national identity, and will look instead at the implications of *political attempts to bring about* such an identity in a society where it is currently lacking or less-than-healthy—especially in a state in which there are currently competing majority and minority national identities. Thus, rather than reflect on the general instrumental value of *having* a widespread national identity within a state, we will enquire (beginning with Section 2.5) about the ethics of *deliberately trying to forge or shape* such an identity. I will argue that there are liberal constraints on the *methods* that can be used to shape identities, as well as on the *content* that the newly shaped identity is intended to have. There are also ethically relevant pragmatic considerations about the wisdom of nation-building in multination states, especially nation-building from the centre that is intended to foster some kind of 'pan-national' unity across the majority and minority communities. The more likely consequence may be the provocation of defensive nation-building projects among threatened minorities.[11] In short, the obvious step beyond the 'first wave' preoccupation with highlighting the potential benefits if your community happens to share a common national identity is to look at the

---

[10] I am including France within the broad liberal-democratic tradition even though the word 'liberal' is obviously problematic in the French political lexicon, where it means something akin to 'pro-capitalist'.

[11] For extended versions of this argument derived in part from analysis of rival nationalist contests in Canada and Quebec, see Trudeau (1965), reprinted in Karmis and Norman (2005a), Laforest (1995, 2001), and Weinstock (1999).

potential problems with trying to deliberately shore up such an identity where it is less than fully formed.

The traditional term for the deliberate forging of identities, 'nation-building', is potentially misleading: it implies that this political activity is essentially about either *creating* a nation out of some other form of community, or making an existing national identity *stronger*.[12] But this omits and distorts much of what is important in nation-building activity. In most cases a national identity already exists, and political actors are trying to shape it *qualitatively*, and not just quantitatively, by addressing the values and beliefs that characterize the national identity in question, as well as the sentiments that bring it to life, so to speak. This should become clearer in Section 2.3. Unfortunately, no other term seems ideal either. It might sometimes make sense to speak of 'national engineering' (which I have not seen in use before) in order to capture the sense in which deliberate nation-shaping activities are really a form of social engineering (a concept that has not played much of a role in political philosophy for a generation or more).[13] But this term too is not quite right.

Again, much of the evolution of national identities happens unintentionally and the ability to deliberately engineer a new identity is often quite limited. For this reason I shall mostly use the more common term 'nation-building', bearing in mind its misleading quantitative connotations.

2.3 WHAT IS A NATIONAL IDENTITY?

Surprisingly enough, many books on nationalism never actually define or discuss at a conceptual level the idea of national identity, and others do so only after using the term casually for quite some time. Obviously, this concept is tied closely to the concept of nation: nation N cannot exist unless there are lots of individuals, N'ians, who identify with N or have an N'ian national identity; and individuals cannot have an N'ian national identity unless N exists and qualifies, in some sense, as a nation. The main difference here is the

---

[12] It is also potentially misleading because the term is widely used in political science and international relations circles to mean, in effect, 'state building', i.e. putting in place the basic institutions of a sovereign modern state. I shall not be discussing this form of nation-building here.

[13] See Popper (1957: 64–70) for a defence of what he calls 'piecemeal social engineering', a terminology that did not catch on. Popper claims this term would be useful 'since there is a need for a term covering social activities, private as well as public, which, in order to realize some aim or end, consciously utilize all available technological knowledge.... Just as the main task of the physical engineer is to design machines and to remodel and service them, the task of the piecemeal social engineer is to design social institutions, and to reconstruct and run those already in existence' (64–5).

kind of 'things' that can be *nations* (i.e. communities) or have *national identities* (i.e. individuals). Both nations and national identities exist because of the beliefs, convictions, sentiments, and attitudes of individual people. As Karl Deutsch said about the 'communicative facility' that he believes underpins national membership, national identity 'is a characteristic of each individual, but it can only be exercised within the context of a group' (Deutsch 1966: 97). In this section it will not be necessary to give a deep or abstract definition of 'national identity': instead I will lay out a number of the beliefs, sentiments, and values uncontroversially associated with national identities in order to understand in a fairly concrete way the principal materials, if you will, that national engineers have to work with. Nationalists shape national identities through subtle and not-so-subtle attempts to instil, eliminate, modify, strengthen, or weaken the beliefs, sentiments, and values that make up individuals' sense of national identity.

The following is a general first-person set of beliefs and sentiments that could be said to characterize and describe someone's national identity. Many of them are typical of identities in general, e.g. of the identities one has as a member of a family or a denizen of a city. Not all of these beliefs need be true, though some of them do. I cannot have a particular national identity solely by virtue of my own thoughts: if I believe I am a member of La-la-land and that there are millions of other members of La-la-land—but if in fact nobody else has ever heard of La-la-land—then I am simply deluded. Nations are imagined communities sustained in the imaginations of people; but not all acts of imagination create nations. Some, but not all, of the beliefs on this list could be considered to be necessary conditions for having the national identity in question; and I think that they are jointly sufficient. I do not pretend, however, that this list is exhaustive. Again, my only aim here is to identify the sorts of beliefs and sentiments that nation-builders or national engineers will be trying to shape.

Here is what I am likely to *believe* or *feel* when I say I have a particular national identity with respect to nation N. That:

[*Beliefs about the world*]

- A real community or society called N exists.
- I am a member of N; that is, I am an N'ian.
- Other N'ians I come into contact with are also inclined to believe I am an N'ian.
- N is a nation; N'ians are a people.
- There is a homeland that properly belongs to N (even if it is shared with other groups).

- You cannot become an N'ian simply by moving to the territory occupied by N; but (unless N is a purely ethnic nation) it is possible to become an N'ian even if you were not born of N'ian parents or in N's territory.
- I automatically consider the children of N'ian parents who are born and raised in N's territory to be N'ians.
- N existed before I was born and will exist after I am dead (this is true even where N did not get a state to call its own until some point during my lifetime).
- N'ians share certain characteristics that tend to distinguish them from non-N'ians, and I am generally able to recognize these characteristics.
- I have 'the ability to communicate more effectively, and over a wider range of subjects, with members of [N] than with outsiders'.[14]
- It is potentially informative to tell strangers (in situations where it is not otherwise obvious) that I am an N'ian (in the way that it is potentially informative to tell them my marital status, profession, sex, sexual orientation, hobbies, etc.). That is, my membership in N is part of my personal identity; I identify with N; my affiliation with N helps people to identify me.

[*Values and Obligations*]

- I believe that it is appropriate for N'ians to be able to govern themselves; there should be political structures that facilitate the collective action of members of N.
- I feel a stronger sense of obligation to fellow N'ians than I feel to non-N'ians, including non-N'ians who are my fellow citizens in a multinational state.
- Some of these obligations I feel I owe to fellow N'ians could involve significant sacrifice on my part.

[*Sentiments and Emotions*]

- I take pride in some of the achievements of N (including those that happened before I was born or in which I played no real role): both large-scale collective achievements (e.g. building a healthy democracy or thriving economy, winning a war) and those of fellow individual N'ians (like artists, athletes, Nobel Prize winners).
- I feel shame for the crimes, misdemeanors, and boorishness of N (including incidents that happened before I was born or in which I played no real role): both large-scale 'crimes' (e.g. systemic racism, belligerent foreign

---

[14] Deutsch (1966: 97) considers this 'wide complementarity of social communication' to be the core of membership in a nation.

policy, or a reckless approach to the environment), and those of fellow individual members (like football hooligans or an embarrassing prime minister on an international stage).

- I tend to be more affected by news of tragedies involving fellow N'ians than I am by similar or worse events involving only non-N'ians. This is especially true of N'ians who are killed 'in service of' N.
- Under certain conditions I can feel either proud or ashamed to identify myself as an N'ian when outside of my national homeland.
- I could live in another state for decades, and even take up citizenship there, but would still consider myself to be an N'ian, even if I also came to feel myself to be a member of this other community or nation as well.
- Although they will make different judgements and have differing sentiments on occasion, the vast majority of my fellow N'ians have similar beliefs and feelings about N.

I need not go into great detail here about any of these claims or why they are typical of national identities or the beliefs, values, and sentiments *closely associated* with national identities.[15] The picture here is, I believe, broadly consistent with both the kinds of socio-historical theories about nationalism that came out of the 1980s and the 'first-wave' normative theories from the mid 1990s.[16] Moreover, I suspect these are the kinds of beliefs and sentiments that many of us can recognize within ourselves, and we do so without any particular shame. The liberal nationalists of the 'first wave' went to some length to defend the now seemingly innocuous claim that national identities are 'defensible parts of personal identity'.[17] I shall assume there is now no real debate about this, even though it is obviously possible for there to be national identities that are in some sense 'indefensible' because of odious normative content, dangerous sentiments, or ridiculously false background beliefs and myths. My aim in this chapter is not to defend the very idea of having a national identity (say, qua liberal), but rather to enquire about when it is

---

[15] I say these are beliefs, etc., 'closely associated' with national identity. There may be good conceptual grounds for having a somewhat narrower definition of national identity as such; although exactly where one draws this conceptual boundary will be a decision not a discovery. My claim is that whether these elements are constitutive of national identity, or merely tend to go along with having a national identity, they are the sorts of things that will be shaped or appealed to by nationalist politics.

[16] I owe a particular debt here to Miller's lucid discussion (1995: 22–7). For an enlightened, and more recent, discussion of the beliefs and sentiments that constitute a social identity, see Appiah (2005: 65–71).

[17] See, e.g. Miller (1995: 31–47), Tamir (1993: chs. 1, 4, 5), Kymlicka (1995a: ch. 5). For a philosophically and psychologically sophisticated discussion of this issue, see Poole (1999: esp. ch. 2).

legitimate deliberately to attempt to shape the identities of others through political and state activity.

Again, the list of features of a typical first-person national identity gives us a good indication of the potential *targets* for nation-building exercises (or material for national engineering projects). Most of these beliefs, sentiments, and values can be modified in some way; indeed, in modern societies many of these things evolve significantly from one generation to the next, if not in the space of months or years. Consider, for example, even the relatively straightforward question of the nation's homeland: over a short period of time members of the nation could come to hold a different conception of what its borders are or ought to be, of whether some other group also has a legitimate claim to the same territory as part of its homeland, of whether both groups can or cannot cohabit the territory in peaceful cooperation, and of how vital some particular chunk of the historic homeland really is to the nation and to the priorities and well-being of individual members of the nation. The evolution of the conflict between Serbs and Kosovar Albanians over the territory of Kosovo is obviously a case in point (see Mertus 1999). Other potential targets for identity modification abound on the above list. The features N'ians take to be characteristics of N'ians change, as do the legal, linguistic, and cultural criteria that immigrants must satisfy before N'ians are inclined to think of them as fellow N'ians. Old heroes can be forgotten, or their heroism can come to be reassessed; new heroes can be found, both among contemporaries and from the distant past. The same is true of the sources of pride or shame in the nation's history—these are always open to both reassessment and revaluation. And, of course, the sense of obligation towards fellow nationals and the willingness to sacrifice (and even to die) for them are historically open to change and manipulation, particularly in times of crisis. These are just a few examples of how different beliefs and sentiments associated with national identities evolve and are shaped by political activity.

2.4 CONSTRUCTING, DECONSTRUCTING, AND RECONSTRUCTING NATIONAL IDENTITIES

Now deliberate nation-building or national engineering projects will typically attempt to shape identities by targeting multiple features of national identities in order to meet certain objectives. Here is a very *non-exhaustive*, but historically significant, list of overlapping general types of identity-shaping objectives and contexts.

2.4.1 Three Archetypical 'Contexts' of Deliberate Nation-Building

2.4.1.1 Category I. Nation-building for the 'nationalization' of the native-born masses

This is surely the most well-documented form of nation-building from the classic age of nationalism, beginning in perhaps the sixteenth century in England and spreading throughout Europe and the other continents well into the twentieth century. Of course, there are disputes among scholars about when any particular nation-building project began, and also about the explanations of how it happened and how successful it ultimately was. These are not my concerns here. I wish only to note the salient details of this archetype of nation-building. Roughly, ideas of a particular national identity arise first among the intellectual and political elite in the 'centre', and are deliberately spread outward to the masses inhabiting the proto-nation's state with the aim of creating a more homogeneous and unified polity and a stronger and more effective state. In the memorable title of Eugene Weber's book (1979), it is the process of turning 'peasants into Frenchmen'.[18] In its purest form this process of nationalization reorients numerous regional, ethnic, religious, and even linguistic identities in its path, but it does not have to contend with full-blown minority national identities. It goes without saying that this kind of project has not always been wholly successful.[19]

2.4.1.2 Category II. Nation-building for the 'nationalization' of national minorities

For all intents and purposes, the project described above is no longer possible. In the modern world, if a diverse state does not already have a widely spread national identity, would-be nation-builders at the centre would almost surely find their efforts countered by minority nationalist political elites already attempting to nationalize regional, ethnic, and religious minorities. That project's last hurrah—and not a largely successful one at that—came in the years immediately following the liberation of the European colonies, mostly from the 1950s to the 1970s. Much more common over the last fifty years are a

---

[18] Weber's controversial theory of French nation-building has been widely debated and is often disputed. See, e.g. Ford (1993).

[19] See Hroch (1993) for a concise discussion of some of the conditions that have tended to improve the chances of this type of nation-building succeeding. This article also proposes a useful scheme for categorizing different versions of this project in states across Europe. See Greenfeld (1992) for a much more lengthy study of roughly this process in England, France, Germany, Russia, and America.

variety of projects that begin with an established national majority group (typically, but not always, with an identity marked by the name of the state itself), and proceed to use state institutions and other means to incorporate the members of national minorities into that larger majority national identity. As noted already, this form of nation-building has been associated with some of the most repressive as well as some of the most progressive nationalist movements in recent history. The most repressive ways to nationalize members of national minorities are to kill them, to chase them away, or to coerce them into changing their names, religions, or the language they use in public life. More progressive majority nationalists have considered 'thinning' out the majority identity, e.g. by de-emphasizing its ethnic roots, or by decoupling it from the majority's language or religion, so that it could be willingly embraced by members of the national minority alongside their existing national identity. We will examine a broader range of 'tools' and strategies for nation-building below. It is now generally accepted that members of national minorities will no longer convert en masse to adopt the larger state's national identity; but it is also clear that most members of national minorities in advanced democratic multinational states are happy to embrace more than one national identity. The proposals for a multinational federal constitutionalism in this book can be conceived of as a modest and concrete manifestation of a strategy to facilitate this kind of dual nationality. Finally, we should note that not all national majorities are interested in converting or incorporating members of national minorities into their identity. This is especially true of majorities with essentially ethnic conceptions of their identity. As we will see in Chapter 5, such national majorities (e.g. Croatians or Macedonians) are willing to share a state with national minorities, but not to consider them to be members of the same nation.

2.4.1.3 Category III. Nation-building for the 'nationalization' of immigrant minorities

Even more ubiquitous in modern democracies are nation-building projects aimed specifically at the assimilation or integration of immigrants into the national 'family'. To say that this project, often under the heading of 'multiculturalism', has been *widely* discussed by political theorists in recent years would be an understatement. It is not my central concern in this book, apart from the way patterns of immigration affect the dynamics of majority and minority nationalist contests.[20] (Immigrants to, say, Quebec or Catalonia will

---

[20] For the special normative and political challenges raised by 'minorities within minorities' see the book of the same title edited by Eisenberg and Spinner-Halev (2005), especially the chapters by Patten, Eisenberg, Moore, and Holder.

find themselves courted by both minority and majority nation-building projects; the issue of who controls the best nation-building 'tools', i.e. who has control over key legislative or administrative jurisdictions such as education, will be an important agenda item in rival nationalist negotiations.)[21] As with the previous two archetypical nation-building projects, there is a broad range of strategies and tools for incorporating immigrants, from the brutal to the progressive. Almost all theorists accept that some forms of encouraging immigrant integration are acceptable, and perhaps even required, in a liberal-democratic state.

I have described these three kinds of nation-building projects in very broad-brush terms as 'archetypes'. They help us understand general motivations behind most of the classic examples of nation-building. Of course, most particular cases will be messier. These three categories are based in part on a distinction between pre-nationalized regional groups, national minorities, and immigrant minorities—categories that are not always easy to apply in practice. This is also not an exhaustive list of cultural minority groups that could potentially be of interest to nationalist entrepreneurs.[22] Something like this general three-part distinction is nevertheless worth bearing in mind as we go on to discuss and evaluate the use of nation-building tools, since these archetypical projects will typically rely on different sets of tools, and target groups with distinct sorts of political demands and minority rights. Before moving on to this normative discussion, however, it is worth highlighting a number of more subtle types of nation-building projects, particularly in advanced modern states where majority and minority identities are already deeply entrenched. The following list, which is also not meant to be exhaustive, highlights the ways in which numerous elements of existing national identities can be targeted by political actors and institutions in attempts to modify identities in qualitative and not just quantitative ways.

(i) **Reprioritizing the national identity**: the attempt to make an existing national identity mean more to people who are currently inclined to identify strongly with some other community or identity group as well. For example, *The Federalist*, can be read as a justification for a constitutional apparatus that

---

[21] To cite one of the clearest examples of the way immigration figures into the contests between established minority and majority nationalists, it is widely recognized that the principal motivation behind Quebec's controversial laws banning commercial signs in English was to ensure that Montreal would present a 'French face' to immigrants, and encourage their integration into the French-speaking rather than English-speaking society. The law requiring immigrants to Quebec to send their children to French-speaking public schools is another obvious (perhaps less controversial) case in point.

[22] For a discussion of a somewhat more complete list, including refugees and *sui generis* groups like the Roma, African Americans, and Russians in the 'near abroad', see Kymlicka and Norman (2000: 18–24).

would eventually shift the primary locus of Americans' patriotism from their states to the country as a whole. This sort of goal for nation-building need not even seek to make the national identity in question the *most* important one, but merely *an* important one. For example, this may be the appropriately modest aim of nation-builders at the centre of a multination state who could not expect to supplant the minority national identity, but who want nevertheless to ensure that alongside it is a certain degree of affiliation with and patriotism towards the pan-state national community.[23] As such, it would amount to a mild version of Category II

(ii) **Sentimentalizing the national identity**: the attempt to intensify some of the various sentiments associated with the national identity, usually with the aim of making nationals more disposed to nationalist forms of argument, rhetoric, and justification, and more inclined to sacrifice on behalf of the nation (i.e. more inclined to accept policies in any domain when they can be called for on nationalist grounds). This could obviously be one (though not the only) strategy for a reprioritizing nation-building project.

(iii) **Desentimentalizing the national identity**: as paradoxical as it sounds, one way in which political leaders may try to shape national identities is to make them *less* intense—especially after a period of sentimentalizing nationalism that has led to unfortunate consequences, such as a costly or humiliating war, inter-ethnic tensions, or irrational economic policies. This would likely go hand in hand with 'reconfiguring' and 'remoralizing' brands of national engineering (below). The general aim would be to make nationals less inclined to be moved by nationalist rhetoric and more inclined to accept, say, liberal-democratic forms of arguments (e.g. in the post-war Federal Republic of Germany, post-junta Argentina, or in post-Tudjman Croatia).

(iv) **Reconfiguring the national identity**: this involves attempting to transform the 'character' or 'content' of an existing national identity, say, to make it more modern, less ethnic or religious, or to change the kinds of myths, heroes, national rivals, etc., that figure in the interpretations people give to their national identities and characters. This process is a multifaceted and continuous one in almost every national society, although it can also be the explicit goal of a political movement including a state or substate government. As noted already, nation-builders might direct this sort of project towards existing members of their own national community in order to make that community and identity more appealing to either immigrants or national minorities.

[23] This is also clearly the aim of identity-building efforts by the European Commission. In promoting Europeans identity and solidarity they are not expecting—or probably even wishing—that people will come to feel European first and, say, French second.

(v) **Remoralizing the national identity**: attempting to change the normative content of the national identity e.g. the kinds of rights and obligations towards fellow nationals, the motivations and sentiments needed to have these rights and obligations taken seriously by members of the nation, the visions of the nation's goals and destiny, or the way the nation thinks of its historic achievements, crimes, or grievances.

Again, any given nation-building project could be pursuing more than one of these general objectives (I–III and i–v) at the same time, and there are surely other possible categories that could be useful in such lists. I mention all these types of identity-shaping projects here as a way to illustrate four general points. First, to locate the concerns of this book primarily within the category of 'archetypical nation-building project II', on the incorporation of national minorities, hopefully at the progressive end of the spectrum. We will also be discussing more nuanced identity-shaping projects like the ones in the (i)–(v) list. Second, when we consider the many types of beliefs, sentiments, and values that can be modified in some way by a nation-building project, it would seem to follow that a liberal ethics of nation-building will not be making any blanket judgements about whether nation-building is just or unjust, permissible or impermissible. Rather we will have to discriminate between many good and bad forms of nation-building and identity-shaping more generally. In fact, I think that it is not difficult to imagine—or to point to historical examples of—particular versions of each of these general projects that would be acceptable in liberal-democratic polities. And it is equally easy, of course, to imagine many that would *not* be acceptable. Third, these lists of different types of nation-building projects reinforce one of the 'storylines' in this book, namely that nation-building in a pluralistic state usually involves some kind of competition between different identities, including different national identities.[24] So any attempt to evaluate some particular nation-building project within nation N (say, Britain or Spain) will have to consider the likely implications it will have for nation-builders among the national minority M (say, Scotland or Catalonia), where N and M claim at least some of the same members (i.e. Scots and Catalans). Fourth, the theme illustrated by these types of projects is just how misleading the quantitative images associated with nation-building are. Most of these projects aim for *qualitative* transformations of an identity, not merely the 'strengthening' of it.

When we think about national identity and national-building in these ways, there seem to be two obvious concerns for a liberal political morality in evaluating any given nation-building project: concerns about the *methods* (what I have sometimes referred to as 'tools' and strategies) that are used in

---

[24] This is also the central theme in Levy's important book *The Multiculturalism of Fear* (2000a).

the attempt to transform people's identities and concerns about the *contents* of the initial and intended identities. We will survey some of the issues these concerns raise over the rest of this chapter.

2.5 CATALOGUING THE *METHODS* OF NATION-BUILDING

In Section 2.3 we 'deconstructed' the idea of national identity into a long list of sentiments, beliefs, and values that are either constitutive of national identity or intimately tied to it. One of the advantages of this way of thinking about identity is that it points to the vast range of political, governmental, and even private or commercial activities that can have an impact on people's sense of national identity. Many of these beliefs and sentiments are in constant flux and change as a result of policies or activities that are not even primarily concerned with identity per se. For example, consider, the enormous impact that networks of communication and information technology—both those that provide links between dispersed fellow nationals and those that link members of a nation to the world outside their state—have on people's identities. Clearly, radio, television, and telephone networks introduced in the twentieth century facilitated the expansion of the 'imagined community' for ordinary citizens: they made it much more likely that fellow nationals would share common sources of information, common stories, and would be more aware of each other's existence. Now in many cases, these information technologies were introduced by, and subsidized by, national governments for nation-building and nation-transforming purposes.[25] But often, these networks were driven by other considerations, such as the opening up of new entertainment markets paid for by advertising revenues. Whatever the original intention, the result can be the same: fellow nationals still end up watching the same shows, laughing at the same jokes, crying over the same real or fictional tragedies, and in general sharing an evergrowing stock of cultural icons and memories. For example, the private sector clearly played a much greater role in the expansion of radio and television networks in the USA than it did in most other Western states. But this does not make American television any less integral to the strength and content of American identity. For example, during the second Iraq War in 2003, many commentators were struck by how much more 'patriotic' and trusting of government

---

[25] This use of radio and cinema by Hitler is the most obvious, and obviously pernicious, example. But almost every state had its own radio stations and sometimes gave itself a monopoly.

sources the private American networks were than the state-owned BBC was in Britain.

This is, of course, an obvious and dramatic example of the role that non-state institutions like CNN can have in shaping and reinforcing identities—even if the primary motivation for doing so was parent company Time Warner's fear of losing advertising revenues if patriotic viewers were put off by news reports critical of the US military. The less obvious examples are in many ways more revealing. The private-sector American media does an extraordinary job at finding a 'topic' every six months or so that will receive an obsessive amount of attention, and which virtually nobody in the country can avoid learning about, having an opinion on, and debating. Considering just the examples from the ten or fifteen years, we find a number of cases involving crimes and criminal trials (O. J. Simpson, Enron, Kobe Bryant, and Michael Jackson), others involving alleged indiscretions by public figures (Judge Thomas and Anita Hill, Bill and Monica, Congressman Condit and Chandra Levy), political events (the Clinton impeachment, the Florida ballot count, the battles over the nomination of Supreme Court judges) and of course terrorist and military events (the Oklahoma bombing; September 11; US military involvement in Somalia, Kosovo, Afghanistan, Iraq, and elsewhere). What is remarkable about these 'events' is that even the least overtly political—such as one involving a former football player who allegedly kills his wife—can become the basis for searching discussions about American state institutions (e.g. the justice system) and American society (violence against women, race relations, the role of the media). The net effect of all of these episodes is to allow the citizens from across a vast and diverse country to connect in ways not dissimilar to gossipy fellow villagers. They transform for individuals what they think America is about, how its institutions work, and what it means to them, and they do this in a way that provides a shared experience for fellow citizens from all walks of life and from all regions. And yet relatively little of this identity-reinforcing and identity-transforming 'village discussion' is directly controlled by political leaders or state institutions, and almost none of it is conducted with the intention of changing people's sense of national identity. Of course, this phenomenon is played out to varying degrees in all modern societies.[26]

I mention this very unmethodical, largely apolitical, process of identity transformation at the outset of a section on deliberate political methods of identity-shaping primarily for the sake of context. Our values, beliefs, and

---

[26] Uncovering the roots of 'banal nationalism' is the central theme of Billig's excellent book of the same title. See in particular his impressive catalogue of nationality-reinforcing content available in the news coverage of a single randomly selected day (1995: 109–19).

sentiments are shaped in many ways in modern societies; many actors and institutions are involved in this process; and much of it happens in ways that nobody in particular was intending. A corollary of this is that no leader or institution in a modern democracy has the power to shape citizens' identities at will. In an open society nation-building powers are limited in numerous ways: they cannot control sources of information; political opponents and political commentators react immediately to explicit signs of their 'playing the nationalist card' and there are real limits on the extent to which democratic governments can coerce and brainwash large portions of the population (e.g. through the schools or the army, or via broadcast and print monopolies). There are certainly places in the world today, and in the past, where political leaders have possessed and used the powers to forge and 'sentimentalize' national identities much more effectively. But in developed Western democracies today the power to influence peoples' beliefs and sentiments in *any* realm (i.e. not only concerning issues of national identity) is much more dispersed.

Still, there is good reason to be concerned about the role that political actors and state institutions play in trying to shape identities. Although they are not guaranteed success in their nation-building projects any more, there is no question that they still can be successful—especially in situations where a large portion of the political class comes to adopt a similar form of nationalism. (And for some purposes, such as winning an election, a nationalist mobilization by one party may be successful even when it shifts the votes of only a tiny slice of the electorate.) Examples of successful elite-driven nation-building in democratic states, within both minority and majority national communities, over the last fifty years abound. In any case, whether political leaders are particularly successful or not in their attempts to use the offices and institutions of the state to shape national identities, their activities are still subject to the strictures of a general theory of political morality or a theory of justice.

What then are the most effective tools that political leaders and state institutions can use to mould national identities? Of course, the answer to this question will vary from country to country and from one era to the next. It will also depend which kind of nation-building project we are talking about. Speeches by charismatic leaders—especially when combined with control over media sources, or if uttered in times of crisis—may go a long way when the object is to sentimentalize or desentimentalize an identity; but this tactic is likely to fall upon deaf ears if the aim is, say, to encourage the assimilation of a national minority into the majority culture.

That said, there are a number of readily identifiable government tools that figure in the explanations for the current shape of most national identities. I will list these with illustrative examples of relatively liberal and illiberal uses of these tools; although a more systematic evaluation of national engineering techniques will be delayed until Section 2.6.[27] Consider:

- Official-language policy:

  Liberal and illiberal examples range from the official recognition of all four minority national languages in Switzerland, which facilitated a strong Swiss identity among members of the linguistic minority groups, on the one hand, to the banning of minority languages in many states in coercive attempts to assimilate minorities into the majority group, on the other.

- Rules for immigration and naturalization (the acquiring of citizenship):

  These have been used in open societies to 'thin out' the ethnic component of national identity and to allow full integration of large numbers of immigrants of diverse ethnoreligious backgrounds; but in other countries strict limitations on immigration and naturalization have been used to preserve an ethnically 'pure' conception of nationality.

- Core curriculum in schools:

  A rigorous core curriculum has been used to advance the equality of opportunity for all children by providing them with linguistic and other skills and teaching the virtues of toleration; but it has also been used to reinforce nationalist mythologies, grievances, and prejudice.

- Compulsory military service:

  This has been a standard way of ensuring the national defence against foreign aggression (which is surely one way to preserve a national identity!); but it has also been used as a school for patriotism where dissent and questioning of the official national ideology are not tolerated.

In addition to these Big Four tools, which have been used pervasively, there a number of others that are either less universal or of generally ancillary importance.

- Fighting and mythologizing about patriotic wars:

  In some cases these would be wholly defensive wars (or defending allied states against aggression), and in other cases they are aggressive or imperialistic.

- Adopting national symbols and holidays.

---

[27] For extensive discussion of actual case studies of many of the nation-building tools on the following list, see Kymlicka (2002).

- Renaming streets, towns, buildings, and geographical features:

    These gestures could be done inclusively, e.g. by including the symbols of constituent ethnic groups (such as the representation of Scotland, England, and Wales in the Union Jack), or by restoring aboriginal place names after a long period of colonization; or these exercises could be carried out in a deliberately partisan way, such as creating a national holiday for a historical figure who was a hero for the state's majority ethnocultural group but a villain for one of the national minorities.

- Control or regulation of national media:

    This could involve some ownership or content regulations to ensure that a national voice is heard (especially in small countries with large neighbours who speak the same language) or, in other cases, a strict state monopoly of television networks controlled directly by the president's office and used for nationalist propaganda (the aim of which may simply be the maintaining of his or her grip on power).

- Promotion of sports, particularly in international competitions:

    Examples abound of healthy and not-so-healthy uses of international sports competitions to promote a national image and to sentimentalize a national identity (and also to distract attention away from the shortcomings of the regime or leadership).[28]

Most of the above nine general policy domains have been employed in national engineering projects in most modern societies. In addition, it is worth noting that in any given state virtually *any* government ministry could find itself in control of a 'national hot-button' policy domain, depending on specific features of the group's history and identity. For example, some national identities are tied closely to particular religions (often thought of as *national* religions), and the state may choose to subsidize or promote this religion in various ways to reinforce the identity. Similarly, every state subsidizes various kinds of cultural practices where these are thought to be historic aspects of the identity. States with official monarchies subsidize and promote the image of the royal family in part as an aspect of national heritage. And for similar reasons some states may feel it necessary to bolster a republican component of the national identity by banning members of a previous royal family from even entering the state. Just about any practice or policy

---

[28] For some fascinating stories of some of the more unseemly nationalist manipulations of football (soccer), see Duke and Crolley's *Football, Nationality and the State* (1996). See also Billig (1995: 119–25).

domain can attract special attention and subsidy if it comes to be seen as something that distinguishes a society from its neighbours. For example, many Canadians see their state-funded universal health care system to be something that is not simply required on grounds of justice and equality, but also a national achievement that distinguishes Canada from its neighbour to the south. This has many consequences for health policy in Canada: it serves to make it more difficult for Canadian governments to use economic or efficiency arguments to justify privatizing aspects of the system, and it also bolsters the federal government's sense of legitimacy in setting health care policy even though this is supposed to be an area of exclusive provincial jurisdiction. There are also examples of peculiar 'hot-button' national issues within minority national communities. These are typically connected with the features of religion, culture, or language that distinguish the minority from the majority in the state. But they can also be very arbitrary-looking from the outside. For example, the Québécois have historical reasons for taking great pride in massive hydroelectric projects, in part because of the way these projects symbolized the power of the new nationalist elites and the Quebec 'state' after the 'Quiet Revolution' in the 1960s. This presumably would make it much more difficult for a Quebec government ever to contemplate breaking up or privatizing the state power monopoly, Hydro Quebec. Again, these are just a few examples to illustrate the general point that in any given political culture, it is possible for almost any policy domain to take on 'national' significance.

Finally, to this potentially long list of both standard and idiosyncratic policy domains that figure in national engineering projects we must not forget to add the significance of basic constitutional choices. Some of these are included in the above list: many constitutions contain symbolic recognition of various aspects of the majority or minority identities, and they may also contain provisions for entrenching official languages or religions, and even for compulsory military service for men. But we must also keep in mind the significance of how constitutions (or other basic laws) decide fundamental issues such as the following.

- Whether the state is unitary or federal; and *if federal* (or involving territorial autonomy for particular groups),
    - how it divides legislative and administrative powers between federal and subunit governments;
    - whether or how it ensures representation of minority communities in federal institutions, like the cabinet, the parliament, the supreme or constitutional court, the civil service, and the military;

- how it fixes the frontiers of federal subunits, and also whether it grants rights for the creation of new subunits (e.g. where national minorities can form a majority);
  - whether it grants rights to secede (especially for national minorities or their subunits).
- Whether it has an electoral system, party system, cabinet system, etc., that encourages strong countrywide, multi-ethnic parties and government coalitions, or rather a sharp division of parties on ethnic lines with governing coalitions that can exclude national minorities.
- Whether it bestows recognition on various constituent groups in appropriate and even-handed ways.

It should be obvious how choices on these sorts of constitutional issues are likely to be driven by, or to promote or discourage, various sorts of national identities at either the majority or the minority level. In effect, many of these provisions decide which nation-building tools will be in whose hands (the majority's or the minority's). I will not say more on these issues here, since they take up the core of the discussion in the following chapters.

As I noted at the outset of this section, a large part of the morality of nation-building or national engineering is concerned with the evaluation of these many methods and tools with which political actors and state institutions attempt to shape people's sense of national identity. It should also be clear that there are many obviously legitimate, possibly even obligatory, ways that identities can be shaped (think of the way the most ideal liberal education will affect the way people reflect on their identities and values); just as there are obviously illegitimate and illiberal ways of doing so (think of forms of education that could only be described as brainwashing). But there is also surely a large 'grey zone' of cases where it is not clear what a liberal democrat should think about policies with identity-shaping consequences. We turn now to the question of what intellectual tools we might have for evaluating the methods of nation building.

2.6 EVALUATING THE METHODS OF NATION-BUILDING

One obvious (if not plausible) candidate for a liberal principle of national engineering is that the state should be *neutral* with respect to people's identities, even their national identities. Something like this principle has been proposed—particularly by opponents of multiculturalism—as directly analogous to the separation of church and state. 'Just as liberalism precludes the establishment of an official religion, so too there cannot be official cultures that have preferred status over other possible cultural allegiances.'[29] And more generally, neutrality with respect to cultural identity could be thought of as a corollary of a principle of neutrality about conceptions of the good. An individual's identities are certainly 'bound up' with his or her conception of the good. For example, the list of components of a national identity (discussed in Section 2.3) includes a number of value judgements as well as sentiments about what kinds of things matter to a person and preferences about what forms of associations a person wants to be involved in. There is also the issue about where the sense of national identity ranks for different individuals among other identities defined in terms of ethnicity, religion, profession, sex, sexual orientation, family status, sports aficionado, etc. Surely, it might be argued, it is not the state's role to be influencing the value or relative value of citizens' various identities.

The withering of ethnocultural neutrality as a viable principle for liberal nation-building is one of the many achievements of the 'first wave' of liberal theorists of nationalism. Simply put, when one looks at the kinds of activities we expect the state to be involved in, and the sorts of things that affect our cultural and political identities, it is simply inconceivable that the state could be neutral when it comes to identity. Kymlicka has focused at length on the role of official (or de facto official) language policy as the most obvious way in which state policies—even if formulated primarily for the sake of efficiency—have an enormous impact on cultural identity:

> Given the spread of standardized and compulsory education, the high demands for literacy in work, and widespread interaction with government agencies, any language which is not a public language becomes so marginalized that it is likely to survive only amongst a small elite, or in a ritualized form, or in isolated rural areas, not as a living and developing language underlying a flourishing culture. Government decisions about the language of public schooling and public administration are in effect decisions about which language groups will survive. (Kymlicka 2002: 17–18)

Even if the state decides to be inclusive by providing services in several languages, this policy would still have an impact on identity (*a*) by excluding at least some of the languages that might be spoken by immigrants, thus forcing them to integrate into one of the mainstream cultures of the state, and (*b*) by promoting a multilingual, Swiss-like conception of the national identity. Consider also that if the state provides public education in only one language in a multilingual, multinational community, it risks disadvantaging

---

[29] Kymlicka (2002:16) is articulating this principle for his opponents. He has Walzer (1992*a*, 1992*b*), Pfaff (1993), and Ignatieff (1993) in mind as supporters of this conception of ethnocultural neutrality.

the members of minority language groups and imperiling their culture. But if it provides schools in different languages, then it risks fragmenting the community and its identity by encouraging children to grow up associating only with members of their own ethnolinguistic group. Either way, its decision shapes identity. And language is only *one* of the identity-sensitive domains in which the state cannot avoid taking some kind of a stand. After having chosen the language or languages of education, it will have to choose what to teach the students in history, social studies, and second-language classes—and so on, all the way down the long list of policy and constitutional choices with identity-shaping potential discussed in Section 2.5: What symbols will be included in the flag? What will the national anthem say? What public holidays will be celebrated? Will the state be unitary or federal? What will be required of immigrants before they can become citizens? How will the mass media be regulated? What will streets and mountains be named? What cultural or sporting activities will be subsidized?

In short, we must reject the principle of identity neutrality because 'ought implies can', and the state simply *cannot* be neutral about national identity. Of course, much the same has been said about the possibility of state neutrality with respect to conceptions of the good, and this is one reason why few liberal theorists now see value neutrality as a foundation of liberalism.[30] That said, there is surely an intuition, which remains attractive to all liberals, behind the idea that the liberal state should be neutral with respect to conceptions of the good, even if any rigorous formulation of this principle seems implausible. For example, we would expect the state to be able to provide 'good reasons' for policies in the areas, just mentioned, on which it must take a stand, especially when these policies are in any way coercive (see Nagel 1987). (Of course, what counts as a 'good reason' and whether those being coerced have to be willing to accept this reason are very contentious issues.) The liberal state is going to be *more* neutral and less coercive than almost any other kind of state, even if it cannot be completely neutral. Liberals from the eighteenth century to the present are instinctively opposed to the state interfering with people's opinions, beliefs, values, sentiments, speech, and activities when these are not harming others. Or at any rate, there is certainly a strong presumption in this direction. I suspect that this is how liberals will

---

[30] For standard arguments in favour of liberal neutrality see Dworkin (1978) and Nagel (1987). For some of the standard arguments against see Nagel (1973), Haksar (1979), and Raz (1986). As Haksar reminds us again and again in his book, we do not really think that the liberal state is neutral between the conception of good that involves, say, raising a family, on the one hand, and the one that takes pleasure in the eating of one's own excrement, on the other.

want to think about the state's role in manipulating aspects of people's identities.[31]

Consider again Kymlicka's critique of Walzer's 'sharp divorce between state and ethnicity' along with his (Walzer's) view that the clearest example of an ethnoculturally neutral state is the USA (see Kymlicka 2002: 16; Walzer 1992*a*: 100–1; 1992*b*: 9). Kymlicka's aim here is not to say that the state *should not* be neutral. He says it *cannot* be—'this idea of ethnocultural neutrality is simply a myth' (Kymlicka 2002: 16)—and so we have to make ourselves aware of all of the ways the state fails to be neutral. He does this in part so that we see the costs, in terms of cultural and economic disadvantage, for members of the society who are not born into the mainstream state culture (or the culture of the national majority). Only by understanding these costs can we start to get a sense of whether there is any injustice going on as a consequence of identity-shaping choices by the state, and if there is an injustice, how it can be prevented, mitigated, or compensated. This is very different from a nationalist argument against cultural neutrality grounded in the belief that the state should be promoting some group's national identity in a vigorous way (not to mention the possible belief that the particular culture in question is inherently superior). In effect, Kymlicka is lamenting that the state cannot be more neutral, and hoping to find ways of limiting the damage caused by its unavoidable partisanship.[32] It cannot be neutral, but it can be more 'inclusive' of other identities, and it can aim to 'thin out' the majority national identity to facilitate nested dual identities for members of minority cultures.[33]

I suspect that this is a common liberal sentiment about the ethics of nationalism—even if it sits uncomfortably alongside other beliefs about the many benefits of a healthy national identity in the modern democratic state. Liberals will instinctively reject any form of political activism or government policy that deliberately manipulates people, subverts their rational reflections and deliberations by whipping up their emotions, exacerbates and exploits ethnic cleavages in the community, or erodes equality of opportunity and political equality. Some forms of nationalist politics certainly fall under all of these headings. In this sense, there is no special liberal morality of nation-building: any political activity or institution will be disapproved of when it

---

[31] For a nicely nuanced discussion of how the concept of neutrality might deal with identity considerations, especially the sort arising in a multicultural society (rather than issues concerned with nation-building in a multinational state), see Appiah (2005: 88–99).

[32] 'Put another way, the standard for evaluating minority rights claims [against majority efforts at nation-building] is no longer ethnocultural neutrality but ethnocultural justice' (Kymlicka 2002: 21).

[33] This sense of 'inclusion' and 'thinning out' are widespread desiderata in theories of multiethnic justice and democracy. For a sophisticated discussion of 'nested' identities see Miller (2000: ch. 8).

seems to undermine traditional liberal values of autonomy, well-being, equality, and justice, especially as these values have been updated in recent years with sensitivity to the rights of ethnocultural minorities. However, one of the novel problems about nation-building in the modern state, is precisely that many of the very policies that are routinely justified on grounds of fundamental liberal principles of justice (universal education, universal health care, redistribution of wealth, political equality) can and *do* have nation-building implications that may favour either a majority or a minority national community in a multinational state.

All of this suggests a check-list approach to deciding whether particular nationalist political activities or government policies are inappropriate from a liberal point of view. 'Inappropriate' is a deliberately vague qualifier here. It covers everything from policies that should be banned constitutionally to those that would merely make a good liberal wince.

Consider something like the following set of questions to evaluate the *methods* of a putative nation-building exercise (we will discuss the evaluation of the *contents* of an identity in Section 2.7).

2.6.1 Basic rights Test

Does the activity or policy violate any individual's basic rights?
This test would, of course, pick out most of the nastiest forms of nationalist politics, including countless activities I have barely mentioned in this chapter because they are so obviously out of the question for a liberal nationalist. These range from genocidal campaigns waged against national minorities, and all of the tactics of 'ethnic cleansing' including the use of paramilitaries and gangs to terrorize minority communities, to a broad range of discriminatory practices designed to exclude minorities from state benefits and employment. Other right-violating policies would include banning minority languages and religions from all forms of public space (e.g. prohibiting their use even in school yards, election pamphlets, wedding ceremonies, or union meetings); prohibiting dissent against official nationalist ideologies and identities by making certain kinds of political speech illegal; or by banning anti-nationalist or minority nationalist politicians from holding office.[34]

Anything violating basic rights in these ways should simply be impermissible in the liberal-democratic state. Many more 'mundane' nationalist policies will be harder to call. How do we decide when particular national minorities have a right to state-funded schools or universities in their own language and with a curriculum over which they have some authority? Should

---

[34] See Kymlicka (2002: 54–8) for a discussion of many of these nationalist tactics as practised in Eastern and Central Europe in the 1990s.

they always have the right at least to *private* schools and universities in their own language? Do long-term residents—especially those who were born in the country, say, of immigrant parents—have a right to citizenship? Are their basic rights violated if they are denied access to citizenship because the state is attempting to preserve an ethnonationalist identity in the majority community? Is it fair to require official-language proficiency as a condition of citizenship? These questions are arguably more controversial in liberal circles than are any of the issues discussed in the previous paragraph. Some liberals would argue that some of the policies referred to in these questions (e.g. denying citizenship rights to long-term residents and their children) do not literally violate basic rights; but they might nevertheless consider them to be illiberal. The following tests are designed to identify other methods of nation-building that seem unacceptable even if they do not, strictly speaking, violate basic rights.

2.6.2 Veracity Test

Do policies, political campaigns, government publications, school texts, etc. involve deliberate lying or misrepresentation in the attempt to promote a particular identity or nationalist sentiment?

There are countless examples, even in democratic societies, of official attempts by politicians and government agencies to cover up facts and events that would undermine nationalist preconceptions—especially when it comes to creating or maintaining myths about contemporary or past patriotic heroes.[35] It is also difficult to know exactly where to draw the line about misrepresentation in contexts, such as school lessons in history, where simplification is a necessity. Some liberals have been willing to argue for the permissibility of sustaining myths of patriotic figures in schools when the benefits of pride and attachment to one's national community outweigh the costs.[36]

2.6.3 Indoctrination Test

Does it exploit the naïveté of the young and uneducated?
Even those who support a certain amount of official patriotic mythologizing, will object to techniques that subvert individual autonomy by brainwashing

---

[35] For a rich array of example from American school textbooks see Loewen's *Lies My Teacher Told Me: Everything Your American History Textbook Got Wrong* (1995).

[36] While noting that 'rigorous historical research will almost certainly vindicate complex "revisionist" accounts of key figures in American history', Galston (1991: 244) argues: 'Civic education... requires a nobler, moralizing history: a pantheon of heroes who confer legitimacy on central institutions and are worthy of emulation.'

those without the knowledge or critical faculties to resist. Coercive nationalist 'education' of military recruits may also fall under this category, even in a volunteer army.

2.6.4 Stigmatization Test

Does it stigmatize internal or external 'enemies' of the nation (especially whole peoples)?
National identities are typically defined by nationalists in ways that highlight relatively small differences between the group in question and some contrasting group such as those in a neighbouring state, or members of a national minority or majority. Extending a theory of Freud's, Ignatieff (1999: 48–61) has called this an example of the 'narcissism of minor differences'. This 'narcissist illusion' can be relatively innocent, for example, when Canadian nationalists play up the fact that Canadian cities are less violent than those across the border, or when British nationalists like Lady Thatcher contrast the supposedly more individualistic, right-respecting British political culture to the collectivist, statist ways on the Continent. Liberals may object in public debates to such comparisons on factual or relevance grounds; but they are likely to be much more concerned when the nationalist contrasts involve especially opprobrious terms, depicting the national rival in ways that are morally inferior or even dehumanizing. Such talk will usually fall within rights to free speech, but it is illiberal nonetheless.

2.6.5 Rabble-rousing Test

Does it subvert democratic processes by temporarily manipulating public opinion?
Stigmatizing 'enemies' of the nation is one of a number of techniques political actors can use to 'play the nationalist card', to whip up nationalist passions temporarily for the sake of a partisan political or personal gain (e.g. winning an election or referendum, or gaining higher ratings and advertising revues for one's TV show or newspaper). Populist rabble-rousing is a standard feature of democratic politics, even if it is absent from any description of an ideal deliberative democratic polity. Again, it usually should be protected by rights to free speech and assembly, but this does not mean that liberals cannot lament its effectiveness and try to counter it and the underlying aspects of the national identity and political culture that make it a viable strategy.

2.6.6 Equal Opportunity for Nation-building Test

To the extent that nation-building exercises aim at incorporating national minorities into the larger state or nation, are these groups given equal opportunities to shape and reinforce their own identities through state institutions?

This 'test' is the thin edge of a very thick wedge buttressing the rights of national minorities.[37] The idea here is that political and cultural identities are not simply the product of free choices in the marketplace of ideas (although this certainly is one factor in their formation), but also the results of deliberate political and state activities and institutions. So there is something intuitively unfair, even unjust, about majority national communities being able to use their control over state institutions and the mass media in deliberate attempts to assimilate national minority groups that, in most cases, never voluntarily assented to membership in the state. Since state institutions can hardly fail to have this effect in a centralized state with a majoritarian democracy and a dominant ethnocultural group, an obvious solution is to grant autonomy for certain national minorities in the form of control over institutions (e.g. schools, television networks). I will say much more about the forms and justifications for such control in Chapters 3, 4, and 5 on federal constitutionalism.

Like many of the lists in this chapter, this one could go on. In the main it is an attempt to highlight kinds of identity-shaping techniques that liberals would likely object to with appeals to traditional liberal values like autonomy and equality. The bottom line, however, is that a tremendous amount of what we might call banal and not-so-banal nation-building will pass these tests. Bear in mind also that some of these are essentially liberal 'wince-tests' designed to articulate high-minded liberal intuitions. When we consider the level of nationalist politics and policy that would be *legally* permitted and even protected within a just constitutional regime, i.e. permitted even though it will make liberals wince, we realize that ongoing nation-building is a fact of life in the modern state. Given the broad range of beliefs and sentiments that constitute an individual's sense of national identity, there will always be a tremendous number of permissible state policies and political exercises with the potential to shape this identity. One cannot fully comprehend the fears and demands of national minorities without recognizing this 'fact' (which is not, of course, to claim that all such fears and demands are legitimate). This is the rationale behind the much more radical final principle in the above list:

---

[37] Satisfying this condition is one of Kymlicka's three conditions for the legitimacy of 'majority nation-building in a liberal democracy' (Kymlicka 2002: 48). See also Costa (2003) and Weinstock (1999).

Nation-building 57

the equal right to nation-building. Again, the long and less familiar foray into federal constitutionalism that will follow this chapter can be understood as a way of making sense of such a right for national minorities. And by the same token, it will provide some recognition of the rights of majority nationalists to continue to pursue a limited range of policies with nation-building implications for national minorities. Finding this balance is a matter of 'negotiating nationalism', of seeking reasonable limits to rival nation-building projects within a common political space.

So far, our evaluation of nation-building has concentrated almost entirely on evaluating the techniques or methods for changing or reinforcing identities. As noted earlier, liberals also have concerns about the *contents* of the identities being shaped. To these we now turn.

2.7 THE MORAL AND POLITICAL RELEVANCE OF THE *CONTENT* OF NATIONAL IDENTITIES

It has been commonplace for almost as long as scholars have been studying nationalism to distinguish between what are, in effect, good and bad nationalisms.[38] This has been done largely by focusing on features of what I have been calling the 'content' of the national identity and most commonly on whether that identity had an ethnic or racial basis, on the one hand, or a more 'civic' or political basis, on the other. This approach tends to reduce the ethics of nationalism to this one issue about the content of national identity: nationalism is acceptable only in cases where it is based on a civic and not an ethnic identity.[39]

What constitutes the *content* of a national identity? How is content related to the set of beliefs and sentiments discussed in Section 2.3, that are typically associated with an individual's national identity? As a first approximation, it would seem to make sense to look for the content of an identity in some of the *beliefs* associated with the identity rather than in the *sentiments*. These beliefs can be descriptive, normative, or a mixture of the two: they are what is involved in trying to answer questions like 'What is an N'ian?', 'Who are the N'ians?', 'How can you recognize an N'ian?'. On this interpretation, the content of the identity is bound up with views about formal and informal criteria for membership in the nation, as well as views about the typical traits

---

[38] For a critical evaluation of this standard modus operandi see Brown (1999). For an early version, see Kohn (1955).

[39] This view is articulated, with a mixture of sympathy and ambivalence, throughout Ignatieff (1993).

of members vis-à-vis non-members. This contrasts with other non-content, 'sentimental' aspects of national identity, which might be elucidated with questions such as 'What does it mean *for me* to be an N'ian?', 'How do I feel about the great achievements and crimes of my fellow N'ians?', 'What sacrifices am I willing to make for my fellow N'ians?'

The clearest way to understand the idea of an *ethnic* national identity is in terms of this kind of content.[40] An individual has an ethnic national identity to the extent that he or she believes that membership in his or her nation is based entirely on descent, i.e. on blood. This will colour all of this individual's answers to the first set of questions in the preceding paragraph. In particular, he or she will be inclined to think that you can be a true N'ian only if you were born of N'ian parents. At the extreme, people with this conception of national identity will include as N'ians the grown children of emigrant N'ians who have never been to N and who don't speak a word of N's national language (and even their children's children, and so on); they will exclude grown children born and educated in N of non-N'ian parents even if these individuals speak only N's national language and will never leave N's homeland.[41] Indeed, at the extreme, someone with an ethnic conception of his or her national identity will not see these people as N'ians even after they are granted citizenship in the N'ian's national state. Also making up the content of an ethnic national identity are likely to be beliefs involving historical myths of ethnic continuity and purity, as well as a host of (no doubt mistaken) beliefs about the 'objective' characteristics of N'ians that distinguish them from non-N'ians, especially the non-N'ians who are internal minorities or foreign neighbours.

Before turning to the contrasting conception of a so-called 'civic' national identity, three remarks about the ethnic conception in the preceding paragraph are in order. First, in its pure form, this kind of national identity is

---

[40] Although it is interesting to note that what people fear (sometimes mistakenly) about ethnic national identities is the intensity of the sentiments they are thought to inspire.

[41] Something rather close to this ethnic conception of nationality was official German policy from 1913 until a new citizenship and nationality law took effect on the first day of the new millennium. The non-German-speaking descendants of ethnic Germans living in Russia for generations could claim an automatic right to citizenship in the German state when the unilingual German-speaking grandchildren of Turkish immigrants to Germany, who were born on German soil, could not. According the German government, the law was changed in part to take account of the fact that 'more than seven million foreigners live in Germany on a long-term basis. One third of them have lived here for more than 30 years; half of them have lived in Germany for at least 20 years'. Moreover, the government adds, the 'lives of most of the foreign nationals living in Germany center around Germany'. 'In practical terms,' it notes, 'these people have become Germans', even if the previous law did not recognize this fact. (Quotations from a press release posted on the site of the German Embassy in the UK, entitled 'Reform of Germany's Citizenship and Nationality Law', http://www.german-embassy.org.uk/reform_of_germany_s_citizenshi.html.)

increasingly rare in the modern world. Nevertheless, if we weaken the conditions just a little bit, then there is a significant ethnic component to many national identities, even in flourishing democracies like Germany, the Nordic countries, and Greece. And this leads to a second point, that the ethnic component in an individual's national identity is usually a matter of degree, and virtually all national identities have some ethnic or 'descent-based' component to them.[42] For example, in every national community the children of nationals born on the national territory are automatically considered to be members of the nation. Where national cultures differ is in the ease with which non-nationals can also come to be (seen as) members of the nation. And this is never simply a question of how easy or difficult it is for them to attain citizenship status in the nation's state (if it has one); although there is certainly an important relation between immigration and naturalization rules, on the one hand, and ordinary people's conception of when a foreigner can come to be regarded as 'one of us', on the other.[43] A final remark is implicit in the way I have been treating national identity and its contents first and foremost as a property of individuals, rather than of groups or political entities. To say that a certain nation has a (relatively) ethnic national identity can only mean that a goodly percentage of the individual members of that nation have such an identity. This is not to deny that national identities are an inherently social phenomenon and the product of social interactions; of course they are, much in the same way that language is.[44] Nevertheless, just as it is only individuals and not groups who can actually speak a language or have an accent, so too it is only individuals who can be the primary bearers of a national identity. Claims about the nature of, say, Québécois identity or a Québécois accent must always be reducible to claims about how most Québécois identify with their community or pronounce (or elide) their vowels. This may seem like a trivial point, but it has significant implications for understanding key issues in the politics of nation-building, and in particular when assessing ethical constraints on the political use of ethnic identities. If the locus of identity is in the hearts, minds, and perceptions of the members

---

[42] See Kymlicka (1995c), reprinted in Kymlicka (2001: ch. 12).

[43] The relationship runs both ways. Politicians in the national state of the N'ians will be reluctant to pass a citizenship law that makes it easy for foreigners to be full citizens in N if the 'native' N'ians cannot really regard these people as true N'ians. On the other hand, a more liberal citizenship law that allows accession to citizenship for immigrants, combined with a strong conception of equal citizenship and non-discrimination, will likely have the effect of de-ethnicizing the national identity of the N'ians. The latter process has been clearly visible in the Anglo-Saxon countries of immigration over the past generation or two, as non-white immigrants have come to be embraced as true members not only of the state, but also of the nation. The same is true, at least for large segments of the population, in France and in Quebec.

[44] Parekh (1995: 258) explores some of the interesting relations between identity and language in his 'The Concept of National Identity.'

of the community, then political elites cannot simply declare the nation's identity to be this or that and thereby make it so. Politicians can certainly speak and act in ways that have a profound impact on the way people reflect on their own national identity, but they cannot literally change the nation's identity with their acts or declarations—just as they cannot change the language by the very act of removing words from, or changing meanings in, the official dictionary. So if it turns out that a significant portion of the population holds an ethnic conception of their national identity, politicians cannot escape any criticism for appealing overtly to that identity just because they have managed to 'civilize' their own conception of the identity. I will discuss such duties relating to the discourse of politics below.

We turn now to the conception of a so-called civic national identity. How would someone with a civic conception of his or her nation, N, answer questions like 'What is an N'ian?', 'Who are the N'ians?', 'What does it mean to be an N'ian?', 'What does it take to become an N'ian?'? Civic nationalists—or at least their intellectual apologists—have tended to answer these questions in one or both of two related ways: first, in terms of membership in a political community like a state or a substate political unit (so the N'ians are simply all of the citizens who happen to live in N, regardless of ethnicity, religion, mother tongue, and what have you) and, second, in terms of accepting certain basic values, including typically the fundamental constitutional rights and duties of the state (so the N'ians are those who believe in liberty, democracy, multiculturalism, or what have you).

Since the recent entry of philosophers into the conceptual debates about the nature of nationalism and national identity it has been noted several times that both of these attempts to conceive of a non-ethnic form of national identity are beset with problems.[45] Both of them fail a test of 'realism', i.e. no actual widely held national identity could truly be characterized in these terms. The first 'territorial' definition is simply an attempt to define any kind of national community identity other than citizenship out of existence. While this can be part of an official state ideology (as it is, say, in France), it will not capture the working sense of national identity actually held by members, who will come to attach other cultural traits besides formal citizenship to 'true' membership in the nation (such as an ability to speak the language, or even to speak it without an accent). The 'shared values' definition is even less realistic: there is no nation in the world that you become a member of simply by espousing certain values; and people do not consider fellow nationals to lose their status as members of the nation just because they reject

---

[45] Karmis (1994), Norman (1995c), Norman (1998c), Weinstock (1996), Kymlicka (2001: ch. 12), Seymour (1998), Schnapper (1998), Yack (1999), and Nielsen (1999).

the allegedly shared civic values. We do not somehow conceptually expel skinhead Nazis from membership in our liberal national community; we are horrified or embarrassed by them precisely because they are *our* skinheads.[46]

There are deeper conceptual reasons why the typical definitions of the civic nation tend to be unrealistic. Neither provides coherent criteria for national membership. The territorial definition begs the question by pushing the issue of membership to the legal level of citizenship. But this provides no rationale for why the state should automatically grant citizenship to children of citizens, or why it does not open its borders to anyone in the world who would like to immigrate. If asked why they should not allow open borders, even elite defenders of the civic nationalist ideology will find themselves talking in more substantive ways about the community having the right to protect 'itself' and its 'way of life' (including social, economic, and democratic achievements) from the onslaught of millions of potential immigrants from the developing world.[47] Similarly, the shared-values conception of the civic nation cannot explain why immigration (or expulsion) should not be allowed for anybody who professes (or rejects) the supposed defining values of the national community.

Civic nationalism has the markings of a generally good idea that looks silly when it is formulated in any specific terms. There is, after all, something very attractive for liberals in the idea of equal citizenship in a political community, where everybody is a full member regardless of ethnicity, gender, religion, or mother tongue. Conversely (and we will pursue this issue more below), there is something very unsettling about a majority ethnic group treating the state as its own and trampling on the civil, political, or cultural rights of members of minority communities. Nevertheless, for the reasons rehearsed above, among others, attempts to conceive of national identities in purely political terms will not work. Or to put it another way, attempts by political leaders or the state to forge an entirely *political* national identity seem futile.

Fortunately, shared ethnicity and shared political values are not the only types of 'identity glue' available. What both the ethnic and civic conceptions of national identity ignore is a range of cultural traits that typically fill out most people's conceptions of their national identity. These are the aspects of language, accent, body language, customs, cultural tastes, culinary tastes, shared memories, etc., that people typically use to recognize each other as

---

[46] I have explored the ideology of the 'shared values' conception of national unity at length in Norman (1995*b*). For recent critique see Henderson and McEwen (2005).

[47] See Carens (1987).

fellow nationals, as well as to recognize others who are not.[48] (Again, we can refer to the list of first-person beliefs and sentiments earlier in this chapter.) These cultural traits can shade into both ethnic traits at one end of a spectrum and political traits at another. Nations that have a significant ethnic component will tend to see many aspects of their religion, their way of life, and their customs, dress, music, and cuisine, as having been passed down to them from time immemorial (even if many of these things in fact arrived relatively recently), and they will sometimes talk as if these essentially cultural artefacts were 'in their blood'. Something similar happens in nations that have a more significant civic or political component to their identity. They will take pride in (and form myths about) their political and social achievements, and they will identify with their political institutions. Some of their heroes will be people who founded or defended these institutions; many of their shared memories will involve essentially political events. The more political components there are to the identity, the easier it should be to accept new members from other national and ethnic origins, be they immigrants or ethnocultural national minorities. Immigrants will not be seen as 'one of us' simply by being in the territory or by espousing certain values; but to the extent that they seem loyal and committed to the national project (which may not involve much more than having a job and feeling grateful to be living in the new land) and begin to share memories and knowledge of at least recent social and political (and cultural and sporting) events, they will come to be seen as members of the national community even if they cannot shake off thick accents and awkward syntax.

It is time to draw together some of the threads of this discussion of the possible contents of national identities in order to see the relevance of identity content to the ethics of nation-building. In particular, how does the nature of the existing or intended content of an identity affect the evaluation of a nation-building (or nation-mobilizing) project?

There is something undeniably compelling about the traditional liberal worry about national identities with a significant ethnic component. This is not because there is anything wrong with individuals having an ethnic identity per se—almost everybody in the world has one, and it can combine comfortably with all sorts of other sources of identity for individuals and provide a potentially significant form of rootedness in the world. The problem is when ethnic identity is combined with the desire for political self-determination that is characteristic of a *national* identity. It seems almost necessarily illiberal to have a political community, like a state or even a province, treated as the 'property' of a particular ethnic group, given that

---

[48] For a ground-breaking explanation of the role of cultural traits in contemporary Québécois identity, see Karmis (1994).

almost all such territories will also be inhabited by individuals who are not members of that ethnic group. This is because it will be difficult to maintain a true sense of equal citizenship when members of the minority feel like second-class citizens in the majority's 'national' state. Whether they are formally second-class citizens (or even non-citizens) or not, minorities in an ethnic nationalist state are likely to get less than their fair share of Rawlsian primary goods, including the 'social bases of self-respect'.[49] They are also unlikely to enjoy political equality, and may find their group permanently outvoted in democratic decision-making whenever their collective interests are pitted against those of the majority. In short, liberal democrats should not generally be keen to associate themselves with ethnonationalist movements.

But this simple judgement leaves most of the live normative issues unresolved. It may be true that liberals would in some abstract thought experiment prefer a world of civic–nationalist political cultures to a world of ethnic–nationalist cultures, but this does not tell us much about what they should do if they find themselves politically engaged in a political culture with a significant ethnic–nationalist component. For example, in such a society, it is difficult to make persuasive public arguments for any major policy (including good liberal policies) without using nationalist forms of justification that appeal to the ethnic roots of the identity. In order to get a clearer sense of the issues about the ethics of nation-building and nation-shaping in such situations, consider the following four general questions:

1. Do liberal political actors in ethnic–nationalist political cultures have duties to engage in identity-shaping projects, such as reconfiguring, desentimentalizing, and remoralizing the identity in order to weaken its ethnic component?
2. Are there ways of securing true equal citizenship in a multiethnic state even if the majority considers the state to 'belong' to their ethnic community?
3. Are there limits for liberals on the use of nationalist arguments to mobilize citizens in favour of various policies (including good liberal policies) when it is known that most of the citizens hold ethnic conceptions of their national identity (even if these liberals themselves have a more 'civic' conception of their own national identity)?
4. Are there liberal ends that are so important that they justify appealing explicitly to ethnic national identities in order to mobilize support?[50]

[49] See Rawls (1971: ch. 2, Section 15).
[50] Questions 3 and 4 are primarily concerned with what we might call the ethics of 'nation mobilizing' rather than 'nation-building'. But they raise issues for political actors since they may want to reshape identities in order to facilitate more appropriate means of mobilizing citizens. For example, they may want to try to reconfigure identities so that citizens will be more likely to be persuaded by liberal, rather than nationalist, arguments.

It is possible (and defensible) to answer each of these questions with a qualified 'Yes'. But this sort of very general answer can still only serve to give, at best, a 'big picture' perspective on liberal intuitions. It will not get us very far in evaluating how actual liberal actors ought to behave in actual political cultures. Nevertheless, at this stage it is useful to note how these general questions point to the sorts of concrete normative issues that liberals face in a nationalist political culture.

The presumption of an affirmative answer to the first question ('Should liberals try to thin out the ethnic component of the national identity in their political culture?') follows from the egalitarian worries about ethnic chauvinism and second-class citizenship just discussed. One way to reduce de facto (and ultimately de jure) discrimination that arises when an ethnic group sees the state (or substate unit) as its own is to try to weaken the ethnic criteria for membership in the nation through what I have called reconfiguring, desentimentalizing, and remoralizing national engineering projects. Of course, this is easier said than done, even for liberal political actors holding high public office; but it does imply a duty to question the myths, values, and sentiments that constitute and sustain the ethnic component of the national identity, and to propose credible alternatives. At the very least, it implies a duty under 'normal circumstances' not to reinforce the ethnic dimension of the existing identity and the sentiments that underlie it; hence the presumption of an affirmative answer to question 3 ('Are there limits for liberals on the use of nationalist arguments to mobilize citizens within ethnonationalist political cultures?').[51] An affirmative answer to question 1 also assumes that some form of national engineering is permissible for liberals (or rather, it presents one of the stronger cases for it being permissible in at least some circumstances for liberals to deliberately try to alter people's national identities).

The second question concerns other ways that liberals could try to secure equal citizenship for ethnocultural minorities in a state run by an ethnonationalist majority. One of the problems with nationalism based on an ethnic identity, again, is that this group is often inclined to see the state as its own (and the same can be true at the substate level for an ethnocultural group that is the majority in a province). While it typically takes a long time—perhaps generations—to significantly 'de-ethnicize' a national identity, it may be possible to 'remoralize' some of its normative political content much more quickly. In particular, it may be possible to change people's conception of

---

[51] The hedge 'under normal circumstances' is a significant qualification of this duty here, since ethnic nationalism is likely to be strongest in times that are, or are perceived to be, precarious. As many liberals and socialists from the former Yugoslavia lamented after the events of the early 1990s, there can be very little room for public reflection on ethnic identity in times of crisis and fear.

homeland in order to accommodate other groups who share a similar historic attachment to the territory, and it may be possible to change the majority group's belief in its *exclusive* 'ownership' of the state. Both these key components of nationalism can be altered through the constitutionalization of various forms of minority rights (including federal autonomy and minority veto rights) and recognition. In other words, there are ways in which an ethnic national identity can be made less objectionable in the liberal state. It is possible for groups with essentially ethnic identities to conceive of themselves as sharing a state. This is likely to be easiest when no one group forms a majority (a state of affairs that holds for about a third of states today), as was the case, say, in Yugoslavia before 1990. But even in cases where one group forms the overwhelming majority of the population, it is possible to formally recognize and afford special forms of representation and autonomy for historic national minorities.[52] All of the major European treaty organizations—including the North Atlantic Treaty Organization (Nato), the European Union (EU), the Organization for Security and Co-operation in Europe (OSCE), and the Council of Europe—currently call upon members to recognize the rights of national minorities; though partly because of the recalcitrance of stalwart nation-states like France and Germany, these organizations stop short of calling for the recognition of historic minorities as full 'partners' in the state. (There is ample evidence in multination states from Canada to Croatia to Indonesia that such recognition might be even more forthcoming were it not for fears that it would fuel secessionist ambitions. I will return to this issue in Chapter 6.)

Question 4 ('Are there liberal ends that are so important that they justify appealing explicitly to ethnic national identities in order to mobilize support?') cuts to the heart of a political morality of nationalism. Since both nation-building and nation-mobilizing are basically forms of politics, and since politics is mostly a means to other ends, a morality of nationalism must consider whether otherwise objectionable means may sometimes justify laudable ends. In short, the moral evaluation of nationalism must be consequentialist to a significant degree. And any consequentialist moral decision-making must contemplate the possibility of having to sacrifice some values for others. In this way, we can certainly conceive of situations in which it might be best, all things considered, for a liberal political actor to behave like an ethnic nationalist. So there are, in answer to question 4, liberal ends that are so

---

[52] Examples abound, e.g. a great many developed states now have significant forms of recognition and special rights for aboriginal peoples as the original inhabitants of the land (in many cases this approach developed after failed and tragic attempts to assimilate these peoples into the mainstream culture). See Levy (2000*a*: ch. 6). The UK is also an early example in the modern world of a state that was explicitly shared by different peoples, as was Canada.

important they justify appealing to and even building up ethnic national identities in order to mobilize support. I have already mentioned the general case of a perennially oppressed ethnic minority. There are good liberal grounds for thinking that such a group is entitled to a substantial array of minority rights.[53] However, there may also be no grounds for thinking that the 'normal' forms of liberal-democratic political activity will be effective for securing those rights. The state may not be democratic, but even if it is, the minority may be too small, too dispersed, or too despised or distrusted to have any expectation of exerting pressure on the majority. There may be no better means for an aspiring political leader from this group—even if he or she is a liberal, and not an ethnonationalist, at heart—than to try to mobilize his or her people in standard nationalist ways, and this may typically involve engaging in what I earlier called a 'nationalizing' form of nation-building, which transforms an existing ethnic identity into a national identity complete with demands for political self-determination. In such a situation it would be unrealistic to imagine that this new national identity would not have a significant ethnic component, since the ethnic identity of the group is precisely the feature that has marked them for oppression at the hands of the majority. Of course, this example of mobilizing an ethnic minority in order to help secure its (liberal) minority rights can only serve as an exception that supports the general presumption against liberals engaging in ethnic identity-building politics. The omnipresent danger in this enterprise is that it will legitimize a kind of discourse that will be much better exploited by one's non-liberal opponents.

2.8 CONCLUSION

This chapter is already rather long, but in many ways it barely begins even to catalogue the inventory of issues that arise once we move from asking questions about the benefits or dangers of *having* a national identity diffused throughout the state, on the one hand, to questions about how we should

---

[53] For the benchmark liberal theory of minority rights see Kymlicka (1995a); for key distinctions between different kinds of minority rights and the arguments for and against granting them, see Kymlicka and Norman (2000: 1–40) and Levy (2000b: 125–60). Of course, there are liberal theorists like Barry (2001) and Kukathas (2003) who have argued against the proliferation of minority rights. But they are not in favour of the systematic oppression of minorities either. In any case, I am concerned here with the legitimacy of nationalist mobilization to demand justice, a democratic political activity that neither need oppose on anti-multiculturalist grounds.

evaluate *attempts to create or transform* these identities, on the other. Kymlicka (2002: 28) understated the case when he recently concluded that 'Western political theorists' have yet to develop 'a consistent theory of permissible forms of nation-building'. It is not as if we have even developed many *inconsistent* normative theories of nation-building. By and large, in this 'second wave' of normative theories of nationalism we are still trying to set the agenda for such a theory. A small part of this agenda involves our choices of terminology, and to this end I have suggested that we beware of the quantitative bias of the traditional term 'nation-building'. It is extremely rare that we are talking about creating something from nothing, or simply making something small, big; or something weak, strong. Instead, we are talking about subtly altering the 'qualitative' content of a long list of beliefs, values, and sentiments of a large number of people. Even to think of nationalist *sentiments* simply in terms of their intensity seems worryingly unsophisticated.

We might be similarly concerned about the quantitative metaphor underlying our talk of 'thicker' and 'thinner' identities. As tempting as it is to rely on these images, I doubt we can really explain what it is that is thickening or thinning about national identities. We think of thin identities as those that are less ethnic and more easily assumable by new immigrants (and perhaps also members of national minorities). This makes contemporary British, French, and American identities relatively 'thin'. But in other ways surely these are also rich and strong, powerful, meaningful, compelling, robust, stable, and historically rooted identities. In how many ways does it really make sense to say they are thinner than, say, the much more 'ethnic' Norwegian or Albanian identities?

Another potentially misleading aspect of the language of nation-building or 'national engineering' is that it implies very *deliberate* attempts to shape identities in specific ways. Of course, history is full of such examples. And we do care about what political actors and state institutions are trying to accomplish and about the real justification for their projects. But it is also important to take into account that much of what comes to inform political cultures and identities is a consequence of policies, institutions, and activities that have been carried out for other reasons. Sometimes the identity-shaping consequences are foreseeable, but often they are not. A wholly consequentialist morality of nationalism will not necessarily be concerned with whether consequences are intended or not, as long as they are predictable. But other ways of evaluating politics and institutions will want to take account of these differences. I have barely broached this issue here.

Once we have a clearer sense of the wide variety of beliefs, values, and sentiments that are associated with national identities, and also of the wide array of political and state activities that can shape these identities, we will have to develop a much more sophisticated understanding of, if you will, the dynamics of 'private-sector' identity-shaping activities. I am thinking of the myriad activities by individuals and corporations ranging from the speech and writings of politicians, political commentators, editorialists, and journalists to the works of novelists, singers, filmmakers, sitcom writers, sporting heroes, advertisers, and so on. I have offered a few speculative comments in this chapter on the cultural and identity influence of these individuals and organizations, but it is very difficult to grasp just how much of an impact they have on the constant evolution of the beliefs, values, and sentiments that shape our identities. As political philosophers we are always inclined to focus on the powerful role of state institutions; but in our modern or postmodern societies in the information age, one wonders whether the lion's share of identity-shaping influences might actually be beyond the normal reach of politicians and governments.

If this is true anywhere, it is true in America. We see there some of the implications of having a rich vein of national identity running through a society. This is a public good (or bad, as the case may be) available to everyone from politicians to the manufacturers of pickup trucks to the makers of infomercials advertising the 'God Bless America' flag-and-bumper-sticker kit with which to decorate your pickup truck. The appeal to national identity to mobilize people to adopt your ideas or to buy your product is yet another central component of nationalism and nationalist politics that has received scant attention so far by political philosophers. It is surely something that serves to reinforce national identities and nationalist sentiments even as it is using these to its advantage. This sort of functional explanation for the persistence of national identities is another aspect of nationalism that deserves more attention.

The last neglected issue about nation-building I want to mention here concerns its alternatives. Several 'first-wave' theorists made of national identity, in Tamir's words (1993: ch. 7), 'a virtue out of necessity'. They showed the potential benefits, for the sake of social solidarity and deliberative democracy, of a healthy national identity. This observation of the potential benefits of a cohesive national identity is by no means a discovery of recent political philosophers. If Greenfeld (1992) is correct, it has been a central driving force in the history of the spread of nationalism from one powerful nation to the next (from England to France to Germany to Russia, etc.). But even if the existence of a strong national identity throughout a society has these benefits, it is not obvious for many reasons that heavy-handed, deliberate attempts *to create* or *diffuse* such an identity will succeed and provide the benefits in a state that is currently divided. As I have noted already, if the centralist nation-building project is designed to assimilate national minorities, there are in fact very good grounds for thinking that it is likely to be counterproductive: it will fuel a minority nationalist project that is much more likely to be appealing to members of the national minority. Weinstock (1999) has suggested we look elsewhere for a basis for solidarity within multinational, divided societies: rather than looking to promote a common identity, we should look instead for policies and institutional arrangements that will inspire trust between the communities. In other words, trust-building might be an alternative to nation-building, at least for majority nationalists trying to hold together their multination state. This is one of many alternatives to nation-building to be found in contemporary debates that argue for the engineering of a so-called post-national, cosmopolitan, or citizenship identity. I have not explored these options in any systematic way here; although the latter three are variants of what many writers have in mind by a very 'thinned out' civic national identity. This book addresses the predicament of multinational states in which the persistence of a plurality of national identities and rival national-identity-shaping projects are a fact of life for the foreseeable future. Over the remaining chapters I will focus on pragmatic and principled considerations for the development of constitutional arrangements that might, where successful, promote the kind of trust that Weinstock has in mind, while also instantiating the minority rights and facilitating the kind of thin national identity that is also at the heart of the Kymlickian project.

2.9 LOOKING FORWARD: FROM NATIONALISM TO FEDERALISM

The focus of this enquiry now shifts from nation-building to federalism, two topics that have rarely been pursued by the same scholars.[54] It is worth reiterating the 'narrative link' I drew between the two at the end of Section 2.6 (on the evaluation of nation-building methods). The simplest solution to the problem of rival nation-building projects in multinational states would

---

[54] It goes without saying that we could nevertheless produce a longish list of scholars interested in both federalism and nationalism who are the exceptions to prove this rule. See, e.g. the various contributor's to Forsyth's *Federalism and Nationalism* (1989), as well as Trudeau (1968), Howse and Knop (1993), Norman (1994), Resnick (1994), Levy (2004), Kymlicka (2001*a*: ch. 5), Weinstock (2001*b*), McGarry (2002), Laforest (2004), Requejo (2005), Linz (2005), and Karmis and Norman (2005*b*) to name a few.

parallel the one some democratic states have adopted to the 'problem' of rival proselytizing religions: let the state be neutral about the value of these rival projects while protecting the rights (and developing the capacities) of individuals to make their own free choices. Unfortunately, this solution is simply not available for the problem of rival nationalisms. Neutrality with respect to nation-building is not possible. There are too many ways that even relatively mundane government policies and institutions (let alone consequential ones, like official-language policy) will make contact with the many contours of moral and cultural personality that make up an individual's national identity. As Moore (2001: 130) puts it, 'It is not possible for the state to be neutral in the sense that it makes no decision on these issues. Nor is it possible to be neutral in the sense of incorporating all traditions, all cultural, ethnic and national claims.' Moreover, standard liberal intuitions (as articulated in the various 'tests' proposed for evaluating nation-building policies, as well as in the discussion of the content of identities) seem to suggest that a fairly wide range of government policies and autonomous political activities with nation-building implications will be *permissible* in any liberal-democratic state. This 'threat' of the nationalizing state will be perceived and felt by many 'identity groups', and many will find themselves unable to resist it (notably, some traditionalist religious communities will have a hard time surviving a nationalizing state's compulsory education system, even if they were not its intended 'target'). Theorists of multiculturalism have highlighted the many ways states have in fact offered special accommodations, protections, and minority rights to these various kinds of groups. Different groups are threatened in different ways and have been, or can be, protected in different ways.[55] Territorially concentrated national minorities can be protected from a nationalizing state through federal arrangements that allow them control over important nation-building powers, such as language policy and education, within a territorial subunit. 'They do not,' as Levy has argued, 'have morally more important claims than still-more vulnerable groups like indigenous peoples and the Roma.' It is their 'particularly strong ability to stand up to a nationalizing state' that avails them to this special constitutional status (Levy 2004: 169).

But what sort of federal status is appropriate for national minorities? What powers of nation-building can they legitimately claim, and which nation-building powers might it actually be unjust for the state to withhold from its

---

[55] Again, see Kymlicka and Norman (2000: 10–30) for a sketch of the variety and justification of different kinds of minority rights for different kinds of groups. Of course, many groups will not qualify for such special rights at all, and many would not qualify for all of the rights they might demand.

national minorities? Do traditional principles of justice, democracy, and constitutionalism—most of which were developed with models of a unitary nation-state in mind—apply in the same way when we want to justify federal arrangements in a multinational state? Or must they be replaced or supplemented with special principles of recognition? What rights, if any, do national minorities have to secede from the state if they cannot secure the powers necessary to be 'masters of their own house'? These are the kinds of questions that will drive the remaining chapters in this book.

Chapter 3 is something of a scholars' interlude and much of it could be skipped over by those interested in pursuing immediately the question of the design and justification of multinational federal arrangements. Chapter 3 is about federal *theory* and *theorists* more than it is about federal institutions per se. Before possibly reinventing the wheel when it comes to federalist theory, we enquire here about what we might plausibly learn from a 400-year-old tradition of debates about federalism in political philosophy. And in particular, we ask whether there are any grounds for maintaining the explicit rejection of federalism by political philosophers during the first half of the twentieth century or the widespread ignoring of federalism as a serious issue in the latter half of the twentieth century. I will argue that this neglect was not justified and that the twentieth-century critique of federalism was neither (*a*) entirely warranted on its own terms, nor (*b*) something that should overly worry a contemporary political theorist wishing to develop a theory of the just multinational federation. I hope that some of this discussion of the history of federalist debates will be of interest to those wishing to start afresh today. But again, if the reader is already convinced about the potential of federal arrangements to reconcile rival nation-building projects in a single state, he or she is invited to pass directly to chapter 4, perhaps after reading only Sections 3.1 and 3.2 (dealing with motivations and definitions).

Chapters 4 and 5 present a normative theory of federalism; or more modestly, because this has never really been done within our tradition of political philosophy, they conduct a survey of the practical, institutional, and normative issues one would have to address in such a theory. Chapter 4 catalogues the options for federal constitutional design, in large part by looking at the options that have been tried by actual federations or confederations. And Chapter 5 asks to what extent our 'traditional' normative theories for justifying political institutions are adequate to the task of choosing among the options for multinational federal constitutions. It proposes that these normative principles be supplemented with principles of (mutual) recognition, including principled limits on nation-building by both sides. Chapter 6 is at once an application of this theory of federal constitutionalism to the design and justification of a secession clause, *and* a challenge to such a constitutional order itself.

If rival nation-building projects are the problem in the multinational state, to what extent and why might federalism be the solution?

3

Should Nation-building be Federalized? Reconsidering the Role of Federalism in Normative Political Theory

[N]ationalist politics is a contest between and among, in Brubaker's words, nationalizing states and state-seeking national minorities.... It is not, as some theorists suppose, simply a matter of belonging to a community larger than the family and smaller than humanity; it is a bitter contest over which of those communities has primary claim on the loyalty of members and on political rights to self-government.

—Jacob Levy (2004: 161)

Secession is the most dramatic form assertions of self-determination can take. Nevertheless... focusing exclusively or even primarily on secession distorts theory and impedes progress in practice. *Achievement of independent statehood is in many cases the least feasible or appropriate exercise of self-determination.* A comprehensive theory of self-determination, therefore, must include not only an account of the right to secede but also a broader normative framework for evaluating and responding to claims to self-determination, and one that does not assume that independent statehood is the natural goal or inevitable culmination of aspirations for self-determination.

—Allen Buchanan (2004: 332, my italics)

3.1 INTRODUCTION: SELF-DETERMINATION AND FEDERALISM

The two quotes above refer, respectively, to the two faces of nationalism in the multinational state: in Levy's, the project to 'determine the self' or nation-building, and in Buchanan's, the project of 'self-determination' or the quest for political autonomy. These two projects are, as we have seen, interrelated in complex and variable ways. Minority nationalists will be engaged in nation-building in part to buttress claims for more political autonomy; they make claims for political autonomy (either within or outside the state) in order to have more freedom to pursue nation-building projects. In the eyes of majority nationalists—who are often less conscious of their own nation-building and self-determination aspirations—these interrelated minority nationalist projects look like a vicious circle: autonomy leads to nation-building, which leads to demands for more autonomy, and so on, until well-mobilized demands for secession are inevitable.

The political sociology underlying this 'vicious circle' is largely speculative. Most national minorities in the world have not been given much political autonomy, so it is difficult to establish a reliable causal connection between minorities getting more autonomy and their expanding nation-building efforts in order to demand even greater autonomy. Moreover, there are some empirical grounds for majority nationalists to be more optimistic. In multinational states with reasonably long traditions of democracy—where minority nationalists have the greatest freedom to mobilize demands for autonomy—there have been very few 'credible' secessionist movements. Even in Quebec, where support for secession does sometimes run higher than 50 per cent in opinion polls and where secession often seems to be just five or ten years away, the best explanation for secessionist demands may be the larger state's *refusal* to grant more autonomy and recognition *within* the state. Part of the reason for the relative unpopularity of the secessionist option in democratic multinational states is that the members of national minorities also feel themselves to be members of the larger nation or state, and they are reluctant to have to choose between these two national identities (as both majority and minority nationalist entrepreneurs would like them to do). That said, we would not even refer to them as *national* minorities or minority *nations* if they were not generally in favour of autonomy and powers of self-government within the larger state.

So secession is rarely the preferred form of political autonomy for national minorities in democratic states; and it is even more rarely the preferred option for the 'international community'. The italicized premise in Buchanan's argument—that 'achievement of independent statehood is in many cases the least feasible or appropriate exercise of self-determination'—is a spectacular understatement. As I noted in the Preface, by the most conservative estimate, there are about four times as many 'nations' (or 'named ethnocultural communities with a national self-consciousness and a desire for self-government that are living in their traditional homeland'[1]) as there are states

---

[1] This 'homeland' requirement is meant primarily to distinguish long-standing ethnocultural minorities from groups of immigrants who have settled voluntarily in a new country. Of course, we would not want to exclude on this basis communities who have been brutally transplanted from their traditional homeland to another region of a larger state or empire (e.g. the Tartars who where expelled from their Crimean homeland by Stalin near the end of the Second World War).

in the world today. When combined with the simple demographic fact that most minority and majority communities intermingle in the way the peoples of Rwanda and the former Yugoslavia do or did, and the brute political fact that the legitimacy of claims to sovereign territory will always be hotly contested, this simple arithmetic points clearly in the direction of Buchanan's conclusion. In the vast majority of cases, self-determination for minority national communities will and should take place within multinational states.

Buchanan's monumental tome is primarily concerned with the case for why and how *international law* should discourage secession while encouraging 'alternatives to secession, in particular by working for greater compliance with existing international human rights norms prohibiting ethnonational and religious discrimination and in some cases by supporting *intrastate autonomy regimes*, that is, arrangements for self-government short of full sovereignty' (Buchanan 2004: 331, my italics). The rest of this book will also focus on these two forms of self-determination: first 'intrastate autonomy regimes' (Chapters 3–5) and then secession (Chapter 6). But I shall do so primarily from the points of view of liberals and nationalists *within* a multinational state, rather than from the perspective of international law. Nothing I argue for should contradict Buchanan's general case for international law; but I will nevertheless envisage autonomy provisions—up to and including secession—that move well beyond what any reasonable international legal regime could demand of sovereign states. This should hardly be surprising. There is nothing unusual about arguing for the justice or desirability of certain institutions within a given state (e.g. free post-secondary education or federalism) while nevertheless refusing to force such institutions upon all states through the blunt mechanisms of international law.

Constitutions are the ultimate battleground for nationalist politics in the multinational state, especially when competing nationalists are duelling for the hearts, minds, and identities of some of the same citizens. Many of the most explicit nationalist demands will call for changes to (or for resisting changes to) the constitution. There are at least two obvious reasons for this. First, because the constitution can determine which national community will get to control which nation-building powers. In a federal or quasi-federal state, the constitution will decide whether it is the central government (typically controlled by the majority group in the state) or the provincial governments (which may be controlled by national minorities) that will have control over particular powers with significant nation-building potential, such as education, health and social services, communications, the military, powers to appoint constitutional court judges, and powers of taxation. Second, the constitution can embody provisions of great symbolic importance to nationalists, be these forms of national recognition or sources of national grievance.

Constitutions sometimes declare that the state is the national state of a particular people; they can declare that the state is inherently indivisible, or that it is a voluntary union or partnership of free citizens or sovereign peoples; they can officially recognize the place or status of minority peoples or nationalities; they can recognize one or more official languages, scripts, or religions; they can recognize certain 'national' holidays, heroes, coats of arms, flags; they can reserve some government posts for members of certain ethnic, religious, or caste groups, and so on. Of course, numerous constitutional provisions may be of both substantive and symbolic importance to nationalists. For example, if only one of several provinces in a federation happens to be controlled by a national minority, and if that province is granted special powers (e.g. control over education, the right to secede, or the right to veto constitutional amendments) that the other provinces do not enjoy, then the people of that province are both symbolically recognized as being unique *and* given special powers to manage their uniqueness.

In addition, numerous constitutional provisions that are neither symbolically significant nor distribute fundamental powers may nevertheless have an impact on minority or majority nationalist politics. This might be how we could characterize constitutionally entrenched electoral systems.[2] It is possible that electoral systems with single-member constituencies (whether in first-past-the-post or two-round elections) will encourage a party system with a small number of strong parties with representation in most regions of the country; this in turn can lead to strong majority governments for parties receiving only a plurality of the votes. Contrarily, some proportional-representation systems would lead to a large number of regional parties and coalition governments in which minority nationalist parties might exert more (or less) influence.[3] Hence, the choice of electoral system could significantly affect how and where majority or minority nationalists are able to pursue their agendas.

In general it is relatively easy to identify which sorts of constitutional provisions will please or aggrieve certain kinds of nationalists. (At least, this is true for observers *within* a given political culture: we will often be surprised to learn that certain obscure issues are deeply contested in some other country.) But evaluating when it is *just* or *legitimate* for constitutions to be written or amended one way rather than another is much more difficult. In other words, we generally know what nationalists want out of the

---

[2] Not all aspects of electoral systems are constitutionally entrenched; many provisions may simply be part of the electoral law that can be changed by the legislatures in question.

[3] This is of course an oversimplified generalization for the purposes of illustration. For a more thorough analysis see Reilly (2001, 2002), and Filippov, Ordeshook, and Schvetsova (2004: ch. 6).

constitution; but what about liberal democrats, including those who are also nationalists or who live in a nationalist political culture? How can we evaluate when specific constitutional provisions or proposals are *just* in a multinational state? As we shall see, it is far from clear even what empirical *political consequences* can be expected from many of the constitutional reforms that are demanded by, for example, minority nationalists.

Most of the rest of this book will consist of tentative steps towards a liberal theory of federalism for the multinational state. I shall also argue for a somewhat more expansive view of constitutionalism than the one typically used when discussing the classic nation-state. Chapter 6, on secession, will be largely a corollary of the theories presented here and in Chapters 4 and 5: it will argue that a secession procedure in a multinational state is perfectly legitimate and should be designed and justified using the principles appropriate for *any* constitutional provision. Part of the argument for such a procedure is that it could help discourage secessionist politics in an otherwise reasonably just multination state while encouraging a more stable realm of autonomy for national minorities as well as a greater commitment to federal partnership. These four chapters, in short, sketch a viable and defensible realm of self-determination for national minorities within, rather than apart from, multinational states. They envisage a world with not many more than 200 states, but in which an ever-increasing number of the 600 to 800 major national minorities would have considerably more room to govern their own affairs and to 'determine their selves' than they typically do today.

3.2 FEDERALISM AND FEDERALIST THEORY: FOR WHOM?

In its most general sense, federalism is an arrangement in which two or more self-governing communities share a common political space. For the sake of brevity and neutrality, I shall henceforth refer to the constituent units of a federation generically as 'provinces'. The standard generic term 'subunit' is not neutral: it seems to imply a hierarchy where the central or federal government is *above* the provincial governments; whereas in its purest form federalism is about coordinating two 'orders' not 'levels' of government, each of which is sovereign in its own competencies. Citizens of federal states are members of both their province—sometimes called a canton, land, autonomous region, or somewhat confusingly, a state—and the larger federal state. They elect representatives in both jurisdictions. Following Ronald Watts in the use of a biology metaphor, we might call this the 'genus of "federal political systems"' (Watts 2005: 234; the remaining quotes in this paragraph are from the same text, pp. 235–7). **Federations** are one of the species in this genus, and their distinguishing characteristic is that 'neither the federal nor the constituent units of government are constitutionally or politically subordinate to the other'. Each has 'sovereign powers derived from the constitution rather than another level of government, each [is] empowered to deal directly with its citizens in the exercise of its legislative, executive and taxing powers, and each [is] directly elected by its citizens'. There are currently twenty-three federations of roughly this type in the world, and of course they vary significantly. Other arrangements that fall within the genus of federal systems include **confederations** (like the EU), where 'the common government is dependent on the constituent governments'; **decentralized unions** (like the UK or the Netherlands), in which there are constitutionally protected subnational governments with functional autonomy even though 'ultimate authority rests with the central government'; as well as arrangements between large states and relatively small territories, islands, or microstates known in the literature as **federacies** (e.g. Denmark–Faeroes, USA–Puerto Rico, UK–Jersey, Finland–Aaland) and **associated statehoods** (e.g. France–Monaco, India–Bhutan, New Zealand–Cook Islands). I shall be discussing the idea of federation most directly; although many of the issues would be equally relevant to confederations and decentralized unions. Indeed, history is full of examples of arrangements of one of these types reforming itself into one of the other types. Decentralized unions can become federations, as Belgium did in 1993; independent states can confederate, as much of Europe has now done; confederations can become federations, as the USA and Switzerland did in the nineteenth century; and federations can become confederal or split up altogether, as when the Soviet Union gave way to the so-called Commonwealth of Independent States and then finally to a collection of independent states *tout court*.

Almost all theories of federalism assume a *territorial* definition of provinces that distinguishes them from other 'consociational' arrangements that involve pacts between groups defined not by the region in which their members live but by ethnicity, language, religion, or class.[4] For this reason, federalism holds out the promise of reconciling liberal-democratic norms of equality and citizenship with sensitivity to the special identities and needs of ethnocultural minorities—as long as these groups are territorially concentrated and able to form the majority in one or more federal provinces. As it turns out, this sort of territorial concentration is characteristic of virtually all of the national minority groups in the developed world that currently contain significant

---

[4] See Lijhardt (1977) and Elazar (1985). For an excellent comparison of the normative stakes in the choice between federalism and consociationalism, see Bauböck (2004).

nationalist movements seeking greater autonomy: the Québécois, Puerto Ricans, Scots, Catalans, Spanish Basques, Galicians, Flemish, Corsicans, Faeroe Islanders, and so on. It is also true of dozens of minority groups in Eastern, Central, and Southern Europe, the former Soviet Union, Iraq, Afghanistan, India, Indonesia, and China (among many others), although most of these groups do not currently enjoy any autonomous status whatsoever. I will focus almost entirely on the possibilities of just multinational federal systems in states that enjoy the most favourable economic and democratic conditions: countries like Canada and the multinational states of Western Europe. It is hoped that any such model could be approximated in at least some of the other multinational states around the world; but it would be facile to think that such arrangements could be easily and directly 'implanted' elsewhere. Of course, this is true of many if not most political institutions and theories of democracy developed with contemporary Western political cultures in mind.

One final caveat before proceeding with the discussion of federalism: the territorial dimension of federalism renders this way of promoting minority national self-determination irrelevant to national minority groups that are not territorially concentrated. There is of course a tremendous body of literature now explaining and justifying special institutions and rights for groups. Some of this theoretical work, from scholars of ethnic-conflict studies, discusses some ways that 'intermingling' minority groups could conceivably enjoy 'virtual', 'province-like' rights or privileges.[5] I will not be able to explore the relationship between these forms of consociationalism and federalism in this book. As I will suggest in a moment, we are still at such a rudimentary stage in the development of federalist theory in contemporary political philosophy that it should be sufficient at this stage to explore the basic structure and justification of federalism for mature multinational states with long-standing, territorially concentrated, democratically minded national minorities. It will remain an open question whether insights from such an investigation could be extended to groups that are not territorially concentrated.

(As I noted at the end of Chapter 2, the rest of this chapter will be a scholarly analysis primarily about the way political philosophers have thought about the theory of federalism throughout in the modern era. Readers interested primarily in the nuts and bolts of a contemporary theory of federalism are invited to skip ahead to Chapter 4. Scholars curious about what we might

---

[5] See McGarry and O'Leary (1993), Horowitz (1985), and Kymlicka and Norman (2000: 12–18).

80   Federalism in Normative Theory

learn from past efforts to 'theorize federalism', including efforts to dismiss such theorizing, are invited to continue with Section 3.3.)

3.3 FEDERALISM AS A PARALLEL UNIVERSE IN THE HISTORY OF POLITICAL THOUGHT AND PRACTICE

In the early 1990s a number of political philosophers nurtured in the vaguely Rawlsian tradition turned for the first time to learn about federalist theory. Some (myself included) found themselves in federal states like Canada, Switzerland, Australia, Belgium, Spain, or South Africa embroiled in massive public deliberations over federal or quasi-federal reforms of their constitutions. Some were evaluating the new confederal directions in which the EU was moving. And many were simply interested in questions of the sort we are discussing in this book, concerning concrete institutional structures for reconciling communities with competing national identities and nationalist projects within a common political space. Of course we knew that our 'mentors'—philosophers like Rawls, Nozick, and Dworkin—were silent on the mysteries of federalism. So too were almost all of their communitarian, feminist, and socialist critics during the 1970s and 1980s (with the notable exception of Charles Taylor in writings aimed at his native Canadian audience).[6] Standard texts in democratic theory generally avoided the topic, as did our field's principal journals, *Ethics* and *Philosophy and Public Affairs*.

Still, as with the topic of nationalism, we knew that there *were* specialists who worked on federalism; mostly from the political science subfield of comparative politics, often publishing in *Publius: The Journal of Federalism* (founded in 1971). We were also aware of a certain number of writings in the history of political thought on federalism. What we found, when we visited these unfamiliar corners of the library, sometimes seemed worthy of the expression Yack used to describe theories of nationalism (quoted in Chapter 1): there are no great theoretical texts outlining and defending federalism; only minor texts by major thinkers and major texts by second-rate thinkers.[7] Of course, this is somewhat uncharitable, both as regards historical thinkers and our contemporary colleagues. It should be noted, historically, that there is

---

[6] See, e.g. the essays collected in Taylor (1993).

[7] As Sheldon Wolin put it in his original foreword to a widely read monograph on federalism by William Riker: 'Although the problems connected with federalism have been of continuing concern to political scientists for more than a century, relatively few theoretical treatises of lasting significance have emerged.' He describes this as a 'failure of theory to keep pace with practice' (Wolin 1964: vii). I thank Jacob Levy for drawing my attention to this foreword.

at least one great text by a great thinker, namely, Kant's *Perpetual Peace*. But this is also an idiosyncratic text from a certain period in European history, and it does not seem to inform contemporary theorizing about federalism the way other aspects of Kant's moral philosophy have inspired recent work in ethics and theories of justice.⁸ *The Federalist* is surely another great text, even if it is basically a compilation of 'op-ed' pieces written to rally support for the world's first truly federal constitution in 1787–8. Tocqueville's *Democracy in America* (1835) is also a great text that deals with numerous elements of that same federal experiment, but its greatness surely lies in its astute political psychology and sociology, not in its normative theoretical insight.⁹

Apart from these—from the first real federalist thinking in the late Renaissance to those from the twilight of the nineteenth century—we do seem to have a history of federalist thought worthy of Yack's quip. There are lengthy and somewhat influential contributions by Althusius (1603) and Pufendorf (1672), and some generally short texts or sections by A-list philosophers like Montesquieu (1748), Rousseau (1782), Lord Acton (1862), and J. S. Mill (1861).¹⁰ This list of pre-twentieth-century classics in federalist thought can be rounded out with longer works by two other figures who might typically qualify as 'second-rate' thinkers in the history of political thought: the antebellum southern statesman, Calhoun (1855), and the French utopian socialist, Proudhon (1863).

The only interruption of the Yackian pattern in the twentieth century is that we generally stopped getting even minor works by the major thinkers. The federal ideal receives barely a glance in any of the twentieth-century Anglo-American texts that staked their claim in the tradition of grand normative political theorizing and that often carried considerable influence for a decade or two: Hobhouse's *Liberalism* (1911), Tawney's *Equality* (1931), Popper's *Open Society and its Enemies* (1944), Schumpeter's *Capitalism, Socialism, and Democracy* (1942), Oakshott's *Rationalism in Politics* (1947), Barker's *Principles of Social and Political Theory* (1951), Dahl's *Preface to Democratic Theory* (1956), Berlin's *Two Concepts of Liberty* (1958), and as mentioned already, Rawls's *Theory of Justice*. Of course, there were important

---

⁸ Of course, *Perpetual Peace* has had an enduring influence on theorizing about international justice.

⁹ See Elster's illuminating analysis in his *Political Psychology* (1993).

¹⁰ Rousseau may have had a book manuscript on federalism go up in flames during the Revolution. So all we are left with is his essay, 'A Lasting Peace through the Federation of Europe: Exposition and Critique of St. Pierre's Project', not exactly his most famous or most widely reprinted work. It is, however, now available in Karmis and Norman (2005*a*), as are all of the other texts (or at least extracts thereof) mentioned in the last two paragraphs, apart from the one by Lord Acton.

writings on federalism throughout the twentieth century, including short critiques by socialists like Laski (1939) and Neumann (1955); panegyrics by European 'personalist' followers of Proudhon like Marc (1969); some reflectively optimistic writings by political figures like EU-founders Spinelli (1966), Schuman (1963), and Monnet (1955) as well as by the soon-to-be Canadian Prime Minister, Trudeau (1968). There have also been a number of important scholarly theorists of federalism like Wheare (1946/1963), Riker (1964), Friedrich (1968), and the prolific Elazar (1987). But it is safe to say that none of these scholars will be remembered for a lasting contribution to grand normative political theorizing more generally, as important as they are to their respective subfields of political science (or in Riker's case, to several subfields of positive political theory).

What are we to make of this curious history of federalist theory? Surely the role of the federal ideal in the standard histories of political thought has been *unjustifiably* neglected in our intellectual tradition. The Western world has had confederations since the Hanseatic League in Germany (1158–1806), the Swiss Confederation (1291–1848) and the United Provinces in Holland (1567–1798), and full-blown, uninterrupted federations since the federalizing of the USA (1789), Switzerland (1848), Canada (1867), and Australia (1901). Throughout this period there has been theorizing about these living experiments that challenges the more simplistic notions of sovereignty and citizenship taken for granted in the standard textbook history of modern political thought, from Bodin and Hobbes to the present. But this federalist theorizing is almost entirely ignored by the mainstream tradition that has generally taken the frontiers of the nation-state as the frontiers of the discipline itself. The EU and the theoretical challenges it poses do not look quite so unprecedented to anyone who has studied the parallel tradition.

The neglect of federalism by political philosophers in the twentieth century deserves special attention, especially if we wish to revive federalism as an important component of the discipline today. Of course, we cannot do justice here to every theorist's particular reasons for passing over federalism. We can surely cover much of the explanation by citing the monumental debates over political economy (capitalism versus socialism) that preoccupied political struggles and political theory for much of that century. To this we can add the growing dominance of central governments in both nation-states and federal states during the two world wars and the great Depression; the general faith in the progressive nature of centralized, technocratic bureaucracies in the service of strong 'national' governments; and finally the widely held assumption that national minority groups would quietly and thankfully assimilate into majority national cultures. Given such intellectual and political currents, it is perhaps hardly surprising that few political theorists in the twentieth century took federalism seriously as a principled way of structuring a modern democratic state.[11]

Many of the factors just mentioned are already evident in the eighth edition (1914) of the great British jurist Dicey's *Introduction to the Study of the Law of the Constitution*.[12] Against those who were urging a federalization of the UK, and even of the British Empire, Dicey argued that:

A federal constitution is, as compared with a unitary constitution, a *weak* form of government.... Yet the comparative weakness of federalism is no accident. A true federal government is based on the division of powers. (Preface to the 8th edn.)
The distribution of all the powers of the state among co-ordinate authorities necessarily leads to the result that no one authority can wield the same amount of power as under a Unitarian constitution as possessed by the sovereign. A federation therefore will always be at a disadvantage in a contest with Unitarian states of equal resources.

In addition to being weak,

[f]ederalism tends to produce *conservatism*. This tendency is due to several causes. The constitution of a Federal state must, as we have seen, generally be not only a written but a rigid constitution, that is, a constitution which cannot be changed by any ordinary process of legislation.... The difficulty of altering the Constitution produces conservative sentiment, and national conservatism doubles the difficulty of altering the Constitution. A system meant to maintain the *status quo* in politics is incompatible with schemes for wide social innovation.

Dicey's final worry qua jurist and democrat (or at least in his attempt to engage with democrats) is:

Federalism, lastly, means *legalism*—the predominance of the judiciary in the constitution—the prevalence of a spirit of legality among the people.... Sovereignty is

---

[11] In an important new contribution to the normative theory of federalism, Jacob Levy identifies another explanation for why 'federalism is almost entirely absent from the work of John Rawls and from the generation of liberal theory he inspired'—an explanation that is intrinsic to philosophical presuppositions rather than to political realities. For this tradition, 'liberalism is synonymous with moral universalism applied to politics'. And if one assumes that 'the task of political philosophy is simply to state what the morally best policies are, then (some seem to have thought) there is nothing normatively interesting to say in favor of a plurality of jurisdictions. A true proposition is, after all, true everywhere.' Given that this philosophical approach 'can barely come to terms with a world of separate states', we should hardly be surprised that it is 'uninterested in subdivisions *within* those states' (Levy forthcoming).

[12] This text continued to be used for decades following Dicey's death in 1923. The ninth edition was published in 1950. The entire eighth edition, quoted here, is widely available in electronic form on the Internet (e.g. http://www.constitution.org/cmt/avd/law_con.htm). I have added italics to the words 'weak', 'conservatism', and 'legalism' in the quotes immediately below. The original pagination is not reproduced in the electronic version of this text, but quotations here can be easily located with computer search functions.

lodged in a body which rarely exerts its authority and has (so to speak) only a potential existence; no legislature throughout the land is more than a subordinate lawmaking body capable in strictness of enacting nothing but bye-laws; the powers of the executive are again limited by the constitution; the interpreters of the constitution are the judges.... Federalism substitutes litigation for legislation, and none but a law-fearing people will be inclined to regard the decision of a suit as equivalent to the enactment of a law.

These three worries about federalism (especially that it is a weak and conservative form of government) would be repeated and sometimes quoted by those few political philosophers, like Laski and Neumann, who even bothered to consider the topic through the mid twentieth century.

For good measure, Neumann also takes direct aim at the most enduring justification of federalism, first articulated by Montesquieu and reiterated by Rousseau, the authors of *The Federalist*, Tocqueville, and even J. S. Mill: namely that federalism promises to combine the democratic advantages of small republican communities with the military and economic advantages of imperial powers, while avoiding the worst defects (such as conformity and tyranny) of either. Call this the '*best of the big, best of the small*' argument. It was assumed by all of its proponents that in this way a federal system could promote both positive freedom (better quality democratic self-determination) and negative freedom (less tyranny from a powerful, remote central government). After analysing these arguments from both the historical figures and their more recent apologists, Neumann (1955:54–5, my italics) concludes:

There are *no values that inhere in federalism as such*, and federalism cannot be defended successfully on the grounds that the inevitable tendency of a unitary state is toward political repression. The testimony of history will not support this assertion, nor will it support the assertion that a division of constitutional power is the best guarantee of political freedom. When to these considerations is joined that of the financial inadequacy or political unwillingness of the smaller units to respond satisfactorily to serious economic troubles, then unrestrained adulation of federalism seems all the more unwarranted.

It is not clear who exactly Neumann is accusing here of 'unrestrained adulation of federalism', though he quotes Montesquieu and (especially) Proudhon, who come close to this. So too do Proudhon's intellectual progeny, including Spinelli and the personalist school in Belgium, who saw in the idea of a European federalism a panacea for the Continent's internecine warlike ways and much else.[13]

---

[13] Federalist panegyrics from Montesquieu, Proudhon, and Spinelli are reprinted in Karmis and Norman (2005a), as are the critiques of Laski and Neumann.

I quote these passages from Dicey and Neumann in part to give some indication why federalist theory—at least as a central component of a normative theory for a liberal-democratic state—fell into disrepute in the twentieth century. These texts were influential, but they were also, no doubt, articulating widely held perceptions. We must also not forget how few federal experiments there were at the time from which to extrapolate general lessons: Dicey's analysis focuses almost entirely on the USA and Switzerland, with a few passing references to Canada. Neumann, writing in the mid-1950s, seems to have mostly the American and the failed pre-Nazi German and Austro–Hungarian experiences in mind.

3.4 RECONSIDERING THE REJECTION

The Dicey–Neumann critique remains relevant, in part, to the extent that echoes of it persist among critics of federalism in both minority-nationalist and majority-nationalist circles. Partisans on both sides of the nationalist rivalry are bound to see a federal system as facilitating weak, conservative, and inefficient governance precisely because of the way it limits each side's nation-building and quests for self-determination. Minority nationalist leaders in control of a provincial government, for example, will be frustrated that the system will not allow them to solve 'their own problems in their own ways' when these problems happen to fall under federal jurisdictions. Likewise, majority nationalists will decry the way the system prevents the construction of efficient 'national' programmes with 'national' standards (rather than a 'hotchpotch' of programmes across the country) when these programmes fall under powers of exclusive provincial jurisdiction. Both kinds of nationalists will disparage the rule by judges when jurisdictional rulings go against them or when their laws are struck down by the constitutional court. And both are likely to resent the inherent conservatism built into the system since constitutions in most federations are notoriously difficult to amend. We will return to the ongoing stakes in these nationalist critiques of federalism when we examine arguments and principles appropriate for the selection of a division of powers and a constitutional amending formula in Chapters 4 and 5. Now obviously, from the fact that some *nationalists* on both sides can find a federal system to be wanting, it does not follow that it is. This is especially true if a given federal system is conceived, in part, as a check on the ambitions of both of these nationalist projects. Levy (2004: 168) has argued that a federal constitution can 'be understood as a kind of treaty, setting out the terms of ongoing peaceful coexistence and shared political life'. It is not obviously a bad thing if such a 'treaty' forbids more radical nationalist leaders from pursuing objectives designed specifically to disturb this 'peacefulness' and 'sharing'. The big question, of course, is how we determine whether the terms of the coexistence and shared political life are appropriate to begin with.

Another reason for looking at the twentieth-century critique of federalism in detail is that it reveals how dramatically the basic terms of the debate over federalism have changed in political philosophy, and in the world, in recent decades. What is most striking to contemporary eyes is how rarely concerns about identity, culture, and ethnicity figure into the history of federalist thought. Of course these concerns occur rather infrequently in the history of political thought in general. But given that they are part of the explanation for the *very existence* of some federations we might have expected cultural considerations to be more apparent in federal theory.[14] Nowadays many are inclined to take federalism seriously, *primarily* as a means of enabling different national communities to secure a reasonable degree of political autonomy within the common political space. There are of course existing federations in uninational states like Australia, Argentina, Germany, or the USA.[15] In these states, debates over federal reform tend to be concerned not with cultural identity but rather with technocratic efficiency, fiscal responsibilities, legal–jurisdictional disputes, or good old-fashioned power politics. Contemporary political philosophers are for the most part inclined to ignore these debates unless they encompass policy areas of special interest.[16] I suspect that most

---

[14] Canada would surely have become a unitary state upon independence in 1867 if Franco-Catholic Quebec had not insisted on autonomy. In the last two decades we have similar minority-nationalist concerns leading to varying degrees of federalization in Spain, Belgium, South Africa, and the UK.

[15] The USA is always a somewhat contested example of a uninational nation-state. Its constitutional structures and much of its political culture certainly treat it that way. But at the margins, so to speak, it does contain classic national minority groups, especially the peoples of federated islands, like Puerto Rico and Guam; the descendents of Mexicans living in what is now the US Southwest when their territory was conquered by the USA; American Indians throughout the mainland as well as Inuit in Alaska, often living on largely self-governing reservations; and native Hawaiians. The American federal system itself is not in any way designed to accommodate this diversity. For a history and some normative analysis of this apparent mismatch, see Kymlicka (2001: ch. 5).

[16] In the USA, for example, issues like abortion and gay marriage are bound up with interpretations of whether or not each state has a right to decide its own position. So one way for a liberal to argue in favour of gay marriage, and against a constitutional amendment banning it, is to say that this falls within the power of the states, not the federal government. This will ensure that at least the more liberal states will make the option of marriage available to same-sex couples. Similarly, many conservatives argue, against *Roe v. Wade*, that abortion law should be left to the states, which would ensure that abortion would become illegal in numerous states. It goes without saying that these are not fundamentally debates about federalism per se. The positions on abortion or gay marriage are not somehow being derived from deeper theories

political philosophers would share Neumann's scepticism about any abstract, general claims about the way federalism per se will promote individual liberty or reduce political repression—at least within uninational federations.

What Neumann's critique does not consider, however, is the way that federal structures can clearly prevent repression and the violation of cultural rights and even human rights in culturally divided societies. One need look no further than post-Communist history of centralized democratic states in Eastern and Central Europe to find a casebook full of examples of government policies deliberately designed to make life difficult for members of national minorities.[17] Consider just the realm of minority language rights. In several of these states minority languages have been banned in 'public' life, especially in schools, higher education, the practice of professions, and of course in parliament and the civil service.[18] Even worse, in some cases the 'public' realm is interpreted so broadly that minority languages were even forbidden within such apparently private realms as union meetings and marriage ceremonies. A territorially concentrated linguistic minority in control of a federal province with competencies in education and language policy would be able to better protect itself from such abuses and whims of a majoritarian central government.

Helping to protect national minorities against cultural and human rights violations is only *one* of the normatively relevant grounds for federation. We will discuss a range of these grounds more systematically in Chapters 4 and 5, including grounds for supporting the central government's role in the political life of minority national communities. This normative and institutional analysis will presuppose a distinction that is now standard in the literature and has been implicitly in play throughout the foregoing discussions: between so-called *territorial* and *multinational* models of federalism. The root difference between these two types of federal systems is in their respective *raisons d'être*. Multinational federations are intended 'to accommodate the desire of national minorities for self-government', principally by creating a province (or provinces) in which one or more minority groups can constitute a clear

---

about how such powers ought ideally to be divided between the centre and the subunits in a federation.

[17] For an extensive survey of these abuses see Kymlicka and Opalski (2002), Kymlicka (2002), and Trifunovska (2001).

[18] It would be fairly safe to assert that some forms of overt legal oppression of minority-language groups has happened in almost every long-standing state at some time or other. Even in Canada, well into the twentieth century, generations of French-speaking residents of the Province of Ontario remained illiterate because their French-language schools were shut down by the Provincial Government. By the end of the twentieth century, however, liberal-democratic opinion almost everywhere considered this kind of oppression of national minority groups to be unjust and, frankly, uncivilized.

majority of the citizens and in which they can exercise a number of sovereign powers. By contrast, a territorial federation is conceived of as a 'means by which a single national community can divide and diffuse power', perhaps accommodating a certain amount of socio-economic diversity at the same time (Resnick 1994: 71; Kymlicka 2001: 190). In principle, a multinational federation (like Canada) and a territorial federation (like the USA) could share many of the same constitutional features. For example, they could both assign the competency of education to the provinces or states rather than to the federal government. But the differing rationales for the two types of federation should also, in principle, lead to different justifications for both specific constitutional practices and rulings by the Supreme Court. Of course, in practice we would expect to see rather divergent political cultures in federations of the two types, not least because of the way minority-controlled provincial governments can be expected to use their powers (such as the control over the school curriculum) in nation-building projects that compete with those typically carried out by central governments in federations and unitary states alike. This book aims to provide some of the groundwork for a theory of multinational federalism. Such a theory will have many points of contact with a theory of territorial federalism, and in general with theories of constitutional democracy. But it also proceeds from the analysis of legitimate nation-building and can be expected to justify multinational federations more radically decentralized than those found in typical nation-state federations, and even than in the relatively modest multinational federal arrangements currently in existence.

Before undertaking this central task (in Chapters 4 and 5), though, I want to return to the more radical critique implied by Neumann's conclusion that '[t]here are no values that inhere in federalism as such'. Some version of this thesis will likely figure in explanations for why most great theorists of liberal democracy in the twentieth century felt no need to integrate possible federal structures into their theories. (We must speculate here, because federalism was ignored more than it was dismissed.) For example, federalism could be seen instrumentally as either (*a*) a pragmatic institutional 'plumbing' issue, akin to a decision about whether or not to have a bicameral legislature, or how to divide up ministerial responsibilities; or (*b*) an example of merely political compromise and power brokering, where regional, or previously independent, elites are unwilling to consent to a closer union.

The latter appears to be Dicey's view. After giving several arguments (including those quoted earlier) for why a unitary state is preferable to a federal state, he admits that federation may sometimes be the only possible constitution 'for a body of states which desire union and do not desire unity' (preface to the 8th edn.). Nevertheless, he continues:

Federalism, when successful, has generally been a stage towards unitary government. In other words, federalism tends to pass into nationalism. This has certainly been the result of the two most successful of federal experiments. The United States, at any rate as they now exist, have been well described as a nation concealed under the form of a federation. The same expression might with considerable truth be applied to Switzerland. (ibid.)

In short, for Dicey there seems to be no principled basis for federalism. It is something you accept as a second best, and you should hope to grow out of it as soon as possible. There can be little doubt that such a view went hand-in-hand with a deeply ingrained nation-state nationalism that welcomed the assimilation of small nationalities (like the Welsh, Scots, and Irish, in the case of Dicey's UK) into great nations.[19] Hence, Dicey's last warning against federalizing the UK is that it would unnecessarily stimulate the 'disruptive force of local nationalism' and 'might well arouse a feeling of divided allegiance' for the UK's subordinate nationalities. He then reminds his readers of the dangers of such divided allegiances by raising examples of then-recent secessions or attempted secessions by the Southern States, the Sonderbund in Switzerland, and Norway. This of course is an early version of the great 'vicious circle' fear of all majority nationalists in multinational states which we discussed at the outset of this chapter: if you give in to minority nationalists' demands for limited autonomy, they will simply use this space for nation-building projects designed to mobilize support for an ever greater realm of autonomy. The political sociology sustaining this fear is not crazy; but nor does it, on its own, constitute a valid moral reason for why majorities should deny minorities autonomy. I shall describe most directly how this fear should be dealt with in federal theory in Chapter 6, in the context of the design and justification of a constitutional secession clause.

Neumann's denial that 'values inhere in federalism as such' is more subtle and less ideological than Dicey's. His main complaint seems to be with specific sorts of claims made on behalf of federalism, namely that federal states are inherently better than unitary states at preventing repression and promoting freedom. Most of his analysis of both political history and the arguments of a long line of federalists—from Montesquieu, Rousseau, and the authors of *The Federalist* to Calhoun, Tocqueville, and Proudhon—tries to

---

[19] The contemporary reader is struck when reading Dicey's text (and others from that era) as to how comfortable he is with conflating the 'United Kingdom' with 'England'. When he speaks of 'Englishmen' he clearly includes among their number the men of, say, Glasgow; the 'English Parliament' is the one with members from constituencies across Great Britain and Ireland; and so on. Well into the book he offers a half-hearted apology—in the Greek sense of 'apology'—when he declares that he will 'purposely and frequently, in accordance with popular language, use "England" as equivalent to the United Kingdom' (1914: n. 95).

refute this necessary connection between federalism and freedom. Neumann's ancillary critique concerns the delicate task of explaining the success of any particular federal system that seems to do a good job preserving freedom. The problem here is that the 'federal arrangement operates always within a specific political, social, and cultural setting and the isolation of the federal element from the setting is obviously extremely difficult, perhaps even impossible'. How do we know if it is the 'federalism' that is responsible for the preservation of freedom and not primarily the choice of a 'presidential or parliamentary democracy', the 'separation of powers' in the central government, the 'party system', or such socio-economic factors as 'the extent of the pluralistic structure of society...the urban–rural ratio...[or] the degree of concentration of economic power'? (Neumann 1955: 44–5) Neumann's rather sensible recommendation is that:

> the value of federalism (as against a unitary state, on the one hand, and a looser form of cooperation on the other) can be determined solely through an empirical analysis of a given political system. (45)

In fact, he does concede that federal systems are in certain instances valuable and that they can sometimes achieve goals not attainable with other systems (54).

There is no reason to disagree with Neumann's basic conclusions, or with most of this critique. It could be that *no* universal generalizations about the valuable consequences of a given type of political institution will survive empirical analysis—especially if all we mean by this is that we can always imagine (or even point to) situations and scenarios in which any given political institution would fail (or has failed). If these are the criteria we are using to judge whether values inhere in a political arrangement, Neumann's conclusion that federalism *as such* has no inherent value may simply follow from a more general claim that no political institution *as such* has inherent value. So it would be a big mistake to assume that the denial of inherent value to federalism *as such* means that political theorists do not have to take federalism seriously when developing normative political theories for the multinational state. On the face of it, there is no intrinsic reason why most democratic theorists should devote so much attention to, say, options and justifications for electoral systems (which would also have no inherent value as such), and so little attention to options for a federal division of powers which, in effect, determines which electorate gets to decide which policies.

In any case, there is not much point in enquiring about the value of institutions as such, let alone about their intrinsic or inherent value. The important normative questions concern not the *value* of institutions (or proposed institutions) but their *justification*. Of course, arguments for the justification of social and political institutions will tend to make some reference to the values or goods they promote (or the disvalue and evils they help prevent), and also to the way their benefits or burdens are distributed. What is clear is that citizens in federal states debate the merits of their constitutional status quo, and of proposed reforms to it, in rich and complex moral language. The same can be said of citizens in the EU, particularly during periods of treaty reform; and also of citizens in pluralistic or multinational states who are contemplating or resisting constitutional reform. They argue about such things as the division of powers between the centre and the subunits, or about the representation of the subunits in central institutions, in terms of whether they are *just, legitimate, democratic, consistent with national identities and collective rights*, or all the contraries, including whether they are *unreasonable, oppressive, humiliating, insulting*, and so on. These debates rarely revolve around merely technocratic or efficiency considerations (although proponents of any given reform will also tend to argue that it is more efficient, and vice versa for opponents), or even about competing interpretations of what is in the common good.[20] A grand normative theory for the multinational state—or to put it less grandly, sound normative theorizing for the multi-national state—must say something about which sorts of arguments and principles are relevant to justifications for basic constitutional structures and reforms in such states. It goes without saying that such a theory should not simply accept all of the patterns of argument and justifications that people in multinational states actually use. Indeed, taking Brubaker's concerns to heart, theorists ought to be especially worried when the terms of debate are tainted by nationalist ideology. That said, any democratic theorist should be interested in understanding the sorts of popular arguments that actually do seem to inspire or motivate citizens' and groups' demands for constitutional reform (or for resisting reform). What is most striking when we catalogue these principles is

[20] Consider the following hypothetical illustration. Imagine a multinational federal state with the following two characteristics: (*a*) each of the provinces currently has the right to its own provincial police force; and (*b*) the federal government finds that it has numerous agencies operating in several federal ministries that gather intelligence relevant to the prevention of terrorism. Now imagine that the federal government announced its desire to reform these two areas: first, by sponsoring a constitutional amendment requiring the provincial police forces to be replaced by a single federal police force; and second, by creating a new federal ministry responsible for intelligence and counter-terrorism. Obviously, the reform requiring a constitutional amendment will be inherently more difficult because such amendments typically require substantial consent from both the provinces and the federal parliament, whereas the latter change can be affected by cabinet or by parliament. But my point is that the public debates over these two parallel reform proposals would be strikingly different. The latter would be debated entirely in terms of efficiency and public security, whereas the former would be resisted by the provinces—especially provinces run by national minorities—as an insensitive federal intrusion, as threatening the liberty of minority citizens, as an unnecessary provocation and questioning of minority loyalties, as an unjustified exercise in federal nation-building, and so on.

that they generally go well beyond the standard foundations of constitutionalism applied to uninational states. In Chapters 4 and 5 I will consider both the 'old constitutionalism' and a range of more popular principles for constitutional reform and justification, and I shall argue for something rather more expansive than the former, while nevertheless calling into question certain hollowed principles in popular (and often heavily nationalist) debates.

3.5 CONCLUSION: RECONCILING THE DISCIPLINARY SOLITUDES

Before turning to concrete constitutional issues I want to pick up a thread left dangling earlier in the chapter. I noted that just as post-Rawlsian political philosophers were typically ignorant of nationalism when the issue thrust itself onto their agenda in the 1990s, they had very little understanding of either the legal-constitutional framework of federalism or the political sociology and history of diverse federal polities. After a quick survey of a 'parallel tradition' of political thinkers who were at times rather enthusiastic about federalism, we discussed some of the reasons for a general dismissal of the subject matter by political philosophers through much of the twentieth century. The lessons we can take from this long history for the sake of contemporary theorizing may be rather limited because, among other things, the cultural-diversity rationale—at the limit, the 'equal right to nation-building' rationale—for dividing sovereignty through federalization is largely absent from this tradition. But the principal reasons given for dismissing the topic as an important component in liberal-democratic theory are also not particularly compelling. Does this mean we have to build a normative theory of federalism from scratch now? Not entirely.

The thread I left dangling concerned the work on federalism by our contemporary colleagues in the social sciences (mostly from political science, history, and law, but also from economics, sociology, policy studies, etc.), particularly since the 1960s and 1970s, and especially over the last decade or so. In a rough and ready way, this literature could be divided into three categories, depending on the degree of normative theorizing involved. To be sure, first, much of this work is empirical or juridical, and a good deal of it involves detailed studies of particular federal states or the comparison of certain elements of two or more federal systems.[21] There is no denying the

---

[21] I will not even pretend that the following citations represent all of the best in the field, but noteworthy examples of this sort of federal scholarship are Wheare (1946/1963), Watts (1999*b*), Lemco (1991), Nicolaidis and Howse (2001), and McKay (2001).

relevance of this sort of research for understanding everything from the broad range of formulas for federal divisions of power or constitutional amending formulas to empirical theories about general sources of stability or the evolution of roles for elites and citizens. But one also finds, second, a significant amount of explicit normative theorizing in this literature: those who know most about the workings of federal systems often do not hesitate to weigh in on how they should be reformed. This is especially true when it comes to recommendations for reform of a particular federal constitution by the social scientists who know that country's constitutional politics inside out.[22] Third, there is also a certain continuing tradition of grander political theorizing about federalism more generally, including its basic principles and justifications along with a certain amount of encouragement for its applicability beyond the current list of twenty-three or so states.[23]

Now any political philosopher will gain invaluable insight from the best examples of all of these kinds of empirical and normative theorizing about federalism coming out of the social sciences. But most of us will also find almost all of it—and most notably the general normative theorizing in the third category—a bit disconnected from the other theories, debates, and styles of argumentation typical of sort of mainstream political philosophizing found, say, in *Ethics, Philosophy and Public Affairs*, or the *Journal of Political Philosophy*. And this is not merely because most mainstream political philosophers have had relatively little to say about federalism. It is also because the federalist theory emerging from the social scientists is almost never set within the context of contemporary theories of justice and democracy more generally. Consider just one important recent book that ought to be required reading for any political theorist interested in federalism: *Designing Federalism: A Theory of Self-Sustainable Federal Institutions* (Cambridge University Press, 2004), written by the eminent political scientist Peter C. Ordeshook and two colleagues, Mikhail Filippov and Olga Shvetsova. Its stated goal 'is to identify the structure of a federal state's political institutions—constitutional and statutory—that best encourage [its] survival and its ability to meet those economic and political objectives that otherwise justify its existence' (3). The book consists almost entirely of 'positive' analysis, including the study of numerous federal states and the use of a host of analytic tools such as game theory and agency theory. They try to understand and explain the role of incentives for various kinds of political actors (including courts), as well as

---

[22] With the same qualifications as in the previous note, see, e.g. Gibbins and Laforest (1998), Beer (1993), Burgess (1995), LaSelva (1996), and Linz and Stepan (1996).

[23] Examples of general normative theorizing about federalism from scholars working primarily in this field include Elazar (1987), King (1982), Forsyth (1981), Hueglin (1999), and Vernon (1988).

the dynamics of various party systems, in order to identify the most effective sources of stability in a federation. But although much of the analysis is 'positive', it serves the essentially normative objective, just quoted. It also aims to identify the most stable and workable arrangements within a range of options available to a reasonably just democratic state. And yet, despite this ever-present normative context, the book is almost entirely uninformed by contemporary normative political theory. Its impressive twenty-eight-page bibliography contains no entries for Rawls or for the other major figures who have engaged with Rawls over the last three decades; nor for any of the authors in the Oxford Political Theory series;[24] nor for any of the major theorists of deliberative democracy;[25] nor for a single article in the 'big three' political philosophy journals I mentioned earlier. This is entirely typical of most books on federalism, including those that are much more self-consciously normative.

My underscoring these bibliographical omissions is not in any way meant as a critique of these works. Rather it indicates how relatively isolated our intellectual worlds are from each other: political philosophers have had little difficulty constructing normative theories for diverse societies without discussing positive theories of federalism, and political scientists have no difficulty recommending federal institutions for liberal-democratic societies without discussing the pluralistic liberal-democratic theories of political philosophers. Of course, one would like to think that both fields could benefit from some cross-pollination, and clearly there has been some.[26] But at this point political philosophers will have to 'translate' and adapt most of the insights from positive federalist theory and experience if they are to reconcile them with the existing structures and concepts of contemporary normative theories. To this task we now turn.

---

[24] There is one exception: *Designing Federalism* deals extensively with the problem of secession, and an extremely influential book on secession by one OPT author, Buchanan (1991), is cited three times, but not discussed.

[25] A well-known article on secession and democracy by Sunstein (1991) is cited in passing.

[26] For some examples of works by philosophers, social scientists, and lawyers writing on federalism who draw liberally from empirical, juridical, and 'mainstream' political-theory sources, see Bauböck (2000, 2004), Bellamy and Castiglione (2005), Buchanan (1991, 2004), Føllesdal (2003a, 2003b), Howse and Knop (1993), Karmis and Maclure (2001), Kymlicka (1998a, 1988b, 1988c, 2001, 2002), Laforest (2004), LaSelva (1996), Levy (2004 forthcoming), McCormick (1999), Norman (1994, 1995a, 1998b), Requejo (1999), Resnick (1994), Smith (1995, 2000), Stepan (2009), Taylor (2009), Van Parijs (2000), Vipond (1991), and Weinstock (2001b). This list could be longer, but it is certainly not endless.

4

Federal Constitutionalism I: Options for Federal Design

> If there is a subject called constitutional design, then there must be alternative constitutional *designs*. Assuredly there are, but even now most constitutional drafters and reformers are, at best, only vaguely informed by anything resembling an articulate theory of their enterprise. Most act on the basis of inchoate and partially worked-out ideas.... Politicians have their own ideas, and these are not so easily dislodged, even with the growth of constitutional design and various sub-fields, such as electoral-system design, as matters for experts.... Before we even reach the contest of explicitly stated theories, we need to recognize the more significant, albeit often subliminal, contest between explicit theories and the more influential, implicit theories espoused by practitioners. The inarticulate theories call out for study. As of now, we lack a theory of their theories.... We also lack a consensus emerging from the articulate theories, whether these relate to electoral systems, presidential or parliamentary structure, or the costs and benefits of centralized or devolved power. [This l]ack of consensus is the first obstacle.
>
> —Donald Horowitz (2002: 19)

What options are there for federal constitutional design in multinational states, and how do we evaluate or justify these options for any given federal state? These are the questions we will explore in Chapters 5 and 6. The pessimistic, or discouraged, observations of this general project by an 'icon' of constitutional design, Donald Horowitz, above, should temper our ambitions.[1] We will certainly not be producing any blueprints for politicians or constitution-drafters. Nor will we be hoping to find a deep emerging consensus among the experts on the optimal design of federal systems. Our aims are much more modest: to look at federal options and to begin to distinguish the moral and political grounds for choosing among them, particularly in states hosting rival nation-building projects for the foreseeable future. The question

---

[1] Horowitz is called one of 'two icons of modern constitutional design' on the back cover of Reynolds (2002). (The other is Arend Lijphart.)

of federal *options* is significantly easier to answer at this stage, not least because there have been so many actual federal experiments from which we can learn. The question of evaluating or justifying the options remains much more open. Of course, one's ultimate answer to the question, 'how do we justify federal institutions?' will depend largely on one's answer to the question 'how do we justify *political* institutions?'; and *that* question constitutes most of political philosophy! We will not be arriving at many ultimate answers here. Instead, as I have indicated along the way, we will look at some of the justifications that are typically given by both ordinary political actors and liberal-democratic political philosophers, and then see to what extent we can develop a workable set of normative criteria. At this very early stage in the development of principles of multinational federal justice, it will be helpful if we can at least identify relevant criteria beyond those that would be sufficient in the context of unitary nation-states like Iceland or Portugal.

The basic challenge in the design of a multinational federation is to coordinate (*a*) the self-government aspirations of more than one national community, and (*b*) the rival nation-building projects by political actors in these communities, especially those in control of government institutions. Once again, we are confronted with the two distinct, but intertwined, strands of nationalism: self-determination and the determination of the (nation's) 'self'. The first coordination challenge—(*a*), clarifying the realms of self-government—is in one sense the more technocratic, legalistic task. It involves defining the self-governing territories, the division of powers that will be handled by the different orders of government, the rules for resolving disputes between these two orders of government, the design of their parliamentary systems, etc. This is sometimes referred to as the 'plumbing' of a federation. As we have noted already, both multinational and territorial federations can in principle share much of the same plumbing. In other words, they might look similar 'on paper'. But in a multinational federation the motivations for selecting among the options for plumbing designs will give rise to the second coordination challenge, (*b*), concerning the contest between rival nation-building projects. Each side will be keen to control the tools most effective for shaping the national identities of its members. But if we are to imagine majority and minority nationalists negotiating the terms of a federation, where they have already ruled out both independence for the minority and a unitary state controlled by the majority, then they will have to accept that they cannot both control all of the nation-building powers they might desire. Again, they will be negotiating limits to their own nationalism.

After a brief discussion of some background issues, in Section 4.1, the bulk of this chapter will look at the wide variety of 'plumbing options' for a multinational federation, in Section 4.2. Throughout the discussion of these options we will take note of the stakes for rival nation-building projects, as well as the kinds of principles that are commonly used (by nationalists and non-nationalists alike) to support demands for reforming federal systems. Section 4.3 turns to another battleground for rival nationalists in the drafting of a federal constitution. In addition to plumbing—the basic design and coordination of two orders of government—most federal (and even non-federal) constitutions also enshrine symbolic considerations of particular importance to nationalists. Contemporary political debates typically focus on the demands of *minority* nationalists for constitutional recognition. But this is largely because *majority* nationalists in most states were historically able to entrench the symbolism of their own nation-building projects into their constitutions right from the start. Section 4.3 will look at the way both majorities and minorities have sought recognition and reinforcement of their conceptions of national identity, as well as some of the challenges of coordinating or reconciling these nationalist visions in the same legal document. In Chapter 5 we will take a more philosophical look at how basic liberal-democratic principles and principles of recognition can be combined in a normative theory of multinational federalism.

4.1 FEDERAL VERSUS NON-FEDERAL INSTITUTIONS

How do we distinguish between federal and non-federal institutions? We could consider a democratic state like France or Italy, with a basically unitary system of government, and ask what constitutional or statutory changes it would have to make to be considered a federation. The architects of a federalizing unitary state would have to address the following six basic questions:

1. What are the *boundaries* of the federal provinces (or how should the boundary issues be decided)?
2. What is the *division of legislative and administrative powers* between the central government and the provinces?
3. How are the provinces and/or their citizens to be *represented* within the central or federal institutions?
4. How are the markets and legal systems of the provinces to be integrated?
5. What will be the procedure for *amending* these and other constitutional structures and provisions?
6. Will the secession of a province be permitted? And if so, what procedures must be followed?

I will say much more about the range of options for answering each of these questions in Section 4.2. At this stage two observations are in order. First, these 'federal' elements of a constitutional regime are not simply grafted onto a set of existing non-federal structures. Unitary states already have institutions and rules in most of these areas: e.g. precisely defined regional units (like cities, counties, cantons, *départements*) with certain legislative and (especially) administrative powers; schemes for representing citizens of different regions in the central parliament; a constitutional amending formula; and so on. If a unitary state goes federal it will be changing its answers to some or all of these questions, not asking them for the first time. And there is not always a clear line between a 'federal' issue and a simple 'democratic' or 'governance' issue. For example, as part of a federal arrangement it may be decided that the provinces will be represented equally in the upper chamber of a bi-cameral parliament (often called the senate). So, this will look like a question of how provinces and their citizens are represented in parliament. But it will also be a question of the design of a parliamentary democracy, since there will have to be rules about how these senators are elected, what the procedures are within the senate, how the senate relates to the lower chamber for purposes of initiating, passing, or vetoing legislation, and so on. When it comes to designing and justifying an entire package of rules to define the institution of parliament, it will not always be entirely clear when we are dealing with a 'federal' element and when it is a 'democracy' element.

Second, relatedly, it would be a mistake to think that all of the special constitutional design features of relevance to multinational accommodation will take place within the more specifically 'federal' features of the constitution. Franz Neumann hinted at this in a passage quoted in Chapter 3 when he noted that when we *do* find a successful federation (where 'success' in his example concerned its ability to preserve liberty) the full explanation for the success will rely on both the federal features and a number of other major political or socio-economic factors. The authors of *Designing Federalism* offer an even stronger warning to would-be federal architects:

the institutional variables commonly attended to in federal design—constitutional clauses pertaining to federal subject [i.e. provincial] representation in a national legislature, the identities of federal subjects, the right or prohibition of secession, the supremacy of federal law, comity, the rights of federal subjects in amending a national constitution, and statements prescribing the policy jurisdictions of federal subjects versus the national government including the authority to tax—*are not the uniquely critical parameters that need to be attended to.* . . . We must also attend to a second level of design that structures political processes generally, with a clear understanding of how constraints of one type interact with institutions that might otherwise seem tangential to federal matters . . . [such as] the authority of a chief executive, the organization of the judiciary, and the structure of a separation of powers [between branches of the national government]. (Filippov, Ordeshook, and Schvetsova 2004: 4, my italics)

Neither Neumann nor the authors of *Designing Federalism* pay particular attention to the sociology of nationalism in ethnically diverse societies. We can therefore supplement their lists of not-necessarily-federal factors of relevance to a well-functioning constitutional regime with, e.g. federally guaranteed minority rights (especially for national minorities that are not living in a province in which they are the majority), and possibly nation-building provisions that aim to promote a pan-national identity and loyalty to counterbalance the possibly destabilizing tendency of nation-building at the provincial level, among many other things. In deeply divided societies, particularly in less-than-fully-democratic states in the developing world, federalism per se will rarely be more than *part* of the solution, and often not even that (especially, of course, when minorities are not territorially concentrated).[2]

Much of this chapter and the next will concern the balancing or 'negotiating' of rival nation-building programmes within a federal constitutional framework. Now we saw in Chapter 2 that the tools of nation-building are not exclusively defined by constitutional powers, let alone by the powers that are implicated in the specifically federal plumbing of the constitution. Nevertheless, there are compelling moral and political reasons for states to allow territorially concentrated national minorities a degree of real self-determination, and with this a right to determine their national 'selves', through a federal system. And once such a structure is in place, it will profoundly shape and colour the competing national discourses and debates. Democratically elected provincial governments—rather than simply intellectuals, poets, singers, and minor party leaders—will now be able to speak on behalf of minority national communities and many of their demands will naturally come to focus on divisions of power and responsibilities between federal and provincial governments. This 'constitutionalization' of power struggles between minorities and majorities (i.e. between provinces and the state) means that even symbolic and 'recognition' issues are likely to be translated into demands for specific political and constitutional reforms rather than for

---

[2] This is surely the only conclusion one can draw from a survey of the literature in the emergent subfield of ethnic-conflict studies. See, e.g. the excellent recent volume *The Architecture of Democracy: Constitutional Design, Conflict Management, and Democracy* (Reynolds 2002), especially Belmont, Mainwaring, and Reynolds (2002), Horowitz (2002), Ghai (2002), Solnick (2002), and O'Leary (2002).

being merely embodied in de facto understandings, historical memories, myths, heroes, folklore, nationalist hymns, sports teams, and so on.[3]

We will now turn to the range of issues and options that are most likely to be contested should different national(ist) communities sit down to negotiate the terms of federation, be this (*a*) a number of states or former colonies coming together to create a new federation or confederation; (*b*) a formerly centralized state deciding to federalize; or (*c*) a federal state considering major reforms.

4.2 BASIC COMPONENTS AND OPTIONS FOR FEDERAL DESIGN

Most of the following seven categories of federal options spring from the six questions at the beginning of Section 4.2.

4.2.1 Subunit Boundaries

Like some many normative questions concerning nationalism and minority rights, the question of just procedures for creating or changing boundaries—whether internationally, or 'intra-nationally'—was absent from the agenda of political philosophy during most of the last half of the twentieth century. As we shall see (especially in Chapter 6), there has been a flurry of intellectual activity over the last fifteen years on the changing of *international* boundaries through secession. But the question of how best to fix or modify the boundaries of *federal subunits* (or provinces) has rarely been posed.[4] Discussions are almost unheard of even in the vast federalist literature by social scientists,

---

[3] Consider just one example using the last-mentioned source of national pride. For generations, and especially during the centralized, authoritarian rule of the Franco regime, the Barcelona Football Club was a source and symbol of pride and national honour for Catalans—especially in its direct battles with Real Madrid or its tellingly named cross-town rival Español (see Duke and Crolley 1996: ch. 3). More recently, however, Catalan nationalists have mobilized behind a much more constitutional and 'federal' demand to allow Catalan teams to compete in international competitions under the Catalan flag. One petition for this demand, presented to the Catalan parliament, garnered more than half-a-million signatures in a province with a population of less than seven million.

[4] See Kymlicka (2001: 110–12), Moore (2001: 137–64), Buchanan and Moore (2003*a*, 2003*b*).

apart from some historical descriptions of internal border changes in India, Switzerland, and the USA, among other places.[5]

Yet the question of provincial frontiers goes to the heart of the federalist 'solution' for minority self-determination. This solution works for a minority group to the extent that its members form the majority (preferably the *vast* majority) within a federal province or provinces, and also to the extent that the vast majority of the members of the group reside in provinces in which they are a majority. It is very rare for ethnocultural groups in federal or quasi-federal states to coincide perfectly with their subunit.[6] So *in principle* federal solutions could be improved in some situations by provincial 'gerrymandering'; by modifying the frontiers of a federal province in order to include more members and fewer non-members of the minority group. I emphasize 'in principle' because in practice such border-changing also poses numerous problems. To the extent that provinces *really matter* in a federation—that they are not as politically and culturally insignificant as, say, counties in the USA—then changing their borders will raise versions of many of the problems with changing international borders. For example:

- The territory ceded from one province to another will invariably contain at least a minority of citizens who are not happy about the change but who are forced to go along with it or to physically move back to their original side of the border. This will often include members of the putative minority group who nevertheless have roots in the province or community in which they were living. But it can also result in the 'stranding' of fellow nationals on the 'wrong side' of a border that can have a lasting impact on the nationalist 'psyche', and can provide a long-standing source of grievance exploitable by nation-building and nation-mobilizing projects.

- The greater the realm of provincial autonomy, the more such provincial-frontier changes can pose material hardships for the citizens whose provincial membership is 'forcibly' changed. There may be a different official language in the new province, and you may not speak it or speak it as well. You may be a member of a profession or occupation that is licensed provincially, and getting recertified may be no easy matter (if you are a

---

[5] There are numerous recent cases of (generally wealthier) towns or boroughs attempting, and in some cases succeeding, to secede from cities in the USA—e.g. Staten Island from New York City, the San Fernando Valley from the City of Los Angeles, and Long Island, Maine, from Portland, Maine. There have also been movements in the Texas panhandle to secede from Texas, and in the Oklahoma panhandle to secede from Oklahoma. See Ulen (1998).

[6] Scotland comes close. No parts of the traditional Scottish homeland are in England, and no parts of the English homeland are in Scotland, even though, of course, there are a great many individual Scots living in England and some English in Scotland.

teacher you may find yourself having to get requalified, to learn a new curriculum, and perhaps even having to teach in a new language; if you are a lawyer, you may even have to work within a new type of legal system).

- The territories that are to be transferred could contain valuable assets (e.g. infrastructure, natural resources, ocean ports, military bases) that will affect the opportunities and tax base for the two provinces involved, as well as possibly, the property rights of owners.

- Similarly, the territory involved may contain historical or religious sites of particular cultural importance to members of one community or another. If either minority or majority nationalists feel that their community has been 'robbed' of assets or 'sacred ground', this narrative could become a long-standing source of national grievance for nation-builders.

So the changing of provincial frontiers, and the transfer of communities and territories from one province to another can directly affect individuals' fortunes and well-being, as well as their shared memories and sentiments; all of which provides a potential source of grievance for nation-building and nation-mobilizing.

There is also a whole range of issues about the justice and legitimacy of the *process* leading to any decision to redraw internal frontiers. In the 'ideal type' of federation (see Watts's definition in Chapter 3), neither the central nor the provincial governments would be entitled to unilaterally change the frontiers of provinces. Provincial boundaries will be defined in a constitution, and since both governments derive their sovereignty from the constitution and neither order of government is superior or subordinate, a true federal amending formula would require the consent of both orders of government for any changes; and also, surely, the consent of any particular provinces having their frontiers modified. In other words, there would be complicated negotiations involving at least two provinces and the federal government, and any changes would have to benefit all parties. One would hardly expect such a process to lead to many if any changes in most federations. It is also conceivable that a federation would agree to a general procedure for changing provincial frontiers by way of 'cascading referendums', where one or more subprovincial domains (such as counties or electoral constituencies) could vote to secede from one province and create a new one or join a neighbouring province. If the vote within that territory is sufficient to legitimize the internal secession procedure (and the threshold in a referendum may be considerably higher than 50 per cent), then contiguous domains could be invited to decide whether they want to join that unit in a new province or remain. Perhaps after such a series of votes, there might have to be another one where all the citizens of all of the contiguous domains vote again to decide whether they want to join together to create a new province. In fact, such an arrangement is more than conceivable; it is similar to a procedure in the Swiss constitution that has been used successfully.[7] The right process may minimize the possibility that nationalist grievances will be created by, for example, heavy-handed central authorities taking 'sacred' territory from one community and giving it to another. But by the same token, an ideally democratic and consensual process may make it more difficult to rectify what nationalists might see as an historically inappropriate provincial boundary.[8]

In general, democratic theory is always on relatively shaky ground when it comes to procedures for redrawing the frontiers of democratic polities. It has been said many times now (by theorists writing on secession) that democracy assumes we know who the people are when we agree that they should rule themselves.[9] But a vote to change frontiers will change the definition of 'the people' who make up the democratic communities involved. It is not clear which set of people should have a say in such a decision. In the case of changing frontiers between provinces, should all of the citizens of each affected province get a vote, and can a failed ratification in one province kill the deal? Or should just the people in the 'breakaway' region itself get a vote? Or should all citizens in the federation have a say? The decision on who should have a say will largely determine the decision itself; but it does not seem possible to democratically decide who should have a say in the first place. We will return to this issue in the discussion of a constitutional secession clause in Chapter 6.

Finally, we can consider issues relevant not to the case of changing provincial boundaries in a 'true' federation where provinces are already sovereign,

---

[7] The Swiss constitution of 1999 lays out an extremely federal and democratic process for altering Canton boundaries in Article 53 covering the 'Existence and Territory of the Cantons' (1) The Federation shall protect the existence and the territory of the Cantons.
(2) Modifications of the number of the Cantons, of the Cantons or their status are subject to the assent of the population concerned, of the Cantons concerned, and of the People and the Cantons.
(3) Modifications of the territory of a Canton are subject to the assent of the population concerned, of the Cantons concerned, and the assent of the Federal Parliament in the form of a federal decree.
(4) Intercantonal boundary settlements may be made by treaty between the Cantons concerned. The German constitution also has a complicated set of rules involving referendums for altering boundaries between its federal subunits, the *Länder*. See Article 29 of its constitution, the Basic Law.

[8] India offers a unique historical example: with the 1956 States Reorganization Act central authorities massively redrew state boundaries in order to make them coincide better with ethnolinguistic communities. There have been several further adjustments to state boundaries, the most recent in 2000 when three new states were carved out of existing states (Mathew 2002).

[9] See, e.g. Barry (1991: 162), Moore (2001: 152), and Beran (1984).

but rather to the situation of a unitary state that is contemplating becoming a federation (or quasi-federation); e.g. the situation of Spain during the transition following the collapse of the Franco regime in the mid-1970s, of South Africa in the 1990s, and potentially of Italy or the UK in the future. At this stage there will clearly be more constitutional freedom for federal architects. What considerations might they (legitimately) use? Consider four approaches to provincial frontier determination: which we might playfully dub the 'Burkean', the 'Gellnerian', the 'Tocquevillian' and the 'Machiavellian' (without implying that each of these approaches would have been endorsed, respectively, by these four dead authors).

The *Burkean approach* is the most conservative, if you will, and would begin with a strong presumption to use existing or well-recognized traditional internal borders when creating new subunits with greater autonomy or sovereignty. (This is clearly the approach that would be used to set the boundaries between England and Scotland and Wales were the UK to federalize.)

The *Gellnerian approach* is the most radical. It would attempt to gerrymander provincial frontiers in a way that satisfied the minority nationalist desire to have their cultural community be roughly *congruent* with their political (i.e. provincial) unit. This would maximize the percentage of members of the national minority group that could participate in their own self-governing community, while minimizing the number of non-members who would find themselves a minority within the national minority's province. (This approximates the approach used in the construction of the post-civil war Republic of Bosnia and Herzegovina, although this example is complicated by the 'ethnic cleansing' that took place during the war. A map laying out the boundaries between the two confederal units, the Bosniac-Croat Federations and the Republika Srpska, is a textbook picture of gerrymandering.)

The *Tocquevillian approach* is for those who fear that the Gellnerian approach might prove to be inherently unstable if nation-building within the minority's province led ultimately to a strong secessionist movement. Tocquevillians would draw boundaries in ways that encouraged long-term pan-national or federal unity, or at least stability. For example, they might be happy to have a province in which the national minority 'M' is in the majority, but in which, say, 30 per cent of the population were members of the national majority 'N', and where, say, 30 per cent of M were residing outside of M's homeland province. Another Tocquevillian strategy might be to create more than one province in which M would form a majority. A Tocquevillian strategy could go hand-in-hand with a Burkean presumption to retain historic community boundaries in cases where these boundaries approximate the desired results.¹⁰ Ideally, the Tocquevillian approach is an attempt to balance the minorities' desire for self-determination with the majority's desire for a stable, unified state.¹¹ In practice it is unlikely to be viewed as an even-handed balancing by minority nationalists. Their nation-building projects could respond to the 'arbitrary' boundary in one of two ways. They could use the cause of their 'stranded' fellow nationals in other provinces as a perpetual source of grievance with which to stoke nationalist flames (to use the language introduced in Chapter 2, this would be an attempt to 'sentimentalize the national identity'). Or they could engage in what we called 'reconfiguring the national identity' by promoting a new concept of minority national identity and membership that coincides with the boundaries of the newly created province.¹²

¹⁰ As a result of Spain's 1978 constitution and the negotiations and processes it laid out, the federal subunits called 'Autonomous Communities' were built out of smaller provinces based on boundaries established in 1833. One of the 'Tocquevillian' effects of this process is that Basques are distributed into two different Autonomous Communities (though they are not the majority in Navarra), and Catalan speakers are the majority in three different Autonomous Communities (Catalonia, Valencia, and the Balearic Islands) and a minority in a fourth (Aragon).

¹¹ This balance is rarely an easy one to strike, of course. Witness, for example, the rioting by thousands of members of the national majority in Macedonia when their government tried to redraw municipal boundaries in ways that would enable the minority Albanians (who make up a quarter of Macedonia's population, and who form the majority in some regions) to make up local majorities with control over their own schools. According to Saso Ordanovski, editor of *Forum*, a weekly magazine in Macedonia, this form of border revision makes the Macedonian majority 'increasingly afraid that Albanians are exercising their territorial interests' (quoted in Nicholas Wood, 'Ethnic Macedonians Riot Over Laws that Aid Albanians', *New York Times*, 24 July 2004, A4). Tito's gerrymandering of federal subunits (republics) in Communist Yugoslavia is another example of a Tocquevillian attempt to promote stability by shifting provincial boundaries to change ethnocultural demographics. It is also an example of the long-term risk that this entails.

¹² Both of these responses to 'stranded' fellow nationals have been favoured at different times by the minority nationalists in Canada and Spain, and also (under different circumstances) in the Republic of Ireland. In Canada, the descendents of French settlers used to consider themselves to be members of a French-Canadian nation (often referred to, until well into the twentieth century, as the French-Canadian race). Roughly 20 per cent of French Canadians lived outside of Quebec, and roughly the same percentage of the population of Quebec were not French Canadians. This larger ethnolinguistic nation was the focus of nationalists through much of Canadian history before and after Canada's independence in 1867. But beginning in the 1960s there was a very conscious decision among nationalist elites in Quebec to 'reconfigure the nation' to fit with the territory of the one province it controlled. So French-Canadian nationalism gave way to Québécois nationalism, and francophones outside Quebec were no longer, properly speaking, members of this nation. In an effort to adopt the trappings of civic rather than ethnic nationalism, Québécois nationalist leaders also now insist that all citizens of Quebec are members of this nation (even though many Anglophones, Aboriginals, and 'allophones' resist interpreting their own national identities this way). A similar situation exists in Catalonia, where few Catalan nationalists now think in terms of their nation including Catalan-speakers in Valencia, the Balearics, Aragon, the south of France, or the city of Alghero in Sardinia (all traditionally home to Catalan speakers). Basque nationalism too has involved a real tension between a political identity (with attendant demands for autonomy) that includes all Basques and one that is confined primarily to the Autonomous Community they control in Spain. On

The *Machiavellian approach* carries the Tocquevillian strategy one step further—forgetting about the balancing act altogether and undermining the minorities' demand for self-determination by explicitly fixing frontiers in ways that prevent the minority from forming a majority in any province.[13] (Other variations include: forcibly resettling minority groups outside of their traditional homelands, or encouraging or forcing their dispersion; encouraging settlement by non-members of the minority in the minority's traditional homeland; and, of course, refusing any kind of decentralization or federalization in order to leave the group a permanent minority within the larger state's national institutions.) This is a clear example of a strategy for majority nation-building that aims to ensure that minority national or proto-national identities remain 'folkloric' by depriving would-be nation-builders from these communities of any of the important nation-building tools of the state.

Given the vital link between territories, homelands, and nationalism, it is not surprising that the question of how best to fix the internal frontiers of federation should be a hotly contested one between minority and majority nationalists. What is surprising is how little attention these issues have received in both normative and positive theories of federalism. In practice, internal border changes in democratic federations are very rare indeed.

4.2.2 The Division of Powers

That there be a division of powers (i.e. of legislative and/or administrative competencies) between the central and provincial governments is almost always seen as a necessary condition for federalism. As the first Dean of post-war federal scholarship, Wheare (1963: 75) put it, 'There must be some matter, even if only one matter, which comes under the exclusive

the evolution of French-Canadian/Québécois nationalism see, e.g. Derriennic (1995: 21–40), Taylor (1993), Carens (1995b), and Seymour (1998); on minority nationalisms in Spain see, e.g. Conversi (1997) and Guibernau (2004). For a similar phenomenon, but for an international dimension, in Northern Ireland, see McGarry (2004).

[13] This strategy seemed to underlie US policy for creating states in the territories it occupied. As Kymlicka notes, it 'would have been quite possible in the nineteenth century to create states dominated by the Navaho, for example, or by Chicanos, Puerto Ricans, and native Hawaiians. At the time these groups were incorporated into the United States, they formed majorities in their homelands. However, a deliberate decision was made not to use federalism to accommodate the self-government rights to national minorities. Instead, it was decided that no territory would be accepted as a state unless these national groups were out-numbered within that state' (Kymlicka 2001: 98). This strategy can also be used in non-federal states where traditional provincial units nevertheless have political weight. As Bauböck notes, 'When in 1789 the National Assembly divided France into eighty-three departments of roughly equal size, this was meant to destroy the historical identities of regions many of which could be identified by cultural and linguistic difference' (Bauböck 2000: 376).

control, actual or potential, of the general [i.e. central] government and something likewise under the regional [i.e. provincial] governments.'

Many people speak or write about federalism as if the division of powers were the *only* essential element of federalism. And quite commonly the division of powers is thought to define *on its own* the realm of self-determination or self-government for the provinces. Both of these views are misguided; but the division of powers is nevertheless a crucial element in the design of any federal system, and it is bound to be contested over time in states where minority nationalists control one or more provinces and majority nationalists control the central government. As we have already noted, the division of power apportions out the tools for the respective minority and majority nation-building projects.

The division of powers for a given federation will generally be defined by the following constitutional provisions:

- a list of the powers controlled exclusively by the central government (typically including national defence, currency, postal service, interprovincial and international trade, copyrights and patents, and the criminal law, among other things);
- a list of the powers controlled exclusively by the provincial governments (these vary widely but sometimes include the regulation of municipalities, health care, and education);
- a list of concurrent or shared powers on which both orders of government can legislate (such as agriculture, transportation, and importantly, taxing powers);[14]
- rules for what to do when federal and provincial legislation in shared jurisdictions conflict;
- a rule for which order of government has the right to legislate in matters not mentioned in the first three lists of exclusive or shared powers.[15]

---

[14] These three lists can be rather long in some cases. The Indian constitution of 1950 listed 97 headings under exclusive control of the central government, 66 under the exclusive control of state governments, and 47 that were shared (see Wheare 1963: 77). Typically they are much shorter.

[15] The tenth amendment to the US Constitution from 1791 makes clear that 'the powers not delegated to the United States [i.e. the central government] by the Constitution, nor prohibited by it to the states, are reserved to the states respectively or to the people'. The somewhat obscure principle of 'subsidiarity' in the Maastricht Treaty can also be thought of as a rule for helping to adjudicate disputes about the division of powers in the EU: 'In areas which do not fall within its exclusive competence, the Community shall take action, in accordance with the principle of subsidiarity, only if and insofar as the objectives of the proposed actions cannot be sufficiently achieved by the member staes and can, therefore, by reason of the scale or effects of the proposed action, be better achieved by the Community.' There is no consensus, political or legal, on how this principle of subsidiarity should operate; but for philosophically sophisticated interpretations see Føllesdal 2003*a*, 2003*b* and Levy (forthcoming).

It must be emphasized, however, that no actual division of powers will be as tidy and categorical as these criteria might have us believe. First, many areas of government policies spill across different traditional jurisdictions, sometimes giving rise to disputes between ministries in the same government, and sometimes between ministries across the provincial-and-federal divide. Second, any rigidly defined lists of competencies are bound to look dated and even inadequate over time. Consider the case of the stated divisions of powers in the founding constitutions of the USA, Switzerland, and Canada from the eighteenth and nineteenth centuries. Governments at the time accounted for a relatively small proportion of GDP, were involved in almost none of the programmes of a modern welfare state, and made no provisions for modern telecommunications, energy production and distribution (including nuclear power), transportation, or pharmacology, for example. How do constitutionalized divisions of power keep up with social and technological innovation? Sometimes by court decisions, which may see affinities between the old (postal service) and the new (telephones or the Internet), and interpret the old division of powers accordingly.[16] Sometimes the constitutional document is actually amended explicitly to assign 'new' powers to one order of government or another; although this is relatively rare given the cumbersome procedures for amending most federal constitutions.[17] A third reason most divisions of powers are 'messier' in practice concerns the use of instruments like the 'federal spending power' by which federal governments make and finance policy in areas of exclusive provincial jurisdiction by offering the provinces money in return for their meeting certain standards or following certain principles in the administration of a given programme.[18]

It is obvious why the division of powers is the flashpoint for so many disputes between rival minority and majority nation-building projects in multinational federations. At various times the ability to set the curriculum

---

[16] Wheare discusses the case of responsibility for aviation, a power that no federal constitution drafted before, say, 1904 would have allocated to either federal or provincial governments. 'In Switzerland this was dealt with in 1921 by an amendment to the Constitution which handed the power to...the [federal] government. But in the United States and Australia the powers of the [federal] governments over aviation are only those which they have in virtue of their control over defence and inter-state commerce and from their powers to implement treaties' (Wheare 1963: 79).

[17] In a very rare instance of such an amendment to the Canadian constitution, in 1964 the federal government was granted permission to legislate (concurrently with the provinces) in the area of Old-Age Pensions (Section 94A).

[18] The federal spending power can be used like a stick or a carrot. The US federal government used a big stick to bring about an important change in a realm of exclusive state jurisdiction by promising to withhold substantial highway spending grants from any state that did not raise its legal drinking age to twenty-one. The Canadian federal government created a 'national' health care system, despite the fact that health care is ruled to be an area of provincial jurisdiction, by large transfers of cash if the provinces followed certain basic principles of universality.

in schools (as provincial governments do in many federations), to indoctrinate conscripted military recruits (as central governments have done even in peace time) or to maintain state television monopolies (a common practice for central governments in Europe through much of the latter half of the twentieth century) have been crucial to nation-building strategies. So too have been the somewhat less obvious strategies of promoting identities and loyalties towards either the province or the state by being seen as the ultimate guarantor of health care and other social services. And as I emphasized in Chapter 2, almost any area of policy can become a lightning rod for nationalist attention in a given federation if one side or the other comes to see it as central to its identity, even if (or especially if) they do so for largely symbolic purposes. Moreover, even in a culturally homogeneous setting, the creation of provincial boundaries (and governments responsible for exercising the provincial powers within those boundaries) by itself will give rise to provincial societies with distinctive political cultures and identities. Provincial elections will involve provincial political elites, parties, and issues. And social policy, which is typically either under provincial control or administered provincially, provides a medium for provincial interest-groups to grow and these groups, in turn, mobilize provincial publics in distinctive ways (see Cairns 1977; Eisenberg 1994: 9–10).

In this context, it is worth mentioning one final kind of nationalist demand with respect to the division of powers that has come to the fore in recent years: so-called 'asymmetrical federalism'.[19] It is typical for multinational federations to contain one or more provinces that are controlled by one or more national minorities, but also to contain numerous provinces that are controlled by citizens belonging to a national majority.[20] In these cases, minority

---

[19] See, e.g. Requejo (1999), (2001), Taylor (1993: ch. 8), Lenihan, Robertson, and Tassé (1994: 127–45), Resnick (1994), Seidel (1994), Gagnon (2001), Kymlicka (2001: 102–10).

[20] For example, Canada has one province with a francophone majority and nine others with anglophone majorities (it also has one quasi-provincial territory in the north especially created to contain an Inuit majority). Spain has six Autonomous Communities in which either a majority or a sizeable minority of the population identifies with one of three minority national identities (Galician, Basque, or Catalan), as well as eleven other Autonomous Communities in which virtually all of the citizens identify themselves first and foremost as Spanish. The Russian Federation has eighty-nine constituent units of six different types, including twenty-one Republics which tend to be ethnoculturally distinct and the most autonomous of the units. The forty-nine *Oblasts* or Provinces are dominated by ethnic Russians and have less autonomy than the republics. Note that in some federations where there is no majority or where the ethnonational communities are more comparable in size, it is more common to have provinces or subunits that match these communities one for one, as in the complicated example of Belgium. For an excellent summary of the structure and history of the current federations of the world, see Griffiths (2002*a*). It is noteworthy that when the possibility of federalization is envisaged in the UK, there is an open debate about whether, in addition to a province each for the Scottish, the Welsh, and the Northern Irish, there should be one or several English provinces.

nationalists typically demand that their provinces have a claim to control powers that the other provinces do not need to control (say, control over immigration and naturalization, or language policy). In practice this amounts to a demand for the transfer of a power from the central government's side of the ledger to the provincial side in the case of the minority province alone. Pragmatic grounds are usually given for this: the distinct identity and needs of the minority province's population requires that it be able to set its own policy in a given domain. But there are also clearly symbolic grounds (the asymmetry of a division of powers helps to recognize and emphasize that group's distinctiveness), otherwise it would be difficult to explain why minority nationalists are typically disappointed with a counterproposal simply to transfer the power to all of the provinces. We will return to this question of the relevance of asymmetry when we discuss symbolism and justification later and in Chapter 5. At this point it is worth noting that 'symbolic' issues are often more substantive than they first appear. In the case of the asymmetric transfer of a federal power to a minority-controlled province, there is also a clear shift in the balance of nation-building powers in the minority nationalists' favour.

4.2.3 Representation in (and Design of) Central Institutions

It is clear why the division of powers is a key part of defining the realm of self-determination and self-government for a minority national community. If that community's province has exclusive control over education, say, then the members of that community will be able to determine (insofar as modern pedagogical methods permit) what their children will learn in school. But since the central government also has exclusive and shared rights to legislate and administer in certain policy domains over the minority's territory, it follows that minorities can also enhance their control over their destiny if they can influence how the central government wields its power. This is partly a matter of having a voice and a vote within central institutions, as minority-rights theorists have long recognized. But it is equally a matter of having central institutions that are designed in ways that will take proper account of these voices and votes.[21] When theorists like Neumann and the authors of *Designing Federalism* warn about the importance of 'non-federal' institutions in the design of a federation, it is some of these central institutions that they have largely in mind.

[21] 'Designed' is not an entirely adequate word in this sentence. Well-designed institutions can be badly run; and many well-functioning institutions operate according to healthy traditions and conventions that were not part of their original design. We need to take these sorts of considerations into account when evaluating actual institutions.

Consider three kinds of central institutions that will have different sorts of implications for minority or provincial autonomy:

- *basic political institutions* for deciding upon policy and overseeing its implementation, namely the executive, the legislature, and the head of state (e.g. a constitutional monarch who may not be a member of either the executive or the legislature);
- the *civil service*, including the military and federal police forces, along with important federal agencies and some state-owned enterprises;
- the *courts*, in particular the court that has the ultimate say over the interpretation of the constitution.

Decisions about majority, minority, and provincial roles in these three types of institutions will profoundly shape the identities and loyalties of different groups of citizens within the state as well as the fortunes of nationalist projects within both minority and majority communities. It is difficult to embark on a discussion of options for representation and design of these institutions without simultaneously invoking rationales and justifications; but as much as possible I shall try to delay the normative enquiry until Chapter 5. Without pretending to spell out the entire range of options for representation and design of these kinds of institutions I will give some examples of the sorts of demands that might be brought to the table at the time of negotiating or renegotiating the terms of federation by, for example, *minority nationalists* (such as Scottish nationalists, were the UK hypothetically to federalize) interested in securing more autonomy for the federal province they control, and *federalists* (such as British nationalists in the same hypothetical federation) interested in promoting a 'pan-national' identity (one that incorporates members of minority or majority nations as well as immigrants). I will not say much here about the demands of straightforward *majority nationalists* (such as English nationalists in this example): sometimes they will make autonomy demands like minority nationalists,[22] sometimes they will conflate the pan-national identity with their own,[23] and sometimes they will be downright imperial in their willingness to subjugate or assimilate minorities.[24] My aim is merely to display a range of options with fairly obvious implications for nation-building projects.

---

[22] For a rare analysis of this phenomenon, see Resnick (2001).
[23] The conflation of pan-national citizenship identity with a majority national identity was well-illustrated by quotes from Dicey in Chapter 3, where he explicitly treats 'English' and 'British' as synonyms.
[24] This sort of majoritarian imperialism was discussed in Section 2.4.1.1, turning peasants (such as Bretons, Catalans, Basques, Corsicans, Occitanians, and Alsatians) into Frenchmen, Kurds into Turks, and so on.

Basic Political Institutions. We would not be surprised to see minority nationalists seeking a bicameral legislature, where the upper house has representatives nominated by the provincial legislatures and acting on the orders of these legislatures or their governments. (This is the way the American system worked until 1913. It is still the model for the German Bundesrat, the upper house in India, and the Council of Ministers in the EU.) This would typically go along with the right of this chamber (or even of a minority within it) to veto federal legislation. In these ways, minority nationalist elites would not only have access to nation-building powers at the provincial level, they would be able to prevent the enactment of some federal legislation with unwanted majority nation-building implications in their province.

Federalists are also likely to be receptive to a bicameral legislature with an upper house in some sense representing the provinces. But they would prefer that the *citizens* of each province elect their representatives to the upper house rather than having them as agents of provincial governments (this is how it is done, e.g. in the US and Australian Senates). Federalists may be in favour of some way of overrepresenting the citizens of either small provinces or minority provinces (small provinces can be overrepresented by having equal representation in the upper house from each province; large minority-controlled provinces would need some more explicit form of overrepresentation). Federalists would also typically allow this house to exercise a veto over federal legislation. So much for the upper house. Almost all democratic theorists and all federations opt for a lower house that represents the citizens of the federation on a roughly equal basis. There may nevertheless be demands that minorities be overrepresented, or that members of the lower house representing minority provinces be given a veto on certain types of culturally sensitive legislation. In the case of asymmetrical federations where, say, one province M has a power P that is otherwise exercised by the federal government for the other provinces, there may have to be special voting procedures in parliament so that members from M do not vote on federal legislation concerning P.

Democratic federations typically do not have formal quotas for representation of provinces, regions, or minority groups within the executive or cabinet. It is, however, typical for there to be strong conventions in diverse federal states to ensure informal forms of representation at that level. In more sharply divided societies, such as Belgium, there can even be parallel ministers in the federal cabinet responsible for administering the same services (say, health or education) for their respective communities. There may also be calls for the head of state or the head of government to be filled by a member of the different constituent cultural communities on an alternating or rotating basis (as the presidency of the EU has been). It is safe to say that federalists are more likely to want any 'ethnically-sensitive' criteria for cabinet selection to be relatively informal and accommodating, in order to promote the idea that the federal government takes into consideration the interests of all citizens fairly and even-handedly. Minority nationalists typically do not press for quotas in the federal cabinet, perhaps because they have no reason to expect that 'co-opted' federal politicians will be minority nationalists even if they are members of the minority national community.

Civil Service. There is no shortage of examples of democratic multinational states in which the central government's bureaucracy, military, police forces, and state-run agencies and corporations have been dominated by members of the majority national community.[25] Surely most have been this way earlier in their history, and many continue to be, especially in the multinational states that have not federalized. The movement to ensure adequate representation and opportunities for members of national minorities is often initiated by minority groups themselves in the name of fairness and equality of opportunity. But it is also embraced by true federalists keen to reinforce the sense of equal citizenship in the federal state; as well as by nation-builders at the federal level trying to promote a pan-national identity that incorporates the notion of equal citizenship for members of the national majority and minorities. In the case of multilingual states equal representation within the civil service often goes hand-in-hand with equal status for minority languages and the delivery of government services in all official languages. Minority nationalists may be politically ambivalent about such reforms of the federal state. On the one hand, they have to be in favour of ending the discrimination against their people. But on the other, they know that if the federal bureaucracy underrepresents their people and does not operate in their language, then they can use this fact to mobilize support for more autonomy. For this reason, they may be inclined to dismiss the achievement of a truly representative and multilingual federal civil service since celebrating this would be seen as part of a pan-national identity-building project designed to counterbalance the attractions of the minority national identity.

Courts. The role of the courts, and in particular the court that serves as the final arbiter of the constitution (call this 'the Court'), is pivotal in a truly federal system. Recall that in the ideal type of federation neither order of government is superior or subordinate; both derive their sovereignty and legitimacy from the constitution. This means that the Court should not be seen as a branch of the central government per se (or of the provincial governments for that matter; although I do not know of any Constitutional

---

[25] In some cases, such as Apartheid South Africa or Baathist Syria or Iraq, central institutions are (or were) dominated by a *minority* group.

Court that could be mistaken for such, not even in the EU). Moreover, one of the important functions of the Court is to rule on jurisdictional disputes between orders of government, disputes that can have very high stakes when both federal and provincial governments are involved in rival nation-building projects. The Court will have to decide which government's programme takes precedence when the division of powers awards both concurrent powers, and also when one government is trying to legislate in a jurisdiction in which the other order of government has an exclusive power. In a federation with a Bill of Rights and judicial review, the Court will sometimes be asked to strike down legislation that is thought to violate basic individual rights and we know that aggressive nation-building legislation may often be seen as a candidate for such judicial review.[26] In short, as much as they might like to, the judges of the Court will not be able to remain on the sidelines during protracted contests between minority and majority nationalists in a federation.

So how can the Court's impartiality and independence be ensured? The simple answer is that these things can never be *ensured*. Courts are made up of judges, who are human and subject to bias; and these judges have to be appointed by humans who are *even more* likely to be subject to bias. Nevertheless, consider three ways of enquiring about independence. First, we can ask, how are the judges nominated, vetted, and appointed to the Court? Second, from which communities do the judges originate? And third—much less clearly defined—how can the judges, and the Court more generally, demonstrate their continued impartiality and independence? Minority nationalists might well demand that a certain quota of judges be nominated by the government of the minority province. They might also demand a certain overrepresentation of 'minority' judges on the Court. Any ruling that went in favour of the federal government against the minority's province that did not also carry the majority of the province's judges would appear illegitimate, whether or not there was a formal requirement for a 'double-majority' in these cases. Federalists would be wary of having judges appointed in a quota system by provincial governments if these judges were being sent to represent the interests of the provinces rather than the constitution per se. They should equally be concerned about any direct appointments by the federal head of government. Expertise and fidelity to the rule of law should be seen as paramount in factors for judicial legitimacy, and in a true federation this may require special arm's-length bodies or commissions that nominate top

---

[26] The classic example here is Quebec's notorious Bill 101 which, among other things, restricts the use of English on commercial signs, and prevents Francophone citizens and most immigrants from sending their children to English-language public schools. There have been several challenges to these parts of the law, but by and large they have been upheld by the Supreme Court of Canada.

candidates for the Court.[27] This could still be compatible with some kind of regional quota system for the origins of judges, as well as public hearings for parliamentary approval of final nominees. Most legal systems also protect judges from being removed by partisan politicians once elected to the Court. In the end, however, the Court will have to prove its own legitimacy by its rulings; and courts tend to be better or worse at this in different eras.

This completes our brief survey of issues around the design of central institutions in a multinational federation. We will return to a select number of these issues in Chapter 5 when we take up arguments for justifying one design over another. It must be said that there are voluminous literatures in various subdisciplines of political science, political theory, policy studies, and constitutional law that deal with the design of parliaments, executives, electoral systems, court systems, and so on. My principal aim here was to look at a range of design options (mostly of a kind that we find in actual federations) and to highlight their implications for rival nation-building projects and for the 'reconciling' of these projects. Minority nationalists typically devote less attention than they probably should to the relevance of central institutions. Their public rhetoric of self-determination leads them to focus on the division of powers and on the powers that they would like to control. But in terms of the rivalry between their nation-building projects and those of the central government, it may be just as useful to focus on their ability to constrain what the central government can do with its powers. Unfortunately, seeking the reform of central institutions may be a game that minority nationalists qua nationalists cannot win. It is very difficult to make the necessary constitutional changes since these require the broad support of the national majority; and if they do succeed in reforming central institutions so that they are less of a threat to minority nation-building, this may play directly into the hands of federalist nation-builders eager to show that the system works for everyone.

4.2.4 Integration of Markets and Legal Systems

This heading of federal design issues will be more or less important in different situations. In some sense, these issues are dealt with in the division

---

[27] Unusual measures like this may be less necessary in states where the main divisions that threaten the perceived impartiality of the Court are ideological; say, right-left, conservative-liberal. At least in these cases there may be some hope that parties of government or Presidents will alternate along these lines, so over time the court will have a balance across the ideological divide. When the main divides are between majority and minority national communities, or between centralists and provincialists, there may never be alternation for the heads of the central government—they may always be from the majority national community and care most about the central government's interests.

of power (which typically specifies concurrent rights to regulate commerce for both orders governments, and regulation of interprovincial and international commerce to the central government, and which divides responsibilities for different aspects of the law) and the design of central institutions (that specifies relations between courts). But in some federal situations the integration of markets and legal systems will demand special attention—especially in cases of deepening confederation, like the EU, where previously independent systems are being merged. There are many examples of the long-standing coordination of different legal systems in federations or otherwise divided societies (including Canada, the USA, the UK, India, Israel, Keyna, and South Africa), especially concerning the coexistence of Roman civil law with British common law, and of family law from secular and religious traditions.[28] There is also an emerging trend to incorporate Aboriginal legal traditions into modern states that are willing to grant substantial autonomy to Aboriginal peoples (see Levy 2000*b*). On the other hand, relatively little reform of markets and legal systems may be required in the case of the federalization of unitary states.

4.2.5 Constitutional Amending Formula

All constitutions—federal or not—need an amending formula. And in almost every case, the formula requires a process and a level of support that is more demanding than that needed to modify statutory legislation. The rigorous amending formula goes to the very heart of the ideal of constitutionalism, where democrats impose 'gag-rules' on their ability to make democratic decisions in order, paradoxically, to strengthen their democracy.[29]

In federal states, a role for both provincial and federal governments in the amending of the constitution is implied by the idea that each order of its government is sovereign in its realm, and that neither order is superior or subordinate. Once the terms of the federation have been agreed to by all parties they cannot be unilaterally changed by one party or another. This basic principle is not in fact followed in a number of the states that are often considered to be federations. In Spain and India, for example, the

---

[28] On incorporation of religious family law, see Shachar (2000); on the coordination of civil and common law see, e.g. Tetley (2000).

[29] The image of a 'gag-rule' seems to owe its currency in contemporary democratic theory to Holmes's important article, 'Gag rules or the politics of omission'. He explores the concept further under the heading of 'autopaternalism' in a companion article, 'Precommitment and the paradox of democracy' (1988*b*). See also Elster (1988: 9).

constitution can be amended by the central government on its own.[30] This is also true in Belgium, where there is nevertheless a mechanism to ensure that each of the constituent communities has its say and gives its assent within the federal parliament itself.

The basic principle for federal amending formulas is also vague about the critical question of provincial autonomy. It claims that neither the provincial governments *collectively* nor the central government can unilaterally amend the constitution. If an actual federation is to satisfy this principle, then obviously it cannot have an amending formula that allows the central government or parliament to change the basic terms of the federation on its own. But how does the basic principle apply to provincial rights? It implies that all the provinces together cannot change the constitution on their own.[31] But it does not imply that the constitution can never be modified against the objections of *any given* province.

Consider the amending formula in Article 5 of the US Constitution: any changes require the approval of two-thirds of the members of both houses of Congress and three-quarters of the state legislatures. This ensures that the states cannot have their constitutional powers changed by an act of Congress, and also that the states cannot band together and change the constitutional powers of Congress. But what it does *not* ensure is that, say, New York State (whose population is greater than most countries in Europe) will never have its powers changed without its consent. Now most New Yorkers are probably not especially worried about this prospect. Any given citizen of New York State is likely to find himself or herself on the losing side of plenty of major political issues and contests, and an amendment against the wishes of the New York State legislature might simply be treated as yet another such incident. Obviously, anybody could be more or less upset depending on what the content of the specific amendment was. But it is unlikely that most typical New Yorkers would be especially upset by *the mere fact that* it passed without New York State's assent.

This is *not* likely to be the reaction of members of a province controlled by a national minority in a multinational federation, however—for reasons that go

---

[30] See the Spanish Constitution of 1978, Part X, section 166–9, which gives rules for amendment by the two houses of the Spanish parliament, the Cortes, along with provisions for statewide ratification by referendum. This is sometimes cited in arguments for why Spain should *not* be counted as a truly federal state. Most parts of the Indian constitution can be amended by the two houses of parliament, although changes to the federal distribution of powers, or to the representation of the states in the federal parliament, also require ratification by 50 per cent of the states.

[31] Note that all of the member states of the EU on their own—i.e. without the consent of the Commission, the Parliament or the Council—can change the EU 'constitution' or basic treaties. This is one of the strongest indications that the EU is more of a *con*federation than a federation.

to the heart of both their interpretation of the federal 'compact' and their quest to be 'masters of their own house'. Obviously, for reasons already discussed, minority nationalists will be worried about any changes to the division of powers or the design of central institutions that either reduce their own nation-building powers, or increase those of the federal government. In the context of a perceived rivalry between minority and majority nation-building projects, it is inevitable that minority nationalists will distrust their majority counterparts to a certain degree. If their rivals are 'conspiring' with other provinces to modify the constitution without the minority province's consent, it will be hard not to assume that their rivals are doing this to gain the upper hand. Even the mere fact that major provisions (especially, again, those with nation-building implications) *can be* modified without the minority province's consent, even if they are not *in fact* modified, is likely to be unsettling to national minorities. Indeed, 'unsettling' is too gentle a term: this possibility could have profound implications for how secure the minority feels in the state, to how loyal they feel towards the state and its constitution, and to how trusting they are of their federal partners. For all these reasons, it is hard to imagine that a national minority would voluntarily agree to give up a right to veto constitutional amendments if it were negotiating the original terms of federation in free and fair conditions. In most actual cases, of course, national minorities did not have such a role in the founding of the federation. We will discuss the relevance of 'hypothetical contract' reasoning to the justification of federal institutions in Chapter 5. For now it is important simply to highlight that national minorities are bound to see their partnership in the state as a nation or a people and not merely as a political jurisdiction like a province. And they will be as reluctant to concede complete sovereignty over the fundamental terms of their partnership as are the member states of the EU today.

Not surprisingly, there is a flip side to the minority nationalists' desire for a veto on constitutional change. Members of the national majority are also reluctant to hand over such a veto for fear that the minority group could use it to frustrate their (the majority's) attempts to be a self-determining, self-governing democratic community. In other words, both of minorities and the majority have fundamentally nationalist reasons for their preferences concerning the minority's or each province's right to a veto over constitutional change. This looks like an issue requiring soul-searching negotiations. It is also bound up with concerns over symbolism and recognition, and for this reason I will discuss it further after looking at the role of these two notions in a theory of constitutionalism for the multinationals state (in section 4.7 and in Chapter 5).

4.2.6 Secession Clause

It is obvious what secession means for minority and majority nation-building projects. Secession is the ultimate dream for hard-core minority nationalists, opening up the possibility that they will be free from most outside interference to shape their identity 'authentically'. For most majority nationalists, the secession of a minority they had been trying to incorporate within a pan-national society and identity represents the ultimate failure. But while it is obvious how both sides will look at secession, it is not at all obvious (*a*) how they should feel about having a legal secession procedure in the constitution, and (*b*) what would be the best design for such a clause. As we shall discuss in Chapter 6, which will be devoted to these questions, very few actual federations have constitutionalized secession. At the same time, it is difficult to conceive of independent states today freely bargaining to create a confederation or federation without insisting on the right to exit.

Secession is, in some sense, the logical extreme of most of the terms of federation. If a province—almost certainly a national-minority province—decides it wants to secede from a federation it is, in effect, asking for:

- a major constitutional amendment (one that will write it out of the constitutional order);
- a radical transformation of the division of powers (it is asking for all, or virtually all, of the federal powers to be transferred to it); and
- a radical diminution of its representation in federal institutions (although it may ask that new supranational institutions be created to manage any continued shared powers between the new state and the rump state, such as a common currency, a free-trade zone, or a common postal service).

If a secession clause is an extension of existing federal rules, such a clause should not appear completely out of place within a modern, progressive federal constitution. I will say no more about this now. Again, a sustained exploration of the constitutionalization of a secession clause will take up the bulk of Chapter 6.

This completes the survey of what is sometimes called the basic 'plumbing' or (more grandly) 'architecture' of federal systems. This plumbing constitutes many of the rules of the game for the federation. Decisions under each of the headings above will generally be entrenched in the constitution; often quite dryly, belying the tremendous stakes that both minority and majority nationalists will attach to these rules. For all of its nation-building significance, for example, the division of powers will typically be reflected in three brief lists of competencies (for federal and provincial powers, and those shared between the two) and a sentence or two about who gets to decide on issues not falling under these three lists. But as important as these plumbing decisions are for the citizens of the federation, they hardly exhaust the pressing issues for federal design and federal constitutionalism in a multinational state. Virtually all constitutions—especially in states with diverse populations and histories of 'identity politics'—also contain what we might loosely describe as 'symbolic language' and debates at constitutional conventions may devote as much or more time to these passages as they do to many of the decisions about plumbing.

4.3 SYMBOLIC TERMS OF FEDERATION

Identifying the symbolic content of any given constitution is not always a straightforward task, especially for an outsider unfamiliar with the special coded language and hot-button issues that might develop in some particular political culture.[32] But of course, often it *is* straightforward, and that is the point. Many constitutions begin with preambles containing declarations of the fundamental values of the state or its people or peoples. They might also cite *principles* that the state 'upholds' or 'takes to be self-evident', or which underlie its constitution, as well as *claims of fact* (especially alleged historical facts),[33] and even *theological* or *metaphysical* claims about, for example, the existence of deities or the nature and divisibility of sovereignty.

---

[32] Consider the rather arcane-looking sentence known as the Second Amendment in the US Constitution: 'A well regulated Militia, being necessary to the security of a free State, the right of the people to keep and bear Arms, shall not be infringed.' A quick check on Amazon.com reveals that literally dozens of books have been published with the phrase 'Second Amendment' in the title—by law professors and gun fanatics alike—to explain this passage and its implications for modern-day gun-control legislation. What is significant for our purposes is the way the Second Amendment anchors historically and constitutionally a particular (and contested) conception of American identity that is bound up with gun-owning, self-sufficiency and distrust of government. All constitutions seem to have passages of this kind that could be skipped over by outsiders reading the document, but which resonate within the political culture of the country concerned.

[33] The Preamble to the Croatian constitution of 1990 (as last amended 2001), for example, begins with an astonishing list of alleged historical facts:

> The millenary identity of the Croatian nation and the continuity of its statehood, confirmed by the course of its entire historical experience within different forms of states and by the preservation and growth of the idea of a national state, founded on the historical right of the Croatian nation to full sovereignty, manifested in:
>
> - the formation of Croatian principalities in the seventh century;
> - the independent mediaeval state of Croatia founded in the ninth century;

What is most striking about symbolic claims and declarations is the way they point so directly to (often contested) aspects of national identity. Indeed, one could start with a list of components of national identity such as the one in Section 2.3, and work backwards to find a wide array of symbolic claims in actual constitutions. For example, with that list of first-person 'identity' beliefs in mind, we notice that most constitutions:

- give a name to the people of the state, often conflating it with the name of the nation to which all or most of the people are declared to belong;
- indicate boundaries of the state, often referring to it as the nation's homeland;
- indicate rights of citizenship (or nationality) by virtue of either blood or birth within the territory of the state;

  - the Kingdom of Croats established in the tenth century;
  - the preservation of the identity of the Croatian state in the Croatian-Hungarian personal union;
  - the independent and sovereign decision of the Croatian Parliament (Sabor) of 1527 to elect a king from the Habsburg dynasty;
  - the independent and sovereign decision of the Croatian Parliament of the Pragmatic Sanction of 1712; the conclusions of the Croatian Parliament of 1848 regarding the restoration of the Triune Kingdom of Croatia under the authority of the Banus grounded on the historical, national, and natural right of the Croatian nation;
  - the Croatian-Hungarian Compromise of 1868 on the relations between the Kingdom of Dalmatia, Croatia, and Slavonia and the Kingdom of Hungary, grounded on the legal traditions of both states and the Pragmatic Sanction of 1712;
  - the decision of the Croatian Parliament of 29 October 1918 to dissolve state relations between Croatia and Austria–Hungary and the simultaneous affiliation of independent Croatia, invoking its historical and natural right as a nation, with the state of Slovenes, Croats and Serbs, proclaimed on the former territory of the Habsburg Monarchy;
  - the fact that the Croatian Parliament had never sanctioned the decision of the National Council of the State of Slovenes, Croats, and Serbs to unite with Serbia and Montenegro in the Kingdom of Serbs, Croats, and Slovenes (1 December 1918), subsequently (3 October 1929) proclaimed the Kingdom of Yugoslavia; the establishment of the Home Rule (Banovina) of Croatia in 1939, by which Croatian state identity was restored within the Kingdom of Yugoslavia, establishing the foundations of state sovereignty during the course of the Second World War, by the decisions of the Antifascist Council of National Liberation of Croatia (1943), as opposed to the proclamation of the Independent State of Croatia (1941), and subsequently in the Constitution of the People's Republic of Croatia (1947) and all later constitutions of the Socialist Republic of Croatia (1963–1990), on the threshold of the historical changes, marked by the collapse of the communist system and changes in the European international order, the Croatian nation by its freely expressed will at the first democratic elections (1990) reaffirmed its millenary statehood. By the new Constitution of the Republic of Croatia (1990) and the victory in the Homeland War (1991–1995), the Croatian nation demonstrated its will and determination to establish and defend the Republic of Croatia as a free, independent, sovereign, and democratic state.

- entrench a range of citizenship rights, including civil, political, and social rights;
- indicate an official language or languages.

In addition, many states' constitutions:

- recognize minority nationalities or national minorities;
- indicate an official religion, along with patron saints or deities;
- indicate an official script or alphabet;
- indicate the nature of official symbols like the flag, the 'national' anthem, or the coat of arms;
- name a particular family with rights to the throne, along with rules for succession;
- state a number of alleged historical facts indicating important shared 'memories' and sources of pride or humiliation;
- indicate certain citizenship duties or responsibilities, especially concerning military service.

All of these provisions correspond to important aspects of the way an individual identifies with his or her state or nation (N or M, in the language of that earlier list of components of national identity); or about what it means to an individual to be a member of that political community (to be an N'ian or M'ian or both). And of course, any of these constitutional declarations can be deeply contested within the state. They can be contested between different cultural or religious subgroups in the state, such as minority or majority national communities; or even between citizens with different ideological views within any one of these groups. The final text of a constitution often represents the victory of some particular cultural or ideological group in the battle to imprint the state with its views and identity.

In short, the nation-building intentions of constitutional symbolism could not be more plain and direct. Nationalists tend to speak most often and explicitly in the language of self-determination, as for example when minority nationalists explain why they need a federal power to be transferred to their province. But debates about constitutional symbolism are first and foremost about nation-building and identity formation; including, in the case of modern democracies, the formation of identities with a significant political content (so-called 'constitutional patriotism'), where citizens are meant to identify with the state's values, principles, institutions, and social achievements. Of course, as we have often seen, nation-building and self-determination are conceptually and causally intertwined, so we should not be surprised to learn that symbolism with direct nation-building implications can ultimately aid self-determination projects as well. This may be especially true in *federations* where symbolic language can guide the constitutional court's interpretation of the constitution in its most delicate rulings over the division of powers and the balance of collective and individual rights. This link between symbolism and real political power reminds us also that constitutional symbolism should rarely be thought of 'merely symbolic' or as constitutional 'window dressing'. Real debates over symbolic language and principles in the constitution are so heated precisely because both sides see the potential substantive, 'non-symbolic' consequences.

Again, nationalists tend not to talk overtly about their quest for nation-building powers. As Brubaker is at pains to point out, they will usually treat the nation as an entity that is already formed and distinct and in need of the particular powers of self-determination that the nationalists are demanding on its behalf. This may be the reason for the increasing popularity of the alternative language of 'recognition' when nationalists are arguing for symbolic provisions in a constitution. In the language of nation-building, nationalists want to place a certain model of what it is to be a member of a particular minority or majority nation into the constitution in order to encourage citizens to see themselves in terms of this model. But entrenching symbolism on these grounds would be a tough-sell in societies with rival nationalisms. Instead, in the language of 'recognition', nationalists argue that the constitution ought to 'recognize' the reality of the existence of a certain nation with certain characteristics and values. If there *was* a process of formation of this national identity—and most reflective nationalists are willing to admit to this much—that process is now said to be sufficiently complete that it is time for the political system to take account of or 'to recognize' this fact.[34] Given that it cloaks the ongoing politics of nation-building in this way, a Brubakerian would presumably argue against our endorsing the language of 'recognition' in political philosophy. We must obviously worry about the dangers of any conceptual scheme or language that obscures our view of nation-building. Indeed, it is a central theme of this book that recent political philosophers have devoted insufficient attention to this face of nationalist politics. Nevertheless, for a variety of reasons that I shall explore in Chapter 5, I believe that the language of 'recognition' also has some advantages in political philosophy and in the public discourse of a multinational state. It may, for example, be much easier to get competing nationalist movements to agree to principles of

[34] Note, it is no part of my argument that nationalists are generally disingenuous about their claims to speak on behalf of a real, existing nation with the characteristics and values they ascribe to it. I am sure that most are genuinely convinced of this. This is what it is to have (or believe in) an ideology. For reasons discussed in the appendix to Chapter 1, I do believe that it is appropriate to acknowledge the existence of a good many nations, even if their characteristics are somewhat less complete and distinct than their nationalist apologists assume them to be.

equal recognition than it would be to get them to accept the equal right of nation-building. In chapter 5 I will offer a number of potentially reasonable principles for brokering rival nationalisms under the rubric of 'principles of recognition'.

The explosion of the discourse of recognition in recent years has been most often associated with minority groups, and in particular with minority groups who are demanding that their existence be recognized in part so that they can make credible claims for special rights.[35] This is certainly true of national-minority groups and their advocates. But we should not infer from the fact that recognition is only sought by or needed by minorities; especially in the context of multinational states. Majorities like recognition too. The difference is that most national majorities (*a*) have already entrenched the recognition of their nation into the constitution, and (*b*) seek their further recognition elsewhere, such as from the international community (through, e.g. military, diplomatic, economic, cultural, or sporting achievements).

Consider, for example, the various forms of recognition and national self-identification packed into the opening sections of the current constitution of the archetypical nation-state, France. The preamble to the constitution of the Fifth Republic (1958) declares that:

The French people hereby solemnly proclaim their dedication to the Rights of Man and the principle of national sovereignty as defined by the Declaration of 1789, reaffirmed and complemented by the Preamble to the 1946 Constitution.

Although France is composed of several ethnolinguistic communities that sociologists would recognize as historic national minorities, the constitution clearly refers only to one French 'people', and the rights in the Declaration and the 1946 Constitution are the classic individual rights of citizenship. The Declaration of 1789 proclaims that the goal of all political associations is to preserve these rights (Article 2). It also includes the 'principle that all sovereignty resides essentially in the nation' (Article 3).[36] Title 1, Article 2 of the 1958 Constitution then declares the following six points:

(1) France is an indivisible, secular, democratic, and social Republic. It ensures the equality of all citizens before the law, without distinction as to origin, race, or religion. It respects all beliefs.
(2) The language of the Republic is French.

---

[35] The list of references on minority rights would be a bibliography on its own. For some useful recent studies, which reassess the voluminous debates on this topic in the 1990s, see Kymlicka and Norman (2000), Young (2000), Gutmann (2003), and Appiah (2005).

[36] It is noteworthy that the 1958 constitution does recognize a different status for Overseas Territories and eventually they would be given the right to secede. No such right is extended to territorial minorities or to Corsicans.

(3) The national emblem is the blue, white, and red tricolor flag.
(4) The national anthem is the 'Marseillaise'.
(5) The Motto of the Republic is *'Liberty, Equality, Fraternity'*.
(6) Its principle is government of the people, by the people, and for the people.

Again, all of this language and symbolism leaves no doubt that France is conceived as essentially a union of equal citizens, where all citizens are members of one and only one nation, France. It represents a victory for a particular conception of the French nation and a defeat for rival conceptions of that nation (e.g. those incorporating certain ethnic, racial, or religions content), as well as for historic rival minority nationalities, such as the Bretons, the Basques, the Catalans, and the Corsicans. And it represents and recognizes this victory not as the result of a long political process, but in some sense as a fact of life.

This language and symbolism would be seized upon by numerous new and newly liberated states in Eastern, Central, and Southern Europe in their post-Communist constitutions. For example, despite the fact that (like France) they contained territorially concentrated national minorities, Croatia, Macedonia, Romania, and Slovakia all declare their states to be 'indivisible' in the opening lines of their constitutions. It is common for states in this region and elsewhere to declare themselves to be the *national state* of the titular nation. Sometimes this nation, like France, is presumed for constitutional purposes to include all citizens regardless of ethnicity (as is the case in the Romanian, Slovakian, and Russian constitutions). And sometimes it is made clear that the state is the national state of a titular nation, but that this state is also shared with members of national minorities who are not members of the titular nation. Consider, for example, in the Preamble to the Macedonian constitution of 1991:

... Macedonia is established as a national state of the Macedonian people, in which full equality as citizens and permanent co-existence with the Macedonian people is provided for Albanians, Turks, Vlachs, Romanics and other nationalities living in the Republic of Macedonia...

Croatia appears to go one better in the Preamble to its constitution (as amended in April 2001), by offering its national minority not merely equality of citizenship and equal individual rights, but also 'national rights':

Croatia is established as the national state of the Croatian nation and the state of the members of autochthonous national minorities: Serbs, Czechs, Slovaks, Italians, Hungarians, Jews, Germans, Austrians, Ukrainians and Ruthenians and the others who are citizens, and who are guaranteed equality with citizens of Croatian nationality and the realization of national rights in accordance with the democratic norms of the United Nations Organization and the countries of the free world.

Again, none of the constitutions I have just quoted from is federal, although the more recent ones do take the rather extraordinary step of symbolically recognizing named national minorities in the fundamental framing characteristics of the state. Compare this to the French constitutional council's steadfast refusal on a number of recent occasions to recognize the existence of a Corsican people.[37]

It goes without saying that an ideal constitution for a multinational federal state will depart significantly from the French model that has proved so popular with majority nation-builders in multiethnic states of late. Again, part of the rationale for this detour through nation-state constitutions was to show how constitutional recognition is as important to majority nationalists as it is to minorities. The difference is that majority nationalists often have a free hand in writing their constitutions—or at least, they do not have to plead with minorities in order to get their symbols recognized. To get a better idea of the symbolism and forms of recognition appropriate for a *federal* state, we can do no better than to look at the shining example of a successful, cohesive multinational federation, Switzerland. A true federation is a simultaneous union of two groups: a union of citizens and union of constituent units (what we have been generically calling 'provinces', but which in Switzerland are called 'cantons'). The 1999 Preamble declares: 'We, the Swiss people and Cantons..., adopt the following Constitution.' And Article 1 proclaims that 'The Swiss people and the Cantons of Zurich, Berne [... and 24 others, each identified by name] form the Swiss Federation.' This simultaneous union of people and constituent units is widely considered to be the fundamental point of distinction between federations and confederations, the latter being primarily unions of constituent units and not of common citizens.[38]

The invention in practice (and, for all intents and purposes, in theory as well) of this kind of dual-union can be traced to the reconstituting of the USA in 1789 after the brief post-revolutionary confederal experiment failed to

---

[37] The Constitutional Council famously declared in 1991 'la mention faite par le législateur du "peuple corse" composante du peuple français est contraire à la Constitution, laquelle ne connaît que le peuple français, composé de tous les citoyens français sans distinction d'origine, de race ou de religion' (décision no. 91–290 D.C. du 9 mai 1991, Loi portant sur le statut territorial de la Corse).

[38] See Karmis and Norman (2005b: 5–7). Of course the real world is never as neatly organized as the theoretical world. Actual 'federal political systems', to use Watts's neutral expression, can be more or less federal, confederal, or unitary depending on how relatively significant the union of either citizens or constituent units is. If they are both significant it is a clear federation. But if the 'union of citizens' aspect is relatively weak, as it is in the EU, then we will consider it to be at the confederal end of the spectrum. And if the 'union of constituent units' aspect is relatively weak, as it is in the case of Spain, then we will consider it to lie somewhere between the federal and the unitary-state end of the spectrum.

provide proper representation of, and governance for, the totality of citizens. The Preamble to that first truly federal state is well known:

We, the People of the United States, in Order to form a more perfect Union, establish Justice, insure domestic Tranquility, provide for the common defense, promote the general Welfare, and secure the Blessings of Liberty to ourselves and our Posterity, do ordain and establish this Constitution for the United States of America.

It is not as unambiguous in its dual-union as the very recently revised Swiss document.[39] Are the 'People of the United States' the people in each of the states that are being united, or are they the people of all of the states as united, or both? Presumably the founders did not expect this to be ambiguous for their contemporary audience. The citizens of this new union clearly identified more strongly with their states than they did with the new 'superstate'.

The 'more perfect Union' was the dual-union. The stated goals of the union seem distributed between the two types of unions: common defence and domestic tranquility seem more like goals relevant to the union of states, and promoting general welfare and securing liberty seem more like the goals of the union of citizens.[40]

---

[39] Interpretation of the precise meaning of this Preamble, or of what the framers intended, is far from an exact science. As Rakove (1996: 18) explains: 'The spare language of the Constitution does not make explicit the broader assumptions about government on which it is clearly based. The preamble to the Constitution cannot sustain the close theoretical analysis that has been lavished on the opening paragraphs of the Declaration of Independence.' *The Federalist* does not seem to discuss the idea of a 'more perfect union', although rival interpretations were certainly debated by Federalist and Anti-Federalists at the time (see Rakove 1996: 149).

[40] It should be noted, however, that a very similar language appears in the previous *Articles of Confederation, 1781*, which really was much more of a union of states than of citizens and called for a 'perpetual', but not perfect, union in its preamble. In the text of the *Articles* the words 'United States' are used as a plural, meaning 'the states united in this pact', not as a singular name of a state. Article III of that short-lived constitution proclaims that 'The said States hereby severally enter into a firm league of friendship with each other, for their common defense, the security of their liberties, and their mutual and general welfare, binding themselves to assist each other, against all force offered to, or attacks made upon them, or any of them, on account of religion, sovereignty, trade, or any other pretense whatever.' The grammar of the clause suggests that it is the common defence, liberties, and welfare of the *states* and not the citizens per se that is being protected by this 'firm league of friendship'. More than 200 years later, the vast majority of Americans clearly identify primarily with their country not their state. Accordingly, one suspects that the words 'a more perfect union', when evoked in political discourse, are interpreted to refer only to the union of citizens, and not to the union of states. Politicians call on Americans to live up to this ideal of 'a more perfect union' by overcoming divisions based on race, class, and ideology, not divisions based on the fact that they live in fifty different states. Consider Bill Clinton's reflections (2004: 951–2) on his Presidency, in which he draws specific attention to the Preamble: 'Had I helped to form a "more perfect union" by widening the circle of opportunity, deepening the meaning for freedom, and strengthening the bonds of community? I had certainly tried to make America the twenty-first century's leading force for peace and prosperity, freedom and security. I had tried to put a more human face on globalization by

The American and Swiss federations both evolved from pre-existing confederations of independent political units. Their challenge was to create a system of states and citizens that could also act like a single state. The challenge for federalism today in multinational societies is somewhat different. It will always be about getting different political units to act in concert, but also to get different *national communities* to cooperate. Although Switzerland has four distinct ethnolinguistic communities, the federation itself is not conceived of as a partnership of these four communities. It is, as we saw, a partnership of equal citizens and twenty-six cantons.

In principle, we might look to the Canadian constitution for advice about reconciling the architecture of federal constitutionalism with the special demands of minority nationalities. After all, Canada was arguably the first federal system to be set up primarily to accommodate cultural diversity: when three British North American colonies decided to create a new state with Britain's blessing, they created a four-province federation, including a new province with a francophone, Roman Catholic majority, because this was a condition of that group's membership.[41] But the Canadian constitutional document has never managed to reconcile all of the competing conceptions of the Canadian federation and its national communities. It went from being an extremely legalistic, 'plumbing-oriented' framework with virtually no symbolic content in 1867, to entrenching the symbolism of *one particular*

urging other nations to join us in building a more integrated world of shared responsibilities, shared benefits, and shared values; and I had tried to lead America through its transition into this new era with a sense of hope and optimism about what we could do, and a sober sense of what the new forces of destruction could do to us. Finally, I had tried to build a new progressive politics rooted in new ideas and old values, and to support like-minded movements around the world.' Note the complete absence of any concern here for the more perfect union of states within the federation. This is emblematic of the transition of the USA from a post-revolutionary confederation to a nation-state that happens to be federal.

[41] This case for Canada's originality in this respect has been argued by the British scholar of federalism, Murray Forsyth, as well as by the Canadian, Will Kymlicka (Forsyth 1989: 3–4, Kymlicka 1998c: 139). It is a matter of public record in the negotiation and ratification process of the new federation that both the creation of a French-speaking and Roman Catholic province, on the one hand, and the adoption of federalism rather than a more unitary state, on the other, were done to accommodate the distinctive situation of the people of Quebec. The first Canadian Prime Minister, Sir John A. Macdonald (1865) made no secret of the fact that he considered federalism to be 'an American abomination, a clear second choice to a unitary state' (Russell 1993: 18), but nevertheless, preferable to the then status quo of divided colonialism. Note also that negotiations leading to the establishment of the Canadian federation took place during and just after the bloody American civil war which many Canadian observers were inclined to blame in part on federalism. As far as Canada's pioneering role in multinational federalism goes, one hastens to add that, in the words of the constitutional historian, Russell (1993: 18–19) 'Not many English Canadians were committed [in the 1860s] to the long-term survival of French Canadians as a distinct collectivity.... Nonetheless, acceptance of the federal solution was the only possible basis on which leaders from the two sections of Canada could work together on a constitutional accord.'

multicultural, but not multi*national* conception of Canadian nationalism in 1982. Repeated attempts by both Canadian and Québécois political elites before and since the 1982 amendments have failed to incorporate the kind of recognition and autonomy demanded by French-Canadian or, latterly, Québécois nationalists.[42] Canada is also home to more than 600 aboriginal communities who have, for the most part, been denied the kinds of self-government rights they demand. Again, there have been high-level attempts to incorporate Aboriginal self-government as a 'third-order' of government (alongside provincial and federal governments) in the Canadian federation; but these too have never managed to be ratified. In short, it seems that Canada's failures to develop a radically multinational federal constitution are in many ways more instructive than the existing constitutional document itself. In a democratic context where the free assent of certain constituent groups is as important for the perceived legitimacy of the constitution as the formal assent of constituent units (the provincial and federal governments), Canadian constitutional history shows the perils of recognizing either too few or too many identities. A detailed look at this history, and the constitutional issues it has struggled with, would distract us from this chapter's survey of federalist options. I shall, however, append to this chapter a brief survey of this history and of some of the recent constitutional proposals Canadians have debated in the so-far futile attempt to incorporate the symbolism of rival nation-building projects within the same constitutional order. Canada has gone halfway down a number of constitutional roads. Other federations might want to turn down some of these same avenues and proceed further along, or they might want to drive right on by.

In order to complete this still-sketchy discussion of federalist options, it is worth taking brief note of issues that straddle the substantive–symbolic divide: the international recognition of federal units. At the more 'substantive' end of the spectrum we note the still mostly hypothetical option, recently discussed by Allen Buchanan, of some so-called 'intrastate autonomy regimes'—of which federalism is one kind—being subject to international law (Buchanan 2004: Ch. 9). His prime cases that might benefit from such arrangements include persecuted minorities (like Kosovars in Serbia-Montenegro) and Indigenous peoples with inherent rights to self-government. The basic idea is that international law, and the international community in general, could play a role in guaranteeing the autonomy and sovereignty of an autonomous unit within a state. The definitions of

---

[42] I hasten to add that the label 'Québécois nationalists' should not be thought to refer simply to an intellectual or political elite. Most francophone Quebeckers think of their group as a people or a nation, and in opinion polls they overwhelmingly support recognition of this 'fact' in the Canadian constitution.

federalism we have discussed so far say that this sovereignty is guaranteed by the constitution; but that can have little meaning when the majority government does not respect the rule of law.

Another federal issue with an international dimension involves the case of the rights of federal provinces to participate within international organizations. This is an important issue for member states of the EU. Federations like Germany, Belgium, or Spain grant exclusive or concurrent powers to their subunits; and yet it is only member-states or 'national' governments that have the right to participate in European Commission and the Council of the EU. Imagine that education is primarily the responsibility of the subunits in a given federation (as it is in Belgium, where it is run by the French-, Flemish-, and German-speaking Communities), and the EU is deliberating about aspects of a common education policy. Who should represent the Belgian federation in those deliberations? A 'national' education minister with very few actual powers, or the subunits' education ministers? Or some combination of both; or some subset of the latter? There are both practical and diplomatic problems with some of the possible solutions. There is also a nationalist dimension to some issues of representation in international institutions, even largely ceremonial ones like the Commonwealth, the Francophonie, the International Olympic Committee or FIFA. Part of what it is to be a nation, as national minorities consider themselves to be, is to be recognized as such in the 'international community'—the 'family of nations'. If national minorities cannot get this sort of recognition controlling subunits in federations, then they have additional motivation to seek it through secession.

4.4 CONCLUSION

This completes a long, and I hasten to add less-than-comprehensive, survey of issues for federal design. My primary aims have been conceptual and descriptive: to distinguish different elements of federal design—the six 'plumbing' issues in Section 4.2, and various types of symbolic recognition in Section 4.3—and to describe options, often with reference to those found in actual federations. The overall purpose of exploring these options, however, is normative and pragmatic: to find ways of reconciling competing nation-building projects within a common political space. Along the way I have given voice to some of the normative and political motivations that typically drive demands by minority and majority nationalists for or against specific options for federal reform. Neither the nationalists' demands nor their real reasons for the demands are in any way self-justifying. They are also not groundless. In a sophisticated political culture the arguments given in public deliberations will often be couched in language drawn from the best general theories of justice and democracy. Of course, liberal discourse can be appropriated in disingenuous ways. But given the interwoven history of liberalism and nationalism we explored in Chapter 1, there can also be a great deal of convergence between what nationalists demand and what liberal-democratic principles permit or even require. In Chapter 5 we will look more closely at the resources within these liberal-democratic theories to provide adequate justifications for federalist constitutional designs. While many of these theories were not designed with multinational states in mind, it is also surprising how useful they can be for justifying federalist arrangements that address the challenge of competing nationalisms. At the same time, we should also not be surprised to find that there are limits in the ability of such theories to resolve a range of normative disputes for which they were not originally developed. This is especially true when it comes to understanding and making sense of the demands for *recognition* that are at the heart of the rival nation-building projects.

After exploring principles relevant for multinational federal constitutionalism (in Chapter 5), we will 'test' these theoretical resources on one major design issue in particular (in Chapter 6)—perhaps the most challenging of all: the design and justification of a procedure for legalized secession from a multinational federation. In sum, throughout Chapters 5 and 6 we will enquire about whether, or to what extent, a multinational federation requires basic normative principles, and a conception of constitutionalism, that diverge from those that would be adequate in a merely 'territorial' federation or unitary state housing a single national community.

APPENDIX

CANADA'S CONSTITUTIONAL ODYSSEY: BOLD ADVENTURES AND CAUTIONARY TALES[43]

The 'constitutional politics of recognition'—the attempt by nationalists or other minority or majority leaders to have their group, and their particular conception of that group's identity, incorporated into the constitution of the

---

[43] The Odyssean imagery for Canada's constitutional history is hard to resist. For a much longer and more authoritative version of that voyage than will be presented here, see Russell (2004), entitled *Constitutional Odyssey: Can Canadians Become a Sovereign People?*

larger state—is a high-risk enterprise. And apart from civil war or a successful secession (so far), Canada has experienced most of these dangers first-hand. Canada began its sovereign existence with a constitution nearly bereft of recognitional symbolism. And in almost every one of the fourteen decades since then Canadians have debated the merits of moving on, in one direction or another, from this humble beginning. The groups vying for recognition (even before the use of this term), the kinds of recognition they demand, the formal and informal processes they have followed, and the forums of debate have all evolved dramatically over the years. This kind of change, especially of the groups demanding recognition and the nature of the identities they want recognized, seems inevitable in a pluralistic democracy. And herein lies one of the great challenges of the constitutional politics of recognition: the constitutional recognition of any given group's identity at a given time may appear antiquated, even to the group's progeny, in time; updating forms of recognition may prove difficult in a federation where constitutional amendment is generally difficult; and recognition of one group may invite a proliferation of demands for constitutional recognition by other groups. To shift Greek mythological metaphors, for constitutionalists this process may appear to be less of an odyssey and more like a Sisyphean life struggle, where every hard-fought success at recognizing a minority within the constitutional order leads quickly to a renewed struggle to cope with the demands of some other minority or of some other subgroup's conception of their identity.

Or maybe opening up a constitution to recognition claims is like a Pandora's box. Maybe it would be best never to open it for the purpose of entrenching recognition. Perhaps, in other words, constitutions should be neutral with respect to recognition and in particular with respect to the recognition of eternally contested conceptions of national identity. If ever there was a constitution that strived for 'recognitionally neutrality' it was the *British North America (BNA) Act of 1867*, Canada's founding constitution, which remained until 1982 an act of the British Parliament. As we noted in Chapter 4, Canada was born as a federation rather than a unitary state specifically to accommodate the demands of an ethnoreligious community. This widely accepted historical fact is still cited and taken into account by the Supreme Court of Canada in its rulings (even though the ancestors of those who made the demand no longer define their identity in ethnoreligious terms).[44] This is not, however, a fact or principle that betrays itself explicitly in the *BNA Act, 1867*. That extremely dry, legalistic document also eschews most of the celebration of individual rights and liberties to be found in the republican constitutions of the USA and France from less than a century

---

[44] See Supreme Court of Canada, *Reference* (1998: para. 59).

earlier. The Preamble to the original Canadian Constitution sums up the purpose of the new state very matter-of-factly:

Whereas the Provinces of Canada [*which would be divided into Quebec and Ontario*], Nova Scotia, and New Brunswick have expressed their Desire to be federally united into One Dominion under the Crown of the United Kingdom of Great Britain and Ireland, with a Constitution similar in Principle to that of the United Kingdom:

And whereas such a Union would conduce to the Welfare of the Provinces and promote the Interests of the British Empire:

And whereas on the Establishment of the Union by Authority of [the British] Parliament it is expedient, not only that the Constitution of the Legislative Authority in the Dominion be provided for, but also that the Nature of the Executive Government therein be declared:

And whereas it is expedient that Provision be made for the eventual Admission into the Union of other Parts of British North America....

In other words: these three British colonial provinces want to federate; their union will be in each of their interests as well as the interest of Britain; they will take responsibility for their own government; and they will eventually incorporate other British territories in North America (which will also be in both their interest and Britain's). Rather than 'liberty, equality, fraternity', the founders sought relief from a colonial arrangement that was no longer serving either colonists or the mother country.

Of course, the *BNA Act* was not really 'recognitionally neutral'. For all the reasons discussed in Chapter 2, no diverse state can be neutral with respect to ethnicity, and especially with respect to nation-building. For one thing, there is a clear reflection of British heritage throughout the Preamble and the following articles that would sit more comfortably with the descendents of British settlers than with the descendents of French settlers. For another, there is what we might call the *conspicuous absence* of recognition. The historical fact that it was the French Canadians' desire for self-government and autonomy that was the principal reason for having a federation rather than a unitary state does not even merit an 'And whereas...'. This would make it much harder for constitutional judges (first in the British Privy Council, and later in the Supreme Court of Canada) to take this fact into account when deciding on issues affecting Quebec's autonomy. And it leaves no constitutional trace of Quebeckers' long-held conception of Canada as a federation founded by two *peoples* (of French and British heritage), and not just by a collection of colonial provinces. The other example of conspicuously absent recognition, of course, concerns Aboriginal peoples, who are barely mentioned and given no special rights. The Constitution did not set an official language or languages, and this may appear to be neutral. But it led to almost a century of English being the de facto official language and the language of government, the civil service, and the military; which in turn, along with other economic and demographic factors, led to a federal government far more likely to pursue the interests and nation-building projects of the English-Canadian elites. Among the nation-building projects with the most impact was Canada's participation alongside the 'Mother Country' in the two world wars, conscription for which was bitterly opposed in Quebec.[45] The federal government was also given extensive power with which to pursue its nation-building agenda, including the extraordinary right to disallow the legislation of provincial governments.[46] Finally we must remember the special form of recognition that comes from the international community, to which Canada showed a decidedly 'Anglo' face for most of the first century after its independence (despite having two long-serving bilingual francophone Prime Ministers in that period). So even though it is considerably 'drier' than most modern constitutions, the *BNA Act, 1867* was far from 'recognitionally neutral'. For more than a century—until Quebec began to make more proactive use of the extensive nation-building powers it was accorded in the Constitution—the Canadian Constitution facilitated nearly unopposed nation-building in the image of the national majority group.

A further set of lessons for what we might call 'multinational federal constitutionalism' came from Canada's partly (or mostly) unsuccessful attempts to reinvent itself early in its second century. After decades of unsuccessful attempts by provincial and federal leaders, the first real overhaul of the constitutional order began in 1982 when, with substantial provincial consent, the government of the then Prime Minister Pierre Elliott Trudeau:

(*a*) 'repatriated' the Constitution, so that it was no longer an act of the British Parliament;

(*b*) added to it a Charter of Rights and Freedoms incorporating the standard list of civil and political rights, along with language rights for both anglophone and francophone minorities in different provinces, and recognition of the multicultural (that is, immigrant-led) diversity of Canada;

(*c*) added recognition of Aboriginal rights; and

---

[45] Consider the title of the 1989 book by the respected English-Canadian historian, J. L Granatstein, *A Nation Forged in Fire: Canadians in the Second World War: 1939–1945.*

[46] The power of 'disallowance' remains in the Canadian Constitution. But as Russell explains, 'Over time, the principle of provincial autonomy—self-government in those areas constitutionally assigned to the provincial legislatures—became so strongly held in the Canadian political system that the federal powers of reservation and disallowance...became politically unusable. This did not happen all at once. It occurred only because the idea that the provinces are not subordinate to but coordinate with the federal government became the politically dominant conception of Canadian federalism' (Russell 1993: 39).

(*d*) added an amending formula that would make it much more difficult to amend in the future.

In the years preceding these constitutional changes the Trudeau governments were also responsible for numerous major non-constitutional changes in Canadian government that had profound national-identity-transforming intentions and effects. These included making both English and French official languages, and promoting bilingualism in the civil service and the military; as well as creating or expanding 'national' social programmes, including health care, and 'equalization' programmes to transfer wealth from rich to poor provinces. In other words, a new kind of Canadian nationalism was emerging, one that incorporated francophones and immigrants into the Canadian nation much more readily than the previous Anglo-Canadian version. And this is what Trudeau was able to entrench in the Constitution.

But by turning a dry, legalistic document into what is sometimes called an 'aspirational' constitution, charged with values and symbolic content, Trudeau opened the door to further demands for recognition of visions of the country and its constituent parts that were not yet constitutionally acknowledged. First and foremost were the demands of Quebec nationalists (demands that were supported by a solid majority of francophones within the province) for constitutional recognition and for reconceiving Canada as a truly multinational federation, not merely a federation of ten equal provinces (Laforest 1995, 2001). The Province of Quebec had been the only province not to ratify Trudeau's constitutional amendments; but these amendments came into force nonetheless. So although Trudeau's Constitution did have legal force in Quebec, the federal government that succeeded Trudeau's tried to reconcile Quebec to the new Constitution by negotiating a package of amendments addressing both symbolic and substantive demands from Quebec. This package, known as the *Meech Lake Accord* of 1987, included major changes that fall under most of the first six headings listed in Section 4.2, broadly conceived: especially the division of powers, representation of Quebec in central institutions, and the amending formula (which would require the unanimous approval of provinces for a much greater range of amendments). Most notably or notoriously, however, the Accord called for 'the recognition that Quebec constitutes within Canada a *distinct society*'.

Although the Prime Minister of Canada, Brian Mulroney, and all of his provincial counterparts agreed to this Accord, it was not ratified by all of the provincial legislatures before the required three-year time limit. Explanations for the 'death of *Meech Lake*' have literally filled several books.[47] The simplest

---

[47] See, e.g. Cohen (1990, 1998), Fournier (1991), and Monahan (1991).

explanations focus on the opposition of the majority of English-speaking Canadians to official recognition of Quebec as a 'distinct society'. Some felt this was a claim that Quebec was 'better' than the rest of Canada; some felt this was inconsistent with the supposed equality of the provinces; and some feared that such recognition would only fuel (rather than appease) a form of minority nationalism that would ultimately be satisfied with nothing short of secession. More complex explanations for opposition to this Accord go beyond discomfort with the 'distinct society' clause. Among other things, opponents objected to the changes to the amending formula that would give every province a veto on most future constitutional changes. Since some of the other provinces and regions in Canada also sought changes to the Constitution, they feared their dreams would be much harder to realize if the *Meech Lake Accord* were passed first.

For this reason, in the crisis that followed the 'death of *Meech*' (during which polls in Quebec temporarily showed support for separation well above the 50 per cent level), a grand attempt was made over a two-year period to fashion a major constitutional revision that would incorporate all of the amendments in *Meech* along with numerous other amendments demanded by other regions and groups in Canada. In particular, some of the less populous provinces were demanding a radical revision of the federal parliament to enhance their power vis-à-vis the provinces of Quebec and Ontario which together have more than half of the total population. This process led to another agreement between the Prime Minister of Canada and his ten provincial counterparts that would be known as the *Charlottetown Accord* of 1992. This was a massive proposal for constitutional reform, incorporating fundamental changes to the parliamentary and judicial system, the creation of a new tier of Aboriginal self-government, the entrenchment of social and economic rights, and changes to federal-provincial relations that went beyond those in *Meech*.[48] It also greatly expanded the number of groups and 'characteristics' and visions of the country that would be officially recognized in the Constitution. I will quote only from this relatively short section at the outset of the long *Charlottetown* document. In the place of the *Meech Lake* clause recognizing Quebec as a distinct society, the proposal was that 'A new clause should be included as section 2 of the *Constitution Act, 1867* [the post-1982 name for the old *BNA Act, 1867*] that would express fundamental Canadian values. The Canada Clause would guide the courts in their future interpretation of the entire Constitution, including the *Canadian Charter of*

---

[48] When reprinted in reference books, the text of the *Charlottetown Accord* runs around twenty pages long.

Rights and Freedoms. This clause would be as follows (I will highlight key concepts in bold-face font):

(*a*) Canada is a **democracy** committed to a parliamentary and **federal** system of government and to the rule of law;

(*b*) the **Aboriginal peoples** of Canada, being the first peoples to govern this land, have the right to promote their languages, cultures and traditions and to ensure the integrity of their societies, and their governments constitute **one of the three orders of government** in Canada;

(*c*) **Quebec** constitutes within Canada a **distinct society**, which includes a French-speaking majority, a unique culture and a civil law tradition;

(*d*) Canadians and their governments are committed to the vitality and development of **official language minority communities** throughout Canada;

(*e*) Canadians are committed to racial and ethnic equality in a society that includes citizens from many lands who have contributed, and continue to contribute, to the building of a strong Canada that reflects its **cultural and racial diversity**;

(*f*) Canadians are committed to a respect for **individual and collective human rights** and freedoms of all people;

(*g*) Canadians are committed to the **equality of female and male persons**; and

(*h*) Canadians confirm the principal of the **equality of the provinces** at the same time as recognizing their diverse characteristics.

The *Charlottetown Accord* would never be ratified. It initially looked popular across the country, and provincial and federal leaders agreed to put it to a referendum (a procedure that was not constitutionally required). After an emotional campaign it was rejected in both Quebec and the rest of Canada. Again, the explanation for this rejection is complex and multifaceted involving conflicting values and principles to be sure, but also ignorance in the ways of constitutional law, lack of trust and confidence in particular political leaders, and all of the standard dynamics of political contests. Support shifted dramatically during the referendum campaign and almost everybody could find some aspect of the very long list of proposed changes to be uncomfortable with. (The Canada Clause, quoted above, was just a small part of the very long constitutional text in the Accord.) Many English-speaking Canadians continued to be suspicious of the recognition of Quebec as a distinct society. And this has led to the standard simplified explanation in Quebec nationalist circles that the *Charlottetown Accord* was rejected in Quebec because it did not go far enough (in recognizing Quebec and giving it new powers), and in the rest of Canada because it went too far.[49]

These recent Canadian episodes illustrate well the challenges of multinational federal constitutionalism and constitutional reform. A more detailed study of the *Meech* and *Charlottetown* proposals for constitutional reform would yield prime examples of each of the basic types of federal-design options (apart from a secession clause), along with insights about how they are interrelated and to how support or opposition is likely to revolve around visions of minority and majority nationalism. For the time being I have highlighted primarily the *symbolic* content of these constitutional accords rather than their proposed 'substantive' changes to the division of powers, central institutions, and so on. This Canadian experience shows the inherent difficulty for a truly multinational federation to find an uncontroversial middle ground between, if you will, a 'pre-modern federal constitutionalism' that espouses little more than an institutional framework with the minimum of public values and principles, on the one hand, and a 'postmodern federal constitutionalism' that attempts to incorporate both the standard liberal-democratic norms *and* the forms of recognition demanded by contemporary identity politics, on the other. I am not claiming that demands for symbolic recognition will always figure among the primary demands of minority nationalist movements seeking federalist reforms. Calculations have to be made about what is expedient and possible at any given moment in history. And as many of the Eastern European examples illustrate well, recognition alone is hardly sufficient. While Albanians might appear to have more recognition as 'a people' in the Macedonian constitution than Quebeckers have in the Canadian, there is absolutely no comparison between these groups when it comes to the real powers of self-government, self-determination, and nation-building. Nevertheless, it seems a safe assumption of federal politics that the more self-confident a national minority is in the exercise of what it sees as its inherent right to self-determination, the more difficulty it will have participating in a constitutional regime that does not recognize this 'fact'—especially if the constitution recognizes majority-national or pan-national ('equal citizenship') visions of the federal regime.

---

[49] This 'conventional wisdom' was repeated as recently as 2003 in the Canadian House of Commons by a (separatist) Bloc Québécois M. P. Claude Bachand: 'English Canada rejected the *Charlottetown Accord* because it gave too many powers to Quebec. Quebeckers rejected it because it did not give them enough powers' (*Hansard*, 27 October 2003).

5

Federal Constitutionalism II: Evaluating and Justifying Options for Federal Design

> We also want to 'defend and develop our own [French-Canadian] nationality'; but we think that is only part of our job; we believe that this special development can and must come about in conjunction with the development of a more general patriotism that *unifies us, without fusing us*, to 'the other elements that make up the population of Canada'.
> —Henri Bourassa (1904, my italics)[1]

> Federalism is a natural constitution for a body of states which *desire union and do not desire unity.*
> —A. V. Dicey (1914: preface to the 8th edn., my italics)[2]

5.1 INTRODUCTION: HYBRID THEORIES FOR HYBRID STATES

Any given federal system is a hybrid, lying somewhere on a continuum between a system of independent states and a unitary nation-state. Some federations or confederations, like Belgium or the EU, have relations between

---

[1] The passage comes from a response by Henri Bourassa—a leading intellectual, newspaper editor, and political figure from Quebec a century ago—to an argument by J.-P. Tardivel, himself the editor of the newspaper, *La Vérité*. The quotations within this quote are from an article by Tardivel. Bourassa at this time believed in the possibility and desirability of French-Canadians nurturing both their French-Canadian and pan-Canadian identities; Tardivel advocates a more exclusive French-Canadian nationalism that wishes 'to see founded at the time appointed by Providence' a French-Canadian nation-state. This debate is translated in Cook (1969: 147–51).

[2] For reasons that should be clear in the discussion of Dicey in Chapter 3, he did not think that it would have been a good idea for the UK or its Empire to give up on the advantages of unity, pure and simple. For the UK: 'This new constitutional idea of the inherent excellence of federalism is a new faith or delusion which deserves examination' (1914: preface).

their constituent units that more closely resemble international relations; while others, like Australia or Argentina, are much closer to the 'unitary nation-state' end of the spectrum. Federal constitutionalism and normative federal theory will also combine features found in theories for evaluating both international and 'intranational' institutions.[3] As Levy (2004: 168) observes, a federal constitution 'need not be imagined as an agreement among individuals seeking principles of justice. It could instead be understood as a kind of treaty, setting out the terms of ongoing peaceful coexistence and shared political life'. More controversially, but I think rightly, Levy (2004: 168) adds: '[T]he principles it embodies needn't even aspire to be fundamental principles of justice (which is not to say that they may be *unjust*)'. These constitutional principles must combine many apparently contradictory elements. They will be a mixture of principle and pragmatism, ideals and compromise, concern for the general welfare and respect for rival identities; aiming to promote both individual autonomy (close to what Isaiah Berlin called 'negative liberty') and collective autonomy (one of Berlin's forms of 'positive liberty'), and committed to reconcile the equality of citizens, the equality of provinces, and perhaps even the equality of founding peoples. To adapt the language of the later Rawls, the underlying morality of a multinational federal constitution will be neither a 'comprehensive moral conception' nor a mere 'modus vivendi' between rival factions; but rather a kind of 'overlapping consensus' appropriate for communities that, as Bourassa and Dicey put it in the quotes above, seek a union without complete unity or fusion.[4]

In short, it would be unwise to think that normative theorizing about federalism should have as its aim the development of a comprehensive theory of federal justice applicable equally to federations, be they at either the 'international relations' or the 'unitary state' ends of the spectrum of possible federal hybrids. My aim here will certainly be much more modest. First, I hope to show how a number of familiar principles from 'classic' (nation-state oriented) theories of democracy and constitutionalism are also appropriate for evaluating options for federal design. Second, I will suggest that this set of principles will need to be supplemented with some additional principles of mutual recognition. The idea here is not to gather elements into a general or fundamental normative theory from which philosophers could derive conclusions about the constitutional options that would be appropriate for any given federation. Rather it is to corral together a manageable set of principles

---

[3] Consider the title of a pioneering study of the federalism in terms of the paradigms of international relations, Simeon's *Federal-Provincial Diplomacy* (1972).

[4] I have explored possible parallels between principles of federalism and these Rawlsian concepts, which were intended for conceptions of justice in Norman (1994).

that could and should inform the debates and negotiations among political actors in federations or potential federations. Returning to some of the conceptual and normative distinctions drawn in Chapters 1 and 2, I will try to identify principles that both liberal democrats in general, and liberal nationalists in particular, should be willing to embrace. We have had a taste of most of these principles already. It is not possible to discuss the nature and rationale for various tools of nation-building and options for federal design without betraying the values and principles they are presumed to uphold or to violate. This chapter tries to make the content of these principles, along with an account of their applicability and shortcomings, a little more explicit.

5.2 PRINCIPLES DRAWN FROM 'CLASSIC' LIBERAL-DEMOCRATIC TRADITIONS: THEIR UTILITY AND LIMITS FOR MULTINATIONAL FEDERALISM

5.2.1 The Basic Rationale for Federating or Federalizing[5]

In order to understand what sorts of institutions or principles are appropriate for a political entity it is sometimes necessary to know why the entity came to exist or why ideally we should want it to. In short, what is the entity's basic purpose or rationale? This question is rarely asked in the context of contemporary political philosophizing about nation-states. It *was* in an earlier era, especially in the social-contract tradition and during the era of the founding of the first modern democratic states. Some version of the protection or promotion of 'life, liberty and the pursuit of happiness' of the individuals inhabiting the state is a good approximation of the rationale presupposed by liberal-democratic theory.[6] As we have noted already, by the time Rawls is writing, the rationale for the state per se is no longer a lively or open question.

---

[5] In cases where it matters how, or whence, a federation comes to be, we might use the verb 'to federate' when we are talking about the coming together of (relatively) independent polities, and 'to federalize' when it is a question of a previously centralized polity becoming a federation.

[6] The famous line comes, of course, from the US Declaration of Independence, adopted on 2 July 1776. The second paragraph of that Declaration illustrates clearly how such a 'rationale' for the state is useful for evaluating the institutional design or the governance of the state: 'We hold these truths to be self-evident, that all men are created equal, that they are endowed by their Creator with certain unalienable Rights, that among these are Life, Liberty and the pursuit of Happiness.—That to secure these rights, Governments are instituted among Men, deriving their just powers from the consent of the governed,—That whenever any Form of Government becomes destructive of these ends, it is the Right of the People to alter or to abolish it, and to institute new Government, laying its foundation on such principles and organizing its powers in such form, as to them shall seem most likely to effect their Safety and Happiness.'

His parties *assume* they will be cooperating in a state; their principal concern is with how to distribute the benefits and burdens of this cooperation. In a multinational federation, however, the question of the rationale for the union will become lively and relevant whenever debates about reform arise.

Imagine we want to evaluate some proposals for reforming, say, the division of powers, or the design of central institutions, for some federation F that contains a majority national community, N, and a minority national community, M. This evaluation will depend in part on (*a*) what the basic purpose or rationale for F was to begin with (e.g. why some previous polity or group of polities decided to federate or federalize), and (*b*) what the motivations for the proposed reforms are. Consider, for example, the 'best of the big, best of the small' rationale that dominated theories of federalism in the eighteenth and nineteenth centuries (which we discussed briefly in Chapter 3): that federations can combine the advantages of small, active democratic communities with the advantages of large empires without the main disadvantages of either. Clearly if this is the rationale behind F, then any proposed reforms should be evaluated, at least in part, by how well they help realize these specific kinds of advantages while avoiding the disadvantages. (This is not merely a hypothetical example: it is part of the basic argumentative structure for the specifically federalist architecture defended in *The Federalist*.[7]) If, however, the main purpose of F was to facilitate the mutual self-determination of, and peace between, two peoples, N and M, whose homelands overlap on the same territory, then it is very likely that a different division of powers and different central institutions would be chosen. The existence of legitimately divergent rationales for different federations is one reason why we will not expect a normative theory of federalism to propose common arrangements for them all.

How do we determine what the basic 'purpose' or 'rationale' for a federation is? In fact, this is likely to be a hotly contested issue in any federation contemplating reform. Even when looking at the same historical documents, debates, and constitution—as scholars and political figures from both the North and the South of the USA were in the decades leading to the Civil

---

[7] The papers in *The Federalist* discuss almost every aspect of government for the new republic. For discussion of the more specifically federalist parts see, e.g., papers 2, 9, 10, 15, 17, 39, and 51. These papers are reprinted in Karmis and Norman (2005a). *Federalist* 9 quotes Montesquieu at length in support of the view that 'a general Union of the States' or a 'confederate republic' is 'the expedient for extending the sphere of popular government, and reconciling the advantages of monarchy with those of republicanism'. In particular, quoting Montesquieu: 'A Republic of this kind, able to withstand an external force, may support itself without any internal corruptions.... As this Government is composed of small Republics, it enjoys the internal happiness of each; and with respect to its external situation, it is possessed, by means of the Association, of all the advantages of large Monarchies.'

War—there can be fundamental disagreements about a federation's *raison d'être*. This is also very likely to be the case in multinational federations where, among other things, M and N might always have had different reasons for wanting (or not wanting) to be federated. And we must not forget that national communities, like M and N in this example, rarely think in unison: within either community there are likely to be competing conceptions of the basic rationale for the federation just as there are for the state or the government in general within uninational states. To add to the diversity of beliefs about the basic rationale, we also observe that views about the rationale change over time. Two parties may even agree that F was founded for some particular basic reason, but argue that this reason is no longer valid or relevant and that it has been supplanted by another. For example, it is a matter of public record that the EU project was undertaken in part for the purpose of preventing future wars between the great European powers.[8] The prospect of such a war now seems so remote that one can hardly expect this rationale to figure prominently in debates about how best to reform EU institutions.[9] Presumptions about the basic rationale for political entities are the very building blocks of ideologies, and multinational states host numerous conflicting ideological currents including different forms of nationalism. Clever constitutional engineering and politics in these contexts will have to propose institutions that can be embraced from different ideological perspectives for different reasons; a feat that will not always seem possible and may require political modesty. Perhaps it is not for nothing that the glorious republican rationales of 'life, liberty and the pursuit of happiness', or 'liberty, equality, fraternity', are replaced in the Canadian and Australian constitutions

---

[8] See, for example, the texts by some of the founders of the movement that eventually led to the EU (Spinelli and Rossi 1944; Schuman 1950, reprinted in Karmis and Norman 2005a). See also Monnet (1955), McKay (1999, especially chs. 1–3), and Burgess (2000: chs. 1–3).

[9] Or consider two other examples of shifting federal rationales. The Confederate States of America—the Southern breakaway republic that precipitated the American Civil War—was clearly founded with a primary rationale of preserving slavery and the economy based upon it. Article I, section IX.4 of its constitution proclaimed: 'No bill of attainder, ex post facto law, or law denying or impairing the right of property in negro slaves shall be passed.' Now one imagines that even if the Southern secession had prevailed, eventually the new republic too would have outlawed slavery. But it is by no means clear what the loss of this original rationale for the Confederate States would have implied for constitutional reform (apart from repealing the articles in the constitution that referred to slavery). That is, it is not obvious that the Confederate States would have had to rejoin the USA once they too banned slavery. Or take a less extreme example. After years of failed attempts by Britain and its British North American provinces to create a new country to the north of the USA, three of the provinces forming a continuous frontier were moved quickly to band together in part through fear of an impending attack by the Yankee armies following their victory in the South in 1865. This rationale for the existence of a united Canada clearly disappeared long ago; but again, it does not follow that the Canadian provinces should have disbanded once the threat receded. Other rationales and reasons for remaining federated emerged or became more prominent.

with the rather less inspired instruction that the Parliament is 'to make Laws for the Peace, Order, and good Government'.[10]

5.2.2 Classical Democratic Theory

We have already noted that traditional democratic theory has difficulty with resolving disputes about borders. It guides 'the people' through issues about how they should rule themselves but it cannot help much with deciding who the relevant self-governing people should be. That said, if the vast majority of people in a region, county, or city strongly desire self-government rights, this surely appeals to basic democratic intuitions even if this fact is far from sufficient to justify granting such autonomy. (It may, for example, merely reflect the selfish desires of a wealthier population trying to create its own political jurisdiction in order to avoid transferring as much of its wealth to poorer neighbours within its current jurisdiction, and principles of justice may tell against such a reform.)

Traditional democratic theory does, however, provide at least two powerful justifications for federalism. The first is a large part of the 'best of the big, best of the small' argument first articulated by Montesquieu in the mid eighteenth century. The idea is that democratic deliberation and participation work best in smaller, closer settings; so there is a democratic advantage to dividing a larger polity up into smaller subunits with real decision-making and administrative autonomy. This argument, as noted, was an important part of the case in *The Federalist*, and it would undergo its first sustained empirical investigation in Tocqueville's *Democracy in America*. It is noteworthy that this argument works just as well in uninational states (i.e. with an ethnoculturally homogeneous population) as it does in multinational states. Of course, once your subunits grow from Rhode Island size to California size (over 35 million), the argument loses some of its intuitive sociological appeal.

Another classic democratic argument for federalism also finds its heritage in *The Federalist* and *Democracy in America*, although this one probably makes a stronger case in ethnically divided societies than it does in ethnically homogenous ones. Any sophisticated democratic theory—and virtually every serious democratic theory since Tocqueville—is concerned about the possible 'tyranny of the majority'. Part of this worry concerns the possibility of permanent minorities. You are willing to accept the legitimacy of majority rule as long as you believe there is a fair chance that you will find yourself in

---

[10] See the Canadian *Constitution Act, 1867*, section 91; and the *Commonwealth of Australian Constitution Act, 1900*, Part V, section 51.

the majority from time to time. Ethnolinguistic and ethnoreligious minorities are among the most vulnerable groups because they can find themselves perpetually outvoted on matters of primary importance to their well-being and sense of self-respect. An insensitive majority can always win votes that set an official language or religion, or that enact policies running counter to the minority's basic values and beliefs. But if such groups are territorially concentrated and enjoy federal autonomy over certain sensitive jurisdictions (e.g. education), they can shield themselves from the will of the majority without at the same time violating the principle of majority rule by imposing their will on the majority. In such situations, federalism is an ingenious solution to this potential problem for democratic theory—or at least a partial solution. The mapping out of federal subunits will almost always trap new minorities within minority-controlled subunits (these new minorities may well be members of the national majority) or strand minorities outside of the subunits their members control. For these reasons federal solutions to the problem of the 'tyranny of the majority' will usually have to be supplemented with other forms of minority rights.[11]

5.2.3 Deliberative Democratic Theory

Put another way, classical democratic theory can deal with some of its 'permanent-minority problems' through the use of a federal division of powers. But in addition to the need for minority rights to deal with 'stranded minorities', there is also the problem of how the province-dominating minorities fare in decision-making within jurisdictions that remain in the control of the central government. Long before the idea of 'deliberative democracy' charmed the community of political theorists in the 1990s, the more progressive federal and divided societies instituted procedures and forms of enhanced representation for minorities in parliaments to protect them from intended or unintended tyranny of the majority. Some procedures, such as veto rights in parliament for minority blocs, may simply appear undemocratic (if nevertheless justified on grounds of justice). However, they can also be seen as clever mechanisms for promoting cross-group deliberation by equalizing blocking power. They force majorities to seek consensus policies. Other long-standing mechanisms in legislatures that should appeal to contemporary deliberative democrats include rules that allow for enhanced and guaranteed representation for minority groups,

---

[11] For a canonical elaboration of the argument that 'federalism is not enough', see Cairns (1992, 1995).

along with procedures to ensure that diverse voices are actually heard in public or parliamentary debates. This logic extends to the design of electoral systems including policies promoting public financing for election campaigns, equal access to television, and so forth.[12]

In other respects, federalism can be seen as essentially at odds with the main thrust of deliberative democracy, and it is perhaps no surprise that the federal idea is completely absent from the most prominent deliberative democratic theories. More than any other current theories in democratic theory, deliberative democracy has been concerned with giving real weight to the views, ideas, concerns, and discourse styles of the disadvantaged, especially minorities. But the aim has always been to enhance their *voice*, while the idea of federal autonomy is that it is essentially a form of *exit*. If a minority-controlled province has exclusive power over education, they do not have to listen to, or patiently try to persuade, the majority on matters of educational policy.[13]

There is one area of federal theory and practice that could be improved by deliberative democratic theory: the processes for reforming and amending the constitution, especially large-scale reforms or overhauls of a sort that might be necessary if existing federal constitutions are to live up to some of the more progressive ideals envisaged in Chapter 4. Most federations have amending formulas that make their constitutions difficult to change. As we discussed, they typically give veto power to either individual provinces or a relatively small block of provinces. As with any veto, this enhances the 'voice' and the bargaining power of its holders. Others will have to try hard to convince the veto holders by listening to their objections and then by modifying their own arguments or the proposal itself, or perhaps by providing other kinds of incentive or compensation. In many federations, including the EU, this kind of negotiating has been conducted primarily by political elites (hence the title of Simeon's famous book, noted earlier, *Federal-Provincial Diplomacy*). Some previously elitist federal political cultures have recently turned more populist and participatory, with the citizens of member-polities voting to approve federal reforms for the first time. These debates, however, have taken place in the absence of large-scale institutional reforms to develop official forums in which citizens might participate democratically.

---

[12] See Reilly (2001), entitled *Democracy in Divided Societies: Electoral Engineering for Conflict Management*, for a theory applied specifically to case studies in Australia, Fiji, Sri Lanka, Northern Ireland, and elsewhere.

[13] The ultimate form of exit, of course, is secession. In Chapter 6 I will argue for rights of secession that follow from the basic logic of federalism. Such a proposal, however, is pro-deliberation. I will argue that federal theory would make secession possible and legal, but difficult enough to discourage secessionist politics in otherwise just democratic federations. Presumably this would provide more incentives for minority nationalists to cooperate within the federation rather than to mobilize support to leave it.

Consequently, experiences with attempts at large-scale 'democratic' overhauls of mature federations in recent years—most notably in Canada, Belgium, and the EU—have not been particularly positive or inspiring. Peter Russell has dubbed these attempts 'mega constitutional politics', which goes way 'beyond disputing the merits of specific constitutional proposals and addresses the very nature of the political community'. According to him:

> Precisely because of the fundamental nature of the issues in dispute—their tendency to touch citizens' sense of identity and self-worth—mega constitutional politics is exceptionally emotional and intense. When a country's constitutional politics reaches this level, the constitutional question tends to dwarf all other public concerns. (Russell 1993: 75)

Mega-constitutional reform debates exhibit many of the traits that most interest theorists of deliberative democracy, including deep distrust and mutual incomprehension between majorities and different minorities on issues that cut close to diverse identities and fundamental values.[14] But so far this kind of debate has been a much less appealing forum for scholarly study by deliberative democrats than the 'town hall'.[15]

5.2.4 Consequentialist Democratic Theory

By consequentialist democratic theory I refer to what has surely been the dominant tradition in the theory of government throughout the history of political thought: roughly, the idea that the best decision-making institutions and structures are those that are most likely to make the best decisions over the long run. It need not be a utilitarian theory in the sense that one's criterion for the 'best' decisions can itself be non-consquentialist and even deontological. It is the idea that Rawls has called 'imperfect procedural justice' and that has gone under various names such as the 'best-results' theory of

---

[14] According to Russell (1993: 74), mega constitutional politics also exhibits the 'qualities of a soap opera: if engaged in over a long period of time, it becomes extremely boring; yet all along it remains gripping as to the final outcome—which never seems to come'.

[15] This may have something to do with the fact that most deliberative democratic theorists are American, and the USA is one federation that has not attempted to overhaul its constitution in the post-war era. For an account of the dynamics of failed constitutional reform on a much smaller scale by an American theorist sensitive to the ideals of deliberative democracy, see Mansbridge's *Why We Lost the ERA* (1986). Elster (1988) gives an abstract analysis of issues relevant to constitution making within a constituent assembly, although he is not particularly concerned in this essay with the special issues arising in a multinational federation or with the process of reforming rather than writing a constitution. For analyses of Canadian constitutional debates that explicitly use contemporary deliberative democratic theory, see Chambers (1996, 2001) and Leydet (2001).

democracy. Although not all theorists of deliberative democracy are consequentialists in this way, a consequentialist could be a deliberative democrat if his or her main reason for enhancing the quality of deliberation was based on a conviction that this would lead to better decisions and better government generally. Many of the most sweeping arguments for and against federalism have also been consequentialist in this way. In Chapter 3 we saw some of the traditional consequentialist arguments *against* federalism: that it would lead to conservative, inflexible, weak, and morally regressive government. All of the components of the 'best of the small, best of the big' argument are also consequentialist; and so the argument for the relevance of this theoretical tradition will be parallel to that discussed under the heading of 'classical democratic theory', above. The smaller polities of federal provinces are presumed to be better able to understand and respond to their own needs than are distant central governments. And by federating with their neighbours they enhance their economic prosperity and military security as well as the mobility and autonomy of their citizens.

Related consequentialist arguments for federalism play up the way different provinces can serve as 'policy laboratories', with each province, in effect, testing out different policies and programmes for dealing with problems that are common to all of the provinces. Programmes (say, to reduce unemployment, welfare dependency, illiteracy, or drunk driving) that work particularly well in one province will tend to be copied in others; and programmes that do not work as well as those in other provinces will tend quickly to be dropped. Federalism also facilitates what might account to a market for residents, firms, or capital that can move from province to province depending on which one creates the most attractive mix of relative advantages.[16] If such a market operates efficiently, the end result should be a competitive raising of standards in all provinces.[17] Of course, as with any market proposal, it is also conceivable that such a market could foster a 'race to the bottom' where provinces do better by lowering social standards than raising them. My point here is not that federalism always produces better consequences, but simply that consequentialist reasoning is a useful way to evaluate federal designs.

Most of the arguments sketched in this section work just as well (or badly) for uninational or multinational states (although in some multinational

---

[16] For an excellent recent discussion of this mechanism, see Levy (forthcoming: sect. I). See also Buchanan (1995).

[17] Probably the most exhaustively studied example of this mechanism concerns the federalization of corporate law in the USA. Each state has its own corporate law and competes for corporate headquarters—a competition that Delaware wins hands-down. For a very consequentialist defence of this competition, see Easterbrook and Fischel (1991).

federations, 'competitive federalism' may be less effective if mobility across provincial boundaries is restricted by language barriers or by ethnic or religious intolerance). We have also discussed how consequentialist arguments can look even stronger for multinational states where federal autonomy protects an ignored, misunderstood, or disliked minority from the 'tyranny' (and sometimes even something approaching real unqualified, un-scare-quoted tyranny) of majoritarian government in the centre. In principle, consequentialist democratic reasoning could do much to guide the design of a 'rational' division of powers, representation scheme in the central parliament, amending formula, and so on. In actual constitutional debates in federations one finds a good many arguments for why reforms would lead to more efficient and effective government overall (e.g. government that is less costly, with less waste from two orders of government delivering the same services, or more responsive to citizens' needs). And this is surely a good thing, not least because debates about such consequences can focus on empirical evidence that both sides of a debate have to take seriously.

Consequentialist reasoning is likely to be less useful in understanding or justifying federal reforms based on considerations of identity; and this may be one reason why identity-based demands are often baffling for members of the national majority who are much more likely to be 'in denial' of their own nationalism. Consider, for example, minority demands for recognition and other forms of constitutional symbolism (Quebec's long-standing demand to be recognized constitutionally as 'a distinct society' or 'a people' being a prime example). Minorities themselves may claim that it is important for purely symbolic reasons that the state recognize their status and role. Majorities may find it hard to believe that minorities would press so hard for something that did not in some way enhance their powers (say, because the recognition affected constitutional court interpretations in the minority's favour), and hence they might become suspicious of such non-consequentialist arguments. Now when political representatives of minorities demand more autonomy, more enhanced representation in the centre, or a constitutional veto, they will almost always use consequentialist arguments of a sort we have discussed already. But these arguments will probably not fully capture the normative force behind the demands. The missing element is perhaps best captured in a case where a demand for political autonomy is made even without much hope that it will lead to better government per se, as when Berlin (1969: 157) attempts to articulate the root desire for decolonization:

Although I may not get 'negative' liberty at the hands of the members of my own society, yet they are members of my own group; they understand me, as I understand them; and this understanding creates within me the sense of recognition that leads the most authoritarian democracies to be, at times, consciously preferred by their members to the most enlightened oligarchies, or sometimes causes a member of some newly liberated Asian or African state to complain less today, when he is rudely treated by members of his own race or nation, than when he was governed by some cautious, just, gentle, well-meaning administrator from outside.

Writing in 1958, Berlin (1969: 157) calls this 'the heart of the great cry for recognition on the part of both individuals and groups, and in our own day, of professions and classes, nations and races'. It is, to put it inelegantly, a decidedly non-consequentialist cry.

In general, consequentialist theories of democracy will be challenged by any claim that certain individuals or groups have a *moral right* to participate in a political process, and that they have this right even if the granting of this right can be shown to lead to worse decision-making or government in the long run.[18] Thus any argument for or against federal options based on intrinsic or inherent rights of certain kinds of groups to exercise certain kinds of powers would probably be non-consequentialist. This, of course, is the essence of nationalist arguments for the supposed right of nation self-determination (even though nationalists also clearly believe that the members of their nation will be better off if they govern themselves for all of the reasons cited earlier in this section). We will discuss how principles of recognition might fit with other normative theories of federalism in Section 5.3.

5.2.5 Classical Constitutionalism

So far we have looked at the relevance of various 'traditional' or 'classical' normative theories and values (i.e. those developed for, and used in, nation-states) for the justification of federalism or of proposals for federal reform. Given that many such reforms will involve constitutional changes, it is also important to consider the relevance of 'traditional' normative theories about constitutions themselves. 'Constitutionalism is the idea...that government can and should be legally limited in its powers, and that its authority depends on its observing these limitations' (Waluchow 2004). Modern federal systems, as understood from Chapters 3 and 4, fit squarely within the constitutionalist tradition: each order of government derives its powers, authority, and limits

---

[18] A prime example of such a theory would be one based on the demands of political equality (see, e.g. Beitz 1990). See also Williams's sustained argument for 'the right to fair legislative representation' (1998). Although there are many theorists who argue against consequentialist or best-results theories of democracy, almost nobody draws out the explicit implication that they would remain committed to their non-consequentialist theory even if it could be shown to lead consistently to worse government. There has always been a 'have your cake and eat it too' quality about many non-consequentialist theories of democracy.

from the constitution, and neither order of government can unilaterally change the constitution. Nevertheless, most normative writings on constitutionalism focus entirely on the justification of this idea within the presumed context of the homogeneous nation-state. The principle challenge of constitutionalism within contemporary debates has been to explain and justify why democrats should believe in 'self-binding' or 'precommitment' strategies that place constraints and limits on majoritarian democratic decision-making. The leading solutions to this alleged 'paradox of democracy' have tried to show that 'without such constraints democracy becomes weaker, not stronger' (Elster 1988: 9). As Sunstein (2001a: 10) puts it: 'In a deliberative democracy, one of the principal purposes of a constitution is to protect not the rule of the majority but democracy's *internal morality*' (my italics). In the unitary state, constitutionalism safeguards democracy's internal morality in numerous ways that are quite familiar, for example, by entrenching basic political and civil rights that cannot be violated by regular legislation, by protecting democratic processes from democratic excesses (such as disenfranchizing certain groups or modifying electoral constituencies to suit the ruling party), by protecting a private sphere from public majority rule, by taking some issues off the ordinary political agenda, and so on.[19] Constitutional provisions maintain their special power in so far as they are (*a*) relatively difficult to amend, and (*b*) upheld by an independent judiciary with widely respected legitimacy.

In multinational federal states, citizens will also want their constitutions to safeguard democracy in all of these ways. But they will find standard discussions of the *purpose* of constitutions to be insufficient for their societies—especially to the extent that they think of the constitution as a kind of 'treaty' governing the relations between their 'national' community and the other constituents of the federation. Sunstein sums up the uninational perspective well when he declares that 'the central goal of a constitution is to create the preconditions for a well-functioning democratic order, one in which citizens are genuinely able to govern themselves' (Sunstein 2001a: 6). Again, the notion of 'citizens governing them*selves*' is always going to be much more complicated in multinational federations where citizens are simultaneously members of two (or more) 'selves', conceived of as self-governing political communities (such as provinces) or as historic national communities. They will be concerned not only about the challenges of *governing* democratically but also about the '*selves*'—how they are recognized, defined, shaped, or protected, and how they relate to each other and to the citizenry. Although

---

[19] See Sunstein (2001a: 96–101) for an impressive 8-point list of 'precommitment' strategies.

contemporary discussions of constitutionalism tend to focus entirely on the 'governing' and not the 'self' part of self-governing, this was not always the case. According to James Tully, when the language of modern constitutionalism emerged in the seventeenth and eighteenth centuries, it was in opposition to both 'ancient constitutionalism', based on custom and irregularity, and 'preconstitutional societies', where life was presumed to be nasty, brutish, and short (Tully 1995: 39–40). By the time of the 1789 French *Declaration of the Rights of Man and Citizen*, the 'picture of the modern constitution', for Tully, 'is of a culturally homogeneous and sovereign people establishing a constitution by a form of critical negotiation. ... The constitution founds an independent and self-governing nation-state with a set of uniform legal and representative political institutions in which all citizens are treated equally, whether their association is considered to be a society of individuals, a nation or a community'.[20] Tully's own argument is that the nation-state nationalism inherent in this dominant model of constitutionalism must now, at least in the case of diverse societies, be 'informed by a spirit of mutual recognition and accommodation of cultural diversity' (Tully 1995: 209). Of course, this has been a major theme in political philosophy over the last decade and a half. Again, in Section 5.3, I will suggest some ways that these kinds of recognition and accommodation can be realized within a multinational federal constitution. In the terminology proposed by Stepan (2005), diverse federations need a form of constitutionalism that can be both 'demos-constraining' and 'demos-enabling'.

5.2.6 Contractualist Constitutionalism

There is one final tradition worth examining when searching for relevant tools from 'classical' normative and constitutionalist theories. This is an idea we have appealed to at numerous points and which in fact is embedded in the title of this book, *Negotiating Nationalism*: namely, that an appropriate design for a multinational federation is the one that would be agreed upon, under reasonably fair and favourable circumstances, by parties representing the citizens and constituent units of the federation. In principle, this contractualist ideal incorporates all of the normative elements we have already discussed, since wise and reasonable parties to such a negotiation would obviously take them into account (e.g. they would want to prevent a tyranny of the majority, to promote progressive deliberation, good government, and

---

[20] Tully (1995: 41). See Tully (1995: 85–91) for an analysis of the French *Declaration*.

so on).[21] There is something so obviously right about this ideal. Just as there is obviously something unsettling about the idea of a historic national minority being forced to work within an arrangement that it could not reasonably be expected to accept voluntarily.

Yet, as stated, this contractualist federalist ideal is far too vague to provide much specific guidance for our normative theorizing about a just multinational federation. Moreover, the most basic attempts to clarify it as a procedure or method run into issues that seem as controversial as the ones we are trying to solve with the method itself. Consider the following questions.

5.2.6.1 How abstract should the initial bargaining situation be?

Surely we would not be expecting something as abstract as Rawls's 'original position', where the parties to the negotiation know nothing about their own identity or of the society or societies for which they are selecting basic principles. It would probably not even be as abstract as the next stage in Rawls's so-called 'four-stage sequence', the 'constitutional convention', where

> the veil of ignorance is partially lifted. The persons in the convention have, of course, no information about particular individuals: they do not know their own social position, their place in the distribution of natural attributes, or their conception of the good. But in addition to an understanding of the principles of social theory, they now know the relevant general facts about their society, that is, its natural circumstances and resources, its level of economic advance and political culture, and so on.... Given their theoretical knowledge and the appropriate general facts about their society, they are to choose the most effective just constitution, the constitution that satisfies the principles of justice and is best calculated to lead to just and effective legislation. (Rawls 1971: 197)

Rawls himself never really considered the special challenges of federal constitutionalism, let alone multinational federalism—a fact betrayed in part by his use of 'society' and 'political culture' in the singular rather than the plural. He imagines a plurality of conceptions of the good but not a plurality of political identities. In order to make this 'constitutional convention' a little less abstract and more relevant to the multinational federal challenge we will have to try to answer some of the following questions.

---

[21] In Rawlsian language, we can look at the idea of a contractual situation as an 'expository device'. Any conditions we apply in our favoured description of such a hypothetical situation can and must be argued for on their own: the contractual story is supposed to help draw out the implication of the assumptions it embodies. See Rawls (1971: 21, 587).

5.2.6.2 What groups or 'units' are the parties representing in the negotiations?

Our answer to this question will have a big impact on the shape of the final arrangement. Yet surely there is no way to answer this from within the contractualist logic itself. It is also problematic to try to answer it 'factually', as we saw in discussions about nationalism and nation-building in Chapters 1 and 2. If we imagine that the proper negotiation should take place between national communities, we may find ourselves being co-opted by nationalist ideologies in ways that Brubaker has warned against. That is, we may end up, in Brubaker's language, reifying political fictions, treating nations as entities rather than contingent events. Again, virtually all sociologists of nationalism agree that these groups and their identities are in continual flux, and also that they are not in any sense 'natural' features of the social world, but are rather constructed by more or less deliberate political projects, and in particular by previously existing political jurisdictions and regimes. In practical terms, this means that if we are looking at the groups existing in a particular country that is contemplating federalization, we are necessarily dealing with groups whose identity and even very existence may be largely determined by the political arrangements that currently exist. But if we radically change the institutions through federalization, these very identities or 'selves' are likely to be gradually but substantially transformed. Why, one might ask, should we privilege the 'corrupted' national 'selves' that pre-dated the federation and that were merely the products of perhaps very non-ideal and unjust pre-existing arrangements? Whatever one thought of Michael Sandel's critique of Rawls's individualist contractualist theory of justice—as a theory that absurdly presupposed that a self could be prior to its ends—one should surely be worried about any abstract contractual situation that treats particular nations as existing 'eternally' and prior to political arrangements.[22]

5.2.6.3 Who are the parties representing the constituent groups?

Now one way to salvage the contractual metaphor is to think of it in much less abstract terms. So we imagine an actual situation where it might seem clear who the relevant groups are. Even if they are themselves political constructs derived from generations or centuries of non-ideal political arrangements, they may simply be the groups that in the real world have to be contended with. (For example, when Iraq was drafting its constitution in 2005, it was clear that the Kurds, the Sunnis, and the Shiites were the groups that would do

---

[22] See Sandel's famous critique in Sandel (1982), and a critique of the critique (with which I am sympathetic) in Kymlicka (1989: 51–65).

the negotiating, no matter how historically and politically contingent these identities were in fact.) Or to put it even more concretely, we may be talking about the reform of some actual federation, and we may decide that the relevant groups are simply the currently defined provinces. If this is how we are thinking about a minimally abstract contractual situation, we still have to think about which parties should get to negotiate on behalf of these groups, what 'point of view' should they be adopting, what motivations should they have, and whose interests do they have to take into account. For example, will they be hard-core nationalists? Or should they represent a more accommodating perspective? We have already emphasized at several points that most members of national minorities in advanced multinational states have overlapping national identities for both their 'minority nation' and the national state. How do we ensure that both of these identities are represented by parties to the (hypothetical) negotiation?

5.2.6.4 *What is the no-agreement 'default' position?*

One of the attractions of contractualist reasoning is that it aims to show us the results of a truly free and fair negotiation. But again, the conditions of 'freedom' and 'fairness' in a contractualist bargaining situation will be highly contested. For example, a free bargain is typically thought of as one that parties can freely choose *not* to make. If we are thinking about the terms of federation or confederation for independent states (such as the six founding members of the European Economic Community in 1957), then it is reasonable to think of the status quo of independence as the no-agreement position. But what should be the no-deal option when we think through, say, the appropriate terms of federation in a unitary state, particularly one with a long history of oppressing, or at least not recognizing, its national minorities?[23] If the status quo is already unjust, and if this is the no-agreement point, minorities may be 'coerced' into accepting only a slight improvement rather than the realm of autonomy and the freedom of nation-building they 'deserve'. And yet, for reasons discussed at the outset of Chapter 3, it does not seem appropriate to model federal negotiations by imagining that full independence for any national minority would be the no-agreement point. This

---

[23] Bauböck (2000: 372–4) has rightly emphasized the potential need for different normative theories to evaluate federal arrangements depending on the type of design problem we are trying to solve. In particular, he recommends distinguishing the following questions: (*a*) why *federate* rather than stay together? (*b*) why *transform* a unitary state into a federal one? and (*c*) why *maintain* a federation rather than centralize the state or break it apart? To these questions we might add a fourth: (*d*) why *reform* the constitution of a federation one way rather than another (or rather than maintain the federal status quo)?

might be how we would think of federating in a world of 600 or 800 nation-states with clearly defined borders and well-established political cultures, national identities, and governance structures. But why should that be thought of as an appropriate idealization for federal theorizing in *our* world? This would make for an especially unhelpful guide to negotiation parameters in the very states where federalization is most needed. As it is, national majorities in ethnically divided unitary states tend to be so distrustful of the 'loyalty' of their national minorities that federalism is an 'F-word' that dare not be uttered in constitutional discussions.[24] This was certainly the case throughout most of the former Communist countries in Europe, apart from a few exceptions where minorities held extraordinary bargaining power.[25] But imagine how much more difficult it would be for minorities even to get to the table to bargain for limited federal autonomy if it were understood that they could opt for independence if they did not like what was on offer?

In short, thinking about constituent groups negotiating the terms of their partnership in fair and reasonable conditions is a potentially useful way of identifying appropriate federal arrangements. But it looks exceedingly difficult to refine this ideal into the sort of normative methodology we find in sophisticated contractualist theories of justice. *Answers to the very questions we are trying to resolve will have to be presupposed in order to make the method work.* And of course, different constituent groups—especially minority and majority nationalists—are unlikely to agree on these various methodological presuppositions.

In Section 5.3 I shall propose, in effect, a different way of salvaging the ideal of a fair negotiation of the terms of federal partnership—or a negotiation on the mutual limitations of nation-building projects—by thinking about concrete and complementary forms of recognition.

5.3 CONSTITUTIONAL RECOGNITION

A theory of constitutionalism is not complete without a theory of recognition. In Chapter 4 I tried to dispel the idea that 'recognition' was some kind of

---

[24] I owe this observation to Will Kymlicka, who attributes such attitudes to many of even the most liberal political actors and analysts in Eastern and Central Europe. See also McGarry (2002: 435) and Stepan (2005: 256).

[25] For example, for obvious geopolitical reasons, Ukrainian Crimea, with its ethnic Russian majority, and home to the Russian navy's Black Sea Fleet, was able to gain a unique status as an 'Autonomous Republic' within the Ukraine. See, e.g. Solnick (2002: 195–9).

'postmodern' battle cry for minorities. All modern constitutions have managed to lavish recognition of the nation-building (or 'nation-built') aspirations of majorities. Indeed, 'recognitional neutrality' is probably impossible in states with nationalizing majorities and minorities—especially where the majority nation shares a name with the state—because states get recognition as members of the international community. What is possible, however, is some kind of 'recognitional parity' or mutual recognition for national communities in a multinational state. In this section, we will look at some of the challenges incorporating this kind of ideal into a multinational federal constitution, as well as some of its implication for concrete decisions about nation-building and options for the design of federal institutions.

Long before Kymlicka burst onto the scene to awaken post-Rawlsian political philosophers to both the *need* for a theory of minority rights and the *resources* within their tradition to build such a theory—indeed, a few years before Kymlicka was born—Berlin (1969: 156–7) articulated some of his basic case:

What oppressed classes or nationalities, as a rule, demand is neither simply unhampered liberty of action for their members, nor, above everything, equality of social or economic opportunity.... *What they want*, as often as not, *is simply recognition* (of their class or nation, or colour or race) as an independent source of human activity, as an entity with a will of its own, intending to act in accordance with it (whether it is good or legitimate, or not), and not to be ruled, educated, guided, with however light a hand, as being not quite fully human, and therefore not quite fully free [my italics].

When Berlin first wrote these words in 1958, they would have echoed the pleas of nationalist leaders from Flanders, Catalonia, or Quebec. That their fellow citizens in Belgium, Spain, and Canada now clearly do see the Flemish, Catalans, and Québécois as 'independent source[s] of human activity' and members of entities 'with a will of [their] own, intending to act in accordance with it' is due in no small way to the effective nationalist mobilization in these regions, often thanks to powers and autonomy given by federal or quasi-federal structures in the constitutional regime. Berlin's words should, to this day, resonate with Hungarians in Romania, Albanians in Macedonia, Turks in Bulgaria, Kurds in Turkey, and so on—the list could name hundreds of national minorities with no real recognition or autonomy. Berlin may overstate his case when he claims that what oppressed national minorities usually want is '*simply* recognition': since they really do tend to want and need rights, prosperity, and real power. But they clearly do fight for recognition, even if it is never a 'simple' matter to know what will constitute an appropriate form of recognition. Perhaps no fundamental feature of the political cultures of multinational democratic states varies more than the ways in which recognition is recognized, so to speak. To be sure, most demands for recognition are non-constitutional: from the most basic anti-racist demand by ethnic and racial minorities to be respected as equal human beings by their fellow citizens to the more rarefied political demand by the Québécois to have an official delegation to the Francophonie, or the very popular movement in Catalonia to have their own team at some international sporting events. Demands by minorities for *constitutional* recognition are also inevitable, however, especially in any political culture where 'constitutional politics' is part of regular politics and where the majority has already taken the liberty to recognize its own visions of the state in the constitution. But here too the ways 'recognition' can be encoded into a constitution, and meanings and powers attached to this encoding, vary profoundly from one multinational state to the next. One will certainly miss much of the 'politics of recognition' if one focuses entirely on demands that the preamble to N's constitution include phrases like 'The M'ians are to be recognized as a nation within N'. In fact, almost any aspect of the constitution can constitute a form of recognition if it is viewed that way by either the majority or minority group. Consider some of the following examples, in addition to the explicit phrase just mentioned:

- The mere fact that the state is a federation can be seen as 'recognizing' at least one group's insistence on its right to autonomy within this state. This is a very plausible explanation of the existence of federations in Canada, Switzerland, Spain, and Belgium, not to mention most of the post-colonial federations brokered by the departing British.[26]
- Similarly, the fact that the provinces have certain powers—such as the right to their own legal system, to set an official language, or to control education—may recognize the special status and needs of minority-controlled provinces, even if the power is given to all provinces symmetrically.
- If a minority-controlled province is given special powers that are not given to other provinces (a so-called asymmetrical federal approach), this can be interpreted as a strong form of recognition (depending on the significance of the powers).
- Similar interpretations can be attached to special forms of representation in central institutions, special roles in the amending procedure, or rights to secede.
- Besides the explicit recognition of M as a people, nation, nationality, or 'distinct society', much significance can also be attached to recognizing M's symbols in the flag or coat of arms, M's religion, M's language and script,

[26] On the tragically but instructively brief history of most of the post-colonial 'Commonwealth' federations, see Watts (1966).

the name that M'ians give to themselves and to the country in their language, and so on.

- There can also be constitutionally entrenched rights, for both individuals and groups, that are especially important to minorities, such as rights to the use of the minority language and religion, and more general rights to preserve and promote their language and culture through their provincial government.

- There is the very important matter of the existence and form of recognition of either the majority national community or the alleged pan-national community (where all citizens, including minorities, are taken as equal members of 'the people' or nation-state). These forms of recognition can sometimes largely negate those granted to minorities.[27]

- Finally, there is a question of who or what else receives special recognition in the constitution. If the 'nationalities and regions' are both granted recognition in the same sentence (as they are in the Spanish Constitution of 1978), that may dilute the importance of the nationalities. If other identity groups, but not national minorities, are given explicit recognition, this may be taken as an insult by national minorities.[28]

---

[27] The Spanish case is instructive here. Spain's historic national minorities (each with its own language), the Catalans, the Basques, and the Galicians, all played an important role in securing quasi-federalization in the drafting of the post-Franco constitution in 1978. And although it does not recognize them by name, the constitution also explicitly 'recognizes and guarantees the right to self-government of the nationalities and regions of which it is composed and the solidarity among them all' (section 2), and it allows the Autonomous Communities to make their own official languages (section 3(2)). But this constitution also screams a kind of nation-state nationalism that will forever offend nationalists in those communities. The first words of the preamble of the constitution are 'The Spanish Nation, desiring to establish justice, liberty, and security, and to promote the well-being of all its members, in the exercise of its sovereignty, proclaims its will to...'. And it quickly goes on to declare: 'National sovereignty belongs to the Spanish people, from whom all state powers emanate' (section 1(2)); 'The Constitution is based on the indissoluble unity of the Spanish Nation, the common and indivisible homeland of all Spaniards' (section 2); 'The mission of the Armed Forces... is to guarantee the sovereignty and independence of Spain and to defend its territorial integrity and the constitutional order' (section 8(1)); 'Castilian is the official Spanish language of the State. All Spaniards have the duty to know it and the right to use it' (section 3(1)); that the flag of Spain must fly on all public buildings of the Autonomous Communities, with their own flags alongside if they wish (section 4(2)); and so on.

[28] Much of the impetus for the movement to amend the Canadian constitution in the late 1980s to recognize Quebec as a 'distinct society' came from the fact that the 1982 overhaul of the constitution (which again was not ratified by the Province of Quebec) gave constitutional recognition for the first time to 'aboriginal peoples' (Part 2 of the *Constitution Act, 1982*) and to the 'multicultural heritage of Canadians' (section 27 of the *Charter of Rights and Freedoms*). (The 'multicultural heritage' is understood as that arising from immigration from places other than the British Isles and France.) There was not nearly the insistence on this particular form of recognition for Quebec during the preceding 115-year period when the much more legalistic *BNA Act* served as Canada's constitution.

In short, the possible forms of recognition, or of denying recognition, are countless. On occasion it will be plain to anyone reading a country's constitution when a particular kind of group is being accorded a significant form of recognition (e.g. in the Swiss constitution, which, as we saw, recognized at the outset twenty-six named cantons as full partners). But in other cases, it will be hard to tell if some explicit constitutional recognition amounts to much for the group in question or (perhaps more to the point) for the judges on the constitutional court. As noted already, Quebec nationalists might like Quebec to be recognized as a nationality apart from Canadians, the way Albanians are in the Macedonian constitution, but Macedonia's marginalized Albanians would trade that window-dressing recognition for Quebec's real political autonomy and clout in a heartbeat. Provisions that are treated as forms of recognition at one stage in the history of a federation may be forgotten as such later. Or, contrarily, provisions that seemed relatively innocent in one era might later be seen by minorities to be oppressive forms of nation-statist recognition.[29] It is also often impossible to predict from the outside, or in the future, what demands for constitutional recognition may become hotly contested battles in the 'politics of recognition'. Explicit demands for recognition and status, especially those requiring constitutional amendment, are often treated as claims of justice. But they are also high-stakes exercises of nationalist mobilization and must be understood within the dynamics of nationalist political movements. Nationalist leaders may have the most noble of intentions in mind. But it is also, for example, not entirely inconceivable that minority nationalist leaders could decide to mobilize a movement in favour of a form of recognition that they know in advance will be refused by other federal partners. Their aim could be less to get the form of recognition for their people than to stir up feelings of humiliation and resentment, which could in turn be used to mobilize their support for a more radical project (or even just to help the nationalist party win its next election).[30]

---

[29] To draw on the example of an earlier note, consider the Spanish constitutional duty to speak Spanish. This may not have seemed particularly significant in 1978 when, thanks to two generations of centralized fascist rule, all Spaniards had been educated in Spanish and spoke it fluently. But it is now much more of a chore or an insult for many younger Catalans and Basques who have been educated primarily in their mother tongue and who may rarely have to speak Spanish in their professional or social lives.

[30] There is something cynical in such a strategy to be sure. But there is nothing intrinsic in nationalism that makes nationalist political figures more or less cynical than those in other ideological movements. Such tactics have been used to mobilize support for both just and unjust causes as long as there has been politics. It would be hard to find a non-partisan political commentator who did not interpret the movement in the run-up to the 2004 elections for a constitutional amendment to ban gay marriage in the USA—a proposed amendment that everyone seems to recognize will never be ratified—as a ploy to get more conservative republican politicians elected.

Where does all this indeterminacy leave the concept of recognition in a theory of multinational federal constitutionalism? I think it is safe to conclude that there is no *particular form* of recognition for minorities (or majorities) that can be identified as a basic condition of justice or legitimacy for all multinational federal constitutions. You cannot conclude that a constitution is illegitimate or unjust simply because it does not name and value minority or majority groups in the preamble, for example. But it is also safe to conclude (in the language of contractualism) that no self-respecting national community would agree freely to a constitutional arrangement that did not in some way—concretely, symbolically, or both—recognize its special situation and (perhaps) the divided loyalties and identities of its members. When ethnocultural groups come to see themselves as nations, this implies, by definition, that they seek self-determination *and* recognition in the family of nations. If a federal arrangement is being held out as a preferred alternative to secession or independence, it must also provide at least a degree of both self-determination and recognition. (Of course, the two often go together, most notably when powers of self-determination, or a right to secede, are given 'asymmetrically' to the minority-controlled provinces only.) In short, although it can be difficult to judge the appropriateness of any *particular form* of constitutional recognition for minority or majority groups, it is much less controversial that some form of recognition is appropriate and that its complete refusal is problematic.

We can also ask, more productively, whether there are any *in*appropriate forms of recognition. Of course, there are. Some of the most obviously pernicious examples involve groups recognizing their own controlling majority nation at the expense of others. Uncontroversially, we would want to denounce boastful and false claims by the titular nation (e.g. that it is a 'master race' or is otherwise superior or more blessed in the eyes of God), or explicit 'negative recognition' or denigration of minorities or other classes of people (as when black slaves were counted as two-thirds of a person in Article 1, section 2.3 of the original US Constitution, or when racial groups or women are refused political rights). More controversially, we will worry in multinational states when constitutions depart from what we might call a language of pure citizenship—where the constitution lays out the structure of the state and its institutions along with the rights and duties of equal citizens—towards a nationalistic language that recognizes only the nation of the majority.[31] It is one thing to declare that the people of the state N are

---

[31] Now there may be good reasons why constitutions for multinational states should not restrict themselves to a language of pure citizenship, especially if they contain an ethnocultural majority nation (like the Macedonians or the Croatians) that all of the citizens do not identify

sovereign and quite another to declare that N is the national state of the N'ians and that the N'ian nation is sovereign, especially when N either explicitly does not include members of a national minority M or where M'ians themselves contest their membership in the majority nation N, even though they accept membership in the state with the same name. Such language could never be written into a constitution with the free assent of the members of the minority M. It is a powerful exercise of nationalist affirmation by the majority trying to assert its mark and its claim on the state. At the limit, it is an attempt to declare a specious Gellnerian 'congruence' between the national and the political unit. In such a context it is difficult to see how a claim for some form of national recognition (along with concrete measures for autonomy and protection from the nationalizing majority) could not be considered legitimate on behalf of a national minority. The only explanation for the presence of constitutional recognition for one community, N, and its absence for another, M, is that N'ians are in the majority and they used their permanent demographic power to get their way. This is a perversion of democracy, not an affirmation of it.

Of course, we should not assume that the only inappropriate forms of constitutional recognition are those secured by *majority* national communities. Specific demands for recognition by national minorities may also be ill-conceived. They may, for example, be demanding recognition of alleged facts—say, from oral history, or about ethnoracial purity—that cannot be supported. The leaders negotiating on a minority group's behalf may also have specifically nation-building objectives in mind that would introduce novel language or contested claims into the constitution.[32] For example, they may want a description of their minority nation that denies the dual, overlapping national identities of many of its members, or that includes groups of people (i.e. minorities among the minority) who do not consider

---

with, but which shares the same name as the state. In this case, the language of pure citizenship may nevertheless be read by most citizens through a nationalist lens. Consider, for example, how more oppressive the UK would feel for the Scottish and the Welsh if the state were instead called 'England', and if the official institutions and public officials made constant reference to 'the English people' for not just the English themselves but for all of the citizens of what we call 'the United Kingdom'.

[32] I believe that the Canadian Constitution does not anywhere use the term 'nation', apart from one sentence referring to 'the general principles of law recognized by the community of nations'. So it might seem inappropriate or problematic were Quebec nationalists to demand that Quebec be recognized as a nation within Canada. This Constitution does, however, accord rights and recognition to 'aboriginal *peoples* of Canada', so a demand for the recognition that Quebec houses 'a people' might make more sense. As it turns out, the Supreme Court (1998: section 3) already takes into account that 'much of the Quebec population certainly shares many of the characteristics of a people'.

themselves to be members of the minority nation. They may also ask for a specific form of recognition as a nation (rather than a national minority, a nationality, a nation within a nation, a people, or a distinct society) not because it would recognize their status within the state, but because they think it would facilitate their eventual secession from the state. At the very least we can argue that it would not be illegitimate for federalist leaders to contest various specific proposals for minority recognition. After all, an essential aspect of the 'recognition of x' is how others *besides* x see x, not simply how x sees itself or wants others to see it. In an ideal world, of course, others will see x for what x really is, and both x and not-x can celebrate this fact. In our world, we should not be shocked if x'ian nationalists see x in ways not fully appreciated by non-x'ians.

This does not tell us what specific form of recognition national minorities may have a right to in a state with a nationalizing national majority. In what follows I will simply speculate about some possible forms and principles of recognition that might be agreed to by majority national communities like N and minorities like M in free and fair negotiations conducted with the aim of securing a long-term or 'indefinite' union within the same federation. With such motivations, under favourable conditions, we might expect agreement on principles that combine, or even harmonize, different groups' visions of the nature, purpose, and function of the union.

5.3.1 Seven Principles of Recognition

5.3.1.1 *Partnership*

The ideal of partnership in a collective endeavour is a quintessential form of mutual recognition. In a multinational federation it will not always be an easy matter to decide who the official or unofficial partners should be (will it just be the federal subunits or other groups as well?). And conceptions of who the partners are can change dramatically over time.[33] But an agreement to treat a significant national minority group as a full partner in the federation provides a powerful opportunity for mutual recognition that should have real implications for decisions about both symbolic and concrete aspects of the federal

---

[33] One hazards to guess that if Canada and Australia were to recast their constitutional identities as 'partnerships' in any way, they would now almost certainly include Aboriginal peoples as partners, even though they were not even considered to be citizens when these states were founded.

architecture (such as a special role in the amending formula or secession procedure).[34]

5.3.1.2 Collective assent

As a corollary of the principle of partnership, the legitimacy of a federal constitution for national minorities will hinge on the belief that they have given their free assent to the arrangement. This is the opposite, if you will, of colonialism. Collective assent fits well with the ideology of a 'contract' between peoples (plural), and not just individual people, that tends to characterize most national minority groups' visions of their participation in the larger state, even in cases where there was clearly no such historical contract. Since most multinational states were founded without the collective assent of the constituent communities, it is important that at some stage there is occasion for the assent to be formally given. This could come through the ratification (perhaps by referendum) of a reformed constitutional agreement, as happened in Spain in 1978. It can also be part of the language of the document itself.

5.3.1.3 Commitment and loyalty

From the point of view of the majority, the collective assent of federal partners cuts both ways: it constitutes a form of commitment and loyalty to the federal project by the national minorities and the majority alike, one that cannot be easily shirked. If minorities want assurance that the fundamental terms of partnership will not be violated without their consent, majorities will expect no less from minorities. The language of loyalty or solidarity is also likely to figure in the wording of a fair multinational constitution. And the principle should have implications for both the federal plumbing (especially the amending formula and the secession procedure) and various conventions in the political culture. It need hardly be noted that should a majority demand that the minority demonstrate its loyalty in the absence of any of the other forms of recognition on this list, this would hardly constitute a form of progressive recognition.

5.3.1.4 Anti-assimilationism

National minorities should be able to expect the majority to commit to their continued existence and flourishing. This principle, in effect, demands that

---

[34] For numerous explorations of the usefulness of partnership metaphors in multinational federations (and in Canada in particular), see the essays collected in Gibbins and Laforest (1998).

the majority renounce significant nation-building objectives and powers. It should be accepted at all levels of the constitutional order and the political culture that it is 'normal', to say the least, that the state contains more than one 'people' and more than one national culture, language, religion, or what have you. As a principle, anti-assimilationism must go beyond a mere modus vivendi acknowledgement by the majority that it is not currently in a position to assimilate the minority. There are tremendous benefits to trust in a federal partnership, and a demonstrated commitment to anti-assimilationism is essential to secure the trust of minorities. A concrete commitment to this principle by the majority will involve reconsidering the exercise of many of the powers that are taken for granted by central governments in nation-states, since these will be seen to have assimilationist effects by the minorities. Control over language policy and education are obvious examples, but there can be many others. For example, most western societies today require immigration to sustain their economies and welfare states, and national minorities will rightly feel threatened if they are not permitted sufficient control over immigration into their territories to be able to promote the integration of immigrants into their national culture (and language). Minorities are also likely to demand that some form of this principle be articulated in a way that can affect judicial interpretation by the constitutional court. In the exercise of concurrent jurisdictions, minorities will sometimes need to be able to argue for the legitimacy of their policies over federal policies when the latter have assimilationist consequences.

5.3.1.5 *Territorial autonomy as national self-determination*

One of the most concrete ways to recognize and to embed the principle of anti-assimilationism into a constitution is to give national minorities territorial autonomy in the form of a federal province exercising powers that will promote the continued existence and flourishing of their group. (Again, as discussed in Chapter 4, this is clearly not sufficient, since powers that remain in federal hands can be used intentionally or unintentionally in ways that threaten minority cultures.) It is also symbolically important that the terms of federation explicitly recognize the right *and the duty* of the minority's provincial government to promote its culture. Such recognition will almost certainly have to be given 'asymmetrically' if it is to be meaningful. That is, in a federal state with one or more minority-controlled provinces and several majority-controlled provinces, it is not sufficient to simply declare that provincial governments have the right and duty to protect the culture of their province. In a radical version of this principle it would be clear that the governments of minority-controlled provinces have a duty to protect a distinct or *national* culture, and also (as a corollary in the interest of the federation) that this constitutes an appropriate form of national self-determination for the group or groups in question.

5.3.1.6 *Equal right of nation-building*

At some level the political culture of a multinational federation must recognize that the previous two principles imply an equal right for both minorities and majorities to engage in national engineering or nation-building. To be sure, this is not the kind of language that is likely to be enshrined in a constitutional preamble. (As we have seen, nationalists rarely admit to their own nation-building projects, that is, to their own desires to 'forge' and shape the identities of the community they claim to represent.) But this is what we are talking about when we say that a provincial government should promote or protect its culture, and when a federal government has a mandate to promote a kind of pan-national citizenship and identity. It is also, in many ways, simply acknowledging the inevitable. As we discussed in Chapter 2, nation-building consequences can be expected from the exercise of a broad range of government powers and democratic political activities, and there is nothing wrong, illiberal, or illegitimate about many of these. Given that the state simply cannot be neutral about national culture and identity, '[a]ll else being equal, national minorities should have the same tools of nation-building available to them as the majority nation, *subject to the same limitations*' (Kymlicka 2002: 27; see also Costa 2003: 68–9). Moreover, in the context of a federal regime in which these other principles are well entrenched, the very idea of 'rival nation-building projects' should not seem as threatening to either the minority or the majority. Once the 'normalcy' of a state shared by more than one national community is accepted, majorities need not fear that a national self-consciousness among the minorities will lead inexorably towards arguments that it can only be 'normal' if the minorities have their own state. Similarly, once the principle of anti-assimilation is well entrenched, minorities should feel less threatened by federal nation-building that 'targets' minority citizens but does not meddle with any aspects of their cultural particularity (e.g. promoting pride in the state's international sporting prowess need not have any implications whatsoever for the minority's distinct cultural heritage).

5.3.1.7 *Multiple and nested national identities*

In most democratic multinational states today, the preceding principle can make sense only if it is widely recognized in the political culture that national identities are not mutually exclusive, and that rival identity-shaping projects

Evaluating Federal Options 167

are not locked in a zero-sum battle. Again, it is 'normal' for members of the Catalan, Flemish, Québécois, and Scottish minorities to feel themselves to be members of two national communities. In Miller's words, 'they do not experience this as schizophrenic, because their two identities fit together reasonably well' (2000: 129). At any rate, this is normal for *citizens* in minority national communities: as Brubaker and Levy remind us, it is not normal for their nationalist leaders. Hard-core nationalists of both minority and majority communities tend to view the world in terms of mutually exclusive national groups. Both types of nationalist are suspicious, to say the least, of any nation-building projects (whether these are explicit or not) by the other side. But many of these suspicions can be seen as misplaced if we recognize explicitly the normal psychology of overlapping dual national identities. In particular, neither side need feel threatened or insecure about the other side's attempt to make minority citizens feel pride in one of their identities, since we have ample evidence that such pride in membership is not a zero-sum issue. In short, finding ways to entrench the language of multiple, overlapping, intertwined, or nested nationality can be good for the flourishing of national identities and good for trust and unity in multinational states, even if it is not necessarily good for nationalist ideologues.

Principles or 'mutual understandings' like these seven must form part of the core of any idea of constitutionalism for a modern, democratic multinational federation. This is not to say that they must necessarily be entrenched in the constitution. In fact, there is not a constitutional document on the planet that includes a set of explicit principles like the ones just proposed. In a broader sense of the 'living constitution' of many states, however, some principles like these are taken for granted.[35] They may be recognized by the population in general, the political class in particular, or, perhaps most significantly, by judges in the constitutional court. Whether they are explicit or not, in multinational federations these principles should sit alongside the fundamental characteristics of any democratic regime that we discussed in section 5.2. Again, none of these seven principles directly implies any particular constitutional provision, just as the principle of protecting against the 'tyranny of the majority' does not imply any particular provision, let alone a phrase using the words 'tyranny of the majority' in the preamble. These principles are mutually reinforcing, and they could be parsed in different ways and in different terms. The basic idea is that they attempt to combine the sorts of

---

[35] A 'living constitution' evolves over time in ways that are not necessarily reflected in amendments to the document itself. In the famous words of the Warren court in the USA, the interpretation of the constitution reflects 'the evolving standards of decency that mark the progress of a maturing society' (in *Trop v. Dulles*, 356 U.S. 86 [1958]). Conservatives in the USA are, of course, inclined to reject the very idea of a living constitution.

recognition and autonomy demands that national minorities would make in free and fair negotiations with the recognition of majority national communities and their concerns for a smoothly functioning, indefinite (if not necessarily eternal) federal union. Put another way, they expand and explicate the otherwise vague, general ideal of 'recognition'.

5.4 CONCLUSION

The basic subject matter of multinational federal constitutionalism and justification is still at such a primitive stage of development that I have barely been able to sketch out some desiderata. Sections 5.2 and 5.3 can be seen as addressing two different audiences and approaches to federal justification. Many theorists who began working on justice in the multinational or multicultural state over the last decade or two write as if a completely novel normative tool kit required for designing and justifying institutions in such a state. For such theorists it is useful to consider just how much of the selection and justification of basic federal options (of the sort discussed in Chapter 4) can be worked out from within some of the classic normative traditions of liberal-democratic thought. At the same time, it is clear that these traditions can only take us so far. Section 5.3 was an attempt to clarify the legitimate demands for recognition in a multinational federal context. These demands cannot be ignored in free and fair negotiations with national minorities on the design of a just state; nor can they be excluded from an adequate theory of constitutionalism for such a state. In many ways, however, the argument in this chapter is a long promissory note. The real intellectual debt can only be paid off by showing how both the elements of the 'classic normative traditions' and the principles of recognition can be combined in the design and justification of particular constitutional structures—i.e. the 'plumbing' issues explored in Chapter 4—for a multinational state. I will try to take at least the first steps in this direction in Chapter 6 where I lay out a federalist approach to a constitutional secession clause (as paradoxical as that might sound). If this were to be a much, much longer book, we would try to do something similar for other basic elements of federalist 'plumbing', such as the determination of provincial borders, the division of powers, representation in central institutions, and the constitutional amendment formula. I will limit myself to the more modest task concerning secession for two reasons: first, it will help show how it is possible to make a rather definitive case for a concrete constitutional proposal despite the fact that our normative tool kit is in many ways so unwieldy; and second, because the topic of secession has received far more attention from political philosophers in recent years than any other aspect of federal constitutionalism. During these debates it has often been suggested that we cannot expect to have an adequate theory of federal divorce without an adequate theory of federal marriage, so to speak. Up until now in this book we have been lining up the essential features of a theory of federal marriage. Chapter 6 will be my attempt to see if the suggestion has been justified—can this really help us with the theory of divorce?

6

A Federalist Theory of Secession

> By virtue of the principle of equal rights and self-determination of peoples enshrined in the Charter of the United Nations, all peoples have the right freely to determine, without external interference, their political status and to pursue their economic, social and cultural development, and every State has the duty to respect this right in accordance with the provisions of the Charter.
>
> Nothing in the foregoing [paragraph] shall be construed as authorizing or encouraging any action which would dismember or impair, totally or in part, the territorial integrity or political unity of sovereign and independent States...possessed of a government representing the whole people belonging to the territory without distinction as to race, creed or colour.
>
> —*UN Declaration on Friendly Relations*, 1970

In the contest between rival nation-building projects in the multinational state, secession is the ultimate stake. For hard-core minority nationalists, almost by definition, it is the ultimate prize; just as surely as it is, for hard-core majority nationalists or federalists, the ultimate failure. Preventing secession—indeed, obviating even the *desire* by national minorities to want to secede—is thus a central design challenge for any given federation. In the broadest sense, of course, any aspect of a political system that contributes to the maintenance of a stable, prosperous, just state with ample autonomy and recognition for constituent groups will also help to prevent secession (and vice versa). But in addition, as we noted during the discussion of federal 'plumbing' options in Chapter 4, federal architects or negotiators may also want to consider head-on the question of what kinds of rules for secession, if any, ought to be inscribed in the constitution.

6.1 BACKGROUND CONTEXT IN INTERNATIONAL LAW

Contemplating the conditions (if any) under which secession would be permitted is one way to think deeply about the nature of the state and of the bonds between its constituent parts. This is analogous to the way in which the rules and conventions about divorce in a given jurisdiction reveal a lot about the institution of marriage there: knowing how something comes apart, or is allowed to come apart, tells us much about how or why it is put together. At one level, secession is a phenomenon of international relations and international law. It is not like a group of people simply emigrating from one state to another. Nor is it, as Buchanan frames the issue,

> simply the formation of a new political association among individuals who repudiate the existing state's authority over them. It is a taking of territory that is claimed by an existing state, accompanied by the assertion that those doing the taking have a right to attempt to exercise over that territory the kind of control that only legitimate states have. (2004: 24–5)

So what does international law say about secession? Even today, it is about as 'liberal' with respect to secession as the nineteenth-century British legal system was about the divorce of a married couple. It gives central governments extensive rights to prevent wayward minorities from exiting the state (and taking some of its territory with them) in roughly the same way that most legal systems used to allow husbands to maintain loveless, and often violent, marriages.[1] Indeed, in one sense the legal regime governing secession is even more 'paternalistic' than the one that used to govern marriage and divorce. At least women sometimes had a choice over whether to enter into a marriage. Very few national minorities ever consented to join the states in which they now find themselves, and yet they cannot simply choose to leave. To be sure, the 'international community' will now *consider* intervening in cases where the repression of a central government involves systematic human-rights abuses or genocide (although the recent history of Sudan is hardly promising); but a central government that simply refused to grant a national minority any autonomy or recognition of the sort advocated in

---

[1] Consider how few words would have to be changed in John Stuart Mill's account of the legal tyranny of husbands and the legal subjection of wives in Victorian Britain to have the same passage apply to the sovereign authority of central governments over national minorities today: 'Men are not required, as a preliminary to the marriage ceremony, to prove by testimonials that they are fit to be trusted with the exercise of absolute power.... The vilest malefactor has some wretched woman tied to him, against whom he can commit any atrocity except killing her, and, if tolerably cautious, can do that without much danger of the legal penalty.... The law, which till lately left even these atrocious extremes of domestic oppression practically unpunished, has within these few years made some feeble attempts to repress them. But its attempts have done little, and cannot be expected to do much, because it is contrary to reason and experience to suppose that there can be any real check to brutality, consistent with leaving the victim still in the power of the executioner. Until a conviction for personal violence, or at all events a repetition of it after a first conviction, entitles the woman *ipso facto* to a divorce, or at least to a judicial separation, the attempt to repress these "aggravated assaults" by legal penalties will break down for want of a prosecutor, or for want of a witness.' (Mill 1869: ch. 2)

Chapters 4 and 5, and prevented any mobilization for secession, would not be acting outside of the bounds of international law. As James Crawford, the Whewell Professor of International Law at Cambridge University, puts it (in effect, drawing out the implications of the *UN Declaration on Friendly Relations*, quoted above):

> In international practice there is no recognition of a unilateral right to secede based on a majority vote of the population of a sub-division or territory, whether or not that population constitutes one or more 'peoples' in the ordinary sense of the word. In international law, self-determination for peoples or groups within an independent state is achieved by participation in the political system of the state, on the basis of respect for its territorial integrity. (Crawford 1997: summary)

In short, baring extreme brutality, secession is permitted only by mutual agreement between a central government and a regional minority.

Although seductive and suggestive, the analogy between secession and divorce is a very imperfect one.[2] In particular, the best proposals for the progressive reform of international law do not point in the direction of a 'no-fault', unilateral divorce for national minorities and their homelands. A 'no-fault' approach to secession could create perverse incentives that would make it harder for minorities around the world to gain *any* form of autonomy. As Allen Buchanan argues:

> a theory of the right to secede that ascribed to federal units the right to secede if a majority of their populations desired independence would create an incentive for the governments of centralized states to resist efforts at decentralization, fearing that [this] would be the first step toward disintegration. (Buchanan 2004: 349)

Like most theorists of secession, Buchanan believes that a right for a minority to secede is generated by '(1) genocide or massive violations of the most basic individual human rights [or] (2) unjust annexation' (2004: 351). But the most important innovation in Buchanan's own moral theory of international law is his persuasive plea to bring federal or 'intrastate autonomy' arrangements within the scope of international law. He argues both that 'a state's persistence in violations of intrastate autonomy agreements' can generate a right to secede—this is his third and final sufficient condition for secession—and that the international community should:

> [a] help broker intrastate autonomy agreements as an alternative to secession, [b] monitor both parties' compliance with such agreements, [c] support the agreements' viability by holding both parties accountable for fulfilling their obligations, and [d]

---

[2] For two thorough accounts of the many ways in which the analogy between secession and divorce is misleading, see Blahuta (2001) and Aronovitch (2000*b*).

provide an impartial tribunal for adjudicating disputes over whether either or both parties have failed to fulfil their obligations. (2004: 358)

Among the grounds Buchanan cites in support of international law being reformed in this way is that it 'gets the incentives right':

> On the one hand, states that protect basic human rights and honour autonomy agreements are immune to legally sanctioned unilateral secession and entitled to international support for maintaining the full extent of their territorial integrity. On the other hand, if, as the theory prescribes, international law recognizes a unilateral right to secede as a remedy for serious and persisting injustices, states will have an incentive to act more justly. (2004: 370)

Buchanan notes that he explicitly had cases like Chechnya, Sudan, Eritrea, the Kurdish region of northern Iraq, and Kosovo in mind when he decided to add the third 'violation-of-intrastate-autonomy-agreement' condition to his theory of secession (2004: 357). All things considered, it is still a theory that envisages secession as a remedy of last resort in bitterly divided societies where there is no other sustainable hope for peace, security and democratic cooperation between central authorities and their regional minorities.

In short, the incorporation of this theory of secession[3] into international law would enhance the prospects of (federal-style) autonomy for national minorities around the world. It would do so better than the status quo, and also better than the (wildly unrealistic) proposal for a 'no-fault' law of secession calling for the 'international community' to support actively the aspirations of any regional or national minority that wanted a state of its own. This 'consequentialism of minority autonomy' argument (i.e. roughly, 'favour the system that will help the most national minorities in the most states') is only *one* of the grounds for supporting at most a relatively modest reform of the status quo. A more complete argument—which I sketch in Norman (1998*a*), and which receives its definitive treatment in Buchanan (2004)—would highlight other favourable consequences, as well as conformity to other desiderata for a sound morality of international law. It is not necessary to defend this morality of secession in international law here, however. I mention it primarily as a background context for a discussion of a morality of secession in constitutional law.

6.2 DOMESTICATING SECESSION

The primary aim of this book has been to identify reasonably ideal, and realizable, principles and institutions for democratic multinational states.

---

[3] Buchanan calls it the 'Remedial Right Only' theory. I have argued for it extensively as well, calling it instead a 'Just Cause' theory of secession. See Norman (1998*a*, 2001*a*, 2003*b*).

How might or should these states differ, institutionally and politically, from their uninational neighbours? Now one way such states differ is that they are *much* more likely to host serious secessionist movements. In the actual democratic multinational states from which I have continually drawn examples, secessionist movements have enduring 'hard-core' levels of support in the 20–40 per cent range within at least one of the territories controlled by national minorities; with opinion polls sometimes registering levels of support above 50 per cent. Given our discussions of national identity, nation-building, and federalism throughout this book, this level of support for secession should not be seen as surprising or ephemeral. It poses a challenge for federal architects or reformers; a challenge that will take up the rest of this chapter. The treatment of secession in international law is a background condition because any successful secessionist movement must eventually make its case on an international stage. As we just saw, it is just a plain matter of fact that international law is not sympathetic to the demands of secessionists in reasonably just, democratic states. If the majority of citizens in a federal province of a multinational democracy voted for independence tomorrow, they could not realistically expect to be recognized by a significant number of states (if any) until they had negotiated the terms of secession with their own central government and that government formally recognized the new state. According to Crawford (1997: summary),

> Outside the colonial context, the United Nations is extremely reluctant to admit a seceding entity to membership against the wishes of the government of the state from which it has purported to secede. There is no case since 1945 where it has done so.

If the central government simply refused to negotiate secession, and did not respond with a brutal or prolonged military repression, then secession would not happen. This is, if you will, the predictable scenario that both secessionists and the central government could anticipate. Our brief look at Buchanan's argument suggests that even an enlightened liberal reform of international law would not move it far enough to significantly improve the chances that, say, national minorities could expect to issue unilateral declarations of independence from democratic states and automatically join the 'family of nations'.

This is hardly to suggest, however, that central governments in democratic states hold all the cards, or that they can simply ignore secessionist demands. In purely practical terms, a clear majority within a province demanding independence—especially if their preference is revealed in a reasonably democratic referendum—will give rise to an uncomfortably high level of uncertainty. Economic consequences will be felt in both minority and majority territories, and the possibility of political violence cannot be ruled out in even the most peaceful of political cultures. In normative terms, this kind of status quo is simply unsustainable. The terms of federation (or union) will lose democratic legitimacy. This is why prime ministers in both the UK and Canada have publicly declared in recent years that they would allow their minority nations (Scotland and Northern Ireland, and Quebec, respectively) to secede if this was their clear desire.[4] Stonewalling the secessionists can be expected to strengthen not weaken the movement's support. And the federal solution to the accommodation of the minority's aspirations for self-determination will be seen as a failure. The fact that international law would allow this situation to fester is almost beside the point. After all, international law does not demand that states grant national minorities *any* of the forms of autonomy or recognition that we have discussed throughout this book; but that is no argument for why these groups should not have access to these things under constitutional law. As noted in the opening paragraph of this chapter, a just multinational federation should be designed and run in a way that both (*a*) discourages such secessionist resentment in the first place, and (*b*), when this is not successful, allows for the possibility of secession in accordance with norms of democracy, justice and the rule of law.

I shall argue that a well-designed secession clause in a federal constitution could potentially contribute to both (*b*) and (*a*), in that order. Put very simply, it could facilitate secession, and in so doing discourage it. That said, it is far from clear how the 'norms of democracy, justice and the rule of law' apply to attempts to secede from a reasonably just multinational federation. We have already touched on one of the challenging issues, i.e. the difficulty with using democratic intuitions to justify procedures for changing borders. Examples of fair and functional secession procedures in the real world are also problematic. Although there has been a wave of secessions recently—from the Soviet Union, Yugoslavia, Czechoslovakia, Ethiopia, and Indonesia—these are hardly examples of states with long-standing histories of democratic federation (and many of these secessions were, in fact, bloodstained). There are also relatively few examples of democratic constitutions with detailed provisions for managing secessionist politics within the rule of law.[5] Most constitutions are silent on the issue, and there are numerous examples, as we have seen, of constitutions that seem expressly to forbid secession by declaring the state to be 'indivisible'.

Before proceeding with enquiries about whether a constitutional secession clause would be inconsistent with norms of constitutionalism, or otherwise

---

[4] See Moore (2001: 212); and 'Notes for a Statement by Prime Minister Jean Chrétien in Response to the Supreme Court Ruling in the Reference on a Unilateral Secession' from 21 August 1998; available at http://www.pco-bcp.gc.ca.

[5] For good international surveys of this aspect of constitutional law, see Suksi (1993) and Monahan and Bryant (1996).

inappropriate or ill-advised, it is worth pausing to consider what such a clause might look like. From the small number of states that have 'legalized' secession we can discern three typical approaches: (i) entrenching a concise principle of the right of secession; (ii) entrenching a detailed procedure for secession; or (iii) interpreting a constitution in a way that 'reads into it' a right of, or procedure for, secession.

(i) The most famous and notorious example of an entrenched principle of secession was in the constitution of the Soviet Union. Article 17 of Stalin's 1936 constitution, and Article 72 of the constitution that replaced that one in 1977, both proclaim that 'Each Union Republic shall retain the right freely to secede from the USSR'. Of course, as with many of the high-minded principles in the Soviet constitutions, it is presumed that Kremlin leaders did not seriously entertain the possibility of this right actually being exercised. The provision in Article 1 of the Anglo-Irish Agreement of 1985, which grants Northern Ireland the right to secede from the UK in order to join the Republic of Ireland, serves a similar function (see Moore 2001: 212). One of the problems with legalizing secession with a concise principle, even if this is done non-cynically, is that it leaves a tremendous number of questions unanswered.

(ii) Hence, a second approach to constitutionalizing a right to secede spells out in much more detail the *process* that would have to be followed for a secession to take place. As far as I am aware, the two best examples of this approach are to be found in the eight clauses and three sub-clauses in section 113 of the 1983 constitution of Saint Christopher and Nevis (or St Kitts and Nevis; both names are official), and in the five sections and five subsections of Article 39 of the 1994 constitution of Ethiopia. In both cases, these provisions were demanded at a time of founding these federations by the nervous minorities themselves as a condition of their participating in the new federations.[6]

(iii) A third approach is more likely in countries with lively secessionist movements but without explicit mention of secession in their constitutions. It is possible that judges in the constitutional court can use other constitutional principles and conventions to *read* a secession clause *into* the constitution. French judges have done this in a way that gives 'Overseas Departments' the

---

[6] See Griffiths (2002b) and Pätz (2002). In 1998, 61.7 per cent of voters on the island of Nevis voted to secede (only 58 per cent of registered voters actually voted), but this fell short of the two-thirds majority required by section 113(2)(b) of the Constitution. Note that Eritrea declared independence from Ethiopia in April 1993, a year before the official ratification of the current constitution, after a UN-supervised vote with 99.81 per cent of Eritrean voters opting for secession. Nevertheless, it was through the process of Article 39(4) 'that Eritrea gained *de jure* independence in May 1993. No other member state [of Ethiopia] has ever attempted to secede' (Pätz 2002: 193).

right to independence from France.[7] And as we will discuss later in the chapter, in 1998, in response to a reference from the federal minister of justice, the Canadian Supreme Court gave an *Opinion* running over 25,000 words on what steps would be required for Quebec legally to secede. Even if a country had some kind of secession clause in its constitution it is entirely possible that the constitutional court would have to rule on specific disputes (i.e. on how to divide assets or debts) that arise over matters that can never be fully spelled out in the text of the constitution.

Again, it is a matter of some controversy whether it is appropriate or advisable for constitutions to deal explicitly with secession. So it goes without saying that there is no consensus among constitutional scholars about what the specific content of such a clause should be. Assuming for a moment that it is not inappropriate for a federal constitution to contain a secession clause (and I will be arguing for this assumption over the course of the chapter), it is reasonable to suppose that the details of the clause could vary as much from state to state as do the details of other aspects of federal plumbing, like the division of powers, design of central institutions, and the amending formula. For the purposes of the discussion to follow, I shall assume that federal architects, negotiators or reformers contemplating the inclusion of a secession clause would have to come up with provisions that answer one or more of the following questions (so clauses would differ depending on which questions they chose to address explicitly and which answers they provided to these questions):

- Is the right to self-determination or to secede for groups or territories trumpeted as a fundamental feature of the federation (e.g. in the preamble or the opening articles, as it is in Ethiopia), or is it a treated as a merely remedial provision in the bowels of the constitution, so to speak (as it is in St Kitts and Nevis)?

- What specific groups or kinds of groups or territories have access to the right? Does it name one entity in particular (like Nevis or Northern Ireland), or is the right granted symmetrically to all units of a particular kind (Overseas Departments, federal provinces), or to all groups of a particular kind (such as national minorities)?[8]

---

[7] See Moyrand and Angelo (1999) for an excellent description of the details and logic of this 'reinterpretation' of the 1958 constitution of the Fifth Republic.

[8] The Ethiopian constitution grants the right to secede to 'Every Nation, Nationality and People in Ethiopia' [Article 39(1)] where these are defined very sociologically as 'a group of people who have or share a large measure of a common culture or similar customs, mutual intelligibility of language, belief in a common or related identities, a common psychological make-up, and how inhabit an identifiable, predominantly contiguous territory' [39(5)].

- What roles are given to subunit or federal assemblies in demanding or approving the initiation of secession proceedings? What special voting rules, if any, are required in these assemblies?[9]
- What roles are given to the people in either the potentially seceding region or in the country as a whole, for example, in a referendum or referenda?[10]
- If there is to be a referendum in the potentially seceding region, how is the precise question to be determined? For example: (*a*) is it fixed in the constitution, (*b*) determined by the government or parliament in the secessionist region, or (*c*) determined by the federal government or parliament?
- What level of support within the secessionist region is deemed sufficient to trigger either negotiations leading to secession or secession itself?[11]
- Who sets the rules for the referendum campaign (e.g. the provincial government or the federal government?), and who organizes, counts, or supervises the actual vote (e.g. either the provincial or federal governments, or both, or even international observers)?
- Is there one referendum only, or more than one with a mandatory waiting period between them? If there is a series of referendums, do they re-pose the same question, or is an initial one merely for a mandate to negotiate secession and the last one an approval of the terms negotiated?[12]
- Is there a provision for sub-regions within the seceding region to opt to stay with the rump state, or for sub-regions in the future rump state to join the seceding region?[13]
- How are federal debts, assets and properties to be divided? Is there a specific formula, or a process for negotiations? If the latter, how is 'good faith' enforced? Is there a provision for binding impartial arbitration?

---

[9] For example, the Nevis Island Legislature must pass a bill demanding secession from St Kitts and Nevis, the final reading of this bill must be supported by two-thirds of all the elected members of the Assembly, and there must be at least 90 days between the first and second reading of the bill. Then, after a successful referendum, the bill is submitted to the Governor General. There appears to be no role in this process for the federal legislature of St Kitts and Nevis.

[10] The United States seceded from Great Britain, and Slovakia seceded from Czechoslovakia, without referenda; to mention but two examples.

[11] The Ethiopian constitution demands simply majority support. In Nevis, as noted, two-thirds of the voters must be in favour. The Canadian Supreme Court says repeatedly that the secession of Quebec would require a 'clear majority', and it gives reason to think that this means more than 50 per cent +1. Another possible threshold in a secessionist referendum might be 50 per cent of eligible voters rather than of votes cast.

[12] Both of the quasi-secessionist referenda in Quebec, in 1980 and 1995, have asked merely for a mandate to negotiate a new confederal arrangement with the Government of Canada.

[13] We discussed this issue briefly in Chapter 4 in the context of the question of how to determine borders for federal provinces.

- Who has the authority to negotiate on behalf of the (potential) rump state? It may not be the federal government or parliament if too many of its members represent the seceding region. Are there provisions for the election of a special negotiating body from the rump?
- How would any final deal providing for secession be approved by the rump state? Would it require a constitutional amendment using the normal amending formula? Or would this be circumvented in the case of secession?
- Is there a 'waiting period' (say, 10 years) from the time of ratifying the clause before secession may be attempted? Is there a waiting period after an unsuccessful secession attempt before the same group may attempt secession again?
- What rights would the new state have to the use of the existing state's currency? What role (if any) would it have in the management of the currency?
- What rights would citizens of the new state have to retain citizenship in the rump state?
- Could the rump state carry on with the same constitution, or would the extraction of the seceding region necessitate immediate adjustments (e.g. to the amending formula or the composition of the constitutional court) that should be either spelled out in advance or dealt with by a constitutional convention at the time of the secession?

Now, obviously, we would not expect *all* of these questions to be answered explicitly in a secession clause in any given constitution. At this stage I would like to highlight two reasons why it might be important to have explicit answers to at least some of the key questions agreed up in the constitution. First, in one way or another, most of these questions would in fact have to be answered during the process of an attempted secession from a well-established federal state. If the answers are not clear and specific, many of the questions will be 'answered' (or ignored) by whichever side of the dispute has the power to impose its will. Second, by entrenching very explicit answers to some of these questions into the constitution, federal architects have the opportunity to do more than prepare the way for orderly secessionist politics, should a popular enough secessionist movement arise. They can also establish a pre-emptive impact on the very nature of nationalist-secessionist movements that might arise. Consider two such impacts. First, as I will explain in Section 6.3.3, the wording of a secession clause can be part of the special recognition that a constitution bestows on specific minority nationalities, and in so doing it may appease minority nationalism rather than fuel it. Second, some specific answers to these questions may have the effect of making secession possible but rather difficult: for example, by requiring enhanced-majority support in a referendum, or a series of referendums that would make it harder for minority nationalists to capitalize on fleeting passions, or by alerting secessionists that they would be sitting across from quite-possibly-hostile negotiators elected specially to represent the interests of the rump state. We will call this a *'rigorous* secession clause', which could be defined as one designed to make secession less likely or more costly for the secessionists than would the procedures that secessionists themselves might 'propose' in the absence of explicit rules to the game. And in this way, it might discourage minority-nationalist leaders and movements from 'playing the secessionist card' to begin with.[14] These two features of a secession clause—its ability to serve as a powerful symbol of recognition and its ability to discourage the formation of secessionist politics—will figure prominently in my case in favour of a secession clause for multinational federations.

6.3 THEORIZING SECESSION, THEORIZING NATIONALISM, AND THEORIZING FEDERALISM

The full case for constitutionalizing secession requires a complex blend of normative arguments about justice, democracy, recognition and the right to self-determination, along with conjectures about the political sociology of multiethnic societies and the dynamics of nationalist politics, as well as views about constitutionalism and statecraft in federal democracies. It is an understatement that this case has yet to be made in a systematic fashion in the existing literature. So far we have little more than bullet-point-like considerations intended to show that one is not necessarily crazy to think that constitutionalizing secession will have numerous benefits, including the possible benefit of making secession less likely in the democratic multinational

---

[14] As we discussed in Section 5.2.5 ('Classical Constitutionalism'), constitutionalism has always been partly about trying to push certain kinds of issues off the table, to remove them from 'normal politics'. Consider the way a rigorous amending formula can discourage political actors from 'playing the constitutional-amendment card'. For example, both liberals and conservatives in the USA would love to have, respectively, a woman's right to an abortion or a fetus's right to life, entrenched in the constitution. But they also know that it would be impossible to get three-quarters of the state legislatures and two-thirds of both houses of Congress to pass either such amendment. So consequently there is no significant movement to amend the constitution in either of these ways. Pro- and anti-abortion activists devote their energies and resources to other battles. (One such battle is the attempt to alter the 'living constitution' by appointing Supreme Court judges who will 'read into the constitution' their preferred interpretation.)

state.¹⁵ The reason for the ragged state of this case is (I believe) relatively easy to identify, but difficult to rectify. So far we have tended to treat the issue of whether (and if so, how) to constitutionalize secession as *an application of a moral theory of secession*. In other words, we develop a theory to identify under what conditions territorially concentrated groups have a *moral right* to secede, and then we ask whether this right should be entrenched in constitutions for multinational states. Instead, I will argue that we have to treat this issue as part of a much broader discussion (or theory) of multinational federalism and constitutionalism of the sort I have been developing over the preceding three chapters: what forms of recognition and political autonomy are appropriate for territorially concentrated minority groups, and how do we balance these forms of minority self-determination and nation-building with the need for stability and some kind of common identity and equal citizenship across the larger federal state?¹⁶

In other words, I will argue that we should treat the issue of constitutionalizing secession as one part of a possible answer to this complex question, rather than as a kind of institutional application of a special normative theory of secession per se. To return to that more-often-than-not misleading metaphor, it has more to do with how we think about the terms of *marriage* in the multinational state than *divorce* from it.

In Sections 6.3.1–6.3.3 we will look at three different patterns of argument for recognizing some kind of legalized secession procedure in the constitution of a multinational state:

1. Arguments that propose to institutionalize more or less directly the prescriptions of a moral theory of secession. Call these *applied moral reasons*.¹⁷
2. Arguments that are concerned with ensuring that secessionist politics, and any actual secession attempt, are carried out within the rule of law according to fair democratic norms (*democratic rule-of-law reasons*).
3. Arguments that a secession clause can enhance the quality and strength of the federal union (*democratic-federalist reasons*).

6.3.1 Applied Moral Reasons

Most philosophers and political theorists were introduced to the normative challenges posed by secession through Allen Buchanan's first book on the

---

¹⁵ There was truth-in-advertising in the original working title of Weinstock's important article 'Constitutionalizing the Right to Secede' (2001a). In draft form it was called 'On some advantages of constitutionalizing the right to secede'.

¹⁶ A rationale for building a theory of secession out of a theory of federation that differs significantly from the one I present here can be found in Bauböck (2000: 366–71).

¹⁷ Note: this shorthand term is not meant to imply that the reasons and arguments in the following two categories are not also grounded in moral theories.

subject, *Secession: The Morality of Political Divorce from Fort Sumter to Lithuania and Quebec* (1991). Written and rushed to press shortly after the fall of the Berlin Wall, this book provided the agenda and vocabulary for a voluminous subsequent literature. Buchanan's morality of secession then, as now, is what I am calling a 'just-cause' theory: roughly, that a group has a right to secede only if either (*a*) it is systematically oppressed or exploited, or (*b*) had its territory unjustly annexed within recent-enough memory. (As we saw, he has since amended the theory to include the injustice of a minority's having its 'intrastate autonomy agreement' systematically violated.) After developing and defending this theory over the first three chapters of his 1991 book, he moves on in the fourth chapter to 'apply' it to the practical problem of whether there should be 'A Constitutional Right to Secede'. Most readers would not bat an eyelash at the opening paragraph of that chapter:

Preceding chapters clarified the concept of secession, identified different types of secession and conditions under which secession can be attempted, and offered a moral framework that provides substantial (though admittedly incomplete) guidance for resolving disputes about secession. But a moral framework without an appropriate institutional embodiment is merely a moral vision; and vision, though necessary for right action, is far from sufficient. This chapter begins building the bridge from vision to action, from theory to practice, by exploring how a right to secession might be included in one exceptionally powerful institution: the constitution of the modern state. (Buchanan 1991: 127)

There is nothing wrong with Buchanan's general advice about the need to move from theory to practice here. What is interesting about his argument in the ensuing chapter, however, is how little of it follows or builds out from his moral theory of secession per se. In fact, he argues explicitly against what he calls a 'substantial approach' that would try to apply his preferred theory of secession directly, for example, by having a constitutional clause that gave subunits a right to secede if they were victims of systematic injustice. (Among other things, this approach raises the problem of the 'biased referee', which I will sketch in a moment.) As an alternative to directly applying his moral theory of secession, Buchanan relies on contractualist, 'veil of ignorance' reasoning that, by the very nature of such reasoning, forbids contracting parties to make use of controversial moral theorizing.[18] I will return to this contractualist argument in Section 6.3.3, below, since I believe that it belongs in the category of 'democratic-federalist reasons'.

---

[18] We examined this normative framework under the heading of 'Contractualist Constitutionalism' in Chapter 5, Section 5.2.6. For Rawls's canonical arguments for forbidding controversial moral reasoning in the 'original position', see Rawls (1971: 136–42).

The applied-moral-reasons approach argues for a constitutional clause that will, as nearly as is practicable, facilitate secessions when and only when they are justified by the best moral theory of secession. But what is the best moral theory of secession? This question was the primary focus of most of the normative literature on secession in the decade following Buchanan's 1991 book. It is now common to distinguish three rival moral theories of secession (there are also a few hybrid theories mixing elements of these three theories):

- **Nationalist theories of secession**, which hold that a territorially concentrated group may secede if and only if it is a nation, and the majority of members of the nation (or inhabitants on the territory it proposes to take with it) want to secede.[19]

- **Choice theories of secession**, which hold that (with certain caveats) *any* geographically defined group may secede if and only if the majority of its members choose to (see, e.g. Gauthier 1994; Philpott 1995; Wellman 1995; and Beran 1998).

- **Just-cause theories of secession**, which hold that a group has a right to secede only if it has 'just cause'; for example, if it has been the victim of systematic and continuing discrimination or exploitation, or if its territory had been illegally incorporated into the larger state against its will (within recent memory) (see, e.g. Buchanan 1991, 2004; Norman 1998*a*, 2001*a*).

Each of these theories springs from important insights about the phenomenon and morality of secession: secessionist movements arise almost exclusively among national minorities mobilized on nationalist lines; we cannot envisage a legitimate secession that does not have substantial popular support, at least within the seceding region; and the international community has only ever demonstrated much sympathy for secessionist movements by peoples who have clear just cause (see Costa 2003: 66–7).

Of course, actual theories of these three types are loaded with details, including caveats and compromises, that try to meet some of the challenges of institutionalizing the theory in the real world. I will not be re-evaluating each of these theories at length here.[20] Nevertheless, a brief survey of the relevance of these theories to the question of whether to constitutionalize secession is in order.

If you really believed that either the nationalist or choice theory was correct about the morality of secession—that any nation or any territorially defined

---

[19] Although this is probably the most common justification used by secessionists themselves, it has relatively few philosophical apologists. See Nielsen (1993), Copp (1998), and Costa (2003).

[20] I explore each at some length in Norman (1998*a*). See also Buchanan (1997, 1998*b*, 2004), Costa (2003), and Moore (2001: chs. 7–8).

group whatsoever should have a state of its own if it wants one—then presumably the question of whether this principle should be entrenched in the constitution is a no-brainer. You would probably enshrine this as one of the fundamental principles in the preamble or opening articles of the constitution, perhaps including a detailed process for carrying out secession later in the document. Can we imagine states that would actually entrench such a principle? Of course we can. We have already seen that the Ethiopian constitution has unambiguously incorporated the nationalist theory of secession lock, stock and barrel. And the constitution of St Kitts and Nevis comes close to entrenching a secession clause inspired by the choice theory, although it permits only the island of Nevis, and not the island of St Kitts (or any other smaller jurisdictions on these islands), to secede. It also requires a two-thirds majority in favour of secession; but we should not assume that this departure from simple majoritarianism is inconsistent with the democratic spirit of the choice theory. The European Union too will permit member states to withdraw unilaterally if they want to.[21] That said, these three examples are clearly exceptions that prove the rule. They can be explained in part by the relative reluctance of certain specific 'partners' to join the federation or confederation in the first place. But in a world where there are upwards of twenty-five ethnocultural groups for every state, it is not surprising that so few states encourage their constituent groups to secede by providing a safe, legal route to do so; especially, when we consider again the intensity of nation-building by majorities (or otherwise dominant groups or coalitions) in control of central governments. Presumably, though, a true supporter of the moral worthiness of either the choice or nationalist theory of secession would be undeterred by the fact that the majorities are reluctant to respect their minorities' 'rights'. They would insist that minorities have a moral right to secede just as surely as individuals have a right to vote and to speak their minds, and that all such fundamental rights should be guaranteed by the constitution.

It is difficult to gauge how widely or seriously held nationalist and choice theories of secession are. There was certainly an 'academic publishing market' for these theories in the 1990s, in part because they stood in opposition to the 'just-cause' theory that Buchanan defended so thoroughly when he initiated the debates. They are defended almost exclusively by philosophers (rather than political scientists or international lawyers), most of whom had written little or nothing about nationalism, international relations, or ethnic conflict

---

[21] There is no formal secession clause in the various treaties that serve the function of the EU's constitution. But it is well-understood that member states can exit unilaterally. This is one of the principal reasons for categorizing the EU as a confederation and not a federation. For more on this distinction see Watts (2005: 233–42).

before they turned to the problem of secession. One literally finds arguments for choice theories that begin by extending principles of individual autonomy or freedom of association—as if choosing the borders of your state was just like choosing your friends or neighbours. These efforts from philosophers are greeted with something approaching scorn by political scientists, such as Donald Horowitz, working in ethnic-conflict studies:

> The renewed activity of philosophers in this field derives, of course, from events. The claims of oppressed ethnic groups to self-determination are bound to have considerable prima-facie appeal when ethnic warfare and genocide are recurrent.... But if interest in the problem is driven by events, the methodology is not, for much of the literature [from philosophers] thus far often displays a thoroughgoing ignorance of the complexities of ethnic interactions.... [A] priori methods that seem appropriate to other issues are utterly unsuitable to this problem. (Horowitz 1998: 199)

Horowitz is particularly concerned about the naivety of the belief that 'minority problems' can be solved by secession since 'nine times out of ten' this will create new minority problems (1998: 199). '[S]ecessionist movements sometimes gain much of their energy from a desire to "deal with" regional minorities, free from the intrusion of the centre' (1998: 198). And although Horowitz is primarily concerned about the implications of international law (rather than constitutional law) promoting secession, he shares Buchanan's fear that encouraging secession is antithetical to the much more practical federalist solution to 'minority problems':

> Articulating a right to secede will undermine attempts to achieve interethnic accommodation within states. As things now stand, the principal reason that states are reluctant to devolve power to territorially concentrated minorities, by means of either regional autonomy or federalism, is their fear that it will lead to secession. That fear is usually unfounded unless the conflict has already dragged on for a long time and the central government has been utterly ungenerous.... The best way to dry up devolution as a tool of interethnic accommodation—and a promising tool it is—is to establish a right, recognized in international law, for territorially concentrated minorities to secede. (Horowitz 2003: 56)

Although this is presented as an argument against reforming international law in ways that might follow from the nationalist or choice theories, it is also an argument against doing this within the constitutional law of a good many multiethnic states. This argument is an example of 'institutional moral reasoning' (see Norman 1998a: 44–50; Buchanan 2004: 22–9): in effect, the moral principle is false because we cannot accept its institutional implications; and secession just is 'an institutional concept' (Buchanan 2004: 23).

What about just-cause theories of secession: Is there any reason to think that they might ground a constitutional right to secede? This question is more interesting than the one involving nationalist and choice theories. Most critics of the idea of constitutionalizing a secession clause are also sympathetic to the just-cause theory.[22] Now clearly, on its own, the just-cause theory of secession tells us little about whether a given state should include a secession clause in its constitution, or what such a clause should look like. The theory does help us decide when groups would have a moral right to secede, but of course there are many moral rights that need not and often *should* not be constitutionally entrenched. Similarly, there are many injustices that do not have specific remedies (let alone radical remedies) laid out in constitutional law. And of course it goes without saying that there are many different constitutional traditions, and it is very difficult to generalize across these traditions.

Still, in Sections 6.3.2 and 6.3.3, I will argue that there *is* a strong case for domesticating secession in certain kinds of states; reasons that go beyond simply entrenching a putative moral right. And if this case is compelling, then we might begin with the assumption that the precise form of the secession clause should mirror, to some extent, the moral considerations that justify secession. In other words, the just-cause moral theory of secession does not imply that there should be a constitutional secession clause; but if there is reason to think that there should be such a clause, then the just-cause theory may help us decide what it should look like. Presumably, just-cause theorists will prefer a clause that makes it most likely that groups that have just cause will be able to secede, and that those without just cause will not be able to secede.

But it is not at all clear how this insight should be institutionalized. I have already alluded to Buchanan's argument against any direct attempt to codify this principle. Although Buchanan himself is the 'father' of the just-cause theory in the recent literature, he also underscores the problem of the 'biased referee' (Buchanan 1991: 138). In secession disputes it is unlikely that a neutral party can be found within the state to judge whether the minority has suffered a sufficient degree or kind of injustice to justify its seceding. Even (perhaps *especially*) in democratic settings—such as those found in multinational states like Canada, Belgium and Spain—the question of whether national minorities have been unjustly treated is a deeply contested one among politicians, lawyers, academics and ordinary citizens. Secessionists and federalists (or minority and majority nationalists) are likely to disagree

---

[22] See, e.g. Sunstein (2001*a*: 106) who argues adamantly against entrenching a right to secede but who readily acknowledges that 'When oppression is pervasive and, and not otherwise remediable, secession is a justified response; of course a subunit is entitled to leave a nation that is oppressing it'. Another critic of constitutionalizing secession, Aronovitch (2000*b*: 33–4), also does not rule out the possibility that it may be appropriate for parties to negotiate a particular secession agreement.

about what kinds of incidents or events can give just cause to secede, about whether such events have occurred, about whether they have been or could be rectified by measures short of secession, about whether any particular violations were significant enough, and so on (see Norman 1998*a*: 50–1).

For this reason, just-cause theorists in favour of constitutionalizing secession have tended not to rely on any party (such as the constitutional court) to decide if there has been just cause for secession. Instead they tend to recommend *procedural* mechanisms that would make it possible for oppressed groups to secede, while discouraging what I have elsewhere called 'vanity secessions', defined as 'secessions by groups lacking just cause'.[23] Such mechanisms include many of the rules (which we saw in Section 6.2) that would make it difficult for secessionist politicians to capitalize on fleeting sentiments in favour of secession (e.g. requirements to hold a series of referendums over a period of years, or conversely a requirement that no more than one referendum on secession can be called within a twenty-year period; see Weinstock 2001*a*: 197). They also typically include qualified or supermajority requirements for secessionist votes, in part to use very strong support for secession as a kind of proxy for whether the group has just cause. In democratic states with relatively strong secessionist movements, core support for secession within the minority's territory rarely exceeds 50 per cent. At least in this sort of country it is assumed that it would take considerable outrage, caused presumably by at least the perception of ongoing injustice, to create a sustained level of support for secession well above the 50 per cent level. For this reason, some just-cause theorists have recommended a secession clause that would call for, say, two-thirds support from voters in the seceding region: real injustice could generate such support, but mere nationalist rabble-rousing could not.

As part of a sustained critique of just-cause theories of secession, Margaret Moore has called into question the justification of such procedural institutions that rely on a correlation between popular support for secession and the justice of a group's cause. She notes: 'This is an empirical relationship, which is intuitively plausible, but unsupported' (Moore 2001: 148). Of course, correlated variables do not march in lock-step. We can think of many possible or historical situations of groups falling outside the generalization. For example, groups with clear just cause to secede but that will not be able to mobilize even bare majority support for secession; perhaps because of a large population of non-group-members on their territory. Or consider groups that are mobilized along minority-nationalist lines to support secession even

---

[23] See Norman (1998*a*: 52). My somewhat playful use of the term 'vanity' has been gently rebuked in Costa (2003: 80–1).

in the absence of just cause. 'It may even be because of *past* injustice or exclusion by the majority group in the state, [rather than] any current injustice committed by that group or the state' (Moore 2001: 148, my italics). As Moore notes, these facts do not 'impugn [the] just-cause theory in itself, conceived in non-institutional terms' (ibid.); but, to put it in the terms I am using here, they do suggest that some just-cause theorists may have underestimated the gap to be bridged from the validity of moral theory of secession to the need for, or content of, a constitutional secession clause.[24]

In other words, even if the just-cause theory is the most plausible account of the morality of secession, it does not seem to imply that there should be a constitutionalized secession procedure, nor can it point directly to any given procedure, should a state decide to give itself one. Does it follow that the just-cause theory, and discussions of the morality of secession more generally, are *irrelevant* to the argument for domesticating secession? I think not. In some sense the just-cause theory is what you end up with once you have eliminated nationalist and choice theories from the field. Nationalist and choice theories provide the self-justification for almost every democratic secessionist movement in the world. And as I noted earlier, the truth of either of these theories would virtually require a right of secession in the constitution of a just multinational state. As Buchanan (1991: 4) argues at the outset of his book, 'a political philosophy [such as liberalism] that places a pre-eminent value on liberty and self-determination, highly values diversity, and holds that legitimate political authority in some sense rests on the consent of the governed must either acknowledge a right to secede or supply weighty arguments to show why a presumption in favour of such a right is rebutted'. In effect, what we are calling just-cause theories are the outcome of these 'weighty arguments' against permitting or requiring secession for any territorial group that fancies a state of its own.

6.3.2 Democratic Rule-of-law Reasons

The next set of reasons for domesticating secession in multinational states is based on:

(a) the possibility or probability that secessionist movements will arise within territories or subunits controlled by national minorities whether there is an explicit recognition of a right to secede or not; and

---

[24] A certain excessive enthusiasm about the constitutional implications of the just-cause theory is evident in some of my own previously published arguments, especially as laid out in a portentously worded section 'From the Just-Cause Theory to a Democratic Secession Clause' (Norman 1998*a*: 50–6).

(b) the perceived advantages of handling secessionist politics and secessionist contests within the rule of law rather than as 'political' issues that lie outside of, or are presumed (by the secessionists) to supersede, the law.

I take presumption (a) to be a reasonable upshot of the discussions of nationalism and nation-building earlier in this book. We shall now look at the case for (b).

In Section 6.3.1 we noted that even where a moral right exists (e.g. the right to secede if you have 'just cause') it does not follow that there must be a constitutional expression of this right. In this section we are considering the converse possibility: that there should be a legal provision for an activity (such as seceding, or attempting to secede) even when there is no right to do it; in fact, even when the activity is morally objectionable. I will not make the case here that 'vanity' secessions are morally objectionable (see Weinstock 2001a: 187); but it will be a strong argument for legalizing secession that holds even if this is the case.

The groundwork for this argument comes from Daniel Weinstock's suggestion that we compare the legalization of secession to cases of legalizing other morally dubious activities. It is a pattern of argument that could be addressed to people who thought that abortion, prostitution, or selling narcotics for recreational use are immoral. One might argue that these kinds of activities are going to happen whether they are legal or illegal, and that there may be reasons to make them legal and bring them out of the black market and within the ambit of government regulation.[25] Weinstock argues that 'there is a case to be made for making legal provision for people to engage in behaviour they have no moral right to engage in' when three conditions are met: (*a*) it is most likely that these people will engage in this behaviour even without the legal right to do so, or even if it is illegal; (*b*) 'the behaviour in question does not involve the violation of an absolute moral prohibition'; and (*c*) 'the consequences of legally unregulated behaviour of the kind in question are likely to be worse than the same behaviour engaged in within legal-procedural parameters designed to offset the foreseeable perverse consequences of granting the right' (Weinstock 2001a: 188).

This seems right as a claim about legitimate public-policy formation in modern democratic states. The question is whether Weinstock is justified in

---

[25] For example, one might argue, that brothels and prostitutes should be registered and required to meet various public-health and safety standards, and that heroin should be dispensed by licensed health clinics to addicts. The 'no back-alley abortions' argument for legalized abortion is like this as well: it is addressed in part to people who think that abortion is (somewhat) immoral, and it argues that since abortions are going to happen anyway there are public-health and compassionate grounds for allowing them to happen in safe hospitals and clinics.

claiming that secession satisfies these conditions. The first issue we have to clarify is what the relevant 'behaviour' is. Is it (i) advocating secession, (ii) mobilizing for and demanding the right to secede, (iii) attempting to secede, or (iv) seceding? These are very different kinds of activities. Surely most people would see the mere advocating of secession (i) to be something that falls within rights to free speech, just as advocating drug use, prostitution, theft, or even revolution do. And similarly (ii), mobilizing a peaceful secessionist movement that demands the right to secede, would seem to be an activity that falls under rights to free speech, freedom of the press, and freedom of association; although obviously such activity would have to be carried out in ways that respect the law and public safety (as J. S. Mill pointed out in *On Liberty*, freedom of speech does not protect every form of speech that might be bellowed out to an angry mob). At the other end of the spectrum, it does not make much sense to think that it is (iv), seceding itself, that is the 'behaviour' to be protected. For one thing, this certainly does not meet Weinstock's first, 'inevitability' condition. For another, as a matter of fact and law, a group cannot secede of its own volition, any more than you can get divorced on your own (even if, in both cases, a territorial group or a spouse can separate de facto). Secession involves becoming a new state, and this requires recognition by other states, including typically the rump state. So what, then, is the behaviour that a constitutional secession procedure would be legalizing?

For the sake of brevity I have referred to this 'behaviour' or political phenomenon as 'secessionist politics'. It is a continuous spectrum of activities ranging from the legally innocuous activity of advocating secession to the legally and morally dubious activities of unilateral declarations of independence (UDI) and armed insurrection; encompassing, in between, the creation of political parties with secessionist platforms, the contesting of elections by such parties, their organizing referendums on independence when they form regional governments, and so on. Within this spectrum the crucial point of constitutional interest is the question of whether there is a legal means for a provincial government (or perhaps a federal party) representing a minority group to prove the democratic will of the group to secede and to trigger fair negotiations with the central government (and/or other partners in the state) to bring about a secession. This stage of 'attempting secession', (iv) above, is crucial because understandings about it will effect the dynamics of the activity at either end of the spectrum of secessionist politics: if popular demands for secession fall upon deaf ears in the central government then, at one end of the spectrum, this could heat up the secessionists' rhetoric and increase the movement's sense of grievance along with its popularity; and at the other end of the spectrum, it could end up promoting the strategies of extremists in the movement who prefer extra-legal options, such as a UDI or violence.

So does 'attempting secession', or secessionist politics more generally, meet Weinstock's three criteria, above, for 'legalization'? I will assume that it satisfies condition (b), that is, that it is not in violation of an absolute moral prohibition. Secessions from reasonably just democratic states can be morally regrettable for many reasons; but surely they are not evil. When more than 99.9 per cent of Norwegians voted to secede from Sweden in 1905 (the tally was 368,392 to 184!), and the Swedes did not contest their wish to secede, it is hard to believe that something absolutely awful happened nonetheless. Of course, few cases would be this unproblematic, but in this case surely we would have been more concerned if Sweden had refused the request to secede, especially if it had reacted with force.

How about Weinstock's condition (a): Is secessionist politics in a multinational state *inevitable* whether or not there is a legal mechanism for secession? To some extent, this question is moot for my argument, since I am only concerned with those cases where there is already significant support for secession. But what *is* close to inevitable in multinational democratic states is that there will be movements calling for 'self-determination', including the right to secede if that is what the group wants. Again, this is true almost by definition: we would not call these groups *national* minorities if their ethnocultural difference were not accompanied by a political will to some form of self-government.[26] It is not inevitable that these movements will ever be strong (i.e. popular) enough to actually attempt, or even credibly threaten, to secede. In cases where they cannot rally strong support for secession, a constitutional procedure that allows secession would never be used. But in cases where strong popular support for secession is within the realm of possibility, it is unlikely that the lack of a constitutional procedure will dampen the support for the secessionist option. So yes, in a qualified, slightly question-begging, sense, secessionist politics is inevitable in the kinds of multinational states we are concerned with here.

And this leads us to consideration of Weinstock's third criterion, (c); the consequences of not having a legal secession procedure may well be worse than the consequences of having one. There are two reasons for this: first, because a popular secessionist movement without a legal means to pursue its political agenda will give rise to political uncertainty, and possibly worse (in some cases, the certainty of violence); and second, because a legal procedure

---

[26] Consider the case of the Friesian minority in the north of Holland—a territorially concentrated group with its own language and identity. They do not manifest such a political will for extensive self-government and political autonomy, and this is why we do not tend to think of the Netherlands as a multinational state, even if it is plainly a multiethnic state.

of the right kind might actually diminish the chance that there will be an attempted secession or even a serious secessionist movement. I will say more about this second point in Section 6.3.3. In the meantime, it is instructive to look at the case of Quebec and Canada as an example of the dynamics of a democratic secessionist movement within a constitutional order that was until recently silent on the legality of secession.

6.3.2.1 *Interlude: a case study of high-wire secessionist politics without a net*

There is much to be learnt from more than three decades of serious democratic secessionist politics in Quebec and Canada. Quebec's independence movement is an explicit model for other national minorities in Western Europe and elsewhere. It is also, no doubt, seen by centralists in other multinational states as the example of what happens when 'too much' autonomy is granted to a national minority. The most important lessons, however, may concern the costs of assuming that the challenge of secessionist politics can be met without addressing the rules for secessionist contests.

In 1968 the first major separatist political party in the province, the Parti Québécois (PQ), was founded with a former Quebec cabinet minister, René Lévesque, as its leader. This party won the provincial election in 1976 (with 41 per cent of the popular vote in a first-past-the-post electoral system), promising not to attempt to secede without first winning a referendum. It held this referendum in 1980—the question asked for a mandate to negotiate 'sovereignty-association', a kind of state-to-state confederal arrangement—and its Yes-side lost by a 60–40 margin. The party would nevertheless win three of the next six provincial elections in Quebec, although never with a majority of the votes, and one time with fewer total votes than the federalist Liberal Party of Quebec. In 1995 a PQ government held another quasi-independence referendum, and this time they came within a percentage-point of winning. It is worth reflecting on the wording of the question used in this referendum. The question on the ballot read thus:

Do you agree that Quebec should become sovereign, after having made a formal offer to Canada for a new economic and political partnership, within the scope of the bill respecting the future of Quebec and of the agreement signed on June 12, 1995?

Yes or No. Intense debate in the Quebec National Assembly could not get the word 'country' added after the word 'sovereign', presumably because the majority PQ government knew full well that polls consistently show that support for Quebec being 'sovereign' is higher than support for it becoming a 'sovereign country'. The bill referred to in the question was a long piece of proposed legislation that calls for a declaration of independence if the offer of confederal partnership is refused. The 'agreement signed on June 12th' was an informal one between the leaders of the three nationalist parties in Quebec. Given how fuzzy this question was—especially as a basis for a UDI—it is perhaps not surprising that some leading intellectual supporters of the Yes-side expressed relief afterwards that they *lost* by one percentage-point rather than winning by such a margin.[27]

What was the federal government's response to this steady escalation of democratic secessionist politics? We walked through part of this history in the appendix to Chapter 4. Throughout this period there were significant attempts to make French-speaking Quebeckers feel more allegiance to Canada: French was made an official language in Canada, and its use within the federal civil service was greatly expanded; there was also a steady flow of 'transfer payments' into Quebec as part of a 'regional equalization' scheme where the wealthier provinces subsidize the poorer provinces, including Quebec. And then, as we discussed in some detail in Chapter 4 and its appendix, there were also two major attempts by the federal government to explicitly recognize Quebec as a 'distinct society within Canada' in the Constitution. (Eventually, the federal parliament passed a resolution declaring Quebec to be a distinct society and promising not to ratify any major constitutional amendment unless Quebec had already done so. Such legislation can, of course, be overturned by a future government.) But on the question of secession itself, successive federal governments, like the Constitution itself, remained silent. Senior federal politicians played active roles in both 'sovereigntist'[28] referendum campaigns (on the No-side), thus legitimizing them to a significant extent. But they never laid out an official policy about how they would respond if the Yes-vote crossed the 50 per cent threshold. They (literally) prayed that that would not happen, and were shocked when it almost did in 1995. Afterwards several academic conferences and think tanks debated what might have happened if the Yes-side had narrowly won the referendum of 1995; and virtually no one imagined that things would have proceeded smoothly or 'rationally'. As one of Canada's leading political scientists put it,

If fewer than 30,000 people had switched to the Yes side, Canada would have been thrown into the deepest political turmoil of its history. We should make no mistake about this. A Yes vote would have produced an unprecedented level of uncertainty about the future: right across the country, while the dollar's value plummeted and interest rates rose sharply, Canadians would not have known whether trade with

---

[27] See Laforest (2004).
[28] Democratic Quebec nationalists prefer the neologism *souverainiste* to *séparatiste*, which they associate with violent extremism.

Quebec would continue, whether the North American Free Trade Agreement would still apply to Canada, what currency they would be using in twelve months, or even whether Canada would continue to exist. (Young 1998: 112)

Several volatile issues—especially concerning the borders of a seceding Quebec state which contained territories inhabited mainly by Aboriginal peoples or Anglophones who voted overwhelmingly against separation—had scarcely been aired in public debates.[29] On the border issue, for example, the federal government had neither challenged nor endorsed the separatists' assertion that a new Quebec state would retain the borders it has as a province within Canada. There had been virtually no public debate on the issue of who would actually sit down to negotiate on behalf of Canada or the potential rump of Canada were secession negotiations to take place (the Government of Canada typically contains a significant number of members from Quebec, so it is not clear that it would be the appropriate body to represent the interests of Canadians outside of Quebec). With issues like this unresolved in advance, many commentators refused to rule out the possibility of extreme turmoil and even violence during a period of attempted secession.

In a moment I will discuss some of the Canadian federal government's more recent attempts to clear up this uncertainty by laying ground rules and conditions for future secessionist attempts. At this point, however, it is worth drawing attention to three lessons from this case that could potentially apply in other open, democratic societies with serious secessionist movements.

First, this history illustrates the difficulty of fixing an arbitrary stopping point for the legality of secessionist politics. If it is permissible to advocate secession, to form parties with secessionist platforms, to have those parties form provincial governments, and to have those governments organize referendums that respect the usual democratic norms—and there are good reasons to think that all of these things should be permissible within a democratic multinational federation—then it would be very difficult for a central government to simply refuse to negotiate secession after a 'victory' for the secessionists. To refuse to negotiate (especially after participating on the No-side in a referendum campaign) would be to declare that this whole decades-long democratic process was a charade. And that kind of response

---

[29] Other issues the federal government had never addressed included the question of whether Quebeckers could retain their Canadian citizenship after secession, how the massive national debt would be divided between the two successor states, and whether Quebec would continue to use the Canadian dollar. Of course, the separatist Quebec government had a clear position on all of these issues: a 50 per cent + 1 vote would be sufficient to trigger the secession process, an independent Quebec would retain the borders it had as a province, Quebeckers could retain their Canadian citizenship if they wanted to, and the new state would use the Canadian dollar and become an automatic member of NAFTA.

could only feed the indignation or *ressentiment* that lies behind secessionists' desire to be masters of their own house.³⁰ Yet, there does not seem to be any obviously best place for central authorities to take a stand against secessionist politics in a free society; at least in a liberal democracy whose constitution is silent on secession. You cannot forbid people to advocate secession, and you cannot stop parties from putting secession in their platforms; and in most federations, you would not be able to prevent regional or provincial governments from holding consultative referendums. (Surely a division of powers that prevented provincial governments from holding consultative referendums would be unfairly tilted in favour of majority nation-builders.) Anti-secessionists can, of course, debate secessionists in all of the usual ways; but this hardly amounts to a strategy for containing secessionist politics.

From the perspective of ordinary citizens, who will have heard their politicians and opinion-makers debate the secessionist option for years, a secessionist referendum campaign will look and feel very much like a normal election campaign; albeit one with much higher stakes. In all likelihood the Yes- and No-sides will be led by familiar political parties and politicians; there will be a concentrated campaign period, with the usual marketing mix of posters, TV ads, rallies, televised debates, etc.; the vote will take place in polling stations supervised by party workers and government election officials; some percentage of voters will vote strategically (e.g. not wanting secession, but wanting a strong showing in order to increase bargaining power); there will be an outcome at the end of the evening with one side receiving more votes than the other; this will be followed by victory and concession speeches from the two headquarters. If the No-side wins, political life will return to normal. (Sort of. Referendums like this leave the body politic badly bruised.³¹)

But if the Yes-side gets more than 50 per cent of the valid votes, citizens will find themselves in an entirely novel situation: a political contest has not just been *decided* according to the rule of law, as happens in an election (coalition bargaining notwithstanding). Instead a new contest for which there are no agreed-upon rules will have just been *initiated*. The seemingly familiar exercise of the referendum had the trappings of electoral democracy, but it could also be described as a grand exercise in power politics masquerading as democracy. The secessionists will be asking for the referendum victory to be

---

³⁰ On the concept of *ressentiment* in nationalist politics, see Taylor (1993: 40–58) Resnick (2000*a*, 2000*b*) Greenfeld (1992).

³¹ It is very interesting that opinion polls in Quebec consistently show a much lower level of support for holding another secessionist referendum than they show for preferring separation. In other words, a significant percentage of people who would prefer to live in an independent Quebec would rather not have the province go through another bruising referendum.

treated just like an election victory, entitling them to the 'spoils'. But in fact, when a constitution is silent on this issue of secession, all they will have received from their victory in a referendum is something equivalent to a show of hands at a trade-union meeting in advance of contract negotiations. For example, '50 per cent + 1' on referendum night might count for very little if it is known that there was a boycott by a substantial number on the other side, a fuzzy question, or if subsequent opinion polls show the support for the Yes-side to be slipping. '50 per cent + 1' would seem to be no more decisively democratic a threshold here than it is for, say, a parliamentary party leader who learns that he or she has received the support of only 51 per cent (or even 71 per cent) of her parliamentary caucus or party membership in annual vote of confidence on her leadership. Without more overwhelming support, such a leader would typically resign and call for the election of a new leader (even if she was willing to stand again herself).[32] Similarly, secessionists receiving only 51 per cent support to negotiate the terms of secession and the creation of a new nation-state might well decide that this was not a sufficient mandate for such a project. I assume that there is nothing in the concept of democracy per se that would *require* them to proceed with secession on the basis of such a fragile mandate.

Let us sum up this rambling first lesson from the Quebec–Canada experience of secessionist politics. It will always be possible and permissible to pursue secessionist politics within the rule of law in a just, democratic state. But if unchecked, this political contest can eventually find itself progressing into an arena where there are no clear or agreed rules for deciding the winner of the contest. It can look like an ordinary democratic process all the way along; but without any rules for an end-game it will have to end up as mere power politics (or potentially worse), not constitutional democracy.

A second lesson from this Canadian case is that if there are no explicit constitutional rules in place to govern of the sort discussed in Section 6.2, above—e.g. for the process of holding a secessionist referendum, selecting the wording of the question, deciding the level of support needed for victory, and assigning rights and obligations on negotiating parties in the event of a victory by the secessionists—if there are no such rules in place, then secessionists will be able to 'set' and in some sense legitimize many of the 'rules' themselves. If the central government later declares the process flawed, or the majority insufficient, it cannot help looking like it is trying illegitimately to

---

[32] Interestingly enough, a leader of the Parti Québécois once did just that. After receiving the support of *only* 76.2 per cent of the delegates in a confidence vote at his party's annual convention in June 2005, Bernard Landry resigned his leadership.

move the goal posts while the ball is in the air. As I will suggest later, the rules about secession that might be agreed to under reasonably fair conditions at the point of a federal state's founding or refounding would likely be much more demanding than those which the separatists would set for themselves. (For example, procedures to prevent 'snap' referendums from being called or fuzzy questions from being asked; establishing qualified majorities for success; and possibly procedures for the democratic partition of the seceding territory or the rump state should majorities living in border regions prefer to stay with the larger state or to join the seceding state.) This suggests some clear advantages to setting those rules in advance in as legitimate a fashion as possible.

A final lesson from the Quebec–Canada case—and this speaks to Weinstock's third condition concerning the legalization of morally dubious behaviour—is that there are several potential costs to having a secessionist political contest go entirely unregulated in this way: costs that are quite possibly worse than the costs of having a legalized secession procedure. We will discuss more of the costs to deliberative democracy of having ongoing secessionist politics a little later. At the very least, as Weinstock has emphasized, such long-running secessionist contests have a tendency to muscle many other issues off the political agenda. They also tend to polarize elections, so that voters will find themselves forced to vote for parties on the basis of whether they are separatist or not, rather than according to their policies on the usual range of socio-economic issues (Weinstock 2001a: 196). Then there are the economic costs of political uncertainty, as well as the increased risk of violence. One of the lessons of the Canadian experience is that ongoing, seemingly never-ending, *secessionist politics can be as unfortunate for the larger state as secession itself.* It is the kind of thing that constitutional engineers should be very eager to discourage at the point of founding or refounding a multinational federal state. A secession clause should be a prime example of moderate rival nationalists agreeing to take measures that will limit occasions for some of the more passionate and unpredictable forms of nation-building and nationalist mobilizations on both sides of the fence.

In sum, a strong case can be made for making secession legal, under carefully constructed conditions, even for those who think (as I do) that secession from a reasonably just democratic federation is rarely justified. If secessionist politics is going to happen anyway, it is better that it takes place within the rule of law—especially if a well-formulated secession clause would actually take away incentives to engage in secessionist politics. This latter point leads us to considerations of deliberative democracy and constitutionalism that we will explore in Section 6.3.3.

6.3.2.2 End of interlude: 'rule-of-law' reasons against domesticating secession

Before moving on from this discussion of 'rule-of-law' *reasons* for domesticating secession, it is worth exploring a 'rule-of-law' *objection*, and responding to it, in part, by commenting on the way Canadian courts and lawmakers have tried to domesticate secession in the years since the 1995 Quebec referendum.

Critics of constitutionalizing secession have cited a number of obstacles to formulating a secession clause. Some of these are objections *in principle* to constitutionalizing secession; for example, arguing that it violates the spirit and ideals of constitutionalism.[33] We will deal with some of these objections in Section 6.3.3. At this point we will consider the objection that the real devil is in the details of a secession clause—where the particular details that will be relevant in some future secessionist contest are just too difficult to predict and too uncertain to fix in the text of the constitution. Part of this objection is well taken. Even the most enthusiastic supporters of constitutionalizing secession must recognize that, as Aronovitch puts it, 'beyond whatever can be stipulated by rules and beyond whatever guidance can legitimately come from valid norms of law...there remains the core need, in the best of circumstances, for the parties to a potential secession to work out, on a partly *ad hoc*, contextualist basis, whether and how it is to happen' (Aronovitch 2000*b*: 34). But Aronovitch wants to go further and suggest that stipulating *anything* about secession in legal texts is ill-advised. He raises three challenges in particular:

1. That it would be impossible to spell out in a secession clause fair rules for dividing assets, debts, and properties. 'This seems to require impossible prescience and/or to pre-empt on all kinds of developments and innovations, economic, international, organizational, even moral; such rules which—if formulable at all—might have seemed fair at the outset may not be at all so after the fact.'
2. 'Similarly, how can there be, and why suppose there should be, a clause deciding once and for all which units or groups qualify for the right to secede?'
3. It is very likely there will be disputes between the secessionists and the central government about how to interpret a secession clause; but the supreme or constitutional court 'seems an unlikely candidate for acceptance as an impartial and effective arbiter for disputes about the right to secession' (Aronovitch 2000*b*: 34–5).

I have so far avoided discussing exactly how a secession clause should be formulated, apart from suggesting that it would be built largely out of answers

---

[33] See, e.g. Aronovitch 2000*b*: 33, Bauböck (unpublished): 32 (quoted in Weinstock 2001*a*: 191), or Sunstein 2001*a*: 95.

to the questions listed in Section 6.2, above. In Section 6.3.3 I will also suggest that a secession clause is best arrived at in constitutional negotiations that include a wide range of constitutional provisions of interest to both the minority (e.g. those promoting autonomy and recognition, while discouraging assimilationist majority nation-building) and the majority (e.g. those promoting unity and stability). The most I will ever argue for here is that a well-formulated secession clause could 'fit' very comfortably within a package of such provisions, perhaps even facilitating the final agreement. It is nevertheless worth addressing some of Aronovitch's concerns here, because they go directly to the issue of whether a constitutional clause can realistically and fairly enhance the protections of the rule of law.

All three of Aronovitch's concerns are legitimate worries, but all three will be at least as worrisome in the absence of a secession clause. For example, while it is possible to imagine a constitutional court failing to interpret contentious aspects of a secession clause in ways that the secessionists will perceive as fair, it is surely much more likely that the court would side with an obstructionist central government if there were no guidance whatsoever in the constitutional text; especially if it were asked to rule in the throes of a secessionist crisis. The same goes for Aronovitch's first concern, about the difficulty in specifying precise constitutional formulas for dividing assets, debts, and the like. In all likelihood, a secession clause would not attempt to specify that level of detail; in which case, the negotiations over these issues would be no more difficult with than without a secession clause. But a secession clause might spell out some processes and principles of good faith for such negotiations, and these could be justiciable in the courts. Again, this could not be worse than having no secession clause at all. Finally, to the concern about a secession clause having to specify which particular units, groups or types or groups would be permitted to secede—this is indeed a difficult problem, with or without a constitutional clause. It is worth noting, however, that it is no more difficult in principle than many decisions that have to be made in federal constitutions concerning the types of units that qualify for special federal 'privileges' such as being a province, getting to send representatives to the second chamber of parliament, getting to ratify or veto constitutional changes, and so on. In practice, it will be federal subunits that would be given access to a secession clause; but provisions could also be made for creating new subunits, or for partitioning seceding subunits so that 'federalist' counties could stay in the rump state and minority-dominated counties in a bordering 'rump' province could join the secession.[34]

---

[34] As discussed in Chapter 4, Switzerland and Germany both have democratic criteria for creating new federal subunits by dividing or combining existing subunits. For an interesting

Aronovitch is correct in highlighting just how much of the detail in a secession would be up for negotiation. But negotiation is a fact of life in intergovernmental arrangements like federations or the European Union. Constitutions do not try to decide all these contests in advance, and constitutional courts gain legitimacy as arbiters precisely because they do *not* systematically favour the central government over the subunits.

Although it was published more than a year afterward, it appears that Aronovitch's article was written before the Canadian Supreme Court's 1998 *Opinion* on secession.[35] This thoughtful and lengthy document does much to highlight the close relationship between legal principles appropriate for secession and those already in place within multinational federal constitutions. After the sorry history of the Canadian federal government's neglect of the constitutional challenge of secession, discussed above—and in particular, after the uncomfortably narrow federalist victory in the secessionist referendum of 1995—the Canadian Minister of Justice formally asked the Supreme Court to consider a number of questions about the legality of secession. As we noted earlier, the Court's subsequent *Opinion*, in effect, *read into* the constitution a modest secession clause, even though the constitution itself does not explicitly contemplate secession. I have discussed this *Opinion* at length elsewhere, and will not rehearse all of that analysis here.[36] The Court's bottom line, so to speak, was: 'A clear majority vote in Quebec on a clear question in favour of secession would confer democratic legitimacy on the secession initiative which all of the other participants in Confederation [i.e. the Canadian federation] would have to recognize.' The judges refused to spell out exactly what would constitute a 'clear question' and what level of support would qualify as a 'clear majority', but they left no doubt that the democratic legitimacy of such a result would require the federal government to negotiate in good faith.[37] Perhaps even more interesting than the bottom line is the reasoning leading up to it. They cited 'four fundamental and organizing principles of the Constitution', namely, 'federalism, democracy,

---

proposal for how this could be used to democratically partition a seceding subunit, see Monahan and Bryant (1996: 15–17). See also Laponce (2000) and Moore (2001: 206–7).

[35] *Reference re Secession of Quebec* [1998], 2 S.C.R. 217. Note: Aronovitch has recently written a searching critique of this *Opinion* [Aronovitch (unpublished)].

[36] See Norman (2001*a*), Moore (2001: 208ff.), Tully (2001), Brown-John (1999), and Walters (1999).

[37] '[T]he conduct of the parties [in negotiations following a clear referendum victory for the secessionist side in Quebec] assumes primary constitutional significance. The negotiations process must be conducted with an eye to the constitutional principles we have outlined, which must inform the actions of *all* the participants in the negotiation process. Refusal of a party to conduct negotiations in a manner consistent with constitutional principles and values would seriously put at risk the legitimacy of that party's assertion of its rights, and perhaps the negotiation process as a whole.' (secs 94–5 of the *Opinion*)

constitutionalism and the rule of law, and minority rights' (para. 32). The argument of the *Opinion* is then structured to show that *each one* of these fundamental principles entails the conclusion concerning the rights and obligations of secession negotiations.

Of course, there is no reason to think that most other constitutional courts would be as receptive to the legality of secession as Canada's—Spain's court, in particular, would probably be quite hostile to any unilateral defiance of the state's constitutionally declared 'indivisibility'. Still, Canada is the third oldest democratic federation; and with a tradition in constitutional law that, on the one hand, follows the American model, and on the other, recognizes the existence of multiple peoples within the state, it is hard to dismiss the relevance of the Court's *Opinion* on secession.[38] In the context of critiques of Aronovitch, Sunstein, Bauböck, and others, it is worth highlighting four aspects of the *Opinion*, in particular. First, although the Court firmly rejected the legality of a *unilateral* secession attempt, it did not find the very idea of secession to be contrary to fundamental ideals or principles of constitutionalism (on the contrary). Second, while the Court would agree with Aronovitch that there is a complicated range of issues that would have to be negotiated to effect secession; it also believes that there are fairly clear rights and obligations for the parties to these negotiations. Third, the *Opinion* gives some grounds for optimism that a constitutional court in a democratic multinational federation need not be hopelessly biased in favour of the federal government; especially when the court is able to consider these issues in 'the cool hour' rather than in the heat of a constitutional crisis. As it turns out, the main political actors in both the federalist and secessionist camps found favour in the *Opinion*.[39]

A fourth and final lesson worth emphasizing here is based on the necessary shortcomings of the *Opinion*. The judges did not want to write new law, and explicitly pointed out a number of issues that would have to be defined by political actors: especially concerning the clarity of the question asked in a secessionist referendum, and the size of clear majority (although they hint

---

[38] See para. 59 of the *Opinion* for an example of the Court's explicit recognition that the majority of people in Quebec possess 'a distinct culture'. This 'social and demographic reality... [that] explains the existence of the province of Quebec as a political unit and indeed, was one of the essential reasons for establishing a federal structure for the Canadian union in 1867'. In para. 125, as we saw earlier, the Court recognizes that 'much of the Quebec population certainly shares many of the characteristics (such as common language and culture) that would be considered in determining whether a specific group is a "people", as do other groups within Quebec and/or Canada....' Aboriginals are also given distinct constitutional rights *as peoples* in Canada.

[39] For reactions by politicians, opinion-makers and academics to the *Opinion*, see Schneiderman (1999).

strongly that a supermajority would not be inappropriate).⁴⁰ In Section 6.3.3, I will discuss a number of distinct advantages to spelling out explicit conditions that would have to be met before a province could trigger secessionist negotiations.⁴¹

In sum, the idea of having a legal procedure for secession fits well with the basic tenets, and more importantly with the spirit, of democratic constitutionalism. In a way, this is a negative argument: life could be much less comfortable in a constitutional democracy if serious secessionist debates, contests and negotiations had to take place outside the well-defined parameters of the law. Within a political culture where support for secession in minority territories hovers somewhere between, say, 20 per cent and 60 per cent, debates about secession will seem very much like any other matter that democratic citizens feel perfectly free to discuss openly (even if these debates can be more emotional and intense).⁴² In such political cultures it should seem outrageous that at a certain point these debates and contests will be required to take place in the near-absence of legal rules. Of course, the idea of a legalized secession procedure would itself look outrageous within certain constitutional traditions, particularly those in which the constitution declares at the outset that the nation and state are congruent and indivisible. But this sort of declaration would seem to have nothing to do with the ideal of constitutionalism and the rule of law per se, and everything to do with the power of nation-state nationalists to put their stamp of recognition on the state.

In Section 6.3.3 we will move beyond the negative argument and look at some of the ways in which a well-designed secession clause could actually serve to enhance the democratic and recognitional features of a constitutional

---

⁴⁰ The judges consistently hint that a 'clear majority' requires more than 50 per cent +1 of the votes. The *Opinion* contains expressions like 'clear majority', 'clear expression', 'strong majority', 'demonstrated majority', 'enhanced majority', 'substantial consensus', and 'clear repudiation of the existing constitutional order' in at least twenty-two places.

⁴¹ After the *Opinion* the Canadian federal government took a small but controversial step towards clarifying how it would determine whether it believed that a secessionist referendum involved a 'clear majority on a clear question'. It did this in a piece of federal legislation, rather than through a constitutional amendment, which in Canada would have required the consent of most of the provinces. For some analysis of this 'Clarity Act', see Norman (2001*a*).

⁴² This statement will be true in democratic states with a history of peaceful democratic changes of government along with mainstream secessionist parties committed to peaceful democratic politics. In other words, among national minorities like those in Flanders, Scotland, Catalonia, the Spanish Basque Country, and Quebec. In other parts of the world—e.g. in numerous jurisdictions in Eastern Europe and the former Soviet Union, India and Indonesia, among many other places—support for secession may be in a similar range but less tolerated within the larger state, if not illegal, and hence less 'normal'. Surely no constitutionalist would prefer the climate for discussion of secession in the latter group of countries to that in the former group.

6.3.3 Democratic-federalist Reasons

It is now time to begin cashing some promissory notes that have piled up during the exposition and argument in this chapter. In particular, I have made two claims at a few points in the argument: first, that the strongest arguments for domesticating secession come not from applying a moral theory of secession, but rather from thinking about appropriate conditions for a fair federal union or partnership between political communities hosting rival nation-building projects within a common democratic state. And second, I have claimed repeatedly that having such conditions entrenched and legitimized in the constitution would very likely reduce the incentives to engage in secessionist politics, and thereby decrease the social and political costs of secessionist politics and secession itself. It is time now to begin to cash out these notes.

Because entrenched secession clauses are so rare in the constitutions of modern states, it is tempting to believe that they could only be justified with some special kind of argument, e.g. an argument based on a moral theory of secession. Another approach, the one taken in this book, asks instead what kinds of arguments or reasons are legitimate for justifying *any* features of federal constitutional design; and then asks whether, upon reflection, these reasons would, for certain kinds of states, justify some form of secession clause. We discussed briefly in Chapter 5 Cass Sunstein's general claim that 'the central goal of a constitution is to create the preconditions for a well-functioning democratic order, one in which citizens are genuinely able to govern themselves' (Sunstein 2001*a*: 6). While this may be *the*—or at least *a*—central goal of constitutions, I argued in Chapter 5 that there are a number of other purposes for constitutions that are either derived from this goal, or sit alongside it. Sunstein himself emphasizes that 'a constitution should promote deliberative democracy, an idea that is meant to combine political accountability with a high degree of reflectiveness and a general commitment to reason-giving' (Sunstein 2001*a*: 6–7). And that it should create 'structures that will promote freedom in the formation of preferences and not simply implement whatever preferences people have' (ibid. 8).

More specifically, Sunstein urges that constitutional clauses should aim for:

- the protection of rights central to self-government;
- the creation of fixed and stable arrangements by which people order their affairs;

- the removal of especially charged or intractable questions from the public agenda;
- the creation of incentives for compromise, deliberation, and agreement; and
- the solution of problems posed by collective problems, myopia, and impulsiveness.

Let us call Sunstein's view 'deliberative constitutionalism'. It does not deal directly with any of the symbolic and recognition goals of a multinational constitution, but it is a clear articulation of the all-important democratic features. I am focusing on Sunstein's account here in part because Sunstein is the most prominent opponent of constitutionalizing a secession clause. As it turns out, Sunstein believes that these goals collectively suggest 'that a right to secede does not belong in a founding document' (Sunstein 2001*a*: 114).

I would like to criticize this argument of Sunstein's in two rather different ways. First, in effect, by accepting his premises but denying that they lead to his conclusions. That is, we can accept his goal of deliberative constitutionalism but deny that a properly designed secession clause would undermine it. And second, we will consider the inadequacy of deliberative constitutionalism, on its own, for thinking through the constitutional challenges of the multinational state.

6.3.3.1 *Deliberative democracy and secessionist politics*

The basic argument against Sunstein's case is this: he is absolutely right about the pernicious effects of ongoing secessionist *politics* on democratic deliberation and political stability—indeed, he may even underestimate the variety and potency of these effects—but he is too quick to assume that secessionist politics is necessarily encouraged by a secession clause and discouraged by its absence.[43] Secessionist *politics* can do all of the things Sunstein fears from an entrenched right to secede, i.e.

> increase the risks of ethnic and factional struggle; reduce the prospects for compromise and deliberation in government; raise dramatically the stakes of day-to-day political decisions; introduce irrelevant and illegitimate considerations into those decisions; create dangers of blackmail, strategic behavior, and exploitation; and, most generally, endanger the prospects for long-term self-governance. (Sunstein 2001*a*: 96)

If anything, Sunstein and others underplay the corrosive effects of secessionist politics on deliberative democracy. One cannot fully understand the

---

[43] I have explored this argument in greater detail in Norman (2001*a*).

psychological and sociological dimensions of secessionist politics merely by imagining rational bargaining situations where one party threatens exit (cp. Sunstein 2001*a*: 102). This is because of the ethnonationalist context of virtually every modern secessionist movement. In order for even cynical threats to secede (i.e. threats by those who do not really want to secede but who want to increase their bargaining power for other demands) to be credible, secessionist leaders must first mobilize 'their people' on inherently divisive nationalist lines. As we discussed in Chapters 1 and 2, this kind of mobilization can take years, and involves continuous agitation by secessionist entrepreneurs and other minority nationalists. They have an incentive to portray almost any decision or action by the central government as an example of insult, ignorance, humiliation, aggression, exploitation, or oppression. But unlike some other forms of 'posturing' to back up threats in political bargaining, this kind of nationalist sentiment is not easily turned off; it can become a background feature of the political culture that ensures that the pernicious effects described in the quote from Sunstein, above, become more or less permanent features of the political landscape. Even non-secessionists in the political culture will find themselves appealing to these sentiments in the course of political argument (see, again, the potentially agonizing liberal-nationalist dilemmas discussed in Section 2.7).

So what can be done through the constitutional engineering of a multinational state to take away the incentives for minority leaders to engage in secessionist politics? *One* part of the answer to this question—perhaps only a small part—is the question of whether a legitimate secession clause would increase or decrease incentives for secessionist politics. This last question is, of course, largely an empirical matter, and the results would vary with the nature of the secession clause, and the historical setting for which it is proposed. Much of Sunstein's argument is directed against entrenching what might be called a 'simple right to secession'; one that presumably could be exercised with something like bare majority support in the seceding province (the Ethiopian clause seems to be like this). But none of the federalist supporters of constitutionalizing a secession clause are arguing for a simple right to secede. As I noted at the beginning of this chapter, the principal advocates for a secession clause have been political theorists who are philosophically opposed to secession in reasonably just democratic states. They propose what Sunstein calls a 'qualified right to secede', or what I am calling a 'rigorous secession clause', one that would be constructed from answers to many of the questions posed in Section 6.2, above; requiring, perhaps, a substantial majority (two-thirds or three-quarters support) in the seceding region to be exercised, among other hurdles and qualifications. The hope would be that the qualifications on secession would be such that minority-nationalist leaders could not expect to mobilize enough support to make secessionist threats credible in the absence of genuine oppression by the central government. And with the prospects of a credible secessionist threat not in the cards, there would be less incentive to engage in the kind of nationalist mobilization that drives secessionist politics. (At the same time, removing this strategic option would have few implications for the otherwise legitimate nation-building projects within the scope of provincial government powers.)

Sunstein does consider the usefulness of a qualified right to secede that required a supermajority or an extended deliberation period. He dismisses both qualifications with a sentence or two. He notes: 'A requirement of a supermajority would certainly limit the occasions for, and seriousness of, secession threats. But in cases in which the subunit can be energized—for reasons of economic self-interest or ethnic or territorial self-identification—the protection would be inadequate' (Sunstein 2001a: 112). But this is too breezy a reply. Surely we cannot dismiss a piece of constitutional engineering simply by imagining low-probability situations in which it might be used to overturn something we like about the status quo. We do not dismiss the legitimacy of a rigorous amending formula (such as that in the US Constitution) simply by imagining that it could potentially be used to repeal some fundamental right or to amend the constitution in some reactionary way. There are empirical conjectures relevant here. It is significant that there has never been a substantial majority within a subunit voting to secede from a federal state with a long history of liberal democracy.[44] And again, none of the most popular Western secessionist movements today—among the Québécois, Flemish, Scots, Catalans, Spanish Basques, and so on—has ever shown sustained levels of support for secession above 50 per cent. It is also significant that there are virtually no serious examples of secessionist movements within flourishing constitutional democracies that are based purely on economic self-interest—the other motivation cited by Sunstein, and also by economists who assume that this would be the natural and compelling reason for a territorial group to want to secede.[45] All of this suggests that a secession

---

[44] The attempted secession of the southern US states is a problematic example, of course, but also one that is not particularly relevant to the understanding of rival nationalism in multinational states today. At any rate, no country that permits slavery can possibly be described as a liberal democracy.

[45] The example of the Northern League secessionist movement in Italy in the 1990s is a fascinating example. It is generally presumed that northern and southern Italians share the same ethnicity, though some secessionist entrepreneurs behind this movement have at times played with the idea that there is in fact an ethnic distinction between the two groups. It has also seemed clear that a critical mass of supporters of the movement had no real interest in seceding from Italy, but rather wanted to reform the system (perhaps by federalizing it) in order to reduce their 'subsidizing' of the south. So it may not be a *genuine* secessionist movement. But even if it

clause that demanded a supermajority significantly higher than 50 per cent might be just the sort of mechanism that could help to do something that Sunstein elsewhere cites as a legitimate aim of constitutional engineering: it would amount to 'a decision to take certain issues [in this case secession] off the ordinary political agenda'.[46] In Sunstein's own words, taking issues off the agenda in this way 'protects' and 'facilitates' democracy. If the tortuous Canadian case illustrates nothing else, it is that the issue of secession cannot be removed from the agenda merely by having the constitution turn a blind eye to it. That many of the new multiethnic democracies in Eastern Europe (which were the explicit targets of Sunstein's advice in the original 1991 version of his arguments) have avoided public secessionist debates is surely explained less by their constitutional prohibitions of secession than by the often heavy-handed intimidation of minorities by majority nationalists.

In short, there is good reason to think—at least in the sorts of countries I am addressing here, in the first instance—that a 'qualified right to secede' can serve as part of a constitutional pre-commitment strategy of the sort that Sunstein himself generally recommends. A crucial question, then, is *who* should be doing this pre-committing? In particular, an important consideration is whether the potentially secessionist minority itself would ever voluntarily pre-commit to an arrangement that made exit significantly more difficult. This question leads to a range of issues that are largely absent from most discussions of constitutionalism in the American tradition, where multinational constitutional accommodation has never really been on the table.

6.3.3.2 *Beyond (or beside) deliberative constitutionalism*

All democratic states have an interest in constitutional structures encompassing pre-commitment strategies to facilitate stable, deliberative democracy. But as we saw in Chapter 5, in multilingual, multinational federations, there is a range of constitutional issues that cannot be fully articulated in the

---

is an example of a genuine secessionist movement that is *not* derived from a minority national identity, it is clearly an exception that proves the rule. Another exception is the southern secession in the US. Of course, at least part of the explanation for the attempted secession of the southern states during the US Civil War is economic. This is one of many ways the case of the US Civil War is *sui generis* in the history of secessionist movements.

[46] In a recent reply to Weinstock, Sunstein concedes that he 'cannot prove the (thoroughly empirical) conjecture that' a secession clause would be more likely to fuel than dampen secessionist politics. And indeed he cites no empirical evidence. He concludes his reply to Weinstock's case for constitutionalizing secession by merely reasserting that 'the more sensible prediction is that [a constitutional right to secede] would undermine, rather than promote, the enterprise of democratic rule' (Sunstein 2001b: 355).

language of deliberative democracy—even if addressing these issues successfully will also help facilitate stability and deliberation. Some of these considerations were listed in Chapter 5 (Section 5.3.1) under the heading 'Seven Principles of Recognition' and include a variety of concepts, values, and principles that can be enshrined in various ways in a constitutional order and in the political culture it helps shape. They include the ideals of:

1. Partnership
2. Collective Assent
3. Commitment and Loyalty
4. Anti-assimilationism
5. Territorially Autonomy as National Self-determination
6. Equal Right of Nation-building
7. Multiple and Nested National Identities

The idea was that these principles of recognition could be instantiated in many different ways, concretely and symbolically. I will now discuss *one* of those possible ways. In what follows I shall very briefly suggest that these overlapping ideals could be partially realized or enhanced with the entrenching of a well-designed secession clause; especially if the insistence by the majority of a rigorous secession clause can be used to facilitate agreement on a number of other recognitional measures of interest to the minority. Here, then, are some of the possible benefits to both nationalist majorities and minorities of such a clause.

(a) **Removing secession as a realistic objective of ordinary politics.** Thus far, I have repeatedly drawn attention to one striking way that a rigorous secession clause might reduce the incentives for secessionist politics—i.e. by making the conditions for secession significantly more difficult than those that would be insisted upon by secessionist entrepreneurs in the absence of explicit rules. We have already discussed this argument in some detail. It is time to explore some less obvious ways a secession clause could facilitate a just federal union.

(b) **A symbol of voluntary assent** (see Principle 2). Even in the democratic world, almost none of the existing national minorities ever gave their initial, democratic assent to their membership in the larger state; and few have had a formal opportunity to assent since. In the less-than-fully-democratic world, of course, the situation for minorities is much worse. Most multinational states are the result of conquests, royal marriages, arbitrary colonial boundaries, and the like, from the distant past. When such conquests are of relatively recent vintage, as they were in the Baltics, minority nations will usually take their first democratic opportunity to exit—and rightfully so. In general, though, when peoples have been sharing the state for many generations, especially under conditions of equal citizenship and democratic elections, exit is not the preferred option. The larger state provides more opportunities, and the intertwining of political and economic systems, not to mention populations and families, make dismemberment messy and risky. But this acquiescence does not necessarily imply voluntary or enthusiastic assent on the part of minorities. When states are undergoing fundamental constitutional reforms, occasions for genuine assent present themselves. And an agreement between national minorities and the central government on a qualified right to secede is a powerful symbol of assent. Why is this? For one thing, it approximates a condition that would now be insisted upon by a sovereign state agreeing to enter a federation. Some kind of qualified escape clause would almost certainly be necessary today to get any independent state to agree to surrender a significant degree of its sovereignty to join a new state or superstate organization, even a free-trade agreement. Second, an unused escape clause can become a symbol of continuous voluntary cooperation—roughly in the way that an amendable constitution is usually seen as tacitly accepted over generations even if it is only rarely amended. Placing the possibility of a secession clause on the table during major constitutional reforms can provide a powerful means for making progress on other constitutional issues; as I shall describe below.

(c) **Partnership and recognition** (see Principle 1). There are, of course, many symbolic and concrete ways that a constitution can enshrine ideals of partnership and recognition—including declarations in the preamble that the country is a partnership, a 'community of communities', a federation of peoples, or what have you; or with specific roles for groups or subunits in, for example, constitutional amendment. Declaring that certain federal partners—whether by name, or by subunit status—have a qualified right to secede is another meaningful way of recognizing such territorial groups as full and willing partners in the state. This is especially true in so-called asymmetrical federations (those in which one or more federal subunits are recognized as homelands for particular national minorities and receive powers not shared by subunits occupied by members of the state's majority group). If only the national minorities' subunits are granted rights to secede, this will help satisfy their desire to be recognized as 'not just another province'—but as, at least symbolically, a nation-to-nation partner.

(d) **Trust-building, anti-assimilationism, loyalty and stability** (see Principles 3 and 4). At the point when states are refounded—especially when this is an opportunity for the democratization of a previously undemocratic state—national minorities are often looking to emerge from a long history of oppression by the majority. In Communist Eastern and Central Europe (ECE), as well as in Franco's Spain, for example, national minorities were subjected to extremely coercive assimilationist projects, typically including the denial of the right to use their minority language in schools and in public life (alas, much of this has continued in the post-Communist era in ECE). For true, voluntary, democratic cooperation to work after such a history, an extended period of good will and trust-building is needed (see Weinstock 1999). The minority is rightly suspicious of the majority; but the majority also has a long-standing suspicion of the 'loyalty' of the minority. In such a situation, an appropriately tailored secession clause could build trust in both directions. For example, in addition to a supermajority requirement, such a clause might also preclude any secession process for the first ten or twenty years. This might assure the minority that the majority would change its assimilationist habits, and it could assure the majority that the minority would not use any breathing space it got to plot its immediate escape. 'Stability' is hardly a principle of recognition, but in volatile multinational states it is likely to assume the status of a basic principle by members of majority and minority communities alike. The kind of secession clause just mentioned could help secure a good measure of it.

(e) **Facilitating fair terms of partnership** (Principles 1–7). I have already suggested ways in which a secession clause need not be thought of as merely a constitutional *artefact*: it can serve a critical role in a negotiating *process* leading to constitutional reform. Again, some kind of escape clause would almost certainly be demanded by independent states agreeing to join a new partnership, as there is implicitly in the European Union.[47] But for the foreseeable future, federations are more likely to arise (or be reformed) by decentralization than by the voluntary union of previously independent states or colonies. And putting a secession clause on the table in such processes of reform creates some intriguing and largely unexplored possibilities. In effect, a minority could agree to accept a rigorous secession clause as a kind of quid pro quo in exchange for greater autonomy and recognition. Or to look at it from the other side, majorities are often reluctant to offer minorities a significant degree of autonomy or recognition (e.g. constitutional recognition of the minority as a 'people' or a 'nation'), because they fear that this autonomy and status will be used by minority nationalists in nation-building projects leading to secession. Of course, individual minority leaders demanding autonomy and recognition will often verbally renounce secessionist ambitions,

---

[47] 'For the European Community, for example, a right to secede may therefore be more sensible, and indeed it will provide a greater incentive to join in the first instance.' (Sunstein 2001*a*: 105)

but by agreeing to accept a secession clause that would make secession an unrealistic goal in the absence of central government oppression, minority groups would be making a concrete, long-term commitment to the larger state; and in so doing they would be acknowledging the fairness of *a particular level* of autonomy and recognition. Roughly speaking, the greater the realm of recognition and autonomy (and the nation-building powers that come with it) that the minority demands, the higher the threshold of 'obstacles' (e.g. the level of a qualified majority vote) the majority could demand in the correlative secession clause. A constitutional accord understood in part as a result of this kind of good faith bargain would legitimize many of the Principles of Recognition:

(i) It would show the 'normalness', for both the minority and majority, of minority nationhood and autonomy within a larger federal state. By accepting a difficult secession procedure in return (in part) for national recognition, the minority itself would have committed itself to the rejection of the belief that the only 'normal' condition for a nation is to control a state of its own. Similarly, the majority could grant this kind of recognition (which they may acknowledge de facto in any case) because they no longer have to fear that it will necessarily lead to demands that, as a nation, the minority has an automatic right to its own state.

(ii) Similarly, it could help uncouple, in the eyes of both majorities and minorities, minority nation-building from secessionist politics. And this in turn could help establish the legitimacy of both orders of government using their sovereign powers in projects with foreseeable and reasonable identity-shaping effects. In other words, it could facilitate an understanding of an equal right of nation-building; nation-building that aimed for neither the assimilation of, nor the escape by, the national minority.

(iii) Both of these potential benefits of a constitutional accord balancing autonomy and recognition, on the one hand, with a pre-commitment to a rigorous secession clause, on the other, should also facilitate the more healthy acceptance and development of overlapping national identities among members of the national minority: they can be committed to their larger state in part because they appreciate the respect and autonomy it accords to their (primary) national affiliation.

In short, thinking about the terms of secession may be a very helpful way to think about the terms of federation. It is a truism in the literature on secession that one of the reasons secession is not usually justified is that it is possible for national minorities to enjoy a sufficient degree of self-determination and self-government within some kind of federal system. As we have seen, some theorists go even further by suggesting that a national minority is done an *injustice* if it is not granted a sufficient degree of autonomy and recognition within the larger state.[48] But thus far political philosophers have given very little indication of how to evaluate whether the degree of autonomy and recognition, and the terms of federation more generally, are just or appropriate. When is enough, enough? 'Veil of ignorance'-style contractual reasoning might give us some very general guidelines, but there will always be too much particular socio-historical information, and too much room for empirical speculation, for us ever to hope to determine precisely from behind a veil of ignorance the best terms of federation for any particular multinational state (e.g. its division of powers, constitutional amending formula, provincial representation in the second chamber of parliament, etc.). But in the rough-and-tumble world of actual constitutional negotiations between national minorities, federal provinces, and central governments, the creative use of a secession clause can help nudge a federation in the direction of arrangements that enhance both the autonomy of minorities and the stability of the state.

Now it could be objected that if a central government is looking for some kind of guarantee that a minority would not use its newly granted autonomy and recognition in a nation-building project leading to secession, then it would be better to have the minority agree not to a rigorous secession clause, but rather to a clause that explicitly rules out secession altogether.

The first response to this objection is simply to accept that in certain situations there might be nothing wrong, from the perspective of multinational federalism, for a group to renounce all rights to secede in exchange for other forms of autonomy, status or recognition. I am not arguing that a just multinational federal constitution *must* contain a secession clause, but only that such a clause is potentially beneficial in a number of ways that matter in multinational democracies. That said, many minority groups can foresee no likely circumstances in which they will favour seceding from their larger state (perhaps this is the way most Welsh, Bretons, Frisians, and Spanish Galicians or Majorcans feel), so in their constitutional negotiations they may very well be happy to renounce permanently a right to secede in order to receive other things they do desire. Other national minorities (and the politicians negotiating on their behalf), however, will find it much more difficult to renounce permanently the independence option, even if they are

---

[48] See the discussion in Section 5.3. See also Bauböck (2000), Weinstock (2001a: 189), Costa (2003: 69–71), Moore (2001: 151).

willing to agree to a clause that would make secession next-to-impossible.[49] So a second response to the objection is that it may be easier for a central government to secure a minority's agreement to a package of reforms if it demands that the minority accept a rigorous secession clause rather than renounce secession entirely. In circumstances where both sides are looking for an agreement—to end years or decades of constitutional disputes, from the point of the federal government, and to secure a more favourable status, from the point of view of the minority—the quid pro quo with a rigorous secession clause should look mutually advantageous.

It may also be a better hedge against secessionist politics in the (distant) future. In stable democracies, constitutional procedures have a way of gaining significant legitimacy over time, no matter how arcane. A secession clause that required, say, a three-quarters majority in the seceding province, might sit almost unnoticed for generations. But should a secessionist movement ever arise, it is very likely, in a society that respects the rule of law, that most citizens would see the secessionists as bound to meet those conditions in order to trigger secessionist negotiations. (Consider how nobody seriously suggests ignoring the Electoral College rules in US Presidential elections, even when these rules dictate a result that goes against the more intuitively legitimate popular vote. People may advocate reforming the rules for future elections, but not ignoring them while they are in place.) But, it is not inconceivable that a secessionist movement could arise long after the inclusion of a constitutional ban on secession, claiming the usual extra-constitutional legitimacy. Simply put: we know that long-standing constitutional procedures—even arcane and inconvenient ones—are almost always adhered to in constitutional democracies, but also that explicit bans on secession in otherwise open societies do not prevent the emergence of secessionist movements willing to move beyond the rule of law. We have already discussed, in Section 6.3.2, why it is generally preferable to deal with secessionist politics within the rule of law.

Perhaps the principal advantage to using a rigorous secession clause rather than an outright ban in exchange for more autonomy or recognition for national minorities, is that this allows for some of the other important symbolic benefits just described (voluntary assent, loyalty, recognition, and so on). Entrenching even a heavily qualified right to secede in the constitution—especially if such a right is granted only to particular, named groups or subunits—can serve as a powerful and permanent symbol of that group's national status *and* willing partnership in the state. For a group to accept such a clause is also a significant gesture of commitment to the state and to a

---

[49] See Weinstock (2001*a*: 201) for an explanation of the moral psychology involved in this position.

political culture that precludes secessionist threats in negotiations between the provinces and the federal government.

6.4 CONCLUSION

In this chapter I have argued for two points: first, that it would often make sense to include a secession clause in the constitution of a multinational federal state; and second, that the reasons for this are best understood not so much by thinking about the morality of secession, but by thinking through the moral logic of multinational constitutionalism. If the case for the second point is plausible, then the case for the first point will necessarily be rather sketchy at this stage—because we are still a long way from having a very sophisticated theory of multinational constitutionalism. Indeed, when it comes to issues about 'entrenching institutional arrangements and substantive rights...constitutional theory remains in a surprisingly primitive state' (Sunstein 2001a: 97), even in the 'cleaner' case of constitutional theorizing for the 'uninational' state. I have argued that an appropriately qualified right to secession would often make sense within the framework of the deliberative constitutionalism that Sunstein advocates: it could provide a better disincentive for secessionist politics than would constitutional silence on the issue. It makes even more sense once we consider the additional roles a constitution plays in states containing more than one significant national homeland. In these multinational states, we should think through the issue of whether or not to entrench a secession clause in much the same way we think through issues such as whether to have a centralized state or a federation, how to divide the powers between federal and subunit governments, how to represent subunits in federal institutions, what role to grant subunits in the process of constitutional amendment, whether to give special powers or forms of recognition to particular groups or subunits, and so on. In a multinational state where these issues are open to free and fair negotiation, the demands of minority national communities will reflect their identities as peoples with their own needs for self-government and recognition; needs that must be balanced against their interest in participating within a stable, self-governing sovereign state with which most of their members also have some level of overlapping national identification. My argument does not conclude that multinational states *must* include a secession clause, nor does it have anything to say about whether 'uninational' states would benefit from such a clause (presumably most would not).

Federalist Theory of Secession

The more general objective of this chapter has been to demonstrate something that could not be easily articulated in a 'meta-theory': namely, the feasibility of marshalling the wide array of relevant normative tools (discussed in Chapter 5) in order to justify specific federal-design options. As summarized in the preceding paragraph, the argument for constitutionalizing secession is still quite incomplete. But we do have a sense of what a much more definitive case for or against such a clause, or for or against certain design options for such a clause, would look like. This case may be a mixture of considerations of justice and minority rights, democracy, recognition, stability, pragmatism and group-interest; but the precise normative cocktail need not look arbitrary, and in particular, there are grounds for believing that, at least under favourable conditions, representatives of national minorities and majorities could agree on both a clause and its moral and political rationale. As I noted earlier, if this book were much longer (or if it were a multivolume work) there could be a chapter (or a book) on the patterns of normative argument for each of the other major 'plumbing' decisions in federal design. A secession clause is a good starting point because (*a*) the issue of secession has received much more attention in recent political theory than, say, the issue of the division of powers; (*b*) it is intimately linked to the rivalry of minority and majority nation-building projects that is at the heart of this book's conception of the multinational state; and (*c*) thinking about a secession clause can facilitate progress in negotiations about how other features of the federal plumbing could be arranged to suit these rival nationalists (as noted, a more rigorous secession clause, which should please *majority* nationalists, may permit them to be less anxious, and more generous, about the level of autonomy and asymmetry for minority provinces in the division of powers, which should please most *minority* nationalists).

Afterword

> Nationalism has torn apart colonial empires and Communist dictatorships, and redefined boundaries all over the world. Yet democratic multination federations have succeeded in taming the force of nationalism. Democratic federalism has domesticated and pacified nationalism, while respecting individual rights and freedoms. It is difficult to imagine any other political system that can make the same claim.
>
> —Will Kymlicka 2001: 91–2

This book has been about nationalism and federalism and the relations between them. The only point of agreement among those who have spoken and written on these two 'isms' is that one is the problem and the other is the solution. If there is one thing that links Victorian gentlemen like Lord Durham or A. V. Dicey, on the one hand, and military strongmen like Saddam Hussein and General Suharto, on the other, it is the conviction that federalism is the problem and nationalism is the solution. Granting autonomy to ethnocultural minorities, on this view, can only exacerbate divisions and heighten instability; the better alternative is to engage in nation-building to infuse the entire population with a common national identity and sense of loyalty to the central state. It is now, of course, much more common to think that nationalism is the problem—the sort of coercive majority nationalism just referred to, as well as the disruptive politics of minority nationalism—and that a federalism that constrains majority nationalists and appeases minority nationalists is the solution.

I have argued that federalism *can be* a solution. I am more ambivalent about whether nationalism is a *problem*. Human-resource managers are fond of saying that 'there are no problems, only challenges!', and perhaps that is how I have looked at the phenomenon and politics of nationalism in this book. Some forms of nationalism are obviously problematic, or worse; and this is why it had such bad press in post-war political philosophy. But as I tried to show in Chapter 2, nation-building is a natural consequence of perfectly legitimate government programmes and political discourse. And mobilizing support for just policies by appealing to aspects of citizens' national identities is also, within limits, a normal part of democratic politics. Nationalism becomes challenging when there is more than one national community—more than one nation-building project—sharing the same state. When at least one of those (minority) communities is territorially concentrated, federalism goes part of the way to meeting that challenge. Everybody writing on federalism in multinational contexts emphasizes that federalism is not a 'panacea' and does not guarantee 'success'. But the clear consensus, not just among theorists of federalism (who would say so, wouldn't they), but also among specialists in ethnic-conflict management and institutional design, is that 'it is hard to see any form of successful accommodation of multiple nations within a single state that does not include federalism' (Simeon and Conway 2001: 364).

So let us say that if multinational states are the challenge, federalism is part of the solution. It may not even be the biggest part of the solution (Filippov, Ordeshook, Shvetsova 2004: ix). It is, however, a part on which 'there is very little contemporary political theory...shed[ding] light' (Kymlicka 2001: 93). The challenge at the heart of this book was not to propose a federal system that would enable multiple nationalities to cooperate within the same political space; but rather, to consider how we would have to retool our normative theories and principles in order to evaluate such proposals. Of course, if a federal solution is going to work in a given setting, the devil is in the details. A federal design that works well in one state might fail utterly if tried elsewhere. In principle, one single institutional choice (such as whether to have education as a federal or provincial power, or whether to include a secession clause) could make the difference between the long-term stability and the early demise of a given federation. This is one reason we have spent rather more time than is typical in political philosophy surveying and categorizing institutional and constitutional options. The contingent nature of federal 'success', along with the extreme variability of nationalist movements and nationalist political cultures, raises a meta-problem for a normative theory of multinational federalism: it is difficult to make any normative claims that are both deep and generalizable on these issues. A normative theory of democracy might tell us that any democratic system should operate on the basis of 'one person, one vote'. But a normative theory of federalism is never going to tell us something nearly that specific; for example, it will not be able to tell us that every federal parliament should have a lower chamber in which every province has equal representation. This is part of what Kymlicka means when he warns that 'Federalism does not provide a magic formula for resolution of national differences'. What it does provide, however, is 'a framework for *negotiating* these differences' (2001: 118, my italics).

Like almost any work in political philosophy, this book has generally worked with some simplifying assumptions or parameters—about options, groups, and principles—concerning the nature of these 'negotiations' to resolve national differences in the multinational state. In addition to focusing primarily, as just mentioned, on *federal* options and mechanisms (rather than, say, electoral systems or consociational features), I have also been almost exclusively concerned with some particular kinds of groups and with the principles they might use to make their case for one set of options over another. I have concentrated on the negotiations between groups that can reasonably be called *national minorities* and *majorities*; groups that are territorially concentrated and have a national self-consciousness and some form of nationalist political culture. I have mostly had in mind national majorities whose conception of their nation includes the members of the minorities (the way French, British, or Canadian nationalism do), but have also entertained the possibility that the majority group, like the English or the Flemish, may not incorporate members of the national minority. In any case, my interest has been in the conflict and rivalry between groups whose leaders vie for control of state institutions in part to carry out nation-building projects. Finally, I have focused on potential negotiations between such rival nationalists within *liberal-democratic settings*, seeking principles and arguments that are likely to be acceptable within such political cultures. Using the issue of a constitutional secession clause as my most detailed case study, I have tried to show that traditional principles of democracy and constitutionalism, supplemented by some reasonable principles of mutual recognition, can facilitate agreements between rival national communities over even controversial federal options.

Of course, the flip-side of this focus on a circumscribed set of options, groups and principles is that I have said very little about a vast array of other political and institutional options, groups, and principles or political cultures. In particular, minority groups that are dispersed rather than concentrated, demographically tiny, or that do not have a national consciousness—many religious groups, indigenous peoples, or immigrant minorities fall under one or more of these categories—have barely shown up on the radar screen. I must emphasize again that the exclusion of such groups from a discussion of federalism is not based on any presumption that these groups are less imperilled or less morally worthy of special protection in the diverse modern state. Powerful and self-confident national minorities like the Québécois, the Catalans, or the Scots, as Levy (2004: 169) has argued, 'have a place of special importance in the constitutionalist argument only because of their particularly strong ability to stand up to a nationalizing state'. But 'the same sorts of reasons invoked for giving special powers within the federation to national minorities also apply' to 'still-more vulnerable groups like indigenous peoples and the Roma'. 'Of course', Levy adds, 'the institutions [for these other groups] will not look quite the same' (ibid.). Alas, our philosophical discussions of federalism are still at such a primitive and incomplete stage, in this book I have barely been able to sketch a case for federal principles and institutions involving the 'textbook' national minorities. This is not, in other words, a comprehensive political morality for the multiethnic state. Based on some of the tentative proposals I have advanced here, however, I share Levy's optimism that federalist principles and institutions could be extended to protect other (though not all) groups from certain aggressive nation-building exercises by a national majority or the federal government it dominates.

I dare say a similar apology (in both the English and Greek sense) is in order for the other conspicuous omission in this book. Federalism holds out the promise of reconciling diverse peoples in multinational states around the world; but I have primarily drawn examples from, and speculated about scenarios for, the relatively successful liberal-democratic states of Western Europe and North America. My aim here has been to try to understand the ways in which the institutions of a multinational federal state, and the principles sustaining or criticizing these institutions, might differ from those of a similarly developed uninational state. By looking at federations or quasi-federations in advanced democratic states, we are obviously able to reduce the number of 'variables' that might explain relevant differences between multinational states, on the one hand, and the uninational states that have generally been presupposed by Western political philosophy, on the other. These advanced federations also provide a wealth of examples of institutions that 'work' (or fail) and of promising proposals for reform. Of course, it would be foolish to think one could simply transplant a successful federal constitution from Western Europe into, say, Indonesia, Sri Lanka, Iraq, or even Croatia or the European Union.[1] Indeed, this is true of many elements of a constitution or political system. So I am not sure that 'pioneering' theorists of multinational federalism need be significantly more defensive about a 'developed democracies' focus than are, say, theorists of deliberative democracy, who also, by and large, do not try to extend their theories to democratizing societies in Eastern Europe or the developing world. As I have noted frequently, there is a growing body of theory and expertise on ethnic-conflict management and institutional design for deeply

---

[1] The numerous attempts to implant designer federal constitutions into short-lived post-colonial federations inspired studies with titles like *Why Federations Fail: An Inquiry into the Requisites for Successful Federalism* (Franck 1968). See also Watts (1966). I have explored the question of the relevance of genuinely federal structures or federal theory for the European Union in Norman (1995a). There is a vast and growing literature on this *sui generis* question. For just the tip of the tip of the iceberg see, e.g. McKay (1999, 2001), Nicolaidis and Howse (2001), Burgess (2000).

divided societies that can be drawn upon to try to extend the kinds of theorizing about federalism presented in this book.² But again, the theorizing presented here is barely developed to the point of clarifying the 'easy' cases, so it is still too early to know what aspects would have to be *merely adapted* and what would have to be *entirely rethought* for more deeply divided and less democratic political cultures. In short, I have asked how a committed liberal democrat, who is perhaps also a nationalist, and who thinks seriously about the sociology and morality of nationalism, should justify federal arrangements in a multinational state. It is not at all clear how much of the answer to this question will be of help for theorists or political cultures that are not committed to liberal democracy, or are blinded by their own nationalistic and theocratic world views (although they may certainly find various federal institutions to be justifiable on other grounds).

Consider just one example. I have been able to presuppose in 'easy case' countries like Canada, Spain, and the UK, the existence of so-called 'nested' national identities, particularly for members of national minorities. This in fact explains much of the dynamic of rival nationalist politics in these states: both majority (or federal) nation-builders in the centre, and minority nation-builders in the provinces, are competing for the loyalty and identity of the same group of citizens who already share both identities. Many theorists of ethnic conflict have emphasized the importance of nested identities in explanations of the viability of federal solutions (e.g. McGarry 2002: 439; Simeon and Conway 2001: 361; Miller 2000: ch. 8). But it is not always clear whether a given multinational state without a long history of democracy has minority groups with sufficiently nested national identities. The final draft of this book was being prepared at the same time as the post-Baathist constitution of Iraq, in the summer of 2005. That constitution turned out to incorporate federalism. Indeed, at the insistence of the Kurdish representatives, the delegates even debated the possibility (which they eventually rejected) of including a secession clause in the constitution. During the constitutional negotiations an editorial cartoon appeared in American newspapers that depicted three Iraqi men, looking like a Kurd, a Shiite and a Sunni, trying to write a constitution. One begins writing 'We the people...', and over his shoulder the second cautions, 'Not crazy about the word "we"', to which the third adds, 'Me neither'.³ This sums up nicely the fear of many observers

---

² See, e.g. Reynolds (2002), Reilly (2001), Filippov, Ordeshook, and Shvetsova (2004), Watts (1966, 1999*b*), Gurr (2000), Stepan (2005).

both inside and outside of Iraq about the viability of federalism if there is not among any of the three major groups, and in particular among the Kurds and Shiites, a significant-enough Iraqi identity to 'nest' alongside their primary ethnic or religious identities. Of course, given the colonial and post-colonial history of Iraq, and in particular Saddam's brutal regime that clearly favoured the minority Sunnis, it is not surprising that Kurds and Shiites might not hold much loyalty or identity for Iraq as such. That said, it is an open question in even very non-ideal federal terrain such as this whether a period of constitutional and civil peace may be sufficient to begin building or rebuilding nested identities among the members of constituent nationalities. There are certainly plenty of encouraging examples of this happening, from the three oldest federations to India and the United Arab Emirates more recently.[4]

In any case, I am not pretending to offer an analysis of the federal prospects for Iraq, but rather pointing out that questions of whether relatively ideal models of federalism are 'exportable' may come down to specific features of the federal proposal and the political cultures of the country in question. It is certainly not the case that federalism can work only when all other features of a wealthy, modern, democratic state are in place. Sometimes constituent groups just have to fear a common enemy, or the costs of civil strife, more than they distrust each other. As Kymlicka puts it, in the passage quoted earlier, federalism provides a 'framework' for negotiating national differences. In the language of this book, these negotiations are literally about the acceptable forms and limits of rival nation-building projects on shared territories.[5] The success of this framework depends, according to Kymlicka on 'an enormous degree of ingenuity, goodwill, and indeed good luck' (2001: 118). *Ingenuity* requires federal theory, both positive (of which there is a wealth) and normative (of which there is still a dearth). *Goodwill* requires the voluntary, mutual taming of nationalism. The more ingenuity and goodwill, the 'luckier' a federation is likely to be.

---

[3] The cartoon is by Jeff Stahler of the *Cincinnati Post* (United Media); it was reprinted in the *New York Times*, Sunday, 21 August 2005, Section 4, p. 2.

[4] The Iraqi constitution was ratified following a state-wide referendum on 15 October 2005. Although this constitution contains provisions for Islamic law that worry secular Iraqis, it must also be said that it offers generous recognition, in both symbolic and concrete forms, of the 'multi-ethnic, multi-religious, multi-sect' (Article 3) nature of the country.

[5] So enlightened Kurd or Shiite leaders (or at least, those who were not simply proposing a federal Iraq to facilitate a quick secession) would do well to ensure that the federal government has sufficient nation-building powers to enable it to foster goodwill and a sense of loyalty across the federation. I have discussed the logic of minority nationalists welcoming a degree of pan-nationalism in Norman (1994).

Bibliography

Acton, J. (1862). 'Nationality', in J. Figgis and R. Laurence (eds.), *The History of Freedom and Other Essays*. London: Macmillan, 1922, pp. 270–300.
Akhavan, P. and Howse, R. (1995). *Yugoslavia, the Former and Future: Reflections by Scholars from the Region*. Washington, DC: Brookings Institution Press.
Althusius, J. (1603). *Politica*, F. S. Carney (trans. and ed.) (Indianapolis: Liberty Fund, 1995). Relevant extracts reprinted in D. Karmis and W. Norman (eds.) (2005a), pp. 27–34.
Anderson, B. (1991). *Imagined Communities: Reflections on the Origins and Spread of Nationalism*, 2nd edn. London: Verso.
—— (1993). 'Nationalism', in J. Krieger (ed.), *Oxford Companion to Politics of the World*. Oxford: Oxford University Press, pp. 574–669.
Appiah, K. (2005). *The Ethics of Identity*. Princeton, NJ: Princeton University Press.
Arel, D. (2001). 'Political Stability in Multinational Democracies: Comparing Language Dynamics in Brussels, Montreal, and Barcelona', in A. Gagnon and J. Tully (eds.) (2001).
Armstrong, J. (1982). *Nations before Nationalism*. Chapel Hill, NC: University of North Carolina Press.
Aronovitch, H. (2000a). 'Nationalism in Theory and Reality', *Philosophy of the Social Sciences*, 30/3: 457–79.
—— (2000b). 'Why Secession is Unlike Divorce', *Public Affairs Quarterly*, 14/1: 27–37.
—— (unpublished). 'Seceding the Canadian Way', Department of Philosophy, University of Ottawa.
Audi, R. (1989). 'The Separation of Church and State and the Obligations of Citizenship', *Philosophy and Public Affairs*, 18/3: 259–96.
Baker, J. (1994). *Group Rights*. Toronto: University of Toronto Press.
Barker, E. (1922). *National Character and the Factors in its Formation*. London: Methuen.
—— (1942). *Reflections on Government*. Oxford: Clarendon Press.
—— (1951). *Principles of Social and Political Theory*. Oxford: Clarendon Press.
Barry, B. (1987). 'Nationalism', in D. Miller (ed.), *Blackwell Encyclopaedia of Political Thought*. Oxford: Blackwell, pp. 352–5.
—— (1991). 'Self-Government Revisited', *Democracy and Power*. Oxford: Oxford University Press, 156–86.
—— (2001). *Culture and Equality*. Cambridge, MA: Harvard University Press.
Bartkus, V. O. (1999). *The Dynamic of Secession*. Cambridge: Cambridge University Press.
Bauböck, R. (2000). 'Why Stay Together? A Pluralist Approach to Secession and Federation', in W. Kymlicka and W. Norman (eds.) (2000), pp. 366–94.
—— (unpublished). 'Self-Determination and Self-Government'.

Bauböck, R. (2004). 'Territorial or Cultural Autonomy for National Minorities?', in A. Dieckhoff (ed.) (2004), pp. 221–57.
Belmont, K., Mainwaring, S., and Reynolds, A. (2002). 'Introduction: Institutional Design, Conflict Management, and Democracy', in A. Reynolds (ed.) (2002), pp. 1–11.
Beer, S. (1993). *To Make a Nation: The Rediscovery of American Federalism.* Cambridge, MA: Harvard University Press.
Beiner, R. (1998). 'National Self-Determination: Some Cautionary Remarks Concerning the Rhetoric of Rights', in M. Moore (ed.) (1998), pp. 158–80.
—— (ed.) (1999). *Theorizing Nationalism.* Albany, NY: SUNY Press.
—— and Norman, W. (eds.) (2001). *Canadian Political Philosophy.* Toronto: Oxford University Press.
Beitz, C. (1990). *Political Equality.* Princeton, NJ: Princeton University Press.
Bellamy, R. and Castiglione, D. (2005). 'Building the Union: The Nature of Sovereignty in the Political Architecture of Europe', in Karmis and Norman (eds.) (2005a), pp. 293–310.
Bennett, D. (ed.) (1998). *Multicultural States: Rethinking Difference and Identity.* London: Routledge.
Beran, H. (1984). 'A Liberal Theory of Secession', *Political Studies*, 32: 21–31.
—— (1998). 'A Democratic Theory of Political Self-Determination for a New World Order', in P. Lehning (ed.) (1998).
Berlin, I. (1958). *Two Concepts of Liberty.* Oxford: Oxford University Press. Reprinted in Berlin (1969), 118–72.
—— (1969). *Four Essays on Liberty.* Oxford: Oxford University Press.
Breuilly, J. (1982). *Nationalism and the State.* Manchester: Manchester University Press.
Brighouse, H. (1998). 'Against Nationalism', in J. Couture, K. Nielsen, and M. Seymour (eds.) (1998), pp. 365–406.
Billig, M. (1995). *Banal Nationalism.* London: Sage.
Blahuta, J. (2001). 'How Useful Is the Analogy of Divorce in Theorizing about Secession?', *Dialogue: Canadian Philosophical Review*, 241–54.
Blais, F., Laforest, G., and Lamoureux, D. (eds.) (1995). *Libéralismes et nationalismes.* Ste-Foy : Presses de la Université Laval.
Blattberg, C. (2003). *Shall We Dance?* Montreal/Kingston: McGill-Queen's University Press.
Bourassa, H. (1904). 'A Friendly Reply to La *Verité*', in Cook (ed.) (1969), pp. 148–50.
Bourdieu, P. and Wacquant, L. (1992). *An Invitation to Reflexive Sociology.* Chicago: University of Chicago Press.
Brown, D. (1999). 'Are there Good and Bad Nationalisms?', *Nations and Nationalism*, 5/2: 281–302.
Brown-John, C. (1999). 'Self-Determination, Autonomy, and State Secession in Federal Constitutional and International Law', *South Texas Law Review*, 40: 567–601.
Brubaker, R. (1996). *Nationalism Reframed: Nationhood and the National Question in the New Europe.* Cambridge: Cambridge University Press.

—— (1998). 'Myths and Misconceptions in the Study of Nationalism', in M. Moore (ed.) (1998), pp. 233–65.
Buchanan, A. (1991). *Secession: The Morality of Political Divorce from Fort Sumter to Lithuania and Quebec.* Boulder, CO: Westview Press.
—— (1997). 'Theories of Secession', *Philosophy & Public Affairs*, 26/1: 30–61.
—— (1998*a*). 'What's so Special About Nations?', in J. Couture, K. Nielsen, and M. Seymour (eds.) (1998), pp. 283–310.
—— (1998*b*). 'Democracy and Secession', in M. Moore (ed.) (1998), pp. 14–33.
—— (2003). 'Making and Unmaking Boundaries: What Liberalism has to Say', in A. Buchanan and M. Moore (2003*a*).
—— (2004). *Justice, Legitimacy, and Self-Determination.* Oxford: Oxford University Press.
—— and Moore, M. (2003*a*). *States, Nations, and Borders: The Ethics of Making Boundaries.* Cambridge: Cambridge University Press.
—— and Moore, M. (2003*b*). 'Introduction: The Making and Unmaking of Boundaries', in A. Buchanan and M. Moore (2003*a*).
Buchanan, J. (1995). 'Federalism as an Ideal Political Order and an Objective of Constitutional Reform', *Publius*, 25/2: 19–27.
Burgess, M. (1995). *The British Federal Tradition.* London: Leicester University Press.
—— (2000). *Federalism and the European Union: The Building of Europe, 1950–2000.* London: Routledge.
Cairns, A. (1977). 'The Government and Societies of Canadian Federalism', *Canadian Journal of Political Science*, 10: 695–725.
—— (1992). *Charter versus Federalism: The Dilemmas of Constitutional Reform.* Montreal/Kingston: McGill-Queen's University Press.
—— (1995). 'Constitutional Government and the Two Faces of Ethnicity: Federalism is Not Enough', in K. Knop, S. Ostry, R. Simeon, and K. Swinton (eds.), *Rethinking Federalism: Citizens, Markets, and Governments in a Changing World.* Vancouver: UBC Press, 15–39.
Calhoun, J. C. (1855). 'On the Relation which the States and General Government Bear to Each Other [The Fort Hill Address]', in D. Karmis and W. Norman (eds.) (2005*a*), pp. 135–46.
Callan, E. (1997). *Educating Citizens: Political Education and Liberal Democracy.* Oxford: Oxford University Press.
Canovan, M. (1996). *Nationhood and Political Theory.* Cheltenham, UK: Edward Elgar.
Carens, J. H. (1987). 'Aliens and Citizens: The Case for Open Borders', *Review of Politics*, 49/3: 251–73.
—— (1995*a*). *Is Quebec Nationalism Just?* Montreal/Kingston: McGill-Queen's University Press.
—— (1995*b*). 'Immigration, Political Community, and the Transformation of Identity: Quebec's Immigration Politics in Critical Perspective', in J. H. Carens (1995*a*), pp. 20–81.

—— (1995c). 'Liberalism, Justice, and Political Community: Theoretical Perspectives on Quebec's Liberal Nationalism', in J. H. Carens (1995a), pp. 3–19.

—— (2000). *Culture, Citizenship, and Community: A Contextual Exploration of Justice as Even-handedness*. Oxford: Oxford University Press.

Chambers, S. (1996). *Reasonable Democracy: Jurgen Habermas and the Politics of Discourse*. Ithica, NY: Cornell University Press.

—— (2001). 'New Constitutionalism: Democracy, Habermas, and the Canadian Exceptionalism', in R. Beiner and W. Norman (eds.) (2001), pp. 63–77.

Clinton, B. (2004). *My Life*. New York: Alfred A. Knopf.

Cohen, A. (1990). *A Deal Undone: The Making and Breaking of the Meech Lake Accord*. Vancouver: Douglas and MacIntyre.

—— (1998). 'Revisiting the Meech Lake Accord, Ten Years Later', in M. Westmacott and H. Mellon (eds.) (1998), pp. 175–86.

Connor, W. (1994). *Ethno-nationalism*. Princeton, NJ: Princeton University Press.

Conversi, D. (1997). *The Basques, the Catalans and Spain: Alternative Routes to Nationalist Mobilisation*. London: Hurst & Company.

Cook, R. (ed.) (1969). *French-Canadian Nationalism*. Toronto: Macmillan.

Copp, D. (1997). 'Democracy and Communal Self-Determination', in R. McKim and J. McMahan (eds.) (1997), pp. 277–300.

—— (1998). 'International Law and Morality in the Theory of Secession', *Journal of Ethics*, 2: 219–45.

Costa, J. (2003). 'On Theories of Secession: Minorities, Majorities, and the Multi-national State', *CRISPP*, 6/2: 63–90.

Couture, J., Nielsen, K., and M. Seymour (eds.) (1998). *Rethinking Nationalism* (*Canadian Journal of Philosophy*, 22/suppl.). Calgary: University of Calgary Press.

Craig, G. M. (ed.) (1982). *Lord Durham's Report*. Ottawa: Carleton University Press.

Crawford, J. (1997). *State Practice and International Law in Relation to Unilateral Secession. Report to Government of Canada concerning unilateral secession by Quebec*, 19 February 1997. Available at http://canada.justice.gc.ca/en/news/nr/1997/factum/craw.html.

Dahl, R. (1956). *A Preface to Democratic Theory*. Chicago: University of Chicago Press.

Denitch, B. D. (1994). *Ethnic Nationalism: The Tragic Death of Yugoslavia*. Minneapolis, MN: University of Minnesota Press.

Derriennic, J.-P. (1995). *Nationalisme et démocracie : réflexion sur les illusions des indépendantistes québécois*. Montreal: Boréal.

Deutsch, K. (1966). 'Nationalism and Social Communication', reprinted in J. Hutchinson and A. Smith (eds.) (1994), pp. 26–9.

Dicey, A. V. (1914). *Introduction to the Study of the Law of the Constitution*, 8th edn. London: Macmillan.

Dieckhoff, A. (ed.) (2004). *The Politics of Belonging: Nationalism, Liberalism, and Pluralism*. Lanham, MD: Lexington Press.

Duke, V. and Crolley, L. (1996). *Football, Nationality and the State*. Harlow, Essex: Longman.

Dunn, J. (1979). *Western Political Theory in the Face of the Future.* Cambridge: Cambridge University Press.

Dworkin, R. (1977). *Taking Rights Seriously.* London: Duckworth.

—— (1978). 'Liberalism', in S. Hampshire (ed.), *Public and Private Morality.* Cambridge: Cambridge University Press.

Easterbrook, F. and Fischel, D. (1991). *The Economic Structure of Corporate Law.* Cambridge, MA: Harvard University Press.

Eisenberg, A. (1994). 'Individual and Group Difference in Canadian Jurisprudence', *Canadian Journal of Political Science,* 27.

—— (2005). 'Identity and Liberal Politics: The Problem of Minorities within Minorities', in A. Eisenberg and J. Spinner-Halev (eds.) (2005), pp. 249–70.

—— and Spinner-Halev, J. (eds.) (2005). *Minorities within Minorities: Equality, Rights and Diversity.* Cambridge: Cambridge University Press.

Elazar, D. (1985). 'Federalism and Consociational Regimes', *Publius: the Journal of Federalism,* 15/2: 17–34.

—— (1987). *Exploring Federalism.* Tuscaloosa, AL: University of Alabama Press.

Elster, J. (1988). 'Introduction', in J. Elster and R. Slagstad (eds.) (1988).

—— (1993). *Political Psychology.* Cambridge: Cambridge University Press.

—— and Slagstad, R. (eds.) (1988). *Constitutionalism and Democracy.* Cambridge: Cambridge University Press.

Eriksen, E. and Fossum, J. (eds.) (2000). *Democracy in the European Union: Integration through Deliberation?* London: Routledge.

Fichte, J. (1807–8). *Addresses to the German Nation,* R. Jones and G. Turnbull (trans.) La Salle, IL: Open Court Publishing (1922).

Filippov, M., Ordeshook, P., and Schvetsova, O. (2004). *Designing Federalism: A Theory of Self-Sustainable Federal Institutions.* Cambridge: Cambridge University Press.

Føllesdal, A. (2003*a*). 'Subsidiarity', *Journal of Political Philosophy,* 6/2/: 190–218.

—— (2003*b*). 'Federalism', *The Stanford Encyclopaedia of Philosophy* (winter 2003 edn.). Available at http://plato.stanford.edu/archives/win2003/entries/federalism/.

Forbes, H. D. (ed.) (n.d.). *Canadian Political Thought.* Toronto: Oxford University Press.

Ford, C. (1993). *Creating the Nation in Provincial France.* Princeton, NJ: Princeton University Press.

Forsyth, M. (1981). *Union of States: The Theory and Practice of Confederation.* London: Leicester University Press.

—— (1989). 'Introduction', in M. Forsyth (ed.), *Federalism and Nationalism.* Leicester: Leicester University Press.

Fosses, E. and Requejo, F. (eds.) (1999). *Asimetría federal y estado plurinacional.* Madrid: Editorial Trotta.

Fournier, P. (1991). *A Meech Lake Post-Mortem: Is Quebec Sovereignty Inevitable?* Montreal/Kingston: McGill-Queen's University Press.

Franck, T. M. (ed.) (1968). *Why Federations Fail: An Inquiry into the Requisites for Successful Federalism.* New York: New York University Press.

Freeman, M. (1998). 'The Priority of Function over Structure: A New Approach to Secession', in P. Lehning (ed.) (1998).
Friedrich, C. (1968). *Trends of Federalism in Theory and Practice*. New York: Praeger.
Gagnon, A. (2001). 'The Moral Foundations of Asymmetrical Federalism', in A. Gagnon and J. Tully (eds.) (2001).
—— and Tully, J. (eds.) (2001). *Multinational Democracies*. Cambridge: Cambridge University Press.
Galston, W. (1991). *Liberal Purposes: Goods, Virtues, and Duties in the Liberal State*. Cambridge: Cambridge University Press.
Gauthier, D. (1994). 'Breaking Up: An Essay on Secession', *Canadian Journal of Philosophy*, 24: 357–72.
Granatstein, J. (1989). *A Nation Forged in Fire: Canadians in the Second World War: 1939–1945*. Toronto: Lester & Orpen Dennys.
Gellner, E. (1983). *Nations and Nationalism*. Ithaca, NY: Cornell University Press.
Ghai, Y. (2002). 'Constitutional Asymmetries: Communal Representation, Federalism, and Cultural Autonomy', in A. Reynolds (ed.) (2002), pp. 141–70.
Gibbins, R. and G. Laforest, (eds.) (1998). *Beyond the Impasse: Toward Reconciliation*. Ottawa: Institute for Research in Public Policy.
Gilbert, P. (1998). *The Philosophy of Nationalism*. Boulder, CO: Westview.
Goodin, R. and Pettit, P. (eds.) (1993). *Blackwell Companion to Political Philosophy*. Oxford: Blackwell.
Graham, K. (1986). *The Battle of Democracy*. Brighton: Wheatsheaf.
Greenfeld, L. (1992). *Nationalism: Five Roads to Modernity*. Cambridge, MA.: Harvard University Press.
Griffiths, A. (ed.) (2002a). *Handbook of Federal Countries, 2002*. Montreal/Kingston: Forum on Federations & McGill-Queen's University Press.
—— (2002b). 'St. Kitts and Nevis', in A. Griffiths (ed.) (2002a), pp. 269–81.
Guibernau, M. (2004). 'Catalonia: A Non-secessionist Nationalism?', in M. Seymour (ed.) (2004), pp. 234–46.
Gurr, T. (2000). *People versus States*. Washington, DC: United States Institute of Peace.
Gutmann, A. (2003). *Identity in Democracy*. Princeton, NJ: Princeton University Press.
Haksar, V. (1979). *Equality, Liberty and Perfectionism*. Oxford: Oxford University Press.
Hardin, R. (1995). *One for All: The Logic of Group Conflict*. Princeton, NJ: Princeton University Press.
—— (1999). *Liberalism, Constitutionalism, and Democracy*. Oxford: Oxford University Press.
Hechter, M. (2000). *Containing Nationalism*. Oxford: Oxford University Press.
Henderson, A. and McEwen, N. (2005). 'Do Shared Values Underpin National Identity? Examining the Role of Values in National Identity in Canada and the United Kingdom', *National Identities*, 7/2: 173–91.
Hesse, J. and Wright, V. (eds.) (1996). *Federalizing Europe? The Costs, Benefits, and Preconditions of Federal Political Systems*. Oxford: Oxford University Press.
Hobhouse, L. T. (1911). *Liberalism*. Oxford: Oxford University Press.

Hobsbawm, E. (1990). *Nations and Nationalism since 1780*. Cambridge: Cambridge University Press.
Holder, C. (2005). 'Self-Determination as a Basic Human Right: The Draft UN Declaration of Indigenous Peoples', in A. Eisenberg and J. Spinner-Halev (eds.) (2005), pp. 294–315.
Holmes, S. (1988a). 'Gag Rules or the Politics of Omission', in J. Elster and R. Slagstad (eds.) (1988), pp. 19–58.
—— (1988b). 'Precommitment and the Paradox of Democracy', in J. Elster and R. Slagstad (eds.) (1988), pp. 195–240.
Horowitz, D. (1985). *Ethnic Groups in Conflict*. Berkeley, CA: University of California Press.
—— (1998). 'Self-Determination: Politics, Philosophy, and Law', in M. Moore (ed.) (1998), pp. 181–214.
—— (2002). 'Constitutional Design: Proposals versus Processes', in A. Reynolds (ed.) (2002), pp. 15–36.
—— (2003). 'A Right to Secede?', in S. Macedo and A. Buchanan 2003, 50–76.
Howse, R. and Knop, K. (1993). 'Federalism, Secession, and the Limits of Ethnic Accommodation: A Canadian Perspective', *New Europe Law Review*, 1/2: 269–320.
Hroch, M. (1993). 'From National Movement to the Fully-formed Nation: The Nation-Building Process in Europe', *New Left Review*, 198: 3–20.
Hueglin, T. O. (1999). *Early Modern Concepts for a Late Modern World: Althusius on Community and Federalism*. Waterloo, Ontario: Wilfrid Laurier University Press.
Hutchinson, J. and Smith, A. (eds.) (1994). *Nationalism*. Oxford: Oxford University Press.
Ignatieff, M. (1993). *Blood and Belonging: Journeys into the New Nationalism*. London: Penguin.
—— (1999). *The Warrior's Honour: Ethnic War and the Modern Consciousness*. New York: Vintage.
Kant, I. (1795). 'Toward Perpetual Peace', in *Practical Philosophy*, Mary J. Gregor (trans. and ed.), Cambridge: Cambridge University Press, 1996, pp. 311–52.
Karlsson, G. (2000). *The History of Iceland*. Minneapolis: University of Minnesota Press.
Karmis, D. (1994). 'Interpréter l'identité québécoise', in A.-G. Gagnon (ed.), *Québec: État et société*, tome 1. Montréal : Québec Amérique, pp. 305–27.
—— (1998). 'Fédéralisme et relations intercommunautaires chez Tocqueville: entre prudence et négation des possibles', *Politique et sociétés*, 17/3: 59–91.
—— (2002). 'Pourquoi lire Proudhon aujourd'hui? Le fédéralisme et le défi de la solidarité dans les sociétés divisées', *Politique et sociétés*, 21/1: 43–65.
—— and Gagnon, A. (2001). 'Federalism, Federation, and Collective Identities in Canada and Belgium: Different Routes, Similar Fragmentation', in A. Gagnon and J. Tully (eds.) (2001), pp. 137–75.
Karmis, D. and Maclure, J. (2001). 'Two Escape Routes from the Paradigm of Monistic Authenticity: Post-Imperialist and Federal Perspectives on Plural and Complex Identities', *Ethnic and Racial Studies*, 24/3: 361–85.

Karmis, D. and Norman, W. (eds.) (2005*a*). *Theories of Federalism*. New York: Palgrave.

—— —— (2005*b*). 'The Revival of Federalism in Normative Political Theory', in D. Karmis and W. Norman (eds.) (2005*a*), pp. 3–21.

Kettler, D. (1987). 'Ideology', in D. Miller (ed.), *Blackwell Encyclopaedia of Political Thought*. Oxford: Blackwell, 1987: pp. 235–38.

King, P. (1982). *Federalism and Federation*. London: Croom Helm.

Kohn, H. (1955). *Nationalism: Its Meaning and History*. Princeton, NJ: Van Nostrand.

Kukathas, C. (2003). *The Liberal Archipelago: a Theory of Diversity and Freedom*. Oxford: Oxford University Press.

Kymlicka, W. (1989). *Liberalism, Community and Culture*. Oxford: Oxford University Press.

—— (1995*a*). *Multicultural Citizenship*. Oxford: Oxford University Press.

—— (ed.) (1995*b*). *The Rights of Minority Cultures*. Oxford: Oxford University Press

—— (1995*c*). 'Misunderstanding Nationalism', *Dissent* (Winter 1995): 130–37.

—— (1998*a*). 'Western Political Theory and Ethnic Relations in Eastern Europe', in M. Opalski (ed.), *Managing Diversity in Plural Societies: Minorities, Migration and Nation-Building in Post-Communist Europe*. Ottawa: Forum Eastern Europe.

—— (1998*b*). 'Is Federalism a Viable Alternative to Secession?', in P. Lehning (ed.) (1998): pp. 111–50.

—— (1998*c*). *Finding Our Way: Rethinking Ethno-cultural Relations in Canada*. Toronto: Oxford University Press.

—— (2000*a*). 'Nation-Building and Minority Rights: Comparing East and West', *Journal of Ethnic and Migration Studies*, 26/2: 183–212.

—— (2000*b*). 'Federalism and Secession At Home and Abroad', *Canadian Journal of Law and Jurisprudence*, 13/2: 207–24.

—— (2001). *Politics in the Vernacular: Nationalism, Multiculturalism and Citizenship*. Oxford: Oxford University Press.

—— (2002). 'Western Political Theory and Ethnic Relations in Eastern Europe' in W. Kymlicka and M. Opalski (eds.) (2002), pp. 13–105.

—— and Norman, W. (1994). 'Return of the Citizen: Recent Work in Citizenship Theory', *Ethics*, 104/2: 352–81.

—— —— (eds.) (2000). *Citizenship in Diverse Societies*. Oxford: Oxford University Press.

—— and Opalski, M. (eds.) (2002). *Can Liberal Pluralism be Exported? Western Political Theory and Ethnic Relations in Eastern Europe*. Oxford: Oxford University Press.

LaFollette, H. (ed.) (2003). *The Oxford Handbook of Practical Ethics*. Oxford: Oxford University Press.

Laforest, G. (1995). *Trudeau and the End of a Canadian Dream*. Montreal/Kingston: McGill-Queen's University Press.

—— (2001). 'The True Nature of Sovereignty: Reply to my Critics Concerning Trudeau and the End of a Canadian Dream', in R. Beiner and W. Norman (eds.) (2001), pp. 298–310.

—— (2004). *Pour la liberté d'une société distincte*. Québec: Presses de l'Université Laval.
Laponce, J. (2000). 'Sovereignty and Referendum: In Defence of Territorial Revisionism'. Paper presented at the Canadian Political Science Association meetings, Quebec City.
LaSelva, S. (1996). *The Moral Foundations of Canadian Federalism: Paradoxes, Achievements and Tragedies of Nationhood*. Montreal/Kingston: McGill-Queen's University Press.
Laski, H. (1939). 'The Obsolescence of Federalism', *The New Republic*, 98 (3 May): 367–9. Reprinted in D. Karmis and W. Norman (eds.) (2005a), pp. 193–8.
Leydet, D. (2001). 'Lifeboat', in R. Beiner and W. Norman (eds.) (2001), pp. 249–62.
Lehning, P. (ed.) (1998). *Theories of Secession*. London: Routledge.
Lemco, J. (1991). *Political Stability in Federal Governments*. New York: Praeger.
Lenihan, D., Robertson, G., and Tassé, R. (1994). *Canada: Reclaiming the Middle Ground*. Montreal: IRPP.
Levine, A. (1998). 'Just Nationalism: The Future of an Illusion', in J. Couture, K. Nielsen, and M. Seymour (eds.) (1998), pp. 345–64.
Levy, J. (forthcoming). 'Federalism, Liberalism, and the Separation of Loyalties'.
—— (2000a). *The Multiculturalism of Fear*. Oxford: Oxford University Press.
—— (2000b). 'Three Modes of Incorporating Indigenous Law', in W. Kymlicka and W. Norman (2000), 297–325.
—— (2004). 'National Minorities without Nationalism', in A. Dieckhoff (ed.), *The Politics of Belonging: Nationalism, Liberalism, and Pluralism*. Lanham, MD: Lexington Press, pp. 155–74.
Lijphart, A. (1977). *Democracy in Plural Societies*. New Haven, CT: Yale University Press.
Linz, J. (1997). 'Democracy, Multinationalism, and Federalism'. Paper presented at the International Political Science Association meetings, Seoul, South Korea, August.
—— and Stepan, A. (1996). *Problems of Democratic Transition and Consolidation: Southern Europe, South America, and Post-Communist Europe*. Baltimore, MD: Johns Hopkins University Press.
Loewen, J. (1995). *Lies My Teacher Told Me: Everything Your American History Textbook Got Wrong*. New York: Simon & Schuster.
Macedo, S. and Buchanan, A. (2003). *Secession and Self-Determination* (Nomos XLV). New York: New York University Press.
Madison, J., Hamilton, A. Jay, J. (1961). *The Federalist Papers*. (ed.) C. Rossiter. New York: Mentor Books. (Originally published 1788.)
Mansbridge, J. (1986). *Why We Lost the ERA*. Chicago: University of Chicago Press.
Marc, A. (ed.) (1969). *La révolution fédéraliste*. Paris: Presses d'Europe.
Mathew, G. (2002). 'India', in A. Griffiths (ed.) (2002a), pp. 172–87.
Margalit, A. and Raz, J. (1990). 'National Self-determination', *The Journal of Philosophy*, 87/9: 439–46.
Mazzini, G. (1995). 'The Duties of Man', in O. Dahbour and M. Ishay (eds.), *The Nationalism Reader*. Atlantic Highlands, NJ: Humanities Press, pp. 87–96.

Macdonald, J. A. (1865). 'Speech on the Quebec Resolutions', in H. D. Forbes (n.d.), 66–92.

MacIntyre, A. (1984). 'Is Patriotism a Virtue?', in R. J. Arneson (ed.), *Liberalism*, Vol III. Aldershot: Edward Elgar, 1992, pp. 246–63.

McCormick, N. (1982 [1999]). *Questioning Sovereignty: Law, State and Nation in the European Commonwealth*. Oxford: Oxford University Press.

McFarlane, K. (1993). 'It's Time to Make Explicit Canada's Raison d'être', *Inroads* 2.

McGarry, J. (2002). 'Federal Political Systems and the Accommodation of National Minorities', in A. Griffiths (ed.) (2002*a*), pp. 416–47.

—— (2004). 'Civic Nationalism and the Northern Ireland Conflict', in M. Seymour (ed.) (2004), pp. 194–213.

—— and O'Leary, B. (1993). *The Politics of Ethnic Conflict Regulation*. London: Routledge.

McKay, D. (1999). *Federalism and the European Union: A Political Economy Perspective*. Oxford: Oxford University Press.

—— (2001). *Designing Europe: Comparative Lessons from the Federal Experience*. Oxford: Oxford University Press.

McKim, R. and McMahan, J. (eds.) (1997). *The Morality of Nationalism*. New York: Oxford University Press.

Mertus, J. (1999). *Kosovo: How Myths and Truths Started a War*. Berkeley, CA: University of California Press.

Mill, J. S. (1861). *Considerations on Representative Government*. In H. B. Acton (ed.), *Utilitarianism, Liberty, Representative Government*. London: Dent, 1972.

—— (1869). *The Subjection of Women*. Classical Utilitarianism Website: http://www.la.utexas.edu/research/poltheory/mill/sw/.

Miller, D. (1983). 'Linguistic Philosophy and Political Theory', in D. Miller and L. Siedentop, (eds.), *The Nature of Political Theory*. Oxford: Oxford University Press.

—— (1993). 'In Defence of Nationality', *Journal of Applied Philosophy*, 10/1: 3–16.

—— (1995). *On Nationality*. Oxford: Oxford University Press.

—— (1998). 'Secession and the Principle of Nationality', in J. Couture, K. Nielsen, and M. Seymour (eds.) (1998), pp. 261–82.

—— (2000). *Citizenship and National Identity*. Cambridge: Polity Press.

—— (2003). 'Liberalism and Boundaries: A Response to Buchanan', in A. Buchanan and M. Moore (2003*a*).

Monahan, P. (1991). *After Meech Lake: The Inside Story*. Toronto: University of Toronto Press.

—— and Bryant, M. (1996). *Coming to Terms with Plan B: Ten Principles Governing Secession*. Toronto: C. D. Howe Institute.

Monnet, J. (1955). *Les États-Unis d'Europe ont commencé*. Paris: Laffont.

Montesquieu, Baron de (1748). *The Spirit of the Laws*, A. M. Cohler, B. C. Miller and H. S. Stone (trans. and eds.). Cambridge: Cambridge University Press, 1989.

Moore, M. (ed.) (1998). *National Self-Determination and Secession*. Oxford: Oxford University Press.

—— (2001). *The Ethics of Nationalism*. Oxford: Oxford University Press.

—— (2005). 'Internal Minorities and Indigenous Self-Determination', in A. Eisenberg and J. Spinner-Halev (eds.) (2005), pp. 271–93.
Moyrand, A. and Angelo, A. (1999). 'International Law Perspectives on the Evolution in Status of the French Overseas Territories', *Revue juridique polynésienne* no. 5. Available at http://www.upf.pf/recherche/IRIDIP/RJP/RJP5.htm.
Musgrave, T. (1997). *Self-Determination and National Minorities*. Oxford: Oxford University Press.
Nagel, T. (1973). 'Rawls on Justice', in N. Daniels (ed.), *Reading Rawls*. Oxford: Blackwell, 1974.
—— (1987). 'Moral Conflict and Political Legitimacy', *Philosophy and Public Affairs*, 16: 215–40.
Nairn, T. (1977). *The Break-up of Britain*. London: New Left Books.
Nathanson, S. (1993). *Patriotism, Morality and Peace*. Lanham, MD: Rowman & Littlefield.
Neumann, F. (1955). 'Federalism and Freedom: A Critique', in A. W. Macmahon (ed.), *Federalism: Mature and Emergent*. Garden City, New York: Doubleday & Company, 1955): 44–57. Reprinted in Karmis and Norman (eds.) (2005a), pp. 207–20.
Nickel, J. (1995). 'What's Wrong with Ethnic Cleansing?', *Journal of Social Philosophy*.
Nicolaidis, K. and Howse, R. (eds.) (2001). *The Federal Vision: Legitimacy and Levels of Governance in the United States and the European Union*. Oxford: Oxford University Press.
Nielsen, K. (1993). 'Secession: The Case of Quebec', *Journal of Applied Philosophy*, 10: 29–43.
—— (1999). 'Cultural Nationalism, Neither Ethnic Nor Civic', in R. Beiner (ed.) (1999), pp. 119–30.
Nootens, G. (1998). 'Liberal Restrictions on Public Arguments: Can Nationalist Claims be Moral Reasons in Liberal Public Discourse?', in J. Couture, K. Nielsen, and M. Seymour (eds.) (1998), pp. 237–60.
Norman, W. (1991). *Taking Freedom Too Seriously? An Essay on Analytic and Post-Analytic Political Philosophy*. New York: Garland Publishing.
—— (1994). 'Toward a Philosophy of Federalism', in J. Baker 1994, 79–100.
—— (1995a). 'The Morality of Federalism and the European Union', *Archiv für Rechts- und Sozialphilosophie*, 59, 202–11.
—— (1995b). 'The Ideology of Shared Values: A Myopic Vision of Unity in the Multi-Nation State', in J. H. Carens (1995a): pp. 137–59.
—— (1995c). 'Les points faibles du modèle nationaliste libéral', in F. Blais, G. Laforest and D. Lamoureux (eds.) (1995).
—— (1998a). 'The Ethics of Secession as the Regulation of Secessionist Politics', in M. Moore (ed.) (1998), pp. 34–61.
—— (1998b). 'Federalism and Confederalism', in E. Craig (ed.), *Routledge Encyclopaedia of Philosophy*, Vol. 3. London: Routledge, pp. 572–4.
—— (1998c). 'Les paradoxes du nationalisme civique', in G. Laforest and P. de Lara (eds.), *L'Interprétation de l'identité moderne: autour de Charles Taylor*. Paris: Édition du Cerf, 1998, pp. 155–70.

Norman, W. (1999). 'Theorizing Nationalism (Normatively)', in R. Beiner (ed.) (1999), pp. 51–66.
—— (2001a). 'Secession and (Constitutional) Democracy', in F. Requejo (ed.), *Democracy and National Pluralism*. London: Routledge, pp. 84–102.
—— (2001b). 'Justice and Stability in Multination States', in J. Tully and A. Gagnon (eds.) (2001), pp. 90–109.
—— (2003a). 'National Autonomy', in H. Lafollette (ed.) (2003), pp. 591–619.
—— (2003b). 'Domesticating Secession', in S. Macedo and A. Buchanan (eds.) (2003), 193–237.
Oakshott, M. (1947). 'Rationalism in Politics', in *Rationalism in Politics and other Essays*. Expanded edn., London: Liberty Press (1991).
O'Leary, B. (2002). 'The Belfast Agreement and the British-Irish Agreement: Consociation, Confederal Institutions, a Federacy, and a Peace Process', in A. Reynolds (ed.) (2002), pp. 293–356.
O'Neill, J. (1994). 'Should Communitarians be Nationalists?', *Journal of Applied Philosophy*, 11/2: 135–43.
Oppenheim, F. (1981). *Political Concepts: A Reconstruction*. New York: St Martin's Press.
Parekh, B. (1995). 'The Concept of National Identity', *New Community*, 21/2: 255–68.
Patten, A. (2001). 'Liberal Citizenship in Multinational Societies', in A. Gagnon and J. Tully (eds.) (2001), pp. 279–98.
—— (2005). 'The Rights of Internal Linguistic Minorities', in A. Eisenberg and J. Spinner-Halev (eds.) (2005), pp. 135–54.
Pätz, T. (2002). 'Ethiopia (Federal Democratic Republic of Ethiopia)', in Griffiths (ed.) (2002a): pp. 132–46.
Pavkovic, A. (2000). *The Fragmentation of Yugoslavia: Nationalism and War in the Balkans*. New York: Palgrave Macmillan.
Pfaff, W. (1993). *The Wrath of Nations: Civilization and the Furies of Nationalism*. New York: Simon & Schuster.
Phillips, A. (1995). *The Politics of Presence: Issues in Democracy and Group Representation*. Oxford: Oxford University Press.
Philpott, D. (1995). 'In Defence of Self-Determination', in *Ethics*, 105: 352–85.
—— (1998). 'Self-Determination in Practice', in M. Moore (ed.) (1998): pp. 79–102.
Poole, R. (1999). *Nation and Identity*. London: Routledge.
Popper, K. (1944). *The Open Society and its Enemies*. London: Routledge.
—— (1957). *The Poverty of Historicism*. London: Routledge.
Posner, R. A. (2002). 'Strong Fiber after All', in *Atlantic Monthly*, January 2002: 22–3.
Proudhon, P.-J. (1863). *The Principle of Federation*, Richard Vernon (trans. and ed.). Toronto: University of Toronto Press, 1979. Relevant extracts reprinted in D. Karmis and W. Norman (eds.) (2005a), pp. 173–88.
Pufendorf, S. (1672). *De Jure Naturae et Gentium Libri Octo*, J. B. Scott (trans.) C. H. and W. A. Oldfather. Oxford: Clarendon Press, 1934. Relevant extracts reprinted in D. Karmis and W. Norman (eds.) (2005a), pp. 35–50.

Pye, L. (1993). 'Political Culture', in Joel Krieger (ed.), *The Oxford Companion to Politics of the World*. Oxford: Oxford University Press, 1993, pp. 712–13.
Rakove, J. (1996). *Original Meanings: Politics and Ideals in the Making of the Constitution*. New York: Alfred A. Knopf.
Rawls, J. (1971). *A Theory of Justice*. Cambridge, MA: Harvard University Press.
—— (1993). *Political Liberalism*. New York: Columbia University Press.
Raz, J. (1986). *The Morality of Freedom*. Oxford: Oxford University Press.
Reilly, B. (2001). *Democracy in Divided Societies: Electoral Engineering for Conflict Management*. Cambridge: Cambridge University Press.
—— (2002). 'Electoral Systems for Divided Societies', *Journal of Democracy*, 13/2: 156–70.
Renan, E. (1882). 'What is a Nation?', in A. Zimmern (ed.), *Modern Political Doctrines*. Oxford: Oxford University Press, 1939.
Requejo, F. (1999). 'Cultural Pluralism, Nationalism and Federalism: A Revision of Democratic Citizenship in Plurinational States', *European Journal of Political Research*, 39/2: 255–86.
—— (2001). 'Democratic Legitimacy and National Pluralism', in F. Requejo (ed.), *Democracy and National Pluralism*. London: Routledge Press: 157–77.
—— (2005). 'Federalism in Plurinational Societies: Rethinking the Ties between Catalonia, Spain, and the European Union', in D. Karmis and W. Norman (eds.) (2005), pp. 311–20.
Resnick, P. (1994). 'Toward a Multinational Federalism: Asymmetrical and Confederal Alternatives', in F. L. Seidel (ed.) (1994).
—— (1998). 'Majority Nationalities within Multinational States: The Challenge of Identity'. Paper presented at the conference on Mythologies of Identity and Contexts of Power, organized by the CSIC, Madrid, October.
—— (2000*a*). 'Recognition and Resentment: On Accommodating National Differences within Multinational States', Presented at Europa Mundi conference on Democracy, Nationalism and Europeanism. Santiago de Compostela, 21–23 June 2000.
—— (2000*b*). *The Politics of Resentment: British Columbia Regionalism and Canadian Unity*. Vancouver: UBC Press.
—— (2001). 'Majority Nationalities within Multinational States: The Challenge of Identity', in F. C. González (ed.), *El espejo, el mosaico y el crisol. Modelos políticos para el multiculturalismo*. Barcelona: Anthropos-Universitat Autónoma Metropolitana, 2001.
Reynolds, A. (ed.) (2002). *The Architecture of Democracy: Constitutional Design, Conflict Management, and Democracy*. Oxford: Oxford University Press.
Riker, W. H. (1964). *Federalism: Origins, Operation, Significance*. Boston: Little, Brown.
Ripstein, A. (1997). 'Context, Continuity, and Fairness', in R. McKim and J. McMahan (eds.) (1997): pp. 209–26.
Rousseau, J.-J. (1782). 'Judgement on Saint-Pierre's Project for Perpetual Peace', in C. E. Vaughan (trans. and ed.) *A Lasting Peace through the Federation of Europe*,

London: Constable and Company, 1917. Reprinted in D. Karmis and W. Norman (eds.) (2005a). pp. 59–86.

—— (1985). *The Government of Poland*, W. Kendall (trans.). Indianapolis, IN: Hackett, 1991.

Ruben, D. H. (1985). *Metaphysics of the Social World*. London: Routledge.

Russell, P. (1993). *Constitutional Odyssey: Can Canadians Become a Sovereign People?*, 2nd edn. Toronto: University of Toronto Press.

—— (2004). *Constitutional Odyssey: Can Canadians Become a Sovereign People?*, 3rd edn. Toronto: University of Toronto Press.

Sade, Marquis de (1795). *La philosophie dans le boudoir*. Paris: Édition 10/18 Gallimard (1999).

Sandel, M. (1982). *Liberalism and the Limits of Justice*. Cambridge: Cambridge University Press.

Schnapper, D. (1998). 'Beyond the Opposition: Civic Nation versus Ethnic Nation', in J. Couture, K. Nielsen and M. Seymour (eds.) (1998), pp. 219–34.

Schneiderman, D. (ed.) (1999). *The Quebec Decision: Perspectives on the Supreme Court Ruling on Secession*. Toronto: Lorimer.

Schuman, R. (1950). 'Declaration of 9 May 1950: The Schuman Plan for European Union', in D. Karmis and W. Norman (eds.) (2005a), pp. 203–6.

—— (1963). *Pour l'Europe*. Paris: Nagel & Guillaume Briquet, 1963.

Schumpeter, J. (1942). *Capitalism, Socialism, and Democracy*. New York: Harper & Brothers.

Seidel, F. L. (ed.) (1994). *Seeking a New Canadian Partnership: Asymmetrical and Confederal Options*. Montreal: IRPP.

Seymour, M. (ed.) (1995). *Une nation peut-elle se donner la constitution de son choix?* Montreal: Éditions Bellarmin.

—— (1998). 'Questioning the Ethnic/Civic Dichotomy', in J. Couture, K. Nielsen and M. Seymour (eds.) (1998), pp. 1–61.

—— (ed.) (2004). *The Fate of the Nation-State*. Montreal/Kingston: McGill-Queen's University Press.

Shachar, A. (2000). 'Should Church and State be joined at the Altar? Women's Rights and the Multicultural Dilemma', in W. Kymlicka and W. Norman (eds.) (2000), pp. 199–223.

Simeon, R. (1972). *Federal-Provincial Diplomacy: The Making of Recent Policy in Canada*. Toronto: University of Toronto Press.

—— and Conway, D.-P. (2001). 'Federalism and the Management of Conflict in Multinational Societies', in Gagnon and Tully (eds.) (2001), pp. 338–65.

Smidt, W. (trans.) (2000). *Constitution of the Federal Democratic Republic of Ethiopia* (adopted 8 December 1994). International Constitutional Law Project. Available at http://www.oefre.unibe.ch/law/icl/.

Smith, A. (1983). *Theories of Nationalism*, 2nd edn. London: Duckworth. (First edition, 1971).

—— (1986). *The Ethnic Origins of Nations*. Oxford: Oxford University Press.

—— (1991). *National Identity*. London: Penguin.

—— (1993). 'A Europe of Nations—Or the Nation of Europe', *Journal of Peace Research*, 30/2: 129–35.
Smith, G. (ed.) (1995). *Federalism: The Multiethnic Challenge*. London: Longman.
—— (2000). 'Sustainable Federalism, Democratization, and Distributive Justice', in W. Kymlicka and W. Norman (2000), pp. 345–65.
Solnick, S. (2002). 'Federalism and State-Building: Post-Communist and Post-Colonial Perspectives', in A. Reynolds (ed.) (2002), pp. 171–205.
Spinelli, A. (1966). *The Eurocrats: Conflicts and Crisis in the European Community*. Baltimore, MD: The Johns Hopkins Press.
—— and Rossi, E. (1944). 'The 1944 Ventotene Manifesto: Towards a Free and United Europe', in D. Karmis and W. Norman (eds.) (2005*a*), pp. 199–202.
Spinner, J. (1994). *The Boundaries of Citizenship: Race, Ethnicity, and Nationality in the Liberal State*. Baltimore, MD: Johns Hopkins University Press.
Stepan, A. (2005). 'Federalism and Democracy: Beyond the U.S. Model', in D. Karmis and W. Norman (eds.) (2005*a*), pp. 255–68.
Suksi, M. (1993). *Bringing in the People: A Comparison of Constitutional Forms and Practices of the Referendum*. London: Martinus Nijhoff.
Sunstein, C. (1991). 'Constitutionalism and Secession', *University of Chicago Law Review*, 58: 633–70.
—— (2001*a*). *Designing Democracy: What Constitutions Do*. New York: Oxford University Press.
—— (2001*b*). 'Should Constitutions Protect the Right to Secede?', *The Journal of Political Philosophy*, 9/3: 350–5.
Supreme Court of Canada (1998). *Reference re Secession of Quebec*, SCC no. 25506 (20 August).
Tamir, Y. (1993). *Liberal Nationalism*. Princeton, NJ: Princeton University Press.
—— (1995). 'The Enigma of Nationalism', *World Politics*, 47: 418–40.
Tawney, R. H. (1931). *Equality*. London: Allen & Unwin.
Taylor, C. (1979). 'What's Wrong with Negative Liberty?', in A. Ryan (ed.), *The Idea of Freedom*. Oxford: Oxford University Press.
—— (1991). 'Shared and Divergent Values', reprinted in Taylor (1993), pp. 155–86.
—— (1992). 'The Politics of Recognition', in A. Gutmann (ed.), *Multiculturalism and the 'Politics of Recognition'*. Princeton, NJ: Princeton University Press.
—— (1993). *Reconciling the Solitudes: Essays on Canadian Federalism and Nationalism*. Montreal/Kingston: McGill-Queen's University Press.
Tetley, W. (2000). 'Mixed Jurisdictions: Common Law vs Civil Law (Codified and Uncodified)', *International Institute for the Unification of Private Law*. Available at http://www.cisg.law.pace.edu/cisg/biblio/tetley.html.
Tocqueville, A. (1835). *Democracy in America*, v. 1. P. Bradley and D. Boorstin (eds.), New York: Vintage, 1990.
Trifunovska, S. (ed.) (2001). *Minority Rights in Europe: European Minorities and Languages*. New York: Springer.
Trudeau, P. E. (1968). *Federalism and the French Canadians*. Toronto, Macmillan.

Tully, J. (1995). *Strange Multiplicity: Constitutionalism in the Age of Diversity*. Cambridge: Cambridge University Press.
—— (2001). 'Introduction', in A. Gagnon and J. Tully (eds.) (2001), pp. 1–33.
Ulen, T. (1998). 'Secession', in P. Newman (ed.), *The New Palgrave Dictionary of Economics and the Law*. New York: Stockton Press.
Van Parijs, P. (2000). 'Must Europe be Belgian? On Democratic Citizenship in Multilingual Polities', in C. McKinnon and Iain Hampshire-Monk (eds.), *The Demands of Citizenship*. London/New York: Continuum, pp. 235–53.
Vernon, R. (1988). 'The Federal Citizen', in R. D. Olling and M. W. Westmacott (eds.), *Perspectives on Canadian Federalism*. Scarborough, Ontario: Prentice-Hall, 1988, pp. 3–15.
Vigneault, G. (1966). 'Mon pays'. Montreal: Éditions du Vent qui vire.
Vipond, R. (1991). *Liberty and Community: Canadian Federalism and the Failure of the Constitution*. Albany, NY: SUNY Press,
Walters, M. (1999). 'Nationalism and the Pathology of Legal Systems: Considering the Quebec Secession Reference and its Lessons for the United Kingdom', *The Modern Law Review*, 62/3: 371–96.
Waluchow, W. (2004). 'Constitutionalism', *The Stanford Encyclopaedia of Philosophy* (spring 2004 edn.). Available at http://plato.stanford.edu/archives/spr2004/entries/constitutionalism/.
Walzer, M. (1992a). 'The Civil Society Argument', in C. Mouffe (ed.), *Dimensions of Radical Democracy: Pluralism, Citizenship and Community*. London: Routledge, 1992.
—— (1992b). *What it Means to be an American*. New York: Marsilio.
Watts, R. (1966). *New Federations: Experiments in the Commonwealth*. Oxford: Oxford University Press.
—— (1999a). *The Spending Power in Federal Systems: A Comparative Study*. Kingston, Ontario: Centre for Intergovernmental Relations.
—— (1999b). *Comparing Federal Systems*. Montreal/Kingston: McGill-Queen's University Press.
—— (2005). 'Comparing Forms of Federal Partnerships', in D. Karmis and W. Norman (eds.) (2005a), pp. 233–54.
Weber, E. (1979). *Peasants into Frenchmen: The Modernization of Rural France, 1870–1914*. Palo Alto: Stanford University Press.
Weber, M. (1948). 'The Nation', in H. Gerth and C. Wright-Mills (trans. and eds.), *From Max Weber: Essays in Sociology*. London: Routledge & Kegan Paul.
Weinstock, D. (ed.) (1994). *Le défi du pluralisme*. Montréal: Lekton-UQAM.
—— (1996). 'Is there a Moral Case for Nationalism?', *Journal of Applied Philosophy*, 13/1.
—— (1999). 'Building Trust in Divided Societies', *Journal of Political Philosophy*, 7/3: 287–307.
—— (2001a). 'Constitutionalizing the Right to Secede', *Journal of Political Philosophy*, 9/2: 182–203.

—— (2001*b*). 'Towards a Normative Theory of Federalism', *International Social Science Journal*, 75–83.

—— (2001*c*). 'Saving Democracy from Deliberation', in R. Beiner and W. Norman (eds.) (2001), pp. 78–91.

Wellman, C. (1995). 'A Defence of Secession and Political Self-Determination', *Philosophy and Public Affairs*, 24/2: 142–71.

Westmacott, M. and Mellon, H. (eds.) (1998). *Challenges to Canadian Federalism*. Scarborough, Ontario: Prentice-Hall.

Wheare, K. C. (1946/1963). *Federal Government*, 4th edn. Oxford: Oxford University Press.

Will, G. (2004). 'Can We Make Iraq Democratic?', *City Journal*, 14/1.

Williams, M. (1998). *Voice, Trust and Memory: Marginalized Groups and the Failings of Liberal Representation*. Princeton, NJ: Princeton University Press.

Wolin, S. (1964). 'Foreword', in Riker (1964), pp. v–ix.

Wood, N. (2004). 'Ethnic Macedonians Riot Over Laws that Aid Albanians', *The New York Times*, 24 July 2004: A4.

Yack, B. (1999). 'The Myth of the Civic Nation', in R. Beiner (ed.) (1999), pp. 103–18.

Young, I. (2000). *Inclusion and Democracy*. Oxford: Oxford University Press.

Young, R. (1998). 'Quebec Secession and the 1995 Referendum', in M. Westmacott and H. Mellon (eds.) (1998), pp. 112–26.

Index

Aboriginal groups xxvi, 47, 65, 86, 105, 116, 129, 133–4, 136–7, 159, 162–3, 194, 201, 217
Acton, J. 81
Afghanistan 44, 79
Africa 40, 80, 86, 104, 113, 116, 150
African Americans xvi, 40, 143, 161, 206
Akhavan, P. 2
Albanians 37, 67, 105, 125, 138, 157, 160
Althusius, J. 81
America xv–xvii, 14, 16, 27–8, 38, 40–1, 43–4, 54, 67–8, 81, 85–6, 89, 106–8, 112, 120, 127–8, 132–3, 143–4, 147, 178, 194, 201, 207, 218–19; *see* United States
Anderson, Benedict xi, xxii, 7, 8, 20
Anderson, Brian xi, xxii
Appiah, K. 36, 52, 124
Argentina 25, 41, 86, 140
Armstrong, John xi
Aronovitch, Hilliard xxi, 172, 186, 198, 199, 200, 201, 239
Articles of Confederation (1781) 127, 143
Assimilation xv, 24, 39, 45, 89, 164–6, 199, 208–11
Asymmetrical federalism 10, 109, 112, 158, 161, 165, 209
Audi, R. 14
Australia 80, 82, 86, 108, 112, 140, 143–4, 146, 163
Austria 121, 125
Austro-Hungarian Empire 85
Autonomy:
   for groups or territories xiii, xx, xxiii, 7, 16–17, 22–6, 48, 56, 65, 73–80, 101–17, 129, 133–4, 140, 144–6, 149, 155–8, 160, 162, 165, 168, 170–215

   for individuals 2, 53–6, 56, 140, 144, 148, 173, 185, 188
   see also nationalism as self-determination; secession

Baker, J. xxiii, 2
Balkans ix, xiv
Baltic republics 208
Barker, E. 2
Barry, Brian xi, xxii, 7, 10, 66, 103
Basques 79, 105, 109, 111, 125, 159–60, 202, 206
Baubock, Rainer xxi, 106
BBC 44
Beer, S. 93
Beiner, Ronald xxi, xxii, 2, 7
Beitz, Charles 150
Belgium xii, xiv, xvii, 30–1, 78, 80, 84, 86, 109, 112, 117, 130, 139, 147, 157–8, 186; *see also* Flemish
Belmont, K. 99
'best of the big, best of the small' argument for federalism 84, 142, 144, 148
Beran, H. 103, 183
Berlin, I. xi, 140, 149, 150, 157
Berlin Wall ix–xi, xvii–xviii, 182
Billig, M. 29, 47
Blahuta, Jason xxii, 172
Blais, F. 2
Blanchard, Martin xxi
Blattberg, C. xx
Bosnia 104
boundaries 24–5, 97, 100, 102–5, 109, 121, 149, 208, 215, 224, 231, 235; *see also* frontiers
Bourdieu, P. 19
Bretons 111, 125, 212

242 Index

Britain xv, xix, 42, 44, 55, 67, 83, 89, 111, 116, 128, 132–4, 143, 158–9, 171, 178, 217; *see* United Kingdom
British North America Act 132–4, 136, 159
Breuilly, J. xi
Brown, D. 57
Brown-John, C. 200
Buchanan, Allen xxi, xxiii, 2, 73, 75, 94, 100, 129, 148, 171, 172, 173, 182, 183, 184, 185, 186, 188
Bulgaria 157
Burgess, M. 93, 94, 143, 218
Bush, George W. 16, 27

Cairns, A. 109, 145
Calhoun, J. C. 81, 89
Callan, Eamonn xxi, 15
Canada xiv–xvii, xxii, 2, 31–2, 48, 65, 79–80, 82, 85–8, 105, 108–9, 114, 116, 128–9, 132–9, 143, 147, 157–9, 162–4, 175, 178, 186, 192–4, 196–7, 201–2, 219
  constitution of 108, 128–9, 133–4, 144, 147, 159, 162
  history of xv–xvii, 12, 21, 28–9, 48, 82, 105, 108, 138, 143, 200–1, 207
  national identity in xvi, 2, 48, 105, 128, 131–8
  see also Quebec
Canadian nationalism 105, 129, 135, 139, 217
Carens, J.H. 2, 13, 61, 106
Catalans xii–xvii, 39, 42, 79, 100, 105, 109, 111, 125, 157–60, 167, 202, 206, 217
Chagnon, Carolyne xxi
Chambers, S. 147
Charlottetown Accord 136–8
China/Chinese 12, 79
Chechnya 173
choice theory of secession 183–8
citizenship x, 2, 10, 36, 46, 54, 58–64, 69, 78, 82, 111, 113, 121–5, 138, 161–2, 166, 179, 181, 194, 209
  in diverse societies 2, 14, 38, 44, 46, 92, 94, 99, 112, 120, 133, 137, 146–7, 152, 217–18
  citizenship identity x, 2, 6, 10, 69, 111
civic nationalism 4, 57–8, 60–3, 69, 105
class (social class) 11, 14, 28, 45, 51, 63–4, 78, 127, 150, 157, 161, 167
Clinton, B. 44, 127
CNN xvii, 44
coercion 24, 46, 51, 55, 210, 215
Cohen, A. 135
Cold War xi, 32
collective rights xvi, 19, 25–6, 30, 35, 63, 91, 123, 128, 133, 137, 140, 163–4, 204, 208
colonial nationalism xv, 23, 38, 100, 128, 133, 158, 164, 174, 208, 210, 215, 220
Colom, Francisco xxi
Communism ix–x, 2, 87, 105, 121, 125, 156, 210, 215
communitarianism x, xvi, 2, 80
confederation xxiii, 71, 78, 80, 82, 100, 104, 116, 119, 126–8, 139, 142–3, 155, 178, 184, 192–3, 200
Connor, W. xi, xiii, xv
Connors, Andrea xxi
consequentialist 15, 65, 67, 147–50, 173
conservative xiii, xv, 68, 74, 83–6, 104, 115, 148, 160, 167, 180
consociational 78–9, 217
constitutionalism viii, xv, 10, 17, 39, 56–7, 71–2, 77, 92, 95, 116, 118, 120, 128, 131, 134, 138–40, 150–3, 156, 161, 167–9, 175, 180–2, 197–8, 201–2, 204, 207, 214, 217
contractualism 118, 141, 152–6, 161, 164, 182, 196, 212
Conversi, Daniele xxi, 106
Cook, R. 139
Copp, D. 183
Corsica 79, 111, 124–6
cosmopolitanism xiv, 169
Costa, Josep xxi, 56, 166, 183, 187, 212

Council of Europe 65, 112, 130
Courts 44, 48, 75, 85, 88, 93, 108, 111, 113–16, 123, 132–3, 136, 149, 160, 162, 165, 167, 175–80, 187, 198–201
  constitutional court 48, 75, 85, 88, 123, 149, 160, 165, 167, 176–7, 179, 187, 199–201
  Supreme Court of Canada 44, 88, 114, 132–3, 162, 175, 177–8, 198, 200
  US Supreme Court 88, 180
Couture, J. 2
Craig, G. M. xv
Crawford, J. 172, 174
Crimea 74, 156
Crimean Tartars 74
Croatia 26, 39, 41, 65, 104, 120–5, 161, 218
culture xiii–xv, xvii–xviii, 2, 7, 9–16, 21, 25, 29, 31–2, 45, 48, 50–2, 55, 63–5, 76–7, 86, 120, 131, 137, 153, 158–9, 164–6, 177, 201–2, 205, 208, 214, 217
  minority or majority cultures, 12, 45, 52, 165
curriculum 46, 77, 88, 102, 108
Czechoslovakia 175, 178
Czech Republic 125

Dahl, R. 225
decolonization 149
deeply divided societies 69, 87, 99, 112, 116, 144–6, 173, 219
Democracy:
  and borders xiii, 24, 37, 55, 61, 101, 104–6, 116, 144, 156, 168, 175, 178, 180–1, 185, 194, 197, 199
  and secession viii, x, xii–xiii, xx, 9–10, 16–17, 89, 94, 97–8, 103, 116, 132, 140, 172, 175, 178, 180–220
  nationalism viii, x, 132, 140, 172, 175, 178, 180–1
  and federalism xiv, 88, 94, 98–9, 116, 131–2, 137, 140, 144–6, 148, 172, 175, 178, 180–1

deliberative democracy 14, 30, 55, 68, 94, 145–8, 151, 172, 197, 203–4, 207–8, 214, 218
'classic' democratic theory xi, xiii, xv, 38, 40, 77, 86, 114, 124, 140–1, 144, 168
Denmark 28, 78
Denitch, B. D. 2, 225
Derriennic, J.P. 106
Deutsch, K. 34, 35, 225
Dicey, A. V. 83, 85, 89, 111, 139, 140, 215
Dieckhoff, Alain xxi
'distinct society' 135–7, 149, 158–9, 163, 193
Diversity xiv–xvi, 24, 86, 88, 92, 128, 134, 137, 143, 152, 188
Doire, Alexandre xxi
D'Onofrio, Eve xxi
Duke, V. 47, 100
Dunn, J. 1
Durham, Lord xv, 215
Dworkin, R. x, 51, 80

Easterbrook, F. 148
education xix, 7, 12, 31, 40, 49–55, 70, 75–6, 87–8, 107, 110, 112, 130, 145–6, 158, 165, 216
  and nation-building xix, 7, 12, 31, 40, 49–55, 70, 75–76, 87–8, 107, 110, 112, 130, 145–6, 158, 165, 216
  and federalism xix, 7, 12, 31, 40, 49–55, 70, 75–6, 87–8, 107, 110, 112, 130, 145–6, 158, 165, 216
Eisenberg, Avigail xxi, 2, 39, 109
Elazar, D. 78, 82, 93
electoral systems 49, 76, 90, 95, 115, 146, 192, 217
Elster, J. 116, 147, 151
emigration 31, 58, 171
empire ix–x, 74, 83, 133, 139, 142, 215
England x–xi, 12, 17, 22, 38, 47, 68, 89, 101, 104, 109, 111, 162, 217–18
equality 46, 48, 52–77, 63, 78, 81, 113, 124–5, 133, 136–7, 140, 143, 150, 157

equal right to nation-building 57, 92
Eritrea 173, 176
ethics xiii–xv, xxii–xxiii, 13, 17, 23, 32, 42, 52, 57, 59, 62–3, 80–1, 93
Ethiopia 175–8, 205
  constitution of 175–8, 205
  secession from 175–8, 205
ethnic conflict x–xiv, 24, 41, 52–77, 59, 64, 66, 79, 99, 104–5, 149, 184–5, 204, 216, 219
ethnic-conflict studies xi, 24, 79, 99, 185
ethnic-conflict management x–xiv, 99, 146, 179, 216, 219
'ethnic cleansing' 13, 77, 104–5
ethnic nationalism 54, 63–6, 75, 105, 205
ethnocultural groups/identities x–xiii, 21, 64, 101, 161, 184
Europe ix–x, xiv–xv, 2, 38, 65, 78–9, 81, 87, 109, 117, 125, 156, 192, 202, 207, 210, 218
  Eastern and Central Europe ix–x, xiv–xv, 2, 87, 156, 202, 207, 210, 218
  Southern Europe 79, 125
  Western Europe 79, 192, 218
European Union xxiii, 65, 78, 80, 82, 91, 107, 112, 114, 116–18, 126, 130, 139, 143, 146–7, 184, 200, 210, 218
  as a federation or confederation xxiii, 17, 41, 71, 77–8, 80, 91, 96, 100, 107, 112–18, 126, 130, 139, 143, 146, 184, 210, 219.
  EU identity 41, 69–70, 81–2, 84, 111

Fabry, Mickey xxii
fairness 3, 12, 17, 20, 24, 34, 54, 63, 70, 87, 111, 113, 118, 144, 150, 152, 155–6, 163–4, 168, 175, 181, 190, 197–203, 210–14
fascism 8, 121, 160
Favell, Adrian xxi
federalism:
  amending formula 85, 98, 102, 116–17, 135–6, 149, 164, 177–80, 206–12
  division of powers 83, 85, 90–1, 96, 106–23, 135, 138, 142, 145, 149, 168, 177, 195, 212
  federalist 'plumbing' 88, 96–9, 119–20, 128–30, 164, 168–70, 177
  history of federal theory xi–xiv, xix, 1, 25, 27, 29, 37, 47, 49, 51, 54, 67–8, 71, 73–94, 105, 113, 129, 131, 138, 147, 158–60, 162, 171, 193–4, 200, 202, 206–10, 219–20
  integration of markets and legal systems in 102, 116–38, 158, 171
  and nationalism 1, 69–73, 75, 77, 80, 89–92, 96–100, 105–6, 118, 131, 135–9, 149, 152, 154, 159–60, 179, 184–9, 206, 215–20
  representation in central institutions 158, 168
  territorial vs. multinational 16–25, 48, 60–1, 70–1, 78–9, 87–8, 96–7, 105, 115–26, 131, 135–53, 163–5, 166–75, 188–90, 194, 201, 206–9
Federalist, The 3, 40, 81, 84, 89, 127, 142–4, 170
Faeroe Islands 78–9
Fichte, J. 7
Filippov, M. 76, 93, 99, 216, 219
Finland 78
first-past-the-post electoral system 76, 192
Flanders 21, 79, 130, 157, 167, 202, 206, 217
Føllesdal, Andreas xxi, xxii, 94
Ford, Caroline xxi, 38
Forsyth, M. 93, 128
Fossum, Jon Erik xxi
Fournier, P. 135
France xv, xvii, xxiii, 12, 18, 21, 25, 30–2, 38–41, 59–60, 65, 67–8, 78, 81, 87, 97, 105–6, 124–39, 152, 159, 176–7, 193, 217
  Départements and Overseas Territories 124, 176–7
Franck, T. M. 218

Freeman, Michael xxi
French Canadians 105, 106, 129, 139
Franco, Francisco xxi, 2, 86, 100, 104, 159
Freedom 17, 74, 84, 89–90, 104, 127, 155, 185, 190, 203
Friedrich, C. 82
frontiers x, 49, 82, 101–6; *see* boundaries.

Gagnon, Alain xxi, 2, 109
Galicians 109
Galston, W. 54
Gauthier, D. 183
gay identity 86, 160
Gellner, E. xi, 4, 7
genocide 24, 171–2, 185; *see also* 'ethnic cleansing'
Germany xv, 2, 7, 21, 38, 41, 58–9, 65, 68, 82, 85–6, 103, 112, 130, 199
Ghai, Y. 99
Gibbins, R. 164
Globalization xiii, 127
Godfrey, Sima xxi
Gosseries, Axel xxi
Granatstein, J. 134
Greece 25, 59
Greenfeld, L. 38, 68, 195
group rights xxiii
Guibernau, M. 106
Gurr, T. 219
Gutmann, A. 124

Hall, John 18
Haksar, V. 51
Hardin, R. 2
health care 7, 12, 48, 77, 107–9, 135
Hechter, M. xvi, 7, 25
Henderson, A. 61
Hitler, Adolf 2–3, 13
Hobhouse, L. T. 81
Holder, C. 39
Holmes, S. 116

homeland 4, 34, 36–7, 58, 65, 74, 101, 104, 106, 121, 159, 214
Horowitz, D. xi, xii, xiii, 79, 95, 99, 185
Howse, Robert xxi, 2, 69, 92, 94, 218
Hroch, M. 20, 38
Hueglin, T. O. 93
Hutchinson, J. 3
human rights 75, 87, 137, 171–3
Hungary 121

Iceland 25, 28–31, 96
identity politics 15, 120, 138
ideology xvii–xviii, 2, 6–8, 19, 46, 60–1, 91, 123, 127, 164
Ignatieff, M. x
imagined communities 4, 19, 34
immigration 12–13, 31, 39–40, 46, 59, 61, 110, 159, 165
India xii–xiv, xxi, 78–9, 101, 103, 112, 116, 202, 220
individual rights 114, 123–5, 132, 215
Indonesia 65, 79, 175, 202, 218
Ingram, Attracta xxi
Ingthorsson, Agust xxi
institutional moral reasoning 185
institutions, justification of xii, xx–xxii, 4–24, 29–33, 39–54, 56–62, 71–5, 79, 90–8, 106–22, 130–68, 173, 177, 187, 214–19
intellectuals xv, 20, 99
international law viii, 75, 129, 171–5, 185
    and secession 17, 89, 100–1, 116–19, 131, 138, 143–6, 164, 168, 170–81, 197, 202
intrastate autonomy 75, 129, 172–3, 182
Iraq 16, 74, 79, 113, 154, 173, 218–20
Ireland 89, 105, 133, 176–7; *see also* Northern Ireland
Israel 116
Italy 97, 104, 206; *see* Northern League

Japan 25
Journet, Paul xxi

justice xi, xiii, 11–15, 24, 30–1, 44–5, 48, 52–77, 96, 102, 140–5, 147, 153–4, 156–61, 168, 175, 177, 180, 187
   theories of 81, 93, 131, 156

Kant, I. 7
Karlsson, G. 28
Karmis, Dimitri xxi, xxiii, 32, 60, 62, 69, 72, 81, 84, 94, 126, 142, 143, 169
Kaufmann, Matthias xxi
Kettler, D. 8
King, P. 93
Kohn, H. 57
Kosovars 37, 44, 173
Kurds 219–20
Kymlicka, Will x, xii, 1, 2, 10, 15, 21, 23, 24, 30, 36, 40, 46, 50, 52, 56, 59, 60, 66, 69, 70, 72, 77, 79, 86, 87, 88, 94, 100, 106, 109, 124, 128, 154, 156, 157, 166, 215, 216, 220

LaCasse, Chantale xxi, xxiii
Laforest, Guy xxi, 2, 32, 69, 93, 94, 135, 164, 193
Landes, Xavier xxi
language:
   language rights 87, 134
   control over language in federation xix, 12–16, 40, 45–7, 56, 70, 75–6, 85, 87–8, 96, 105–11, 115, 120, 145, 158, 165, 171, 184, 211, 217
Laponce, J. 200
LaSelva, S. 93, 94
Laski, H. 82, 84
Landry, Bernard 196
legitimacy:
   of amending formula 206
   of constitutions/constitutional courts xx, 17, 54, 56, 66, 200, 213
   of national identities 15
   of orders of government/government policy 54, 211

Lenihan, Don xxii, 109
Lemco, J. 92
Levy, Jacob xiii, xiv, xxi, 2, 5, 21, 22, 66, 69, 70, 72, 73, 80, 83, 85, 94, 107, 116, 140, 148, 167, 217
Leydet, Dominique xxi, 147
liberalism xiv, xvii–xviii, 9–24, 29–32, 41–2, 63, 66, 70, 77–8, 85, 87, 92, 94, 96, 131, 141, 168, 217–18
   liberal theory 9–13, 15–16, 66, 77, 83
   and nationalism 9–15, 49–68, 131, 141–69
Lijphart, A. xiii, 95
Linz, J. 69, 72, 93
lower house 112, 117

MacDonald, Chris xxii
Macedo, S. xxiii, 2
Macedonia 105, 125, 157
MacIntyre, A. x
Maiz, Ramon xxi, xxiii
majorities xix–xx, 39, 97, 99, 105–9, 124, 145, 147, 156–61, 164, 166, 184, 197, 208–17
   majority nationalists 24, 39–40, 57, 69, 74, 85, 89, 97, 102, 106–7, 111, 114, 119, 126, 130, 156, 170, 186
   national majorities xx, 24, 26, 39, 124, 156, 217
majoritarian democracy 56
Mansbridge, J. 147
Mathew, G. 103
Marc, A. 82
Margalit, A. 2
marriage 86–7, 169–81
Martin, Dominic xxi
Marxism 7
Mazzini, G. 7
McCormick, N. xi, 94
McDonald, Michael xxii
McFarlane, K. xi, 94
McGarry, J. 24, 69, 79, 106, 219
McKay, D. 92, 143, 218
McKim, R. 1, 2

Meech Lake Accord 135–8
Mertus, J. 37
Milde, Michael xxi
military service 16, 46, 48, 122
Mill, J. S. 4, 7, 26, 81, 84, 171, 190
Miller, David xvi, xvii, xxi, 1, 2, 3, 15, 18, 30, 31, 36, 52, 219
Milosevic, Slobodan 3
minorities xx, 16–21, 24, 32, 39, 42, 56, 66, 71–4, 77, 78–9, 87–91, 97–9, 105–13, 118, 124, 126–34, 144–9, 166–84, 186–211, 217
    minority nationalists 74–7, 89, 96–7, 105–7, 110–19, 122, 146, 170, 180, 205, 210, 215–21
    national minorities 122–30, 155–219
    see also ethnocultural groups/identities; religion
Mishra, Sangeeta xxii
Monahan, P. 135, 175, 200
Monnet, J. 82, 143
Montesquieu, Baron de 81, 84, 89, 142, 144
Moore, Margaret xxi, xxiii, 2, 6, 39, 70, 100, 103, 175, 176, 183, 187, 188, 200, 212
'more perfect union, a' 127–8
Moyrand, A. 177
Multiculturalism x, 39, 49, 60, 70
multinational states xii–xxi, 17, 22, 29, 39, 69–70, 74–7, 79, 89, 91, 95, 113, 124, 131, 143–4, 148–9, 155, 161, 164, 166–7, 173–4, 181, 186–8, 191–206, 208, 210, 214, 216, 218
    definition of xii–xxi
    plea for xiii, 172
myths x, 4, 36, 41, 54, 58, 62, 64, 100

NAFTA 194
Nagel, T. 51
Nathanson, S. 2
nation, definition of ix–xx, 3–5, 18–22
nation-building 24, 39–40, 57, 69, 74, 85, 89, 97, 102, 106–7, 111, 114, 119, 126, 130, 156, 170, 186

definition of 24–6, 29
justification of xviii–xx, 21, 49–68, 71, 88, 96, 186, 219
methods of 43–9, 54
national identity xii, xvi, xix, 3–4, 12–13, 17, 25–43, 46–7, 49–52, 55–70, 97, 99, 105, 111, 113, 121–3, 132–5, 174, 207, 215
    components of 4, 33–42, 121–2
    nested national identities 52, 166–7, 219–20
national self-determination 5, 24–5, 79, 165
national sentiments 12, 15, 26, 28, 35–43
nationalism i–xviii
    definition of xii, xvi–xvii, 3, 5–7, 11, 21, 25, 44, 57, 64, 215
    as self-determination and determining the 'self' xiii, xv, xviii, 2, 5, 16, 22–43, 66, 73–5, 77, 79, 84–5, 96, 99, 101, 105–6, 115, 122–3, 138, 150, 161, 165, 170, 172, 177, 180–1, 185, 191
    'first wave' theories of xviii, 1–3, 5, 15, 24, 29, 30, 32, 36, 50, 67–8, 175
    'second wave' theories of xviii, 2, 67
NATO 65
Nazis 61, 85
Netherlands 78, 82, 191
Néron, Pierre-Yves xxii
Neumann, F. 82, 84, 85, 90, 98, 99, 110
Nickel, J. xiii
Nicolaidis, K. 218
Nielsen, Kai xxi, 2, 60, 183
Nootens, G. 14
Northern Ireland 106, 146, 175–7
Northern League 206
Norway 89

Oakshott, M. 24, 79, 99
O'Leary, B. 24, 79, 99
O'Neill, J. x
Oppenheim, F. 3
OSCE (Organization for Security and Co-operation in Europe) 65
Ouattara, Ibrahim xxii

Parekh, B. 59
parliament 48, 87, 91, 98, 100, 112, 117, 136, 145, 149, 178, 179, 193, 199, 212, 216
  representation in 47–8, 65, 76, 91, 98, 111–17, 119, 127, 130, 135, 145, 149–50, 158, 168, 212, 216,
  see also lower house, senate, upper house
partition 197, 199–200
Patoine, Tony xxi
patriotism x, xv–xvi, 2, 27–8, 41, 43–4, 46, 54, 122, 139
Patten, Alan xxi, 39
Pavkovic, A. 2
Peonidis, Filimon xxi
personalists 82, 84
Philpott, D. 183
political culture and nationalism xiv, xvii–xviii, 7–16, 25, 31–2, 48, 55, 63–4, 76–7, 86, 120, 131, 153, 158, 164–6, 202, 205, 208, 214, 217
political rights 73, 134, 161
political stability xx, 204
Poole, Ross xxi, 2, 28, 36
Popper, K. 2, 33
Posner, R. A. x, xvi, 27
post-modern 68, 138, 157
post-nationalism 69
Potter, Andrew xxi
Pourtois, Herve xxi
proportional representation 76
Prosperi, Paolo xxii
Proudhon, P.-J. 81, 82, 84, 89
provinces 12–16, 24, 62, 64, 76–9, 87, 97, 99–114, 117–19, 122, 128, 135–6, 146, 148, 158, 165, 174, 192–5, 199–202, 205, 209, 213, 216
  'province' as generic term for 'federal subunit' 16, 24
Pufendorf, S. 81, 233
Puerto Rico 78–9, 86
Pye, Lucian 233

Quebec:
  history of 28, 32, 48, 59, 74, 105, 128, 133–9, 157, 159–62, 175–82, 192–202
  nationalism in 12, 86, 105, 128, 133–9, 157–62, 175–82, 192–202
  secessionist movement in 12, 48, 59, 86, 105, 114, 128, 133–9, 157–62, 175–82, 192–202
  see also Canada

race xvi, 14, 35, 44, 105, 124, 126–7, 150, 157, 161, 170
Rakove, J. 127
Rawls, J. x, xi, 7, 14, 30, 63, 80, 83, 94, 140, 141, 147, 153, 182
Raz, J. 2, 51
recognition xx, 17, 71, 97, 124–6, 132, 135, 150, 156, 158–63, 167, 208–10
  constitutional recognition viii, 97, 126, 132, 135, 156, 158–62, 210
  and nationalism 124
  principles of xx, 17, 71, 97, 124, 150, 163, 167, 208
refugees 40
Reich, Rob xxi
Reilly, B. xiii, 76, 146, 219
religion xiii, xix, 8, 15, 39, 47–50, 60–2, 78, 122, 124, 126–7, 145, 158–9, 165
  ethnoreligious groups/identity 31, 46, 132, 145, 217, 220
Renan, E. 4
representative democracy 113, 152
Requejo, Ferran xxi, xxiii, 69, 72, 94, 109
Resnick, Phil xxi, 69, 88, 94, 109, 111, 195
Reynolds, A. 95, 99, 219
Riker, W. H. 80, 82
rival nationalisms ix, xix–xxi, 17, 27–40, 55, 57, 69–72, 95–100, 108, 114–15, 123–31, 140, 166, 170, 183, 197, 203, 206, 217–20, 239
Roma 40, 70, 217
Romania 125, 157

Rousseau, J.-J. 81, 84, 89
Ruben, D. H. 18
Russell, P. 128, 131, 134, 147
Russia xii, 38, 58, 68
Rwanda xiii, 75

Sade, Marquis de 8
Saddam Hussein 215
Sagos, Nick xxi, xxii
Sandel, M. x, 154
Scotland xix, 42, 47, 79, 89, 101, 104, 109, 111, 133, 162, 167, 175, 202, 206, 217
  and the UK xii, xiv, xvii, 25, 58, 65, 78, 83, 86, 89, 104, 109, 111, 116, 139, 175–6, 219
  nationalism in xix, 42, 47, 79, 89, 101, 104, 109, 111, 133, 162, 167, 175, 202, 206, 217
Schmidtz, David xxi, 106
Schnapper, D. 60
Schneiderman, D. 201
Schuman, R. 82, 143
Seidel, F. L. 109
senate 98
secession:
  choice theory of 183–4
  constitutionalization of 65, 99, 119, 127, 171, 173, 186, 188, 198, 203, 215
  design of secession clause 131–8
  and divorce 52, 169, 171–2, 181
  and federalism xiii, xviii, xx, 69–73, 75, 77, 80, 89–92, 96 100, 105 6, 118, 131, 135–9, 149, 152, 154, 159–60, 179, 184–9, 206, 215–20
  in international law viii, 75, 129, 171–6, 185
  just-cause theory of 182–8
  nationalist theory of 5–8, 184
secession clause xx, 17, 72, 89, 103, 119, 138, 168, 175–88, 198–219
secessionist politics xx, 17, 146, 175–214
Second World War 117, 134, 220

self-determination vs. determination of the 'self' 23–43, 73–5, 152
self-government 23–4, 73–5, 87, 96, 106–10, 129, 133–44, 159, 191, 203, 212, 214
separatism 138, 192, 194, 197
'September 11, 2001' xvi, 16, 27
Serbia 26, 57, 121, 129
Serbia and Montenegro 121, 129
Seymour, Michel xxi, 2, 60, 106
Shachar, A. 116
shared values 60–1, 128
da Silveira, Pablo xxi
Simeon, R. 216, 219
slavery 143, 206
Smith, Anthony xi, xxi, 3, 5, 20, 30, 94
Smith, G. 94
socialism 3, 7–8, 64, 80–2, 121
Solnick, S. 99, 165
Somalia 44
South Africa 80, 86, 104, 113, 116
sovereignty xix, 75, 82, 92, 102, 104, 113, 118–21, 124, 127–30, 159, 192, 209
sovereigntist 193
Soviet Union ix, xii, 38, 58, 68, 78–9, 175–6, 202; *see also* Russia
Spain 42, 80, 86, 104–6, 109, 116–17, 126, 130, 157–9, 164, 186, 210, 219, 225
  constitution of 159; *see also* Basques, Catalans, and Galicians
Spinelli, A. 82, 84, 143
Spinner, J. 2, 39
Sri Lanka 146, 218
St Kitts and Nevis [St Christopher and Nevis] 176–8, 184
Stalin, Joseph 74, 176
states: *see* multinational states; uninational states
Stepan, A. 93, 94, 152, 156, 219
Stewart, Fiona xxii
Sudan 171–3
Suksi, M. 175, 236
Sunstein, C. 94, 151, 186, 198, 201, 204, 205, 206, 207, 210, 214, 233

Sweden 19, 191
symbolism, constitutional 6, 122–9, 149
symbolism and recognition 97, 110, 118, 132
Switzerland xiv, 46, 78, 80, 82, 85, 89, 101, 108, 126–8, 158, 199
  constitution of 108, 126–8, 158, 199
  federalism in 126–8, 158, 199

Tamir, Yael xxi, 9, 10, 15, 16, 30, 36
Tawney, R. H. 81
Taylor, Charles xi, xxi, 2, 15, 80, 94, 106, 109, 195
territorial integrity 159, 170–3
Tetley, W. 236
Tocqueville, A. 84, 89, 144
Tojo, Hedeki 2
Toscana, Manuel xxi
Trifunovska, S. 87
Trudeau, P. E. 32, 69, 82, 134, 135
Trust 7, 30, 32, 69, 137, 165, 167, 210
Tudjman, Franjo 41
Tully, J. 2, 152, 200
Turkey 21, 58, 111, 125, 157
Turp, Daniel xxi
tyranny of the majority 144–5, 152, 167

Ulen, T. 101
Ukraine, Ukrainian 125, 156
unilateral declaration of independence (UDI) 190–3
uninational states xii, 10, 17, 29, 86–7, 92, 144, 148–9, 177, 214, 219
United Kingdom xv, xix, 42, 44, 55, 67, 83, 89, 111, 116, 128, 132–4, 143, 158–9, 171, 178, 217; *see also* England, Great Britain, Northern Ireland, Scotland, Wales
United Nations 126, 170, 174
UN Declaration on Friendly Relations 170–2
United States xvi, 44, 86, 89, 106–8, 112, 117–20, 127, 141, 161, 178, 206
  Civil War 128, 132, 143, 207
  constitution of 107–9, 112–20, 127, 141, 161, 206–7, 213, 227, 232
  history of xvi, 44, 86, 89, 106–8, 112, 127–9, 131–43, 147, 155, 178
  minorities in 74, 155, 173, 192, 227, 232
  upper house 112
utilitarianism 3, 28, 147

Van Parijs, Philippe xxi, 94
vanity secession 187–9
Vernon, R. 93
Vigneault, G. 28
violence x, xiii, 44, 171, 174, 191, 194, 197
Vipond, R. 94

Wales 47, 89, 104, 109, 212
Waluchow, W. 150
Walzer, M. x, 50, 52
Watts, Ronald xxi, 77, 92, 126, 158, 184, 219
war x–xi, 2–3, 10, 16, 27, 30, 32, 35, 41, 104, 106, 128, 132, 143, 147, 207, 215
Weber, E. 38
Weber, M. 4, 7
Weinstock, Daniel xxii, 2, 32, 56, 60, 69, 94, 187, 189, 197, 198, 207, 210, 212, 213
welfare state 10, 108, 165
Wellman, C. 183
Wheare, K. C. 82, 92, 108
Will, G. xv
Williams, Melissa xxi
Williams-Jones, Bryn xxii
Wood, N. 105

Yack, B. 7, 60, 80
Young, I. 124, 194
Young, Mary and Maury xxii
Young, R. 194
Yugoslavia xiii, 64–5, 75, 105, 121, 175; *see also* Bosnia; Croatia; Kosovars; Macedonia; Serbia; Serbia and Montenegro

Lightning Source UK Ltd.
Milton Keynes UK
UKOW05n1059230916

283646UK00008B/80/P